Finding Your Hispanic Roots

FINDING YOUR HISPANIC R·O·O·T·S

George R. Ryskamp

Published by Genealogical Publishing Co., Inc.
1001 N. Calvert St., Baltimore, MD 21202
Second printing, 1997
Library of Congress Catalogue Card Number 96-77405
International Standard Book Number 0-8063-1517-2
Made in the United States of America

Contents

Acknowledgments ... ix
Preface ... xi
List of Illustrations ... xiii
Chapter 1 Introduction to Hispanic Family History Research ... 1
What is Family History? ... 1
What is Hispanic? ... 2
¡Sí, Se Puede!—You Can Do It! ... 3
What is Research? ... 5
Chapter 2 Research: Where to Begin ... 9
The Research Process ... 9
Summary ... 25
Chapter 3 Research: Organizing and Evaluating Information ... 27
For Document and Research Notes: Filing Systems . 28
Pedigree Charts ... 31
Family Group Sheets ... 34
Biography Cards or Individual Records ... 36
Selecting a Genealogy Computer Program ... 37
Chapter 4 Hispanic Family History Research in an LDS Family History Center ... 39
The Family History Center System ... 39
FamilySearch ... 40
Ancestral File ... 41
International Genealogical Index ... 41
The Family History Library Catalog ... 51
Summary ... 61
Chapter 5 Tracing the Hispanic Immigrant in United States Records ... 63
U.S. Record Sources ... 63
Summary ... 80
Chapter 6 General Spanish Research Techniques ... 81
SECTION A: Language and Handwriting ... 81
Spanish Paleography ... 82
The Language of Old Spanish Records ... 87
Areas of Special Handwriting Problems ... 91
Capitalization and Punctuation ... 94
Abbreviations ... 95
Accent Marks ... 97
Numbers ... 97
SECTION B: Naming Systems ... 98
Surnames (*Apellidos*) ... 98

Given Names (*Nombres, Nombres de Pila*) 103
Titles 104
SECTION C: Doing Research by Correspondence ... 105
General Suggestions 105
Correspondence Log 107
Basic Elements in a Genealogical Research Letter .. 108
Chapter 7 Determining Objectives and Starting Work in Original Sources 111
People Analysis 111
Locality Analysis 112
Records Analysis 117
Locality and Records Analyses Sample 124
Beginning Research in Original Sources 124
SELECTED BIBLIOGRAPHY of Hispanic Locality Reference Works by Country 129
Chapter 8 Civil Registers 145
The Records 145
Consulting Civil Registers 153
Chapter 9 Catholic Church Records 157
Organization of Parish Sacramental Records 157
General Procedure in Parish Research 159
Bautismos (Baptisms) 167
Matrimonios (Marriage Records) 176
Defunciones, Colecturías o Entierros (Death, Collection, or Burial Records) 176
Confirmaciones (Confirmations) 183
Locating Parish Records 184
Non-Parish Administrative Records 188
Chapter 10 Marriage Records 193
Pre-Marriage Investigations 193
Canonical Impediments to Marriage 195
Marriage Parish Register Entries 196
Common Phrases of Marriage Records 199
Catholic Church Diocesan Marriage Dispensations .. 202
Chapter 11 Census Records 209
The Value of Census Research 209
Local Censuses 210
Regional and National Census Records 211
Indexes 216
Locating Census Records 216
Chapter 12 Spanish Military Records 219
Historical Organization of the Spanish Military 220
Military Ranks and Promotions 223
Record Types 224
Where to Find Military Records 229

Chapter 13 Notarial Records 235
Spanish Notarial Laws 236
Locating the Records of a Specific Notary 237
Arrangement and Indexing of *Protocolos* 240
Notarial Documents—General Format 242
Notarial Documents—Specific Types 247
Judicial, Governmental, and Ecclesiastical Notaries 252
Glossary 255
Appendix Hispanic Genealogical Societies in the United States .. 279
Index 281

Acknowledgments

In contemplating the many people who contribute to a work such as this, one recognizes how deeply he is influenced, supported, and assisted by others. First and foremost, I acknowledge that this book would not have been written without the love and support of my wife, Peggy—travel companion, research associate, editor, friend, confidante, at times my harshest critic, and always my most ardent supporter. Our four children—Erin, Rix, Jonathan, and Jordan—have endured much, most frequently in the absence of parents who were traveling, researching, teaching, and writing, but also in the recent lifestyle change as I left my law practice to become an assistant professor of history.

Finally, I acknowledge the contributions of many friends in California, Utah, and Texas without whose experiences, support, and encouragement this book would not be as rich as it is. In the last three years Brigham Young University has provided me with research and secretarial assistance. Lastly, I recognize the numerous genealogy clients and students whose work on their ancestry has given me the opportunity to learn about many of the things about which I have written in this book.

Preface

While indexing this book I attended the 17th annual Conference on Hispanic Genealogy and History, hosted by the Hispanic genealogical societies of Texas. That conference, held in Monterrey, Mexico as part of the celebration of the 400th anniversary of the city's founding, was a truly international event. Participants came from such varied locations as Mexico City, Michigan, Florida, and California as well as from throughout Texas to learn from academic historians and genealogists from Mexico and the United States about the rich culture that they share as descendants of Mexico and Spain, and about how to search for and find more about their own Hispanic ancestors. During those four days I watched as the conference attendees exchanged information, found with excitement new "cousins," and made thrilling discoveries about ancestors after years of searching. All of this was symbolic of the dramatic changes taking place in the world of Hispanic genealogy since I began to write the first edition of *Tracing Your Hispanic Heritage*[1] back in 1977.

Testimonials from those who had used *Tracing Your Hispanic Heritage* and requests for copies of it reassured me of the continuing need for an updated version. New topics in the index dealing with such diverse areas as computers, impediments to marriage, microfilming, family history centers, centralization of parish records, and many reference book titles indicate that this new edition of *Tracing Your Hispanic Heritage* offers much that was not in its predecessor. When I returned from Mexico I again found myself teaching a family history class at Brigham Young University, in which we reviewed the following quote from Norman Cantor's and Richard Schneider's *How to Study History*:

> [The study of history] allows for a new level of self discovery and a new degree of empathy with other people. Everyone has a social as well as a personal self. We are all part of all that we have met and all that we have inherited from our families and communities. Historical study allows the student to perceive how the world of today came into existence and how the texture of experience that distinguishes his particular family and community was built up by a complex combination of forces and events over many decades and perhaps centuries. Historical study allows the student to understand why he is the way he is as an American, a Canadian, a Northerner, an Anglo-Saxon, an Italian, a Jew, a Roman Catholic, etc., and also allows him to understand the historical process which has conditioned other people whom he encounters. *History is therefore a road to self knowledge and a*

[1]Ryskamp, George R., *Tracing Your Hispanic Heritage*. Riverside, Calif.: Hispanic Family History Research, 1984.

means of understanding the attitudes and motives of people of disparate backgrounds.[2]

Juxtaposing this statement with my experiences at the conference in Monterrey, I realized that I had been watching and participating in a multitude of experiences resulting in new levels of self-discovery and empathy with other people. There is no better vehicle to accomplish that than the study of one's own family history. Assisting those with Hispanic ancestry in that quest of discovery is the purpose for which this book was written, and to them it is dedicated.

George R. Ryskamp
16 September 1996 (Mexican Independence Day)
Brigham Young University
Provo, Utah

[2]Norman Cantor and Richard Schneider, *How to Study History* (Wheeling, Ill.: Harlan Davidson, Inc., 1967), 3.

List of Illustrations

Figure 2-1	Photograph of family member, Santander, Spain	12
Figure 2-2	Printed death announcement, Costa Rica	13
Figure 2-3	Mexican passport issued by the State of Aquascalientes, Mexico, 1919	14
Figure 2-4	Military discharge papers found in a descendant's home	17
Figure 3-1	Jeri Bebout's first pedigree chart	29
Figure 3-2	Jeri Bebout's extended pedigree chart	32
Figure 3-3	Selected genealogical programs	37
Figure 4-1	Sample IGI microfiche page, #2951 of Mexico (1992 IGI edition)	44
Figure 4-2	Sample IGI microfiche cards for Nayarit, Mexico (1992 IGI edition)	45
Figure 4-3	Baptismal record from parish of Compostela, Mexico (FHL 0652402, page 117)	46
Figure 4-4	List of regions from the 1994 IGI edition on CD ROM	50
Figure 4-5	FHLC Locality Section microfiche headings for Mexico (1993 edition)	54
Figure 4-6	Mexico—FHLC Topics (Edition 2.01, 1993)	56
Figure 4-7	FHLC records for Xicoténcatl, Tamaulipas, Mexico (1993 edition)	59
Figure 5-1a	Marriage certificate from Catholic church, Florence, Arizona	65
Figure 5-1b	Original marriage entry (literal copy), parish records, Florence, Arizona	66
Figure 5-2	Page from 1900 U.S. federal census, Florence, Arizona, p. 202	67
Figure 5-3	Family copy of death announcement in *San Jose Mercury Herald,* San Jose, California, December 1934, p. 26 ...	69
Figure 5-4	Great Register of Placer County for the year 1892, Placer County, California, p. 1 (FHL 977088)	70
Figure 5-5	Page from the passenger list for the Port of New Orleans for the S.S. *Chalmette,* October 16, 1916	71
Figure 5-6	Mexican Border Manifest Card, 1942	73
Figure 5-7	Preliminary Form for Petition for Naturalization, Immigration and Naturalization Service, 1927	74
Figure 5-8	1877 Court Order of Naturalization of Jacinta Acuna, Placer County, California, Certificates of Citizenship Vol. A (1874–1879), p. 54 (FHL 1479768)	75
Figure 5-9	U.S. Social Security SS-5 Application	76

Figure 5-10 Alien Registration Form by United States Department of Justice-Immigration and Naturalization Service, 1940 78
Figure 5-11 World War I Draft Registration Card, Pleasanton, Alameda County, California (FHL 1530653) 79
Figure 6-1 Example of Spanish handwriting styles, 1100–1500 A.D. 83
Figure 6-2 Alphabet chart, reprinted from *Spanish Handwriting* (Salt Lake City, 1979) 85
Figure 6-3 Examples of confusing letters *f, i, j, s,* and *t* 92
Figure 7-1 Page from *Diccionario geográfico del Salvador,* volume 1 115
Figure 7-2 Political divisions of Latin America, Spain, and Portugal 117
Figure 7-3 Principal types of records and where they can be found 120
Figure 7-4 Page from *Censo-Guía de Archivos Expañoles* 122
Figure 7-5 Page from *Diccionario geográfico de Guatemala* 125
Figure 7-6 Sample research log 127
Figure 8-1 National Civil Registers of Latin America 146
Figure 8-2 Certificate of birth from the Civil Register of Montellano, Savilla, Spain, 1880 148
Figure 8-3 Pages of Marriage Civil Register Colonia Juarez, Chihuahua, Mexico, 1912 (FHL 773944) 151
Figure 8-4 Supporting marriage information, Civil Register, Atitalaquia, Mexico (FHL 657687) 152
Figure 8-5 Letter to the Secretary of the Civil Register *(Secretario del Registro Civil)* 154
Figure 9-1 Parish sacramental register 158
Figure 9-2 Extract form, Civil Register/Parish, Birth/Baptism 161
Figure 9-3 Extract form, Civil Register/Parish, Marriage 162
Figure 9-4 Extract form, Civil Register/Parish, Death/Burial 163
Figure 9-5 Baptismal certificate from Daymiel, Spain copied from *Archivo Histórico Nacional* (Madrid, Spain), Sección de Ordenes Militares 168
Figure 9-6 Extraction of baptism in figure 9-5 168
Figure 9-7 Extractions of death entries from figure 9-8 180
Figure 9-8 Pages of Death Register 1788, Logrosan, Caceres, Spain (FHL 1458682) 181
Figure 9-9 Letter to the parish priest 185
Figure 10-1 Parish marriage entry, Cabra, Cordoba, Spain, 1910 198
Figure 10-2 Marriage record from Argentina showing race as designators 200
Figure 10-3 Marriage Dispensation Petition from Guadalajara Diocese, Mexico for parties from Saltillo, 1701 (FHL 168605) 203
Figure 10-4 Canon Law Blood Relationships Chart 204

Figure 11-1 Page from a colonial census, Saltillo, Coahuila, Mexico, 1777 (Archivo Municipal de Saltillo, Sección Presidencia) 212
Figure 11-2 Page from 1907 Municipal Census Vallodolid, Spain (Archivo Municipal de Vallodolid) 213
Figure 11-3 Cover page from 1869 Argentine Census 214
Figure 11-4 1869 Argentine Census page from Santa Catalina, Jujuy 215
Figure 12-1 *Hoja de Servicio* of Miguel de la Torre Balbontin from Archivo General Militar de Segovia 221
Figure 12-2 *Hoja de Servicio* de Jose de Zuñiga, Archivo General Militar de Simancas, Secretaria de Guerra, Legajo 7279, 110 (FHL 1156342) 226
Figure 12-3 Published transfer order list from Servicio Histórico Militar, Madrid, Spain 227
Figure 12-4 *Padrón del Presidio de Sinaloa,* published in *Spanish American Genealogist,* 1979, p. 559 230
Figure 13-1 First page of list of notaries from the province of Madrid, Spain, Antonio Matilla Tascón, *Inventario General de Protocolos Notariales* (Madrid: Ministerio de Cultura, 1980), p. 171 241
Figure 13-2 Index page from a *protocolo* 243
Figure 13-3 Published extracts from notarial records, Israél Cavazos Garza, *Catalogo y Sintesis Archivo Municipal de Monterrey, 1726–1756* (Monterrey, Mexico 1986), p. 42 244
Figure 13-4 Format of notarial documents 246
Figure 13-5 *Inventario de bienes de difunto* from *Archivo Histórico Provincial de Caceres, Protocolos, Legajo* 1615, year 1739, p. 77 251

Finding Your Hispanic Roots

CHAPTER 1

Introduction to Hispanic Family History Research

All of the people were warm and brave, full of joy of life, full of poetry, determined to hold on to their own rich culture in spite of incredible odds.

(A description of Hispanics in New York)[1]

This book is for people who are interested in people. You may not have fully realized it, but you are reading this book because of an interest in a group of real people—your ancestors who spoke Spanish and lived in Mexico, Central or South America, Spain, the islands of the Caribbean, or the United States. This book will help you come to know those ancestors. The process whereby you come to know those people is called Hispanic family history research. This introductory chapter will define that process and answer questions you may have about getting to know your ancestors. The rest of the book will discuss the process of doing Hispanic family history research, or in other words, how you can become acquainted with the many individuals who make up your ancestral family.

WHAT IS FAMILY HISTORY?

Genealogy is defined by Vicente de Cadenas y Vicent, the eminent Spanish genealogist and royal *Cronista de Armas*, as the science of determining family relationships.[2] The genealogist builds a pedigree composed of related family units whose individual members are identified by specific names, relationships, dates, places, and events. The family historian takes the process further. Unlike the history learned in school, which was concerned with kings, politicians, battles, and famous dates, family history discovers and reassembles the details of our ancestors' lives. The family historian begins with the information the genealogist assembles, places it within the broad sweep of national and regional history, and then searches to include even the details of daily living where registers, mementos, and old buildings permit him to do so. Family history is not just a cold scientific study or a mere rambling through collections of dusty old books — it is fundamentally human. Good family history research has "a note of color, or charm, or humor to help us know our ancestors better and more tangibly."[3]

As you begin your quest, be prepared to answer a question you are sure to be asked: Why are you doing genealogy? The answer varies from person to person. For some people it is a hobby, like collecting coins or stamps — they collect baptismal, marriage, and death certificates. Others become interested out of curiosity or a desire to know about their own progenitors, or about history or some aspect of it. For still others, family history and a similar study, local history, are an important means of preserving their cultural and linguistic heritage.

Some people pursue genealogy to aid in the study of other sciences such as genetics, biology, medicine, demography, economics, or sociology. Still others are motivated by deep religious purposes. While Mormons are a well-known example of this, such a spiritual motivation is not limited to members of one church. Whatever the religion, that spiritual motivation is often combined with a love for family, as is well expressed by the Spanish genealogist Jesus Larios, a devout Catholic, in the opening paragraph of his *Curso de genealogía*:

> Genealogy is as ancient as the family. You could say that it was born with the family. It was the desire of God, Creator of the human family, that we honor our fathers, with which word he wishes to signify our ancestors, and this desire was later placed upon us as a law from the summit of Mount Sinai. . . a mutual and reciprocal love unites, even beyond death, parents and children, grandparents and grandchildren, ancestors and descendants and relatives within a family.[4]

WHAT IS HISPANIC?

A dictionary definition of the word "Hispanic" reads as follows: "Of or relating to the people, speech, or culture of Spain and Portugal, or Latin America."[5] While this definition is accurate, it cannot express the extension or diversity of the Hispanic people, found from the southwestern United States to the southern tip of South America and from Spain to the Philippines. Through a colonial experience, which began a century before the earliest Anglo-American colonies were established and lasted fifty to one hundred years longer, Spanish characteristics and institutions interacted — sometimes peacefully, sometimes violently — with indigenous peoples to form new nations and cultures. Wherever early Spanish colonizers traveled, they brought with them the language, culture, institutions, and record systems of their homeland. Contemporary Mexicans, Guatemalans, and other Latin Americans, although Hispanic, are not Spanish. They have combined — not only culturally but through bloodlines — the languages, people, and culture of Spain with those of indigenous cultures to form dynamic new races and cultures. Your ancestors were a part of that process.

Most Hispanics will find that their ancestry has more than just Spanish and Native American lines; it might include French, German, Eastern European, Italian, African, or Portuguese lines as well. Just as the United States has been a melting pot, so have the countries of Central and South America.

The statistics of immigration to Latin America show the diversity of that heritage. Before the end of the colonial period around 1820, an estimated 12 million Spaniards had emigrated, primarily to Mexico, Central America, and South America. The immigration that followed in the next century, however, was considerably greater. Out of a total of 54 million people coming from Europe to the American continents between 1820 and 1920, 20 million went to Latin America, primarily to Argentina, Brazil, Cuba, and Uruguay.[6] Large numbers of those came from Italy, Spain, and Portugal. However, English, Irish, French, and German surnames are also found in Central and South America. Among this diversity of heritage, both immigrant and indigenous, you will search for your unique heritage — your ancestral families.

¡SÍ, SE PUEDE! — YOU CAN DO IT!

Another exciting fact about doing Hispanic family history research is that chances for success are better in Spain and her former colonies than anywhere else in the world. Saul Vela, Chairman of the Fifteenth Annual Conference on Hispanic Genealogy and History in Corpus Christi, Texas, in 1994, adopted the motto *"Sí, se puede!"* ("Yes, you can do it") to encourage families to do Hispanic family history research.[7] In Hispanic countries most families can trace their ancestry into the seventeenth century; in Spain many can find lines back into the fifteenth century and even earlier. The author has personally traced several lines of common laborers from Spain and Mexico into the early 1500s.

According to the English Garter King of Arms Sir Anthony Wagner, there are four main factors affecting success in tracing a pedigree: **status**, **record**, **name**, and **continuity**.[8] Looking at each of these in turn helps explain why possibilities for success in Hispanic research are better than for other cultures.

Status refers to the position a family or individual held in the social structure. Generally, it is easier to trace a prominent family than a more humble one. Prominent families appeared in more records due to the positions they held, the lands they owned, the wills they left, and the special masses they commissioned. Fortunately, parish registers in Hispanic countries recorded people of all social classes, not just those with high social status. Therefore, records beyond the parish are essential only in tracing a pedigree before the sixteenth century, when parish records began, or in cases where parish records have been destroyed.

Records of Hispanic countries are unmatched anywhere in their quality, quantity, and availability. Spanish parish records are the oldest in the world. Nearly all of them begin soon after the Council of Trent in the 1560s, which made such records mandatory throughout the Catholic world. By the time the Americas were colonized, these record systems were thoroughly accepted and were immediately transferred to the New World where the earliest records, in Lima, Peru, begin in the year 1537.

The availability of Hispanic parish records is often lessened by two historical circumstances: Most Hispanic countries have passed through a large number of wars; and the Catholic Church has frequently been the target of passionate outbursts of destruction. Fortunately, even where records have been destroyed gaps can usually be bridged by using other records such as civil registers, notarial records, military records, tax lists, and censuses. Nearly every family can achieve some success, even in areas where records have been heavily devastated by wars and revolutions.

Spanish records are not only the oldest in Europe but also the best in terms of quality. While in most countries baptismal records give only the name of the child baptized and the name of one or both parents, generally after 1790 (and in many cases before) Hispanic baptismal certificates give the names of the child, both parents, and all four grandparents, and even may state the locality where all were born. Although they generally only begin in the late 1800s, the civil registers of most Hispanic countries are even more detailed. Those of Spain have been described as "the fullest in Europe or of any country in the world."[9]

Name is the next factor in successful family history research. Fortunately, surnames were consistently used in Spain for centuries before the colonial period, even before the advent of parish records; naturally, this facilitates the tracing of a family. By the end of the nineteenth century, Spain and most Hispanic countries had adopted a unique system wherein every person has two surnames. Both are used on all official documents, as well as in referring to oneself and being referred to by others. The first surname is the paternal, like that which we all use. The second is the maternal surname, or what we call the mother's maiden name. Therefore, if Juan Gomez Jimenez and Maria Vega Fernandez marry and have a son, Jose, he would be named Jose Gomez Vega.

Of equal importance to the Hispanic family researcher is the fact that a Hispanic woman never changes her name. Even though Maria Vega Fernandez is married, her death certificate will list her as Maria Vega Fernandez, probably adding the comment that she was the wife of Juan Gomez Jimenez. This custom eliminates the problem frequently encountered in American or British research of trying to find the mother's maiden name.

Continuity, the last factor, relates to the family continuing in the same place of residence or occupation for several generations. Staying in one town or small region makes the work easier and family members more readily identifiable. Continuity in a trade also makes tracing records from one generation to the next easier, especially in the urban areas. Doctors, lawyers, notaries, soldiers, professors, shopkeepers, and silversmiths are all good examples of occupations where continuity is likely to exist.

Working-class people in Spain, especially in rural areas, generally remained in the same area for many generations. Extensive mobility usually indicated an occupation that required travel and/or middle- or upper-class social status. In Hispanic America, with its expanding frontier, mobility was greater. Continuity is therefore diminished, often making it necessary to search extensively for earlier generations in another town, region, or country. Fortunately, the great detail of Catholic parish records and governmental records on the Spanish frontiers often compensates for this lack of continuity.

One last word on the researcher's chances of success. Some people ask if they can really research family history themselves, or if it would be better to hire a professional researcher. Occasionally, you might need to consult an expert to help decipher difficult handwriting or to gain access to special limited-access record collections, but nearly anybody with patience, diligence, and a willingness to study can research Hispanic family history. The only other qualification is a basic knowledge of Spanish, which can be obtained by two or three semesters of Spanish at a local university.

WHAT IS RESEARCH?

Val D. Greenwood, in *The Researcher's Guide to American Genealogy*,[10] defines research as an investigation aimed at the discovery and interpretation of facts and the revision of accepted theories in light of new facts. For the family historian this process involves searching out documents and then studying them carefully to find relevant information pertaining to his family lines. He uses the facts he has collected to build a pedigree of his ancestors, to reconstruct their lives in the context of their time and place, and eventually to write a family history.

Research in family history is not different from research in other areas. It must be accomplished with care so that the end product is accurate and easily understood. To help attain this goal, the following rules for genealogical research have been translated and adapted from *Curso de genealogía*[11] by Jesus Larios.

1. Prefer written sources to oral sources. This means that you believe written documents rather than the exciting family tradition that you are a descendant of royalty as Aunt Maria has always told you. Sometimes this is hard, especially for Aunt Maria, but it is essential to accurate research. This does not mean we totally ignore oral tradition. It is often an indispensable guide to the written sources about the family. If, however, there is a conflict between a written source and an oral source, the written source should be considered correct until proven otherwise.

2. Prefer primary sources to secondary sources. Primary sources are those noted by an observer at the time of the incident and recorded soon afterward, preferably without bias about what is being recorded. For example, a baptismal certificate is a primary source for the baptism and birth, since it was recorded by the priest who, as an unbiased observer, performed the baptism and then recorded it in the parish book. Such a source would be preferred over a military record for the same person made twenty years later and listing a different date or place of birth. Perhaps in this case the young soldier lied about his age to get into the service. A record made years after the event, by someone who was not a witness or who might have reason to change the facts, is a secondary source. This means that secondary source materials, such as those in a published family history or a *limpieza de sangre* (purity of blood) pedigree, should be carefully checked against primary sources.

Sometimes an original document can contain both primary and secondary source elements. Spanish baptismal certificates are excellent examples of this. They are primary sources for the baptism and, in most cases, for the birth they record; however, they are only a secondary source for the names and birthplaces of grandparents. Always give more credence to those documents or sources whose author is nearest in time and place to the event being recorded. Remember that the best source is a firsthand witness who records the event very soon after it occurs.

3. Prove any fact or relationship with at least two documents. The apostle Paul gave good advice when he said, "In the mouth of two or three witnesses shall every word be established." Almost any document can be wrong. Even baptismal certificates sometimes omit the name of the child being baptized or give an incorrect name for the father or mother. The people who make records are human and therefore subject to error. Checking each fact against another independent source reduces possibility for error.

There are three words the family historian should adopt as standards for good research: thoroughness, breadth, and accuracy.

Thoroughness means we do not leave records unchecked, but glean all pertinent information. There are several practical guidelines to achieve thoroughness in research. First, copy all information in any sources dealing with a surname you are researching, even if no relationship can be established at the time. For example, in one case a line appeared to have been lost because the death record of the woman being researched recorded her as the widow of Juan Perez, yet she appeared everywhere else as the wife of Domingo Moreno. Upon sitting down to analyze his material, the researcher discovered a marriage entry he had copied earlier showing the woman's marriage to Juan Perez, which listed her as the widow of Domingo Moreno. That entry had been copied before he knew the names of the individuals concerned, but he had been copying all events for that surname. Thoroughness always pays off.

Another principle that helps achieve thoroughness is to work on family groups. Many times the record of a brother or sister of the direct ancestor will be more complete or accurate than that of the direct ancestor. Sometimes even the record of a first cousin will provide some needed piece of information not available for those of the direct-line family.

Breadth is essential to quality research. It would be hard to understand the men and women of the generation that lived through the Great Depression and the Second World War without having some concept of those events. Without knowing about the Mexican Revolution (1911–1919), it would be impossible to really understand the life of someone who was born in Mexico in 1890.

Perhaps of equal or greater importance is a knowledge of local history. Like family history, local history concerns itself with the events that touched the lives of our ancestors most directly. The building of a new church in the village, the transfer of the town to a different ecclesiastical jurisdiction, or the flooding of a river in the valley were probably more important in our ancestor's life than the fact that a new king had been crowned. A family history researcher looks for such details as he works, supplementing his research by searching out local histories and local history records from the places from which his ancestors came.

Accuracy is the research standard where the science of genealogy has suffered most throughout the centuries. An old Spanish saying that describes a person who lies well says he "lies like a genealogist." As Jesus Larios said, "Genealogy must be a reflection of the truth."[12] Since any mistake in relationship on a pedigree is multiplied exponentially by each generation, the time, energy, and money lost because of such a mistake alone should make our striving for accuracy imperative. To achieve accuracy, accept nothing but documented facts for the family history that will be your final product. This may mean accepting a few horse thieves, illegitimate children, and real scoundrels, but even the most royal and noble of lines will have the same and much more. It may also mean doing extra work to prove something conclusively, but in no other way can your research stand the test of criticism so rightfully leveled against many genealogists in the past. Accuracy is obtained by copying and accepting only facts, by doing a total job in keeping with our standard of thoroughness, and in documenting and recording every step. Remember in all of this, ¡*Sí, se puede*! You can do it!

---

1. *Time*. 5, 16 October 1978.

2. Vicente de Cadenas y Vicent, *Rudimentos de la Genealogía* (Madrid: Hidalguía, 1975), 1.

3. Ibid., 14.

4. Jesus Larios, *Curso de genealogía* (Madrid: Hidalguía, 1972), 3.

[5] *Webster's New Collegiate Dictionary* (Chicago: Consolidated Book Publishers, 1979).

[6] Octavio Cabezas Moro, "Emigración Española a Iberoamérica: Evolución Histórica y Características Sociológicas," *Migraciones Latinas y Formación de la Nación Latinoamericana* (Caracas: Universidad Simón Bolivar Instituto de Altos Estudios de América Latina, 1980), 140–179.

[7] Saul Vela, *Proceedings, Fifteenth Annual Conference on Hispanic Genealogy and History* (Houston: Hispanic Genealogical Society, 1994), iv.

[8] Gerald Hamilton-Edwards, *In Search of Ancestry* (London: Phillimore, 1976), 12.

[9] Ibid., 158.

[10] Val D. Greenwood, *The Researcher's Guide to American Genealogy*. 2nd ed. (Baltimore: Genealogical Publishing Co., 1990), 1.

[11] Jesus Larios, *Curso de genealogia* (Madrid: Hidalguía, 1961), 22–25

[12] Jesus Larios, *Tratado de genealogía heráldico y derecho nobiliario*. 2nd ed. (Madrid: Hidalguía, 1984), 22.

CHAPTER 2

Research: Where to Begin

The beginning genealogist is often like the beginning skier. With all the enthusiasm he can muster, he begins a headlong flight down the most advanced hill, without a thought about instruction or direction. The beginning skier frequently ends up buried in a snowbank. Likewise, the beginning genealogist often finds himself overwhelmed by the quantity of materials in the library or archives where he has rushed to find everything he can about his family surname. The wise beginning skier first seeks out instruction to learn basic techniques. The wise beginning genealogist does the same. The purpose of this chapter and the two that follow is to outline the basic approach that the beginner would take in doing Hispanic family history research. By following these fundamental research and organizational techniques, the researcher should not find himself, after many hours of work, buried in a snowbank of disorganized data, much of which is either irrelevant and/or incomplete.

THE RESEARCH PROCESS

Hispanic family history research is, above all else, research. The steps and patterns to be followed apply to any researcher, whether he be a chemist, a general historian, or a family historian. Research can be divided into five basic steps. The first is to discover what has been done before. Frequently, others have already spent hours in search of information about your ancestors, and much time can be saved by knowing what has already been done. In family history research this step is called the *preliminary survey*. After outlining the other four steps of research, this chapter will deal entirely with the procedures to follow in completing that preliminary survey.

The second step of the research process is to analyze the material collected and evaluate the various parts of it, sifting out those which are irrelevant or inaccurate. Chapter 3 of this book explains how material collected during the preliminary survey, as well as during later research from primary sources, can be organized and evaluated. Using the material that has been collected and evaluated, the researcher then completes the third step: determining objectives and developing a plan of research (see chapter 7). The fourth step is to follow that plan in gathering new data from primary sources and to record that data systematically, ensuring a complete and accurate record of all completed work. The remaining chapters of the book deal with the aspects of that process. The fifth step is to review the new data to determine if the objectives established in step three have been fulfilled.

The research process is cyclical. Depending upon the information found in step four, the fifth step yields two options: (1) repeat the entire process beginning with the preliminary survey, adding the recently found information, or (2) go directly to step two in evaluating the information uncovered in the primary source material.

For example, suppose that Juan Pastor Pons begins to do his family history research. Knowing that his mother's surname is Pons and that her family came from Guadalajara, Mexico, he would do a preliminary survey for information relating to members of the Pastor or Pons families who lived in Guadalajara. After collecting that material, he would organize and evaluate it. That evaluation might indicate that he set for his objective the locating of birth records of his father and mother in the Civil Register in Guadalajara, Mexico. Under step four he would then gather that data by writing to or going to the Civil Register in Guadalajara. (To ensure a complete record, he would request literal copies of the entire birth certificate.) Under step five he would evaluate each certificate by reading the information and placing it on the same family group sheets that he had previously set up for his parents and grandparents as part of step three.

In our example Juan Pastor Pons now has two alternatives that he can follow. Remember that the research process is cyclical; once Juan Pastor Pons has completed step five, he will return and begin again. The point in the process to which he returns depends upon the information he gathered in step four and evaluated in step five. Suppose he learned that his grandfather was Francisco Pastor Zamora, and that he was born in Guadalajara. Juan Pastor would then return to the second step above and analyze this information. He would estimate that his grandfather was born about twenty-five to thirty years before the birth date of his father. He would then determine as his objective, under step three above, to search for the birth or baptismal record of his grandfather Francisco Pastor Zamora.

Suppose that Juan Pastor Pons has also found that his maternal grandmother was Maria Rodriguez de la Pena from Guadalajara, and his maternal grandfather was Aurelio Pons Canals from Barcelona, Spain. He would then return to step one to do a preliminary survey for those surnames. The fact that the maternal grandmother, Maria Rodriguez de la Pena, was from Guadalajara would not eliminate the necessity of further preliminary survey work, since the surname Rodriguez de la Pena was not known when the previous survey was completed. He will now check all of the preliminary survey sources described later in this chapter for the Rodriguez de la Pena and Pons Canals families in the Guadalajara area, and the Pons Canals family in the Barcelona area. Having found all of the information that has already been collected or written about the Rodriguez de la Pena and the Pons Canals families, including perhaps a written family history, Juan Pastor Pons then repeats all of the research steps for each new surname and geographical area. As the genealogist/family historian continues to search his family lines, he will repeat this research process again and again.

Preliminary Survey

The preliminary survey has a two-fold objective. The first is to learn all that your relatives know about the history of the family. The second is to identify all of the research already done on the family. The preliminary survey is accomplished in four steps: (1) check for all home and family sources; (2) interview other family members; (3) check for information about family history research done about the family in the FamilySearch® indexes of The Church of Jesus Christ of Latter-day Saints; and (4) check for any printed biographies or histories dealing with the family or its individual members.

Check of Home and Family Sources

As a beginning researcher, you may be unaware of the wealth of genealogical and family history material in your own home. A search should be made in basements, attics, and garages for anything about the family and its early members. At the very bottom of that old trunk may be a letter from a great-grandfather in Spain to his son in Uruguay; military papers showing that a grandfather fought in the Mexican army during the Mexican Revolution of 1911–1919; or a long-forgotten birth certificate, which will yield the name of the small town in Cuba where your ancestor was born. Especially significant, along with written documents, would be pictures, clothing, or tools that had belonged to family members. Any of these things give a greater reality to the life of that person. After your own home has been thoroughly searched and all of the various sources, documents, and personal objects of the family have been gathered together in a single place, you will want to see what family source material can be found in the homes of parents, grandparents, aunts and uncles, and even cousins.

The following list of home and family sources that a person of Hispanic ancestry may encounter can serve as a guide in your searching. Since lifestyles vary from one nation to another, an attempt has been made in compiling this list to include sources that might be found in the home of a family from Latin America, Spain, or Portugal.

1. Vital records. This category includes government or church records of major life events such as births or baptisms, marriages, and deaths. While in some cases such certificates were issued directly at the time of the event, in most cases the copies to be found in homes will be certificates issued by civil or religious authorities years afterward, when they were requested to prove the facts surrounding the event. Birth and baptism certificates are most commonly found because of a variety of situations such as obtaining a passport or visa, being married, or requesting social security, which require proof of birth. Likewise, death or marriage records may have been obtained to settle an estate or to make a claim for a pension. If your family has come in recent decades from one of the many Spanish-speaking countries or is currently living in one, a copy of the *Libro de familia* (Family Book) may also be found.

Vital records from all countries are particularly helpful because they often identify specific places and dates, information that can give a starting point for your research. Vital records for your immigrant ancestors are especially valuable, as they can give clues about the country of origin. By providing names of parents, and usually in the case of modern Hispanic birth or baptismal records the names of grandparents, a single certificate may also give the researcher a small pedigree from which he can begin his research.

2. Photographs. Photographs are a particularly important home source. Perhaps more than any other single item, photographs make the family members we are researching seem personal and alive. Photographs labeled with names and/or dates are especially valuable in helping you reconstruct the lives of your ancestors. In some cases photographs may have the name of the photographer and the address of his studio, which can give you additional clues in identifying the area of ancestral origin (see figure 2-1).

It is challenging when the people who are pictured in photographs are not identified. The best solution to this dilemma may be to have copies of the picture made and send them to the oldest living members of your family, asking if they can identify the individuals shown. If the person lived in a small town, another alternative is to send a copy of the picture to the town's newspaper, asking for their help. These approaches frequently not

Figure 2-1 Photograph of family member, Santander, Spain

Rogad a Dios en vuestras oraciones
por el descanso del alma de

Don Samuel Bonilla Picado

Nació el 14 de Abril de 1895. Hijo de don Manuel Bonilla Arias y doña Juana Picado Jiménez. Contrajo matrimonio en 1918 con doña Esperanza Vargas Jiménez. Falleció el 27 de Octubre de 1934.

ORACION

Señor Misericordioso y Eterno, enseñadme a conformarme siempre con tus designios adorables. Eres compasivo Padre, consuélame en mis penas y da el descanso eterno al alma de vuestro siervo **Samuel Bonilla Picado,** para que, libre del cautiverio del Purgatorio, vuele a las regiones de la Gloria Celestial y desde allí interceda por los que aquí en la tierra lloramos su separación. Te lo pedimos así por los méritos de Nuestro Señor Jesucristo, que contigo vive y reina por los siglos de los siglos. Amén.

———

(Un Padrenuestro y Ave María a Jesús Sacramentado por el descanso de su alma).

Figure 2-2 Printed death announcement, Costa Rica (author's copy)

only identify the individuals in the picture but also bring a wealth of other information concerning your family.

3. Printed Materials. Many families printed announcements in limited quantities for distribution to friends and relatives. The most common of these are wedding invitations. In the past, death announcements were also widely distributed and can frequently be spotted by the black border on the envelopes in which they were sent or on the paper on which they were printed (see figure 2-2). In addition, in Catholic countries both baptisms and first communions were often announced by formal printed invitations or announcements.

4. Passports, visas, work permits, and citizenship or naturalization papers. This category refers to any of the various documents involved in the process of a person leaving his country of birth or citizenship, immigrating to a second country, and in that country taking out citizenship. A passport usually carries the given name and double surname of its holder as well as that of the spouse, and also indicates the holder's nationality, profession, marital status, place and date of birth, residence, color of eyes, color of hair, and any other particularly identifying characteristics (see figure 2-3). It is also possible that the names, ages, and sex of children under a certain age could be included, as well as the picture, signature, and fin-

Tax No. 22566

PASAPORTE NUME A EL PASO, TEXAS, E. U. A.

No. 32567.

EL GOBIERNO DEL ESTADO LIBRE Y SOBERANO DE AGUAS=CALIENTES:

Concede seguro y libre pasaporte en favor del C. AURELIO ESCOTO, originario de Encarnación de Díaz, Estado de Jalisco, según lo ha comprobado ante este Gobierno con información de testigos fidedignos que presentó, habiéndosele eximido del certificado del acta de su nacimiento; reside en esta Capital y se dirige a EL PASO, TEX., ESTADOS UNIDOS DE NORTE AMERICA, con el solo objeto de buscar trabajo para atender a su subsistencia.

Se suplica a las autoridades civiles y militares de los lugares por donde transite le impartan las garantías necesarias y le concedan facilidades para que pueda llegar a su destino.

FILIACION

Hijo de Tiburcio Escoto y de Ma. Refugio Muñoz.................
Edo. civ. casado......
Edad 33 años..........
Oficio jornalero......
Estatura regular......
Complexión regular....
Color moreno..........
Pelo negro............
Frente ancha..........
Cejas negras..........
Ojos oscuros..........
Nariz regular.........
Bigote negro..........
Boca grande...........
Barba razurada........
Señas particulares....
Ligera cicatris vertical sobre la nariz....

FIRMA

Personas que lo acompañan: su esposa Ma. Refugio Muñoz y su hija menor..................

CONSTITUCION Y REFORMAS.
Aguascalientes, 19 de Agosto de 1919.
EL GOBERNADOR CONSTITUCIONAL

EL SRIO. GRAL. DE GOBIERNO
LIC.

U. S. Immigration Service, EL PASO, TEX.
AUG 26 '19
(Da)

Figure 2-3 Mexican passport issued by the State of Aquascalientes, Mexico, 1919 (author's copy)

gerprints of the holder. Passports are and were issued either by the national governments and/or by the civil governors in the provinces or states of many Hispanic countries, including Spain and Mexico.

Unfortunately the use of passports as a necessary requirement for leaving most countries has only been adopted in the twentieth century. A variety of approaches and systems governing exit were used in the nineteenth century. The most popular merely involved going to a port and signing on to a ship. In most cases documents proving that a man had already served in the military were the only ones needed to emigrate. In some cases, such as for migrant workers coming into the southwestern United States, a work permit issued at the border was necessary to obtain work. After 1926 an alien registration card was issued. Look for such documents preserved among the important papers of your immigrant ancestors. They may provide clues as to their place of origin in the mother country.

Once in the country of his destination, some type of action was necessary for your ancestor to achieve citizenship. If this was sought, proof of that citizenship application will likely have been preserved.

5. Legal papers. This category encompasses a wide variety of records usually relating to financial or property transactions. These were originally written to establish or transfer ownership of property, both real and personal. Since they were official documents proving a right of ownership to specific property, they were usually carefully preserved, even for several generations beyond the period of actual contact with the property. These documents can usually be recognized and distinguished from other kinds of papers by the fact that they will have been written and witnessed by a notary and/or carry an official stamp or seal.

Included in the category of legal papers are *capitulaciones matrimoniales* (marriage contracts), *actos de cesión* (cession acts, relating to the relinquishment of a particular right or power), *actos de cambio* (acts relating to a change or transfer), *actos de compra/venta* (the papers relating to the purchase/sale of property or right), *actos de donación* (relating to gifts of property or powers or rights), *testamentos* (wills), *cuadernos particionales* (books relating to the division of properties or rights), *contratos de alquileres* (lease or rental contracts), *derechos de sucesión* (succession rights), *inventarios* (inventories, usually relating to some transfer or sale of property or rights), *declaración de herederos* (declaration of heirs, relating to the rights to certain properties given by the courts to the heirs of an intestate person), and *tutorías* (guardianship papers). In addition, similar papers of a less official nature would be *extractos bancarios* (financial statements or bank extracts), and *polizas de seguros* (insurance policies). For the family historian, these documents can provide a wealth of information as to the activities, interests, and social position of the ancestral family, as well as perhaps the only link to the particular locality from which the family originated.

6. Old letters. Letters written by your ancestors can contain fascinating family history information. Notes as to the activities of a family member, as well as his opinions relating to personal, family, local, and national events, will appear in letters. Many times letters may be the only link with the mother country. Such was the case for one family in Uruguay. Their great-grandfather had remained in Spain and had written a series of letters over a twenty-five year period to a son in Uruguay. Sixty years later, as the great-granddaughter began the search for her family's origin in Spain, the only clues were those contained in the letters. In addition to naming localities, the papers gave important information as to the activities of the family members. The last of the letters was written by a cousin on paper bordered in black, indicating the great-grandfather's death. The entire collection of letters is a treasure-trove of family history and genealogical information for that family.

7. Military records, decorations, etc. Since compulsory military conscription has been a regular part of Hispanic life in most countries for at least a century and a half, military documents are frequently found among the effects of those with Hispanic ancestry. Such documents are usually papers showing release from military service, as they were frequently required before an individual was permitted to emigrate (see figure 2-4). Military documents may indicate the name of the person, the rank which he attained, the regiment with which he served, and the place where he enlisted; they may also include information of a more personal nature, such as his place of birth, occupation, and age. Not only can this information assist in locating the place of origin, but it can also be of great value in indicating where to look for additional military records.

8. School and occupational records. These documents cover a wide variety of materials relating to the educational and occupational activities of one's ancestors. Those relating to educational activities might include registration information from a particular school or college (*colegio* or *universidad*) in which he registered; exam papers; diplomas or titles which were obtained; awards for particular activities in school; records of grades (*notas*) or of graduation from one level to another.

Occupational records are of an even wider variety. They might include special permits such as those which were issued to street vendors, bakers, and many other classes of workers; personal business cards or advertisements; or membership in the *gremios* or *sindicatos* (unions, guilds, or syndicates), which were organized in some larger cities and among some rural farm workers. Of special interest will be work permits issued by immigration authorities.

9. Newspaper clippings. In the home country, mention in a local newspaper would most likely have been limited to the upper class. However, once an individual arrived in the Americas, he may well have achieved local status, and information relating to his activities and origins would be found in local newspapers. Frequently, such newspaper clippings were preserved by other family members or friends and can provide a unique source of information relating to the family, its activities, and its origin.

EL [illegible] y en su nombre el [illegible]

CONCEDO PASE Á LA SITUACIÓN DE SEGUNDA RESERVA, *con arreglo á lo prevenido en el artículo 7.° de la ley de reclutamiento de 11 de julio de 1885, modificada por la de 21 de agosto de 1896, y en virtud de lo dispuesto en* [illegible] *orden de* [illegible] *á* José Reyes Ortiz [illegible] *, de* [illegible] *natural de* Cabra *, Juzgado de primera instancia de* [illegible] *, provincia de* Córdoba *, de oficio* Jornalero *edad* 20 *años, su estado* Soltero *. Fué alistado en el reemplazo de* 1902 *, tuvo ingreso en la Zona de reclutamiento de* [illegible] *, y pasa á* Cabra *provincia de* Córdoba *, que corresponde á la demarcación de la Reserva de* Córdoba [illegible] *, causando alta en* [illegible]

Queda enterado de las prevenciones insertas al dorso, á las cuales dará exacto cumplimiento, y de que á los doce años desde su ingreso en Caja le será recogido este pase y obtendrá su licencia absoluta.

Córdoba 1º Octubre 1908

Anotado al folio 61 *núm.* 1886

DE CÓRDOBA N.º 12

Esta licencia no es válida si no lleva el sello en seco del DEPÓSITO DE LA GUERRA. **(Real orden de 27 de mayo de 1890, D. O. núm. 118).**

Figure 2-4 Military discharge papers found in a descendant's home (author's copy)

10. Documento nacional de identidad o cédula personal (national identity document or personal document). In most Hispanic countries, beginning in the late nineteenth century or early twentieth century, laws were passed relating to the issuance of a personal document (*cédula personal*) which all citizens were required to carry. Locating such a document among the personal effects of an ancestor can be significant, since the point of issuance will probably be the Civil Register of the district in which the family resided at the time.

11. Memberships in private clubs, civic or nobility organizations, and political parties. Political parties and social clubs involved people of all levels of society, both in Hispanic countries and among Hispanics in the United States. Membership, and especially the office held in any of these, may have been certified by a diploma, certificate, or other type of document which may be found in the collection of family sources within one's home. Such documents can be particularly significant, not only because they can offer a glimpse of the active social life of the individual ancestor but also because they can lead to more extensive records kept by the organizations to which he belonged. Records of this type are kept in such a wide variety of locations that the only reasonable clue to locating an individual's membership may be in finding some mention of it among family members.

12. Diaries, biographies, or autobiographies. Neither diaries nor autobiographies are commonly found in Hispanic cultures. However, the move to a new country may have prompted the Spanish immigrant to record information about his life or the lives of his immediate ancestors.

13. Written family histories (published and unpublished). Written family histories are much more common among the nobility of Hispanic countries than among the lower classes. However, as in the case of autobiographies, immigration to another country may have spurred the individual to record his family origins in a family history. Since many of these were of interest only to the family, they will be found in unpublished manuscript form. A discussion of published family histories is found later in this chapter.

14. Medical records. Medical record cards, X-rays, medical analyses, and dental and eyeglass prescriptions can all contribute to a knowledge of the ancestor and how he looked. Such information is most likely limited to the twentieth century, due to the more extensive availability of doctors.

Contact Other Family Members

The second step in a preliminary survey, after having made a thorough search for home sources, is to check with other family members. There are two goals to accomplish in doing this. The first is to make a record of their memories and feelings about the family. It is very likely that older family members such as grandparents, great-aunts and uncles, or cousins from a different branch of the family may have memories that have not been passed on to you or your immediate family. Frequently, the memories of other family members can add new dimensions to your knowledge of the lives and personalities of direct-line ancestors, and also may provide clues to the town of origin in the mother country.

The second purpose in making contact with other family members is to ask them to help you in the search for home sources. Many times original documents from the immigrant ancestor will have been passed down through a different branch of the family.

Contact with other family members can be accomplished in three ways: (1) a questionnaire; (2) a personal letter; or (3) a personal visit. The questionnaire is basically a form letter listing a series of questions relating to the family and information that you want to know, such as the following: Do you remember your grandfather, Juan Garcia? Do you have any idea where he came from in Mexico? Do you have, or know someone who has, any old documents relating to Juan Garcia? A space can be left for short answers at the end of each of the questions on the questionnaire.

The questionnaire is the least desirable approach in contacting other family members, since it is the least personal and will be less likely to get an interested response from your family members. However, this survey approach can be used to reach a large number of relatives easily and can identify those who do have documents and/or interest in developing a history of the family.

A second and better approach is to write a personal letter to each family member. This letter could include many of the same questions as the questionnaire and should follow the basic principles of writing letters to relatives outlined in chapter 6. Ideally, the letter would be an initial contact that could be followed up by a personal visit with those who show interest.

A personal visit is the most effective way to contact family members, especially those who are older. Specific questions asked in a personal visit will frequently elicit stories or information that may not have been included in a response to a survey or letter and yet could add color and detail to a developing family history.

A successful interview is nothing more than a relaxed visit, a way of getting to know a living family member better. Advance preparation is the key to such an experience. Review all the information you can about the person to be interviewed, so that meaningful questions can be asked about her life. Show a personal interest in her, since this will help in soliciting good responses regarding her feelings and memories of the family. Background information may be gained from reading life sketches or diaries, going through scrapbooks, or talking to other family members. It would also be helpful to review general background materials on the historical events of her lifetime. For example, if anybody in her family were a veteran of the Mexican Revolution (in which women fought as well as men), it would be of value to check briefly in a history book about the battles in the area where he or she would have fought. Use this information to plan a series of questions that will help her to recall the events of her life. Be careful that your questions avoid any preconceived prejudices concerning the family or family members, and allow her to stay comfortable and focused.

A permanent, detailed record of the interview is essential to making it a valuable research tool. Again, pre-planning helps. Depending on the circumstances, information from a visit may be preserved by video or tape recording, longhand or shorthand notes taken during the interview, or notes written down immediately after the visit. Of these choices, a tape recorder or video camera is the best and should be used whenever possible. If tape recording, use a good-quality recorder with a microphone that can be set to the side and yet still record the entire conversation adequately. A video camera should be on a tripod or operated by a second person, not the interviewer. Before the interview, practice using the tape recorder or video camera so that you are relaxed and confident with it. After the interview is completed, the tape or film should be checked to make sure that all of the interview was clearly recorded. If it was not, the interviewer should immediately take notes about the things that are unclear.

Remember that your purpose is to establish positive relationships and learn more about your family, and you want the interview to be a positive experience for both of you. Be creative in your questioning. Rather than asking "Yes" and "No" questions, use those that will elicit longer answers and bring forth memories. The stories and details that are most interesting are sometimes at the subconscious level, and it may take time and some meandering to bring them to the surface. Sometimes a variety of approaches may be necessary to bring particular details back to mind.

Potential questions will vary, depending on the reason for interviewing that particular person. If the relative is a direct-line ancestor, such as a great-aunt or grandmother, the researcher will want to preserve details about her childhood memories and her adult years, as well as her attitudes on a wide variety of things. If the relative is a cousin on a collateral branch of the family, limit questions more to her memories of the common family line and information that she may have relating to the researcher's direct-line ancestors.

As the interview proceeds and new thoughts or questions come to mind, make short notes but don't interrupt the person who is speaking. If she makes mistakes, be careful not to correct her as this might be offensive. If there are particularly sensitive areas in the family history, it might be a good idea to save questions about those until near the end of the interview or perhaps even a later time, when a feeling of confidence and relaxation has been developed between the two of you.

Whether the interview was recorded on tape or film or by notes, the following information should be recorded and placed with the interview: the name and age of the person interviewed, your name, the date of the interview, and a general summary of the information covered.

Generally, questions that an interviewer will want to ask fall into four categories.

1. Discuss memories that the person has of deceased family members. The emphasis here should be on the personalities of deceased family members, stories about them, and the kinds of personal and intimate details that records and even photographs do not show. Inquiries about activities such as military involvement, immigration, travels, or occupations can all be particularly important. When trying to trace the immigrant ancestor over the ocean or across the border, even the smallest of details remembered as a child can be helpful in locating the place from which the ancestor came. Comments as to the climate, the language (even isolated words that were spoken), particular historical events that were remembered, any geographical characteristics, monuments, memories of the town, etc., can all aid in locating the particular place of origin. Also search for genealogical data such as names, dates, places, and relationships.

2. Talk extensively about her memories of earlier years. Where does she remember living? What types of clothing were worn? What was a typical day like? What were special holidays? What were their Sunday activities? What kinds of work experiences did they have? Did they live in the city? If not, what was life like on the farm or in farm camps? What was social life like? Did they date? Did they have chaperons? These kinds of questions can not only give us insight into her life but also shed light on the position of the family, and may give additional insight into the lives of family members who are now dead.

3. Ask about her adult years. School or other training, jobs, courtship, marriage, the birth of each of her children, the houses where she lived, her regular routine, her political involvement or other civic activities, and many other subjects can be discussed. Depending on the purpose of the interview, this topic can be more limited if your primary interest is her contact as a child with some of your deceased ancestors.

4. Inquire about memories of world or national events that would have affected the life of the person who is being interviewed. The Spanish Civil War, the Great Depression, the two World Wars, and the Mexican Revolution are the types of events that would have had an impact on Spaniards, Mexicans, and Hispanic Americans. Also inquire about fashions and how they have changed and about what kinds of changes technology has brought. Ask questions about politics and try to elicit general comments on major world events through which she has lived.

As you contact other family members, you will be able to collect a variety of material for use in compiling a factual and yet intimate family history.

Some of the most fascinating material you collect will be based on family oral traditions, such as descent from royalty or "the ancestor who accompanied Cortez in the conquest of Mexico." Frequently, due to the natural desire to improve upon the condition of the family, many traditions, although based on fact, are clearly exaggerated. Family traditions may help to locate a place of origin in the mother country or even pinpoint the original family home, or in other ways further the genealogical search, but all such family traditions should be verified by documentation before they are accepted as true.

Check the FamilySearch® Indexes of the LDS Church for Research Previously Done on the Family

Once a thorough search of sources available within your own family has been completed, the second part of the preliminary survey is to evaluate what research others have done that could tie in directly with your own family. The first place to check is the indexes of The Church of Jesus Christ of Latter-day Saints. Members of this church, usually known as the Mormon Church, have a deep religious interest and motivation in doing genealogical research. The extensive genealogical work they have done has been compiled by topics into several excellent indexes, which will be discussed in greater detail in chapter 4.

All of these indexes are available at the Family History Library in Salt Lake City, and at the more than 1,200 family history centers located in local Latter-day Saint churches throughout the world. Because of the value of these indexes and the wide variety of record sources from Hispanic countries that is available on microfilm through these family history centers, the indexes are grouped together in a computer program called FamilySearch. This database contains the following indexes:

1. Ancestral File™, containing over 20 million names
2. International Genealogical Index™, containing over 240 million names
3. Social Security Death Index, containing over 50 million names
4. Military Index, containing over 20,000 names

Check for Printed Family Histories, Biographies, and Collected Genealogies

The fourth and last step in the preliminary survey is to find out what printed genealogies, biographies, or collected genealogies are available on the family or family members. This involves four separate kinds of searches: (1) searching for information on family surnames in biographical dictionaries and genealogical encyclopedias, (2) searching for biographical information on family members, (3) searching for monograph histories of your family or a collateral branch thereof, and (4) identifying other people who are doing research on the same families or in the same geographic area(s).

The first of these can easily be accomplished nearly anywhere in the world. There are a wide variety of biographical and genealogical encyclopedias and dictionaries available for Spanish surnames. Perhaps the most famous and extensive is Garcia Carraffa's *Enciclopedia heráldica y genealógica Hispano-Americana,*[1] which currently includes eighty-eight volumes published from 1920 to 1967, covering the letters AA through URR. The first two volumes of this series are a study of the science of heraldry, and the remainder of the volumes are an alphabetical list of noble and semi-noble families from throughout Spain and her former American colonies. The family information is organized by surname and involves a brief account of the history of each family, tracing it down to its most recent noble member. Most entries also include illustrations of coats of arms and frequently have a limited bibliography, which can lead the genealogist to more extended monographic family histories.

Automated Archives, Inc. of Orem, Utah, published on computer disks a set of 1,000 surname histories by Lyman D. Platt, entitled *Spanish Surname Histories.** These histories, which have a heavy Spanish American emphasis, originally appeared in *Vista* magazine. Each provides a brief history of the surname, its etymology and a series of references to individuals of the surname who have been famous or found in Spanish American regional sources. A similar series has appeared in the Orange County, California newspaper *Excelsior*, and has been compiled and published by the Society for Hispanic Historical and Ancestral Research.

Almost every Hispanic country has national and regional dictionaries and encyclopedias, which can be of greater value to the researcher because they include many families, surnames, and individual biographies which are not noble in origin. Examples from Mexico of this type are *Diccionario biográfico de Tamaulipas*[2] and *Diccionario biográfico de Saltillo.*[3]

Another type of regional series is typified by the *Diccionario onomástico y heráldico vasco*[4] by Jaime de Querexteta. This six-volume series lists in alphabetical order nearly all of the Basque names which can be found. While it does not give a family history for most of them, it will indicate if the name is unique to a particular region, and may be a clue in helping to locate the particular area in which you should search. For example, the surname Anacaba is listed as meaning *pastizal de gamones* (feeding grass of small mountain goats) and as originating in the area of the province of Vizcaya. Perhaps more helpful would be a reference such as that for the surname Mendiguchía, which the author found totally accurate in predicting the town of origin as Elgueta, Guipuzcoa.

A more modern biographical approach is taken by the *Indice Biográfico de España, Portugal y Iberoamérica.*[5] This four-volume index identifies about 200,000 historical individuals from Roman times to the early twentieth century; it is compiled from 306 biographical encyclopedias, dictionaries, and collective works covering 700 original volumes from Spain, Portugal, and Latin America, published from the seventeenth to the early

---

*A list of the surnames covered appears in *Hispanic Surnames* by Lyman D. Platt (Baltimore: GPC, 1996).

twentieth century. Those works were photocopied and the references from all 700 volumes were then separated and arranged in alphabetical order. That collection is now filmed on 1,070 microfiche, available through the family history centers of the LDS Church (microfiche sets #6002170-6002172).

Other books dealing with biographical data on immigration are also available. One is Peter Boyd Bowman's *Indice geobiográfico de más de 56 mil pobladores de la América hispana*[6] (Vol. 1: 1493–1519, Vol. 2: 1520–1539), which lists the earliest immigrants to the Spanish colonies. The bibliography at the end of chapter 12 of *The Source*[7] is illustrative of the kinds of books that can be used as a starting point for the researcher seeking to identify his own areas and periods of research.

The third type of printed information to search for in completing the preliminary survey is articles or books published about the family. These books will give the family history and sometimes include a list of living family members at the time of publication. Once again, these are found primarily for noble families or for families that have achieved some particular status in Spanish or Hispano-American society, although many descendants of poorer immigrants in the U.S. have written family histories. The only volume listing large numbers of family histories is *Una bibliografía de historias familiares de Latinoamérica y los Estados Unidos*, by Lyman D. Platt (Salt Lake City: IGHL, 1990.).[8] *Hispanic Surnames and Family History* by Lyman Platt (Baltimore: Genealogical Publishing Co., 1996) includes an extensive bibliography of family histories in the United States and Latin America, and lists the Spanish surnames for which histories exist.

Beyond Platt's books several different sources may be checked, many of which are given in the reference works listed in the paragraphs above. Others appear as articles in periodicals such as *Hidalguía*. The Family History Library in Salt Lake City, as well as most large university and public libraries in the United States and Latin America, have large numbers of Hispanic family histories in their card catalogs. As you search for printed materials like those discussed above, check the catalogs for major university collections, many of which are available through local universities or major public libraries on computerized search systems and can be ordered through inter-library loan. You may also find items of interest from local libraries from the area in which the immigrant ancestor settled in the United States. In addition, an occasional perusal of the Family History Library Catalog™ found in the FamilySearch program in the local LDS family history centers may yield a new acquisition of particular relevance. There may also be articles published in major historical and genealogical periodicals relating to the immigration patterns for a particular locality or time period.

As these searches are done, you will want to check each index under Spanish surnames, migration, emigration, and immigration, as well as the specific surnames, countries, and localities being researched, both in the

United States and in the likely country and region of origin. You may also want to consult the card catalog or published indexes for the national library (*Biblioteca Nacional*) in your ancestors' mother country. These, as well as hundreds of libraries in the United States, may be searched through computerized catalog systems such as RLIN and WORLDCAT, available through the Internet at most libraries with inter-library loan services. Ask your librarian for direction and assistance in using these computerized catalog systems.

When a particular region in the mother country has been identified as the origin of the family, a letter to the provincial historical archives or to the city library in the provincial capital may also bring a list of histories of families that might be related to the family being researched. Naturally, any person making a trip to do research in the mother country should stop at these libraries to check for possible family histories before doing extensive research, as this may save a large amount of time.

The final step is to identify others working on the same families or in the same geographic areas you are. There are a growing number of Hispanic genealogical societies in the United States, as well as Hispanic genealogical computer bulletin boards on the Internet. Some of these people may have already researched your family lines or in your locality. You will find that "networking" — the sharing of information, expertise, and enthusiasm — helps everyone. This book's Appendix lists Hispanic genealogical societies in the United States.

SUMMARY

In summary, the preliminary survey brings together all that you and your living family members know about your family and determines if anyone outside your immediate or known family has done research on your family lines. With this information you will now be ready to follow the steps outlined in the next chapter of organizing and evaluating what you have found in order to determine your research objectives.

---

1. Alberto Garcia Carraffa and Arturo Garcia Carraffa, *Enciclopedia heráldica y genealógica Hispano-Americana*. 88 vols. (Madrid: Nueva Impenta Radio, 1932–1963).

2. Carlos Gonzalez Salas and Fidel Zorilla, *Diccionario biográfico de Tamaulipas* (Ciudad Victoria: Universidad de Tamaulipas, 1984).

3. Ignacio Narro Etchegaray and Martha Durón Jiménez, *Diccionario biográfico de Saltillo* (Saltillo: Archivo Municipal de Saltillo, 1995).

4. Jaime de Querexeta, *Diccionario onomástico y heráldico vasco* (Bilbao: La Gran Enciclopedia Vasca, 1970–1975).

[5] Victor Herrero Mediavila and Lolita Rosa Aquayo Hayle, *Indice Biográfico de España, Portugal y Iberoamérica* (New York: K.G. Sur, 1990).

[6] Peter Boyd Bowman, *Indice geobiográfico de más de 56 mil pobladores de la América hispana*. 2 vols. (Mexico: Fondo de Cultura Económica, 1985).

[7] Loretto Szucs and Sandra Luebking, *The Source*, 2nd ed. (Salt Lake City: Ancestry, 1996).

[8] Lyman D. Platt, *Una bibliografía de historias familiares de Latinoamérica y los Estados Unidos* (Salt Lake City: IGHL, 1990). A catalog of all IGHL Publications can be obtained by writing to: IGHL, 316 W. 500 N., St. George, Utah 84770.

CHAPTER 3

Research: Organizing and Evaluating Information

Don Vicente de Cadenas y Vicent entitles his practical kit for family genealogy *Memorandum de la genealogía familiar*[1]. *Memorandum* comes from the Latin word meaning "that which must be had in memory." In English and Spanish it has the additional meaning of a book, file, or report in which things that one wants to remember are noted. This chapter will help you to create your own *memorandum*, to record in an organized and effective way what you want to remember about your family.

A good organizational system does more than merely file information and documents away for later retrieval. The process of organization itself provides a means of analyzing and evaluating the information you have gathered, and organizing it for rapid comparison with new information. As more details are found, a good organizational system can save hours of time by helping you to quickly correlate your new data with the old, evaluating the new knowledge it gives you of the family or the direction you will continue to search.

The personal computer has greatly facilitated this process by allowing for easy storage and retrieval of large amounts of data, which can be rearranged and presented in a wide variety of ways: pedigree charts, descent charts, family group sheets, individual information sheets, sorted lists, etc. In addition, computer programs allow for adding new data from large computerized databases, as well as from the personal databases of other family historians. For a modern and serious family historian, the use of a genealogy computer program is crucial. Nevertheless, an understanding of the traditional paper forms for organizing your genealogy will assist you in understanding the process of doing research in ways that the computer may not.

This entire chapter deals with files, forms, and computer programs. There are many types of forms and several different types of filing systems available. Those described in this chapter have not been chosen because of an inherent superiority over a wide variety of others, but because the author and his students have found them to be the most useful for the beginner working with Hispanic records. The individual researcher should pick a system that suits his needs and temperament best. Any system chosen should provide for minimum duplication, rapid retrieval of information, simplicity in filing, accurate recording of all information obtained, clear indications as to source, and a means of organizing and evaluating new material in comparison with that already discovered, recorded, and filed.

FOR DOCUMENT AND RESEARCH NOTES: FILING SYSTEMS

Whether using a computer program or paper forms, a separate filing system must be created for storage and retrieval of research notes and copies and extracts of original documents. There are four potential systems of filing and categorizing documents and materials gathered from genealogical and family history research: (1) by family units into maternal and paternal family lines, or for each individual surname; (2) by the names of each of your ancestors who appears as a parent on the pedigree chart (discussed later in this chapter) with each file containing information about the family; (3) by each geographical area from which your ancesters came — country, province, or parish; or (4) by record types, e.g., parish records, notary records, civil records, military records, etc., maintaining the original order and numbering of the source archives.

Instructions describing the use of particular filing systems or forms frequently become complicated and difficult to understand. To make the instructions clearer, a real person and her ancestry have been chosen to illustrate the filing process: Jeri Lyn Bebout, daughter of Leroy Bebout, Jr., and Alberta J. Fuertes. (See figure 3-1 for Jeri Bebout's first pedigree chart.) When Jeri began her research, three of her four grandparents were dead. She did, however, have uncles and aunts living throughout the United States as well as in Spain. Letters to them and conversations with her mother and grandmother yielded large amounts of information and documents of the types discussed in the preceding chapter.

Being confronted with a mountain of papers, photos, and family memorabilia, Jeri realized that she needed a system for organizing that material. Her initial action was to file all of the material into separate large files, one for her paternal Bebout ancestors who came from the United States, and the other for her maternal Fuertes ancestors who came to California from Valencia, Spain. For several personal reasons she was more interested in beginning work on the Spanish line than on the other; therefore, the family file for the Bebouts was temporarily left as it was.

Jeri found that the file for all of her maternal lines was still too extensive to be manageable. She then divided that file into two family files, one for the Fuertes side of the family (her maternal grandfather), and the other for the Varea side of the family (her maternal grandmother). No further division was necessary on her grandfather's family file at that time since he was dead, and her grandmother knew very little about the Fuertes family.

Jeri still found the Varea file to be unmanageably large. For this reason she tried a different approach in filing the Varea information, creating a

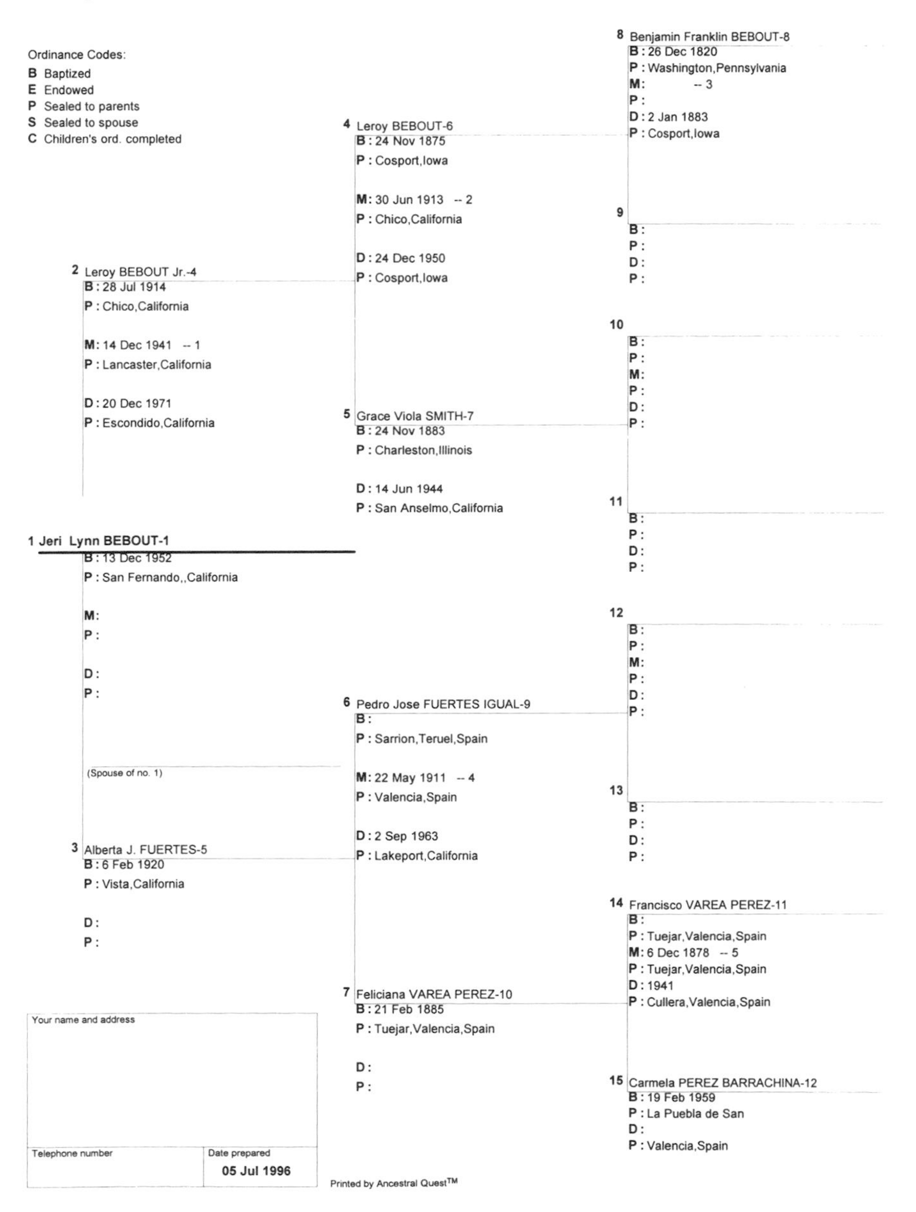
Pedigree Chart
Chart no. 1
Ordinance Codes:
B Baptized
E Endowed
P Sealed to parents
S Sealed to spouse
C Children's ord. completed
1 Jeri Lynn BEBOUT-1
B: 13 Dec 1952
P: San Fernando,,California
M:
P:
D:
P:
(Spouse of no. 1)
2 Leroy BEBOUT Jr.-4
B: 28 Jul 1914
P: Chico,California
M: 14 Dec 1941 -- 1
P: Lancaster,California
D: 20 Dec 1971
P: Escondido,California
3 Alberta J. FUERTES-5
B: 6 Feb 1920
P: Vista,California
D:
P:
4 Leroy BEBOUT-6
B: 24 Nov 1875
P: Cosport,Iowa
M: 30 Jun 1913 -- 2
P: Chico,California
D: 24 Dec 1950
P: Cosport,Iowa
5 Grace Viola SMITH-7
B: 24 Nov 1883
P: Charleston,Illinois
D: 14 Jun 1944
P: San Anselmo,California
6 Pedro Jose FUERTES IGUAL-9
B:
P: Sarrion,Teruel,Spain
M: 22 May 1911 -- 4
P: Valencia,Spain
D: 2 Sep 1963
P: Lakeport,California
7 Feliciana VAREA PEREZ-10
B: 21 Feb 1885
P: Tuejar,Valencia,Spain
D:
P:
8 Benjamin Franklin BEBOUT-8
B: 26 Dec 1820
P: Washington,Pennsylvania
M: -- 3
P:
D: 2 Jan 1883
P: Cosport,Iowa
9
B:
P:
D:
P:
10
B:
P:
M:
P:
D:
P:
11
B:
P:
D:
P:
12
B:
P:
M:
P:
D:
P:
13
B:
P:
D:
P:
14 Francisco VAREA PEREZ-11
B:
P: Tuejar,Valencia,Spain
M: 6 Dec 1878 -- 5
P: Tuejar,Valencia,Spain
D: 1941
P: Cullera,Valencia,Spain
15 Carmela PEREZ BARRACHINA-12
B: 19 Feb 1959
P: La Puebla de San
D:
P: Valencia,Spain
Your name and address
Telephone number
Date prepared
05 Jul 1996
Printed by Ancestral Quest™

Figure 3-1 Jeri Bebout's first pedigree chart

file for each of her direct-line ancestors on the Varea side of the family. She therefore had a file for Feliciana Varea Perez, her grandmother; another file for Francisco Varea Perez, her great-grandfather; and a third file for Carmela Perez Barrachina, her great-grandmother. The only difficulty she found with making files for each individual was when an aunt in Spain mailed her the will of her great-grandfather, Francisco Varea Perez, which contained information about her grandmother as well as her great-grandfather. To solve the dilemma as to which file to put the will in, she filed the original under her great-grandfather, Francisco Varea Perez, and made a photocopy to put in the file for her grandmother, Feliciana Varea Perez. She might also have created a list of documents for each file, and in her grandmother's put the notation, "For will of Francisco Varea Perez."

At this point Jeri had employed two of the four systems listed above. She might have made use of the third type of filing system by dividing all of her information into files according to the area in Spain from which her ancestors came. These might simply have been the province of Teruel and the province of Valencia or, perhaps more likely, the parish of Tuéjar in the province of Valencia, and the parish of La Puebla de San Miguel in the province of Valencia, Spain. The area file works well when the family remains in a single area for several generations, but does not work as well if the ancestors over the first two or three generations moved frequently and lived in a number of different geographical areas. For example, as Jeri traces her paternal American ancestry the system of creating files for each individual will probably be best, since her American ancestors changed from one area of the country to another within a generation, and within two generations are found in four different states.

In Spain and many areas of Latin America, however, most ancestral lines are found in a particular area after a generation or two, and large amounts of research can be done in a single geographical unit, usually the parish from which the family originates. For this reason Jeri, like many Hispanic researchers, adopted the geographical filing system for the Varea line as research progressed.

The fourth type of filing system places all records of a similar type from the same archives together. For example, all civil vital records from a town would be in one file, church parish records would be in another, all wills and notarial documents would be in a third, military records would be in a fourth, etc. If you are using this system, be sure to indicate on the family group sheets the type of record source used, so that the original record can easily be found. Usually this reference is the same as the source archives, which makes it easy to consult the original again later.

Any filing system should be flexible and organized, allowing you to find the material you need as quickly as possible. As your research expands, you will want a filing system that can be modified and extended to adapt to your needs.

No matter what combination of the above filing systems you adopt, it is important that you keep consistent notes and carefully file them following each research experience. All notes should indicate the place where the research was done, e.g., the parish archive of San Miguel, Spain; or the Family History Library in Salt Lake City, Utah. The following information should also be recorded: the name of the person doing the research; the date the research was done; and an indication as to how to retrieve the information, e.g., a library call number, microfilm number, type of parish book and volume number, and for any of these, the page or pages where the information was found. The purpose of source notes is to have your sources of information listed so clearly that it is possible to later find and review the original documents. This also makes it easier for another person to check the validity of the research.

Detailed extracts should be made of any original records you consult. Be sure to copy exactly all the pertinent information given, avoiding the use of abbreviations not found in the original record. Use either file cards or letter-size paper, depending on what works the best for you and your filing system. The first can be more manageable, but the latter has the advantage of making it possible to file not only notes but also photocopies of documents. If photocopies are taken of original documents, be sure to record all of the source information along with the date and place of the research. With the growing availability of laptop computers, these notes may be directly entered in computer research files. Whether you choose to use a computer on-site or not, extracts and notes should still be taken and maintained separately from your family group sheets or computer databases. The ability to consult these extracts and notes at a later time will prove extremely valuable in the on-going process of analysis and conclusion that research in original sources demands.

PEDIGREE CHARTS

Once the initial sorting has been accomplished and a simple filing system adopted, the researcher should create a pedigree chart showing himself and each of his direct-line ancestors, i.e., his parents, grandparents, great-grandparents, etc. This pedigree chart will serve as a guide or skeletal outline for the research to be done on your family lines. Take a work copy of the pedigree chart with you when you go to parish or other archives, or read a microfilm, to immediately record new information that you find.

If you are using a computer program, it is usually helpful to print a pedigree chart that begins with the most recent ancestor born in that parish. This will help to keep the search organized, especially when you find a new generation not recorded on the pedigree. The pedigree chart can serve as a guide telling how far back you have gone, in what area you last worked, and where you need to proceed. To understand how the pedigree chart can do this, look again at Jeri's pedigree chart (figure 3-2) for the

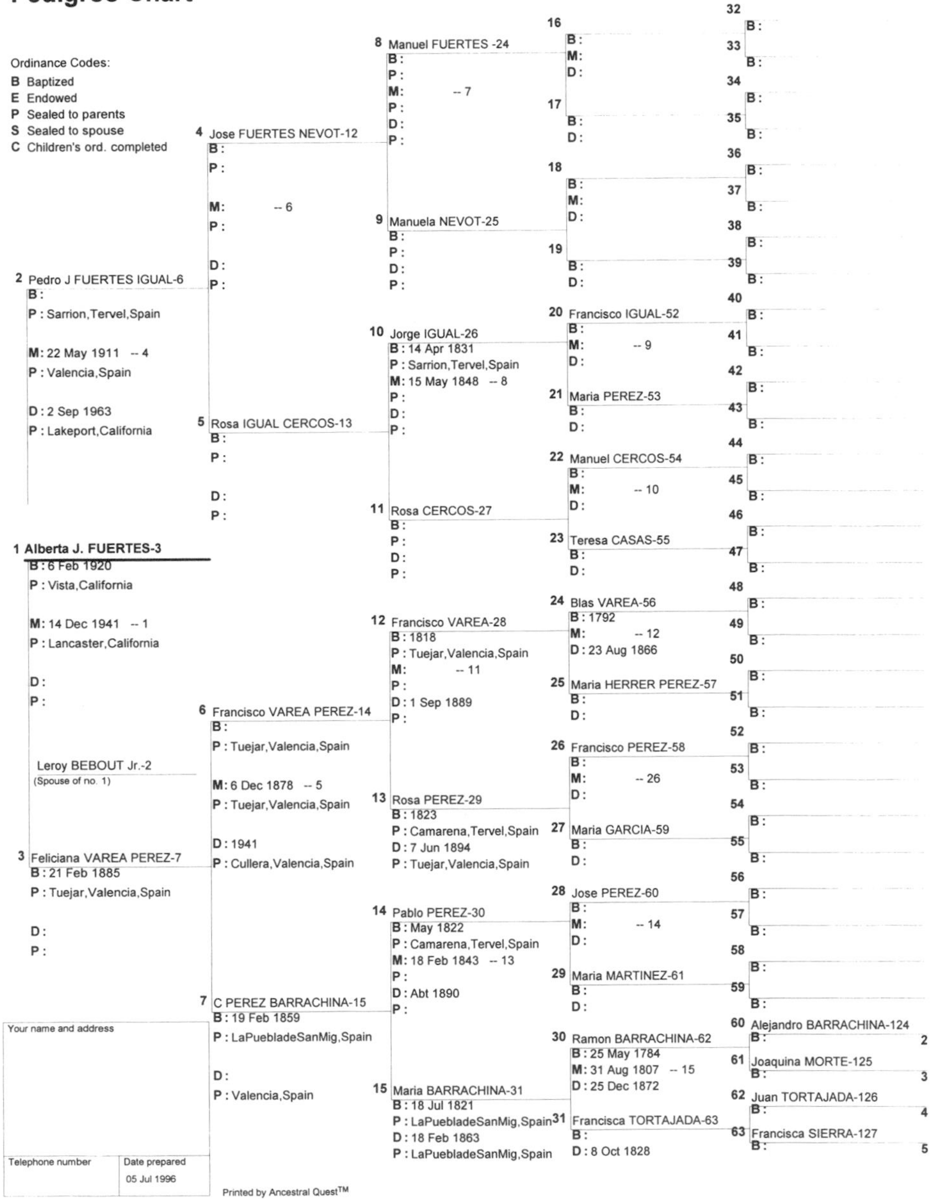
Pedigree Chart
Chart no. 1
Ordinance Codes:
B Baptized
E Endowed
P Sealed to parents
S Sealed to spouse
C Children's ord. completed
1 Alberta J. FUERTES-3
B: 6 Feb 1920
P: Vista,California
M: 14 Dec 1941 -- 1
P: Lancaster,California
D:
P:
Leroy BEBOUT Jr.-2
(Spouse of no. 1)
2 Pedro J FUERTES IGUAL-6
B:
P: Sarrion,Tervel,Spain
M: 22 May 1911 -- 4
P: Valencia,Spain
D: 2 Sep 1963
P: Lakeport,California
3 Feliciana VAREA PEREZ-7
B: 21 Feb 1885
P: Tuejar,Valencia,Spain
D:
P:
4 Jose FUERTES NEVOT-12
B:
P:
M: -- 6
P:
D:
P:
5 Rosa IGUAL CERCOS-13
B:
P:
D:
P:
6 Francisco VAREA PEREZ-14
B:
P: Tuejar,Valencia,Spain
M: 6 Dec 1878 -- 5
P: Tuejar,Valencia,Spain
D: 1941
P: Cullera,Valencia,Spain
7 C PEREZ BARRACHINA-15
B: 19 Feb 1859
P: LaPuebladeSanMig,Spain
D:
P: Valencia,Spain
8 Manuel FUERTES -24
B:
P:
M: -- 7
P:
D:
P:
9 Manuela NEVOT-25
B:
P:
D:
P:
10 Jorge IGUAL-26
B: 14 Apr 1831
P: Sarrion,Tervel,Spain
M: 15 May 1848 -- 8
P:
D:
P:
11 Rosa CERCOS-27
B:
P:
D:
P:
12 Francisco VAREA-28
B: 1818
P: Tuejar,Valencia,Spain
M: -- 11
P:
D: 1 Sep 1889
P:
13 Rosa PEREZ-29
B: 1823
P: Camarena,Tervel,Spain
D: 7 Jun 1894
P: Tuejar,Valencia,Spain
14 Pablo PEREZ-30
B: May 1822
P: Camarena,Tervel,Spain
M: 18 Feb 1843 -- 13
P:
D: Abt 1890
P:
15 Maria BARRACHINA-31
B: 18 Jul 1821
P: LaPuebladeSanMig,Spain
D: 18 Feb 1863
P: LaPuebladeSanMig,Spain
16
B:
M:
D:
17
B:
D:
18
B:
M:
D:
19
B:
D:
20 Francisco IGUAL-52
B:
M: -- 9
D:
21 Maria PEREZ-53
B:
D:
22 Manuel CERCOS-54
B:
M: -- 10
D:
23 Teresa CASAS-55
B:
D:
24 Blas VAREA-56
B: 1792
M: -- 12
D: 23 Aug 1866
25 Maria HERRER PEREZ-57
B:
D:
26 Francisco PEREZ-58
B:
M: -- 26
D:
27 Maria GARCIA-59
B:
D:
28 Jose PEREZ-60
B:
M: -- 14
D:
29 Maria MARTINEZ-61
B:
D:
30 Ramon BARRACHINA-62
B: 25 May 1784
M: 31 Aug 1807 -- 15
D: 25 Dec 1872
31 Francisca TORTAJADA-63
B:
D: 8 Oct 1828
32 B:
33 B:
34 B:
35 B:
36 B:
37 B:
38 B:
39 B:
40 B:
41 B:
42 B:
43 B:
44 B:
45 B:
46 B:
47 B:
48 B:
49 B:
50 B:
51 B:
52 B:
53 B:
54 B:
55 B:
56 B:
57 B:
58 B:
59 B:
60 Alejandro BARRACHINA-124
B: 2
61 Joaquina MORTE-125
B: 3
62 Juan TORTAJADA-126
B: 4
63 Francisca SIERRA-127
B: 5
Your name and address
Telephone number
Date prepared
05 Jul 1996
Printed by Ancestral Quest™

Figure 3-2 Jeri Bebout's extended pedigree chart

Igual line, which begins with Rosa Igual Cercos (number 13). Jorge Igual (number 26, the father of number 13) was born and married in Sarrión. Since no information is given about the birth date of his mother (number 53), it would appear that further work should be done in Sarrión. By the same logic, research should also be conducted in Mora de Rubielos on Jorge Igual's father, Francisco Igual (number 52).

Pedigree charts are found in many shapes and forms. Some are perpendicular, with the person whose ancestors are being recorded frequently superimposed upon a drawing of a tree. Others can be found developed in the form of a square, a fan, a rectangle, or a circle. Various types of pedigree charts can be purchased in many book stores or at the local family history centers of The Church of Jesus Christ of Latter-day Saints, or a researcher can even make his own. At the touch of a button, genealogy computer programs can create a pedigree chart from data already entered.

Sosa Numbering System

No matter what type of pedigree chart you use, the Sosa system of numbering can be helpful to you in locating, classifying, and cataloging your ancestors. The Sosa system is a mathematical numbering system originally developed by the Spanish genealogist Jeronimo de Sosa, first used in a family history he published in the year 1676.[2] It was later adopted by German genealogists and propagated worldwide in the nineteenth century. The Sosa system simply assigns a number to each person appearing on the pedigree chart. Number 1 is the individual researcher, 2 is his father, 3 is his mother, 4 is his paternal grandfather, 5 is his paternal grandmother, etc. Even if you are using genealogy computer programs that assign each individual a unique number, the Sosa number can still be used as an identification number for direct-line ancestors. Simply give children of each direct line ancestor the father's Sosa number plus a letter.

The following are some of the principal advantages of the Sosa numbering system:

1. The Sosa system allows the researcher to file and identify his ancestors ad infinitum. A specific ancestor can then be rapidly located and a relationship established merely by reference to the numbers.

2. It is possible to know the sex of any ancestor. All even numbers refer to males and all odd numbers (except the number 1, which is the researcher) indicate that the ancestor is female.

3. Any person's parents will have a number that is twice the person's number for the father and twice plus one for the mother. For example, the parents of No. 14, Francisco Varea Perez, would be 2 x 14, or 28, for the father (in this case Francisco Varea), and 28 + 1, or 29, for the mother (in this case Rosa Perez). The wife of any male ancestor can therefore be identified by merely adding 1 to his number.

4. The system allows you to do the genealogy of any single ancestor independent from the others while allowing for potential completion of

all family lines. For example, since Jeri Bebout was only interested in working on her Spanish line, she then could locate the ancestors of her mother by following her mother's number, 3; her mother's parents, 6 and 7; her mother's grandparents, 12, 13, 14, and 15; etc. Although Jeri did not begin to do her father's research, the pedigree chart she developed left numbers available for all of those ancestors.

5. The Sosa system avoids potential problems with maintaining relationships where identical names or frequent surname changes occur. Identifying each ancestor with a particular number avoids confusion.

6. The Sosa system pedigree chart can serve as a cross-reference to all of the other material recorded and filed about the family. Mark on the family group sheet and biography cards the Sosa number of the individual whose information is recorded on those forms. In addition, if the individual system of filing is used, the Sosa number can be marked on those files.

Contents and Use of a Pedigree Chart

Each pedigree chart should contain the following information:

1. Names and surnames of each of the direct-line ancestors. In preparing family group sheets, type the surnames in capital letters. By doing this, the various surnames can be rapidly spotted when you are using the pedigree chart. This is an optional feature on most computer programs.

2. Birth and death dates for each ancestor and marriage date for each couple. (This is usually included under the husband's name.) At a minimum, a pedigree chart should show at least the approximate year for each of these events. Being able to identify even the approximate year in which each major event occurred gives you a guide to your research. Dates on a pedigree chart are best recorded with the day first, followed by the month (abbreviated with letters or written out, but not written as numbers), and then the year. Write "16 Feb 1565" rather than "Feb 16, 1565"; "16-2-1565"; or "16-II-1565."

3. Places of birth, death, and marriage. Places are as essential as dates in guiding the researcher as he works. A town should be given for each ancestor, and to avoid confusion, a province and/or country should be included where possible. Standard abbreviations may be used for countries, states, and provinces, but any abbreviations should be avoided for towns and parishes.

FAMILY GROUP SHEETS

The primary place for recording information not appearing on the pedigree chart is the family group sheet, a form upon which all the information is recorded about a single family group. On this form there is space for the same basic information on the husband and the wife as appears on the pedigree, as well as information about other marriages, if any, and parents' names. In addition, the family group sheet allows spaces for the names of each of their children as well as their children's dates of birth and baptism, places of birth, dates of death, marriage dates, and spouses' names. It should also provide a place for the sources of this information to be recorded. Note that all computer programs organized by families assign an identification number to each marriage, and the family that marriage created.

The Sosa identification number that a husband and wife have on the pedigree chart should appear in the left-hand margin or upper-right-hand corner of each family group sheet. Your family group sheets can then be arranged in numerical order. In addition, this helps the researcher to determine the family group sheet of the parent or child of any ancestor (and rapidly locate that sheet) by merely dividing the Sosa number of the ancestor by two to find his child's sheet or multiplying by two to find his parent's.

In numbering the family group sheets with the Sosa number, adaptations can be made for including all of the family group sheets relating to a particular family. For example, if the direct-line ancestor was married more than once, the other marriages should be recorded on a separate family group sheet. On that family group sheet, the spouse who is the direct-line ancestor receives the same number he is always given, and no number is recorded for the non-direct-ancestor-spouse. This sheet is then filed directly after the family group sheet upon which the two direct-line ancestors appear as husband and wife. In many cases extensive information will be encountered about the children of a brother or sister of a direct-line ancestor. For such cases family group sheets can be given the number of the father, followed by a letter on the family group sheet listing the brothers and sisters as parents. In this way family group sheets can be kept in order for a large number of collateral lines down to the level of the first cousins of all direct-line ancestors. This same numbering system can be used for personalized identification numbers when using a genealogy computer program.

Family group sheets are not only the basic repository for storing and organizing data about your ancestral families but also the key point in evaluating that data. When you discover a new source of information about an ancestor, you will want to look first at your pedigree chart to locate him and find his assigned number. Using that number, you can then locate the family group sheet where the ancestor appears, either as a child or parent, and compare information on the recently found source with other information already known. Copy the basics of your new information onto the family group sheet with an indication as to the source. The source document should then be placed in a file as discussed at the beginning of this chapter.

Suppose Jeri Bebout finds a will for a brother of her ancestor Carmela Perez, giving the name of the brother's wife. She would find Carmela Perez on the pedigree (see figure 3-2), where she appears as number 15, as well as Carmela's parents, Pablo Perez and Maria Barrachina, who are numbers 30 and 31. Jeri would then turn to the family group sheet for numbers 30 and 31, which has been filed numerically under the Sosa number. By looking at that family group sheet, she would ascertain how much information is known as to the births, marriages, and deaths of numbers 30 (Pablo Perez) and 31 (Maria Barrachina) and all of their children (number 15 Carmela Perez, as well as her brothers and sisters). She could check the family group sheet to see if the information about the brother's spouse was already known. If she finds that it is not recorded, Jeri would record the name of the spouse and indicate in this person's notes that the will was her source of information. If she later finds a marriage certificate for the brother and spouse, Jeri would again check family group sheet number 30–31 and record the date given on the marriage certificate, as well as its source.

You would go through the same evaluation process with a computer program, where your first step would be to look up the individual record of the person for whom you have new information. It is important to remember, however, to also check the family group for consistency and related information about brothers and sisters.

BIOGRAPHY CARDS OR INDIVIDUAL RECORDS

As a family historian you are interested in developing not only a genealogical record of your family containing names, dates, and places but also a record of your family members as real people who lived, died, and had a variety of experiences. In order to become familiar with each ancestor individually, you may find it helpful to set up a biography file. Use one card for each of the direct-line ancestors and, if desired, for each of their brothers and sisters. The Sosa number and pertinent information from the family group sheet should be recorded on each card or envelope. The Sosa number can then be used for filing and cross-referencing between your pedigree charts and/or family group sheets and biography cards. All of your information about an individual should be listed on the biography cards, especially the type of biographical material that cannot be listed on the family group sheets.

Each biography card, or the notes in the individual computer record, would contain information such as occupations, education, dwellings, and the names of *cofradías* and other clubs to which the person belonged. These cards, envelopes, or individual record notes then become a repository of information that will flesh out the life and character of that particular ancestor.

SELECTING A GENEALOGY COMPUTER PROGRAM

For most family historians today, the use of a genealogy computer program is essential. The most commonly used is the **Personal Ancestral File®** (PAF) published by The Church of Jesus Christ of Latter-day Saints. At a cost of under $40.00, it is one of the most affordable of the many genealogy programs available. In addition, use of PAF is possible without charge at LDS family history centers. Although PAF is an excellent program, it nevertheless has weaknesses in certain areas, such as searching, note entering, and printing quality. Utility programs to remedy these problems can be purchased or obtained through shareware by contacting a PAF

Figure 3-3

Selected Genealogical Programs*

Ancestral Quest: Incline Software, PO Box 17788, Salt Lake City, UT 84117-0788; 800-825-8864 or 800-273-1521. Www.ieighty.net/~ancquest/ns_aq.html

Brother's Keeper 5.2: John Steed, 6907 Childsdale Rd., Rockford, MI 49341; 616-866-3345. Our world.compuserve.com/homepages/Brothers-keeper/homepage.htm

Family Connections: Quinsept, Inc., PO Box 216, Lexington, MA 02173; 800-637-7668.

Family Origins for DOS, Windows: Parsons Technology, One Parsons Dr., Hiawatha, IA 52233; 800-223-6925 (orders).

Family Roots 4.3 for DOS and 3.7 for MAC; Quinsept (see FC).

Family Tree Maker 3.02, the Banner Blue Division, Brøderbund Software, 39500 Stevenson Place, Suite 204, Fremont, CA 94539; 510-794-6850.

MacRoots II: Itasca Softworks, RE.1 Box 408, Bagley, MN 56621, 218-785-2745.

Personal Ancestral File 2.3: Church of Jesus Christ of Latter-day Saints, Salt Lake Distribution Center, 1999 West 1700 South, Salt Lake City, UT 84101; 800-537-5950 cr. card.

ROOTS III or ROOTS IV: COMMSOFT, Inc., PO Box 310, Windsor, CA 95492-0310; 707-838-4300; 800-32ROOTS. Www.sonic.net/~commsoft/commsoft.html

The Master Genealogist 1.2: Bob Velke, Wholly Genes Software, 6868 Ducketts Lane, Elkridge, MD 21227; 410-796-2447.

**Excerpted from Joan Lowrey, Software of Genealogy: Features and Comparisons (La Jolla, 1994), 3–4, with some additions from the author.*

User's Group.[3] For excellent instruction on how to use PAF and the various utilities included with it, see *Personal Ancestral File 2.31 User's Guide*[4] by Joan Lowrey.

You can also purchase other commercial programs that provide capabilities and user friendliness not found in PAF. Figure 3-3 provides a list of a few of the many programs available, along with the manufacturers' addresses. As you select a program, be certain it provides GEDCOM capability, or the ability to transfer data to other programs or input data from files such as the LDS FamilySearch files. Other factors to consider are capacity questions, such as number of individuals and number of children in a family, what charts and reports are printed, how much information can go in a field, and what is the merge capacity. Check current editions of the *National Genealogical Society Newsletter* in the Computer Interest Group section for information and evaluation of various programs.

---

1. Vicente de Cadenas y Vicent, *Memorandum de la genealogía familiar* (Madrid: Hidalguía, 1975).

2. Jesus Larios, *Tratado de genealogía, heráldica y derecho nobiliario* (Madrid: Hidalguía, 1984), 69–73.

3. Check on the Internet for current addresses for PAF User's Groups, such as those in Silicon Valley, California, and Provo, Utah.

4. Joan Lowrey, *Personal Ancestral File 2.31 User's Guide* (La Jolla, Calif.: Joan Lowrey, 1995).

CHAPTER 4

Hispanic Family History Research in an LDS Family History Center

If you live in the United States, the first place you will want to go beyond your home in doing Hispanic research is the family history center in one of the local meetinghouses of The Church of Jesus Christ of Latter-day Saints. This may seem strange when you are researching countries and cultures that are predominantly Roman Catholic. However, information is available in and through the family history center that will assist anyone beginning Hispanic research. In many cases, for a relatively small cost, the family history center will provide you with many weeks, months, and even years of research. For example, it is possible in the family history center to find records for most areas of Mexico and some areas of Spain that will enable you to run ancestral lines back into the seventeenth or even sixteenth century.

THE FAMILY HISTORY CENTER SYSTEM

Most people interested in family history have at least heard of the world's largest collection of genealogical records, assembled by The Church of Jesus Christ of Latter-day Saints (more commonly known as the Mormon Church) in a library at their headquarters in Salt Lake City, Utah. That same church also operates a system of over 1,400 family history centers located in local Mormon churches throughout the world. Each family history center is operated under the auspices of the local Mormon congregation, with volunteers who donate their time to maintain the library facility and to serve the public. Each center is open to the public at no charge. Non-Mormons are very welcome; in many areas the majority of the family history center patrons are not members of The Church of Jesus Christ of Latter-day Saints.

Each family history center contains a minimum of two microfilm readers, two microfiche readers, a copy of the International Genealogical Index (IGI) on microfiche, a copy of the Family History Library Catalog (FHLC) on microfiche, and a collection of reference works in both book and microfiche format. Most now also have at least one IBM Personal Computer with a CD ROM reader. A volunteer consultant is available to answer questions and assist you in using the IGI, FHLC, and other reference materials.

Before visiting a family history center, you should have already searched out all of the information available through home and family sources as discussed in chapter 2. Hopefully, you will have been able to identify a town or towns, or at least a state, from which your ancestors came in Mexico, Spain, or other Hispanic country. If you have not been able to identify a specific locality in the ancestral country, you may need to do additional research in records of the United States for ancestors residing here, as discussed in chapter 5. Often the volunteer consultant at the family history center can provide some guidance in using U.S. records.

Unfortunately, in many cases the volunteer consultant at the family history center will not be aware of the wealth of Hispanic information available. The purpose of this chapter, therefore, is to provide the beginning Hispanic researcher with information on materials available at the family history center for research in Mexico, Spain, or any other Hispanic country, and instructions for their use.

FAMILYSEARCH

The LDS Church has created a package of genealogical computer programs and databases called FamilySearch. These are available on CD ROMs in most family history centers. The FamilySearch programs and databases are:

A. Ancestral File
B. International Genealogical Index (IGI)
C. Military Index
D. Social Security Death Index
E. Personal Ancestral File (PAF)
F. TempleReady™
G. Family History Library Catalog

Only the Ancestral File, International Genealogical Index, and the Family History Library Catalog will be discussed here. The Military Index and Social Security Death Index will be discussed in chapter 5. Currently, the Military Index contains only records of U.S. soldiers who died in Vietnam and Korea. Once that database is expanded to include U.S. Civil War records, its value for the researcher will increase immensely, but only if he or she had ancestors in the United States at that time. The Social Security Death Index would be valuable for any Hispanic who has had ancestors or collateral relatives in the United States who died while receiving Social Security benefits. Be sure to follow through by writing for the death record and the Social Security application form for anyone who is found. Many times this gives an exact place of foreign birth. The Personal Ancestral File was discussed in chapter 3. TempleReady is used only to submit individual names for the performing of religious ordinances and entry in the International Genealogical Index.

ANCESTRAL FILE

The Ancestral File is a pedigree-linked computer database of genealogical information submitted by individual researchers, both Mormon and non-Mormon. The more than 20 million names contained in the Ancestral File represent the researchers' efforts in searching their ancestral pedigrees and collateral relatives. As of 1994 there were relatively few Hispanic families represented in the Ancestral File. You should, however, check to see if your ancestors or collateral relatives are there, as the Hispanic database will grow with the increasing interest in family history among Hispanics. Each of us, as we research, should contribute our findings to the Ancestral File so that others may benefit from our efforts. Information on how to contribute to the Ancestral File, as well as on how to use it for research, is contained in free handouts available at your local family history center.[1]

INTERNATIONAL GENEALOGICAL INDEX

The International Genealogical Index, found at each family history center, is a collection of over 200 million individual entries for persons from all over the world. Thirteen percent of these are from Latin America! Its primary purpose is to index certain religious ordinances performed by members of the Mormon Church for persons who are deceased. Due to its incredible value as a genealogical research tool, it is equally significant to the non-Mormon researcher. As this is a continually growing index, it is republished in expanded form about every two to four years, both in microfiche and CD ROM format. This chapter will discuss the 1993 edition, the most recent at the time this book was prepared.

There are two excellent places to obtain general information on how to use the International Genealogical Index. The article entitled "The International Genealogical Index," appearing in the July 1983 *New England Historical and Genealogical Register,*[2] was written with an emphasis on the value of the IGI to the non-Mormon researcher. The handouts prepared by the LDS Church on using the IGI[3] explain in detail the use of this index. These materials will be especially useful when you later become involved with the intricacies of cross-referencing to the original source for an entry in the IGI.

The International Genealogical Index can serve the Hispanic researcher generally in the following ways:

1. As a finding aid to locate genealogical data. For example, if you only know that an ancestor was born in the Mexican state of Sonora, the IGI provides an excellent means of searching for persons baptized or married in Sonora who could be that ancestor. Considerable time can be saved by use of this index.

2. To identify areas of Hispanic countries where a particular surname appears with great frequency, in an effort to identify the home area of a particular ancestor.

3. To locate original records.

4. To see if other people have been researching that line. This applies in those cases where the IGI entry is not from a Name Extraction Program, but from a submission by an individual.

Looking for Your Ancestors in the IGI on Microfiche

The initial discussion here will focus on use of the IGI in microfiche format, with a subsequent discussion of variations in the computer version. The 1993 IGI on microfiche is divided into twenty-five regions, each of which is designated by a letter. There are six regions of interest to the Hispanic researcher:

M-Southwest Europe is divided into the following countries, listed in alphabetical order: Azores Islands, Canary Islands, Gibraltar, Madeira Islands, Portugal, and Spain. (Note that Cape Verde and the Madeira Islands are found under X-Ocean Islands, Atlantic Islands.)

O-United States is divided into the fifty states, listed in alphabetical order. Entries from the vast areas of the United States that were once part of the Spanish Empire and/or Mexico may be found under the current state names. Some colonial era entries in states such as New Mexico are found under that state in the Mexico region.

Q-Mexico is divided into thirty-one states, listed in alphabetical order. These entries cover all of the geographical area that is part of Mexico today.

R-Central America is divided into the following countries, arranged alphabetically: Belize, Costa Rica, El Salvador, Guatemala, Nicaragua, and Panama.

S-South America is divided into the following countries, listed alphabetically: Argentina, Bolivia, Brazil, Chile, Colombia, Ecuador, Guiana, Guyana, Honduras, Paraguay, Peru, Surinam, Uruguay, and Venezuela.

T-Caribbean is a single index of all of the entries for the Caribbean islands, including the Bahamas, Bermuda, Cuba, Dominica, Dominican Republic, Grenada, Haiti, Martinique, Netherland Antilles, Puerto Rico, Saint Lucia, Saint Vincent, Trinidad and Tobago.

Former Spanish and Portuguese colonies also are found in Asia (U), Africa (V), and Ocean Islands (X). Of particular interest to the Hispanic researcher may be Cape Verde (Ocean-Atlantic), Galapagos (Ecuador), Guam (Ocean-Pacific), Morocco (Africa), Mozambique (Africa), Philippines (Asia), Portuguese Timor (Asia), and Portuguese West Africa (Africa).

Under each country or state, the entries are arranged alphabetically by surname, and within each surname by first given name. Within identical first given names, names are arranged alphabetically by second given name, and then chronologically. To better understand how the IGI is arranged, turn to figure 4-1. This is a page from the seventh microfiche card for the Mexican state of Nayarit, numbered Q-0849. It is one of 440 pages appearing on the card, and page number 2,951 for Nayarit. Suppose that you wanted to find Margarita Jimenes, born in Compostela, Nayarit, about 1830. You would first go to the card drawer containing microfiche records for Mexico and find Nayarit. (Note that the process of finding a name is the same in the IGI for other Hispanic countries, except that you will be searching the entire country instead of only one state.) The tops of the cards for Nayarit appear in figure 4-2.

The name "Margarita Jimenes" would appear on card Q-0849. (Q is for Mexico, and 0849 means it is the 849th card for Mexico.) "Jimenes" would appear on this card because it comes alphabetically between "Hernandez, Mari" and "Lopez, Margarit," which appear at the top of card Q-0849. Under "Jimenez" you will find entries for all of the various spellings and abbreviations of that name, for example, Jimenes, Gimenez, Ximenez, Ximenes, Xez., Ximz. Those entries are all arranged alphabetically under "Jimenez" by the first name of the individual. If you were to spell this name "Ximenez," and look it up under *X*, which appears on card Q-0855 (see figure 4-2), you would find an entry that says, "Ximenez, see Jimenez." Similarly, under "Gimenez," you would find an entry that says, "see Jimenez."

It should be noted that on the IGI, unlike a Spanish alphabetization system, the second surname is totally ignored for alphabetization purposes. Therefore, in figure 1, "Maria Anselma de Jesus Ximenes Arrayan" follows "Maria Anselma Jimenes Garcia." The given names, however, utilize the second names, and the various "Marias" are arranged alphabetically in accordance with their second names. Be sure to check under all spellings of a name, as well as under common abbreviations such as "Ma." for "Maria." Also be sure to check under all possible combinations of given names. Since Maria is such a common name, women frequently used their second given names later in life. An "Isabel Gomez" found on a marriage record may have appeared as "Maria Isabel Gomez" when baptized. Some common abbreviations may also be misfiled. For example, "Juo.," the abbreviation for Juan, is under "Julio."

Return to figure 4-1 and search for the Margarita Jimenes for whom we are looking, who was born about 1830 in Compostela, Nayarit, Mexico. One Margarita appears, whose name is marked on figure 4-1 with an arrow. A search of the other Margaritas shows that one was not born in Compostela, and the other was born in 1750 and married in 1765. Although we are quite sure the one marked with an arrow will be the one we are looking for, we should consult the original record for verification and con-

31 **JIMENEZ, MANUELA** — PAGE 2,951

COUNTRY MEXICO — STATE: NAYARIT — AS OF MAR 1992

SERIAL/SHEET	NAME (M=MALE F=FEMALE H=HUSBAND W=WIFE) / FATHER / MOTHER OR SPOUSE OR RELATIVE	SEX	TYPE	EVENT DATE	TOWN, PARISH	B	E	S	SOURCE: BATCH/FILM No	SOURCE: SERIAL/SHEET
	JIMENEZ, MANUELA									
1337	JIMENES, MANUELA — BENITO MARES	W	M	06FEB1883	NAYARIT,SAN PEDRO LAGUNILLAS,SAN PEDRO			05NOV1981OK	M602454	1297
	XIMENES LOPES, MARCELINO	M	C	20JUN1824	NAYARIT,COMPOSTELA	06JUN1984AZ	17AUG1984AZ	16OCT1984AZ	C602055	0526
0723	MARIANO XIMENES/SEBERINA LOPES									
	JIMENES, MARCELINO — TELESFORA GONZALEZ	H	M	27MAY1878	NAYARIT,TUXPAN,SAN MIGUEL			30NOV1982SG	M602435	0282
1840	JIMENES, MARCIANA — JUAN MESA	W	M	29APR1879	NAYARIT,ROSAMORADA,ROSAMORADA			14AUG1980OK	M601691	0104
	JIMENES ARIAS, MARCOS	M	C	30APR1870	NAYARIT,SAN PEDRO LAGUNILLAS,SAN PEDRO	24NOV1984LA	25JAN1985LA	01FEB1985LA	C602453	1575
0057	POLONIO JIMENES/LEONARDA ARIAS									
	JIMENES SALCEDO, MARGARITA $	F	C	22JUL1861	NAYARIT,IXTLAN DEL RIO,IXTLAN	17SEP1988IF	19JAN1989IF	22MAR1989IF	C607213	0317
2214	ANASTACIO JIMENES/JESUS_ SALCEDO									
3128	JIMENEZ ARREARAN, MARGARITA	F	B	1870	NAYARIT,RUIZ	23JUL1987MX	23JUL1987MX	01AUG1987MX	0792308	18
	REYES_ JIMENEZ/ISABEL ARREARAN									
0425	JIMENES CARRILLO, MARGARITA	F	C	04AUG1872	NAYARIT,SAN PEDRO LAGUNILLAS,SAN PEDRO	15SEP1984LA	08DEC1984LA	02JAN1985LA	C602453	1920
	ROMAN JIMENES/YRINEA CARRILLO									
0884 1163	JIMENES ANDRADE, MARGARITA DE LA LUZ	F	C	14JUN1826	NAYARIT,COMPOSTELA	08MAY1984AZ	01JUN1984AZ	11OCT1984AZ	C602055	0844
	MARIANO JIMENES/JUANA SEFERINA ANDRADE									
	XIMENES, MARGARITA FELICIANA — JOSEPH BONIFACIO	W	M	16JUN1765	NAYARIT,COMPOSTELA			14MAY1986OK	M602057	0922
2953	GIMENES, MARGARITA FELISSIANA	F	C	09JUL1750	NAYARIT,COMPOSTELA	11MAR1987SE	14APR1987SE	16AFR1987SE	C602052	1680
0586	LUIS GIMENES/MARIA DE LOS DOLORES									
	XIMENZ. FONSECA, MARGARITO	M	C	21JUL1812	NAYARIT,ACAPONETA,LA ASUNCION	21NOV1981LG	27FEB1982LG	01APR1982LG	C602442	2065
2062	ANASTACIO XIMENZ./RAFA. FONSECA									
0004	JIMENEZ CALDERA, MARGARITO	M	C	15JUN1851	NAYARIT,COMPOSTELA	08FEB1989AZ	30MAY1989AZ	08JUN1989AZ	C602056	2495
0298	EBARISTO JIMENEZ/REGINA CALDERA									
	JIMENEZ, MARGARITO — PAULA HERNANDEZ	H	M	15OCT1872	NAYARIT,TEPIC,EL SAGRARIO			13DEC1988GU	M607222	1091
0086	JIMENES, MARGARITO DE JESUS	M	C	26JUL1833	NAYARIT,SAN PEDRO LAGUNILLAS,SAN PEDRO	10FEB1988JR	09MAR1988JR	22MAR1988JR	J602452	0550
3220	JOSE YLARIO/MA. DE JESUS JIMENES									
	JIMENES, MARIA — DIEGO JIMENES/MARIA LUISA	F	C	02APR1650	NAYARIT,JALA,NUESTRA SENORA DE LA ASUNCION	15APR1982OG	31JUL1982OG	05AUG1982OG	C602381	0421
0731	GIMENES, MARIA — LEANDRO MARIA ARIAS	W	M	04OCT1795	NAYARIT,COMPOSTELA			16MAY1986OK	M602057	2211
0448	JIMENEZ GRADILLA, MARIA	F	B	02JUL1893	NAYARIT,JALA	05AUG1987MX	07AUG1987MX	08AUG1987MX	0790243	46
	VICENTE JIMENEZ ALVAREZ/REFUGIO GRADILLA MACEDO									
0065	JIMENES LOPEZ, MARIA ... DE JESUS	F	C	27OCT1851	NAYARIT,SAN PEDRO LAGUNILLAS,SAN PEDRO	28MAR1986IF	06MAY1986IF	11JUN1986IF	K602452	1212
	MANUEL JIMENES/MA. PETRA LOPEZ									
1812	XIMENEZ, MARIA ALBINA — ENRRIQUEZ DEDIOS	W	M	09OCT1817	NAYARIT,COMPOSTELA			02JUN1983PV	M602058	0039
	XIMENES, MARIA ALEXANDRA	F	C	17MAR1737	NAYARIT,JALA,NUESTRA SENORA DE LA ASUNCION	21APR1982OG	04AUG1982OG	06AUG1982OG	C602381	5199
0017	NICOLAS LORENSO/THOMAS_ XIMENES									
	XIMENES HERNANDEZ, MARIA ALVINA DE JESUS	F	C	18DEC1820	NAYARIT,SAN PEDRO LAGUNILLAS,SAN PEDRO	19SEP1981AL	18NOV1981AL	19JAN1982AL	C602451	1792
3808	YSIDRO XIMENES/ANA JOSEFA HERNANDEZ									
	GIMENES, MARIA AMBROCIA	F	C	26DEC1795	NAYARIT,COMPOSTELA	06DEC1986WA	28MAR1987WA	11APR1987WA	C602053	4246
3653	TORIVIO/JUANA GIMENES									
3545	JIMENES GARCIA, MARIA ANSELMA	F	C	24APR1861	NAYARIT,ACAPONETA,LA ASUNCION	12OCT1988PV	05NOV1988PV	17NOV1988PV	C602449	0528
	LUCIANO JIMENES/NESTORA GARCIA									
3036	XIMENES ARRAYAN, MARIA ANSELMA DE JESUS	F	C	26APR1821	NAYARIT,SAN PEDRO LAGUNILLAS,SAN PEDRO	19SEP1981AL	18NOV1981AL	20JAN1982AL	C602451	1824
	BENTURO XIMENES/MA. ANNA DE ARRAYAN									
	GIMENEZ, MARIA ANTONIA	W	M	07JUL1765	NAYARIT,COMPOSTELA			14MAY1986OK	M602057	0927
0528	JUAN DE DIOS BAPTISTA									
	JIMENEZ ALCANTAR, MARIA ANTONIA	F	C	14JUN1838	NAYARIT,COMPOSTELA	10MAY1984AZ	06JUN1984AZ	16OCT1984AZ	C602055	3107
0906	JUAN DE DIOS JIMENEZ/BERNARDA ALCANTAR									
0449	XIMENES, MARIA ANTONIA — /GERMANA XIMENES	F	C	25JAN1863	NAYARIT,JALISCO,SAN CAYETANO	21OCT1981LG	05FEB1982LG		C602463	0752
1228	XIMENES VIERRA, MARIA ANTONIA CHRISANTA	F	C	08OCT1803	NAYARIT,ACAPONETA,LA ASUNCION	30NOV1983OK	09MAR1984OK	27MAR1984OK	C602441	5116
2844	JOSE ANASTACIO XIMENES/MARIA ENCARNACION VIERRA									
0417	JIMENES CASTILLO, MARIA ANTONIA ESTEFANA	F	C	19SEP1841	NAYARIT,ACAPONETA,LA ASUNCION	01OCT1983IF	07DEC1983IF	27JAN1984IF	C602447	0028
0939	JOSE MARIA LEON JIMENES/MARIA ROSALIA CASTILLO									
2646	XIMENES, MARIA ATANACIA DE LA CRUZ	W	M	05AUG1820	NAYARIT,COMPOSTELA			02JUN1983PV	M602058	0178
	JOSE CANDELARIO CARDENAS									
0541	XIMENES, MARIA BARBARA	W	M	08JAN1815	NAYARIT,COMPOSTELA			20MAY1986OK	M602057	2733
	JOSE ALBINO SANDOVAL									
2107	XIMENEZ MEDINA, MARIA BASILIA	F	C	23JUN1833	NAYARIT,ACAPONETA,LA ASUNCION	22JUL1983LG	28SEP1983LG	08NOV1983LG	C602445	0180
	JUAN XIMENEZ/MARIA YSIDRA MEDINA									

Δ= ENTRY ALTERED FROM SOURCE; $,∂,>=RELATIVES NAMED IN SOURCE. SEE "SYMBOLS" IN INSTRUCTIONS.

A = ADULT CHRISTENING B = BIRTH C = CHRISTENING D = DEATH OR BURIAL ALL OTHERS = MISCELLANEOUS
F = BIRTH OR CHRISTENING OF FIRST KNOWN CHILD M = MARRIAGE N= CENSUS W = WILL

Figure 4-1 Sample IGI microfiche page, #2951 of Mexico (1992 IGI edition)

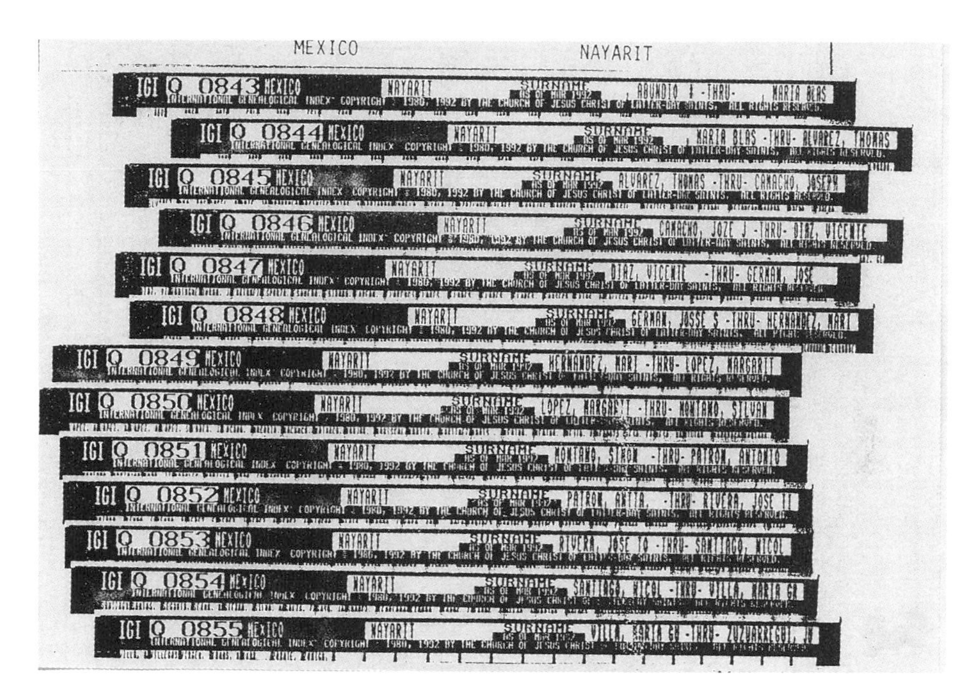

Figure 4-2 Sample IGI microfiche cards for Nayarit, Mexico (1992 IGI edition)

tinue researching her life for full confirmation. Analyzing figure 4-1, the information provided in each column is as follows:

1. The name of the person. As indicated above, surnames appear first, followed by given names. In the marriage entries the surname and given name of the spouse follow. In the birth or baptismal entries, the names of the parents follow on the same line or on the next line. The symbols @ and # indicate that more information appeared on the original than appears in the IGI entry (such as names of grandparents of the child being baptized). These systems were implemented a number of years after the extraction program began, so even if the entry does not have a symbol, the original record may contain significant additional information. For example, figure 4-3 illustrates the original record from the baptismal records of the parish in Compostela, Nayarit, Mexico, for Margarita de la Luz Jimenes Andrade. Obviously, the information recorded in the original record is considerably more extensive than what appears in the IGI entry shown in figure 4-1.

2. Sex. Male (M) and female (F) for birth entries, or husband (H) and wife (W) for marriage entries.

En la Yglesia Parroq.l de Compostela en Catorse
de Junio de mil ocho cientos, veinte, y seis
años el B.r C.r Y.o Aguilera bautizó solemnemente
a una parbula de seis dias de nacida a [illegible]
a q.n puse por nombre Margarita hija de h. l. de
Mariano Jimenez y de Ramona Josefina Andrade
Abuelos Pat.s Mariano Jimenez, y Narcisa
Tobar: Mat.s Felipe Andrade, y Andrea Lopez,
Padrinos Anto. Sanchez y Victoria Flores, a q.
adverti su oblig.n y parentesco, y p.a const.a lo firme
Mariano Flores

En la Yglesia Parroq.l de esta Ciudad en diez, y nue-
te de Junio de mil, ocho cientos, veinte, y seis a.
el B.r C. Y.o Aguilera bautizó solemnem.te a un Par-

Figure 4-3 Baptismal record from parish of Compostela, Mexico (FHL 0652402, page 117)

3. Type. This refers to the type of original record from which the entry was extracted. The nine possible types of events are listed at the bottom of each page. All of the entries on this page (and the vast majority of those from Hispanic countries) have been taken from Catholic parish records of baptisms and marriages, or from civil registration records of births and marriages. "C" refers to a christening (Catholic baptism) record; "B" to a birth record; and "M" to either a Catholic or civil marriage record.

4. Date. This is the date of the baptism, birth, or marriage event.

5. Locality. The title headings "Town" and "Parish" refer to the location in which the event was recorded.

6, 7, 8. Ordinance information. The columns titled "B," "E," and "S" relate to Latter-day Saint religious ordinance information and are of interest only to Mormons searching their ancestry. Information concerning these entries can be found in the reference works mentioned previously.

9. Source. The final column gives the batch/film number and serial sheet on which the original entry is found. (The serial sheet number refers to the sheet in that batch and is of little use to the Hispanic researcher.) As the batch/film number provides the means of locating the original entry, it is important to copy this information.

The batch/film number refers to the film number of the original submission or record from which the entry was created. If preceded by C or M, an entry on the IGI Batch Number Index refers to a specific baptism or marriage film number in the Family History Library collection. The Batch Number Index lists all of the batch numbers in alphabetical/numerical order. For example, we can use it to look up the batch number C602055, which is the batch number for the IGI entry on Margarita Jimenes Andrade. Three columns appear in the Batch Number Index, as follows:

BATCH	SOURCE	PRINTOUT
C 602055	C 652402	None

The first column is the batch number. The second column is the source for that batch number. Because most Hispanic entries were extracted from original parish records, this will generally be a Family History Library film number referring to film of the original source. The source number listed above, 652402, is the film number for the baptismal records of the parish in Compostela, Nayarit, Mexico, for the time period 1822–1838. If you were searching for Margarita Jimenes Andrade as one of your ancestors, you would then order film 652402. When the film arrived, you would look on the film for the date 14 June 1826, and there you would find the baptismal record reproduced as figure 4-3. The third column indicates whether a printout of the information extracted from that film is available. For Hispanic records there are generally no printouts.

What if you want to know whether an entire parish has been extracted and placed on the IGI? To determine this, turn to a small set of microfiche cards known as the Parish and Vital Records List. Look under "Mexico," the country name; then under "Nayarit," the state name; and then under "Compostela," the city name. There, under "Nayarit, Compostela," an entry reveals that extensive records are available for Compostela, Nayarit, Mexico. However, not all of these records have been extracted and placed on the IGI at this time. Only those *without* a double asterisk between the batch number and the film number have been placed on the IGI. Other available records may be extracted and placed on future editions.

When the 1992 edition of the IGI was prepared, a decision was made to exclude a large number of names previously appearing in the 1988 edition with the words CLEARED in all the Ordinance Information Sections for the entry. Eventually these excluded entries should appear in later editions. As a result of this decision, up to 25 percent of the names appearing in the 1988 IGI under some Mexican states were excluded from the 1992 edition. The 1994 addendum restores some of these names, but not even the majority. If you do not find a name you are searching for, inquire if a copy of the 1991 or 1988 IGI versions are available and also check those.

Nearly all of the entries in the Mexican section of the IGI have come from records listed on the Parish and Vital Records List as a result of the Name Extraction Program being carried out in Mormon churches throughout the world. You may find batch numbers that do not begin with *C* or *M*. In this case consult the introductory sources mentioned at the beginning of this section on the IGI or the family history center consultant, for information concerning other types of sources that exist and how to trace them from batch numbers beginning with other letters or numbers.

What if the Ancestor Is Not Listed?

A researcher should never assume that his ancestor will not be found in a certain location simply because he cannot find the name of the ancestor listed under that location on the IGI. The original records may not have been extracted. To see if this is the case, check the Parish and Vital Records List. Also check the 1988 or 1991 IGI editions, if they are available.

Alternatively, the names found on the original sources may have been omitted, misinterpreted, or indexed incorrectly. For example, in one IGI entry the surname of the father of Maria Antonia Estefana Jimenez Castillo was incorrectly entered as "Jimenez Castillo." The correct name of the father was "Jose Maria," and his surname was "Leon Jimenez." The surname of the child should therefore have been "Leon Castillo," rather than "Jimenez Castillo."

Be careful in analyzing IGI entries, as common surnames may have been mistaken for given names. A good example of this is the name "Martin." It is also important to check all of the possible spellings and abbreviations of a surname, as it is possible that the name has not been listed under the standardized spelling. For example, on the Mexican IGI

"Ximen," "Ximines," and "Xims." all appear as abbreviations or spelling variations of the name "Ximenes," which is itself cross-referenced to "Jimenez." On the same microfiche card appear entries for the surname "Zepeda," under which there also appear entries for the surname "Sepeda." "Zepeda" is listed as a separate standardized spelling, although it is a fairly common derivation of the more common surname spelling "Cepeda." Therefore, great care must be taken in exploring the various possibilities for spelling a name, and the possible combinations of the double surname system.

A final reason that an ancestor may not appear in a baptismal or marriage record from a certain location is that the records themselves may have been destroyed or lost. His name might still appear in different types of records for the area, which have not been extracted for the IGI.

In spite of its many difficulties and drawbacks, the IGI is an incredible tool that will eventually index nearly all of the parish baptismal and marriage records available from Mexico and from certain areas of Spain where microfilming has been done, such as Gerona, Lugo, Albacete, Caceres, Ciudad Rodrigo, and the Basque countries. It is currently possible to trace entire family lines in some of the Mexican states with initially nothing more than the IGI. However, it should be noted that in such cases you must ultimately check the original sources, keeping in mind the possibility that extensive additional information may be found, and the possibility of misinterpretation by those who did the indexing.

The International Genealogical Index is becoming a primary tool for locating individual ancestors and tracing family genealogies in Hispanic countries. While Mexico is the Hispanic country with the greatest number of IGI entries, many other Hispanic countries also have extensive entries. Extensive microfilming of parish records has been completed in some regions in other Hispanic countries, such as the Basque countries and Santander, in Spain. As later editions include more and more of the parish records currently being extracted, the IGI will have even greater value for the Hispanic researcher.

IGI on CD ROM

The IGI on CD ROM is faster to search and has both advantages and disadvantages over the microfiche edition. Again, your first step in a search is to select a region. Although assigned different letters, the CD ROM regions are divided in a similar fashion to the microfiche edition. See figure 4-4 for a list of the regions as they appear on the computer screen. After selecting the region you want, a Surname Search Menu appears as follows:

A. Individual Search (Birth/Christening information, etc.)
B. Marriage Search
C. Parent Search (Individual index sorted by parents' names — you may find children grouped together by parents in this index)

```
Main International Genealogical Index 3.05--
Esc=Exit  F1=Help  F2=Print/Holding File                    05 JUL 1996

        SELECT REGION OR COUNTRY OF THE WORLD TO SEARCH
      Use     and press Enter to select one of 20 regions.

A. North America [Canada and USA-including Alaska & Hawaii; etc.]
B. British Isles
C. Wales
D. Germany
E. Denmark
F. Finland
G. Iceland
H. Norway
I. Sweden
J. Continental Europe [Excludes GERMANY, Scandinavia, SW Europe]
K. Southwest Europe [Italy, Malta, Portugal, Spain,..; NOT Greece]
L. Mexico
M. South America
N. Central America [From Belize and Guatemala to Panama]
O. Asia [China, Japan, Middle East, Philippines, SE Asia, etc.]
P. Africa [Algeria, Ghana, South Africa, etc.]
Q. Southwest Pacific [Australia, NZ, SW Pacific Islands, etc.]
R. Ocean Islands [Atlantic Islands, Indian Ocean Islands]
S. Caribbean Islands [West Indies]
T. World Misc.
U. If unsure of the region, press U or F11 to see a country list.

   F11=Country List to Identify Region          Esc=Cancel
```


Figure 4-4 List of regions from the 1994 IGI edition on CD ROM

The ability to separate marriages from individuals is a clear advantage of the CD ROM over the microfiche version. Also, the possibility to list all children of the same parents is a helpful feature not possible on the microfiche. Once you have selected a search, you are given further options to filter, or limit, your search. One of the filter options, exact surname spelling, should never be selected. The other options presented can be very helpful when you are searching a common name. One will limit the search to names in a select area, such as a state in Mexico or a specific country in southwest Europe or South America. The other allows you to specify a range of years to be searched. (In many cases, though, there would be a great advantage to searching all of Mexico.)

Note that the various spellings of "Jimenez" all appear, but not any of the abbreviations, such as "Xz." or "Xiz.," which must be searched separately. Sometimes, but not always, the program will include persons whose second surname is the one for the entry. The program does not, however, search for second given names. Therefore, when looking for someone with an unknown first given name, it is easier to search the microfiche version.

The program will also allow you to go from the individual search to a marriage or parent search for that program and vice versa. Ultimately, the only difference in the information available is that the computer gives you the film number source, eliminating the need to check the batch number index.

THE FAMILY HISTORY LIBRARY CATALOG

While the Ancestral File and International Genealogical Index are excellent indexes and reference tools which may make it possible to trace a family for several generations, they do not replace the need to consult original record sources. In most cases even the records that are indexed on the IGI contain considerably more information than does the actual IGI entry. Also, since the IGI for Hispanic countries is primarily composed of entries from Catholic parish records, a wealth of other valuable records is not accessible through a search of the IGI.

Of greater ultimate value to the Hispanic researcher in the local family history center is access to the microfilm collection of the Family History Library in Salt Lake City, Utah. The family history center system provides local access to almost the entire collection of 1.8 million rolls of microfilmed records from all over the world. Approximately 40,000 rolls are added to the collection yearly. Many of the new additions are from Hispanic countries. Almost all of the existing parish and civil registration records from Mexico and Guatemala have been filmed and are available. In addition, in many areas of Mexico the notarial records, diocesan records, censuses, and a variety of other materials have also been microfilmed. Parish records have been cataloged from twenty of the sixty-two dioceses in Spain. Filming of parish records continues, and records from national and provincial archives are also currently being filmed in Spain and in other Hispanic countries.

In 1979, with the introduction of the computerized cataloging system, the main library began the reproduction of the Family History Library Catalog on microfiche for distribution to the local family history centers. In 1991 an edition was released on CD ROM. The most recent editions, which were released in 1993 and January 1994, list all of the library materials, including new acquisitions through 1992, cataloged and placed in the computer system. (Note that new acquisitions not cataloged when the FHLC was filmed will not appear in the catalog and yet may be available to the researcher. If you do not find references for a particular locality, you should write to the Family History Library in Salt Lake City, requesting a check of the main card catalog and the new film manifests to determine if there are records available for your particular location.)

Your local family history center will have a simple form that can be filled out to order microfilm. For a fee of $3.00 your film can be delivered from Salt Lake City and held in your family history center for three weeks. The payment of $4.50 entitles you to have the film held on loan for six months. With the approval of your family history center director, $6.50 will place the film on indefinite loan. In most cases one microfilm of parish records will contain two or three parish books, covering a period from a few years to seventy-five or eighty years. All of the records for a particular parish are generally covered in six to twelve films, except for the records of very large metropolitan parishes, which can have fifty to one hundred films or more.

Organization of the Family History Library Catalog on Microfiche[4]

The Family History Library Catalog in microfiche format is composed of four sections:

1. Author-Title section (green stripe). This section contains all of the records found in other sections, and lists them in alphabetical order by author or title.

2. Locality section (yellow stripe). This section consists of records of localities, such as countries, states, counties, municipalities, parishes, and other entities.

3. Surname section (red stripe). This section contains family names and names of individuals who appear as the subjects of family histories, newsletters, bibliographies, biographies, and similar records.

4. Subject section (blue stripe). This section lists records by subject for general categories, or those covering such a large geographical area that locality assignment is impossible.

The Author-Title section will be of primary interest if you are looking for a particular book, such as Garcia Carraffa's *Diccionario heráldico y genealógico de apellidos españoles y americanos*. If you know the name of the author it will be faster and easier to search in the Author-Title section than to attempt to find a listing for the book under Spain or Mexico in the Locality section. Also, when searching for notarial records you can look up the name of the notary in the Author-Title section to see if his records have been filmed.

The Subject section can be similarly used. For instance, if you are interested in consulting a book on Spanish paleography, you would look under "Paleography, Spanish." The references indexed in the Subject section of the catalog will be quite general in nature.

As discussed in chapter 2, the Surname section should be consulted to find out if any published works are available for the family lines you are searching.

The Locality Section

The Locality section is the most valuable section of the FHLC. It contains more listings of original records from Hispanic countries than any other section. Considerable microfilming has been done for many of the Hispanic countries, as indicated by the number of microfiche cards for each of the following countries in the 1993 version:

COUNTRY	NUMBER OF CARDS	COUNTRY	NUMBER OF CARDS
Argentina	3	Guatemala	2
Bolivia	1	Honduras	1
Brazil	10	Mexico	21
Central America	1	Nicaragua	1
Chile	3	Paraguay	1
Colombia	1	Peru	2
Costa Rica	1	Philippines	25
Cuba	1	Portugal	10
Dominican Republic	1	Puerto Rico	1
Ecuador	1	Spain	39
El Salvador	1	Uruguay	1

Mexico will serve as the primary example throughout the following discussion, as it is the country whose records have been most extensively microfilmed. (Over 99 percent of the existing parish records from before the year 1900 have been microfilmed.) The concepts, however, apply to all countries.

In the 1993 edition of the FHLC Locality section there are twenty-one locality cards for Mexico. (See figure 4-5 for their title headings.) Each of the microfiche cards contains twenty columns of computer-generated catalog entries, indexing over 120,000 rolls of microfilm.

National General Categories

The first card for Mexico (0001) is entirely an index of Mexican towns. The index cross-references the name of the town to the Mexican state under which the town records will be found in the Locality section. If you know the name of the town but are uncertain as to the state in which it is located, you should begin here by identifying to which state the municipality or parish belongs. This process is discussed in chapter 7.

Following the town index in the FHLC are the general subject headings for all of Mexico. Figure 4-6 shows the 1993 general subject headings (from CD ROM version) for Mexico, which are those that may be found throughout the Locality section. Commentary on the use of items found under each of the subject headings is beyond the scope of this chapter. However, it would be helpful to put card 0002 on a reader and browse through it to get a feel for these entries. The subject heading "Archives and Libraries," for example, is always a source for access to large collec-

FHLC FICHE--MEXICO	
MEXICO	0001 (0667)
TRONCOSO MEXICO	0002 (0668)
PUBLIC RECORDS	0003 (0669)
CHIAPAS JITOTOL (MUNICIPIO) CENSUS	0004 (0670)
COLINA CHURCH RECORDS	0005 (0671)
DISTRITO FEDERAL LA MAGDALENA CONTRERAS CENSUS	0006 (0672)
GUANAJUATO LEON CHURCH RECORDS	0007 (0673)
HIDALGO ACTOPAN (MUNICIPIO) CHURCH RECORDS	0008 (0674)
JALISCO AUTLAN (MUNICIPIO) CIVIL REGISTRATION	0009 (0675)
JALISCO PUERTO VALLARTA CHURCH RECORDS	0010 (0676)
MEXICO CHAPA DE MOTA CHURCH RECORDS	0011 (0677)
MEXICO TULANTONGO CHURCH RECORDS	0012 (0678)
MICHOACAN TINGAMBATO CHURCH RECORDS	0013 (0679)
OAXACA MAGDALENA PENASCO (MUNICIPIO) CENSUS	0014 (0680)
OAXACA SANTA MARIA PENOLES CHURCH RECORDS	0015 (0681)
PUEBLA HEROICA PUEBLA DE ZARAGOZA NOTARIA	0016 (0682)
PUEBLA XCCHIAPULCO (MUNICIPIO) CIVIL REGISTRATION	0017 (0683)
SAN LUIS POTOSI TANCUAYALAS (MUNICIPIO) CENSUS	0018 (0684)
TLAXCALA TZOMPANTEPEC CHURCH RECORDS	0019 (0685)
YUCATAN CACALCHEN (MUNICIPIO) CIVIL REGISTRATION	0020 (0686)
ZACATECAS VILLANUEVA CHURCH RECORDS	0021 (0687)

Figure 4-5 FHLC Locality Section microfiche headings for Mexico (1993 edition)

tions relating to the entire nation or to large regions. Under that heading for Mexico are several indexes or guides to collections in the Archivo General de la Nación in Mexico, a guide to the Franciscan Archive of the National Library of Mexico, and guides to notarial record collections in Mexico City and in Monterrey, Nuevo Leon. Every researcher who is looking beyond parish records should consult the "Archives and Libraries" subject heading for his state and country.

Some record types, while rich in local and family history, are national in origin and will be found listed in the general subject headings. One of the important record sources of this type is "Military Records." Look under "Mexico-Military Records" and note the cross-reference to records in Spain for the colonial period and to the Archivo General de la Nación for later periods.

The subject heading "Church Records" will generally provide information concerning Inquisition records from the colonial period. Church directories may list directories giving all parishes in the country. "Emigration and Immigration" will provide references to works on specific emigration, such as to the United States or to Alta California during the colonial period. This heading will also refer to collections containing passports, passenger lists, naturalization records, and other sources concerning the often difficult-to-document passing of an ancestor from one country to another. Subject headings such as "Directories," "Gazetteers," and "Maps" can provide sources for ways to locate small towns and villages where ancestors originated. A variety of gazetteers are available for Mexico, from a four-volume geographical/historical dictionary published in 1888–1891 to a 750-page United States Board on Geographic Names gazetteer. (See chapter 7 for an explanation of how to use these reference sources.)

State General Categories

The FHLC Locality section is arranged from larger geographical units to smaller geographical units. This means that the first listings in the Locality section for Mexico, as described above, are followed by each of the Mexican states in alphabetical order. (Note that this is English language alphabetical order, so that Chihuahua appears before Coahuila.) For each Hispanic country the major geographical unit will be followed by a smaller one; e.g., Spain by each province; Venezuela by state; Nicaragua by department.

Within each state, the listings begin with general records relating to the entire state, listed under many of the same subject headings as in the general section for the country (see figure 4-6). Note that some headings will have only one entry, while others have several. Note also that every heading listed on figure 4-6 does not appear for each state. Headings of general interest include "Church Directories," "Directories," "Gazetteers," "History," and "Maps," which may provide significant local geographical and historical information.

Also very important, where available, are entries found under "Church Records" in the general section for each state. Records maintained by the Catholic dioceses are listed here or under the city where the bishop resides. Also note listings under "Land and Property." Chapter 9 describes these records and their use by the family historian. *The Morelia Project in Mexico*, by C. Douglas Inglis, published in *World Conference on Records*, Vol. 9 (1980), describes these records for the diocese of Michoacán, with excellent commentary concerning the adequacies and inadequacies of the cataloging of these records in the FHLC.

Under the Mexican state of Jalisco in the category of "Notarial Records" are listed the records conserved in the Public Archives of the capital city of Guadalajara. These records are arranged by the names of the notaries who wrote them, many of whom served outside Guadalajara. Chapter 13 describes the excellent genealogical information contained in notarial records, and how to access and use those records.

Local Record Listings

The general listings are followed alphabetically by smaller local divisions. For each local entity, there will first appear records for the general

	TOPIC	# OF RECORDS
1.	Archives and libraries	9
2.	Archives and libraries — Indexes	1
3.	Archives and libraries — Inventories, registers, catalogs	5
4.	Bibliography	9
5.	Biography	39
6.	Biography — Dictionaries	3
7.	Biography — Indexes	1
8.	Business records and commerce	1
9.	Business records and commerce — Bibliography	1
10.	Census	6
11.	Census — 1960	1
12.	Census — Bibliography	1
13.	Census — Indexes	1
14.	Census — Inventories, registers, catalogs	1
15.	Church directories	11
16.	Church history	96
17.	Church history — Bibliography	1
18.	Church history — Inventories, registers, catalogs	1
19.	Church history — Sources	1
20.	Church records	14
21.	Church records — Inventories, registers, catalogs	1
22.	Civil registration	1
23.	Colonization	7
24.	Colonization — Sources	1
25.	Court records	2
26.	Description and travel	10
27.	Description and travel — Guide-books	1
28.	Description and travel — Handbooks, manuals, etc.	1
29.	Directories	2
30.	Emigration and immigration	21
31.	Encyclopedias and dictionaries	1
32.	Ethnology	1
33.	Gazetteers	14
34.	Genealogy	27
35.	Genealogy — Handbooks, manuals, etc.	6
36.	Genealogy — Indexes	1
37.	Genealogy — Periodicals	8
38.	Genealogy — Sources	10
39.	Handwriting	1
40.	Heraldry	5
41.	Heraldry — Periodicals	2
42.	Historical geography	6
43.	Historical geography — Dictionaries	1
44.	History	95
45.	History — 1540–1810	1
46.	History — 1548–1817	1
47.	History — 1810–1821	2
48.	History — 1821–1861	1
49.	History — 1867–1910	1
50.	History — Bibliography	11
51.	History — Handbooks, manuals, etc.	1
52.	History — Indexes	1
53.	History — Periodicals	1
54.	History — Sources	17
55.	Jewish history	2

Figure 4-6 Mexico — General FHLC Topics (Edition 2.01, 1993)

	TOPIC	# OF RECORDS
56.	Land and property	9
57.	Land and property — Law and legislation	1
58.	Language and languages	1
59.	Law and legislation	5
60.	Law and legislation — Sources	1
61.	Maps	29
62.	Maps — Bibliography	5
63.	Migration, Internal	1
64.	Military history	9
65.	Military history — Bibliography	1
66.	Military history — Biography	1
67.	Military records	1
68.	Military records — Bibliography	2
69.	Minorities	20
70.	Minorities — Bibliography	1
71.	Names, Geographical	1
72.	Names, Personal	6
73.	Native races	23
74.	Native races — Bibliography	1
75.	Native races — Ethnology	6
76.	Native races — Folklore	3
77.	Native races — Genealogy	4
78.	Native races — Genealogy — Indexes	1
79.	Native races — History	7
80.	Native races — History — Bibliography	1
81.	Native races — Indexes	1
82.	Native races — Nobility — Genealogy	2
83.	Native races — Social life and customs	1
84.	Newspapers — Bibliography	1
85.	Nobility	12
86.	Nobility — Genealogy	1
87.	Notarial records	1
88.	Officials and employees	2
89.	Officials and employees — Biography	2
90.	Officials and employees — Directories	1
91.	Periodicals	2
92.	Politics and government	10
93.	Politics and government — Guide-books	1
94.	Politics and government — Handbooks, manuals, etc.	1
95.	Politics and government — Sources	2
96.	Population	3
97.	Population — History	1
98.	Postal and shipping guides	5
99.	Public records	2
100.	Public records — Bibliography	1
101.	Schools	1
102.	Slavery and bondage	1
103.	Social life and customs	13
104.	Social life and customs — Handbooks, manuals, etc.	1
105.	Societies	4
106.	Societies — Bibliography	1
107.	Statistics	4
108.	Taxation	1
109.	Taxation — Bibliography	1

Figure 4-6 (continued) **Mexico — General FHLC Topics (Edition 2.01, 1993)**

entity by that name; then, for those entities that are municipalities, the same name will appear with the word *municipio* in parentheses after it. These listings relate to the municipalities, which are the local political governing units. In many cases a municipality will be made up of several smaller entities, both political and ecclesiastical. Frequently, those smaller units are listed in the description of the civil register or parish records. In some cases the civil registers are kept at the municipality level; in other cases the records of each municipality are divided among various sub-units, such as the parishes that are included in a municipality. When possible, you should identify the municipality to which a particular town or parish belongs, because the records might be found at the municipality level. In each category (Mexico, individual states, parishes, and municipalities) you might find any of the subject headings listed in figure 4-6. In the larger municipalities and cities, you will frequently find listings for census records, land and property records, notarial records, diocesan records, and archives. Generally, however, categories other than civil registration and church records are found only under Mexico, General, under each individual state, and under the largest cities.

When you begin your research, you should take the smallest geographical unit in which you are aware the ancestor resided (or probably resided) at the time of his birth or marriage, and search under that unit for records. For example, if your ancestor came from Xicotencatl in Tamaulipas, Mexico, you would look under Mexico, Tamaulipas, Xicotencatl. The first entry that appears (see figure 4-7) is for "Church Records." These records cover the time period from 1755 to 1934. Basic information concerning the town is provided, followed by a listing of the various volumes and their corresponding film numbers. The principal parish of Xicotencatl is named Dulce Nombre de Jesus, and it included parts of several other parishes. The next entry, under "Civil Registration," lists the principal civil registration records for Xicotencatl municipality (municipio). A third entry under Xicotencatl Municipality lists the 1930 census for that area. The FHLC can assist the Hispanic researcher in locating records and can increase your understanding of area geography. Use of the information in conjunction with maps can help you determine the larger political units to which smaller towns belong.

If I had an ancestor who was born in 1875 in Mexico in the town of Rincon de Romos, in the state of Aguascalientes, I would look in the Locality section of the FHLC under Mexico, Aguascalientes, Rincon de Romos. The first entry, "Church Records, Rincon de Romos," indicates that Rincon de Romos includes the principal parish of San Jose de Grazia, as well as Pabellon, Cosio, Ojocaliente, and Mineral de Asientos. Parish records from 1769 to 1962 are available on microfilm. I would then determine that baptismal records for 1875 would be on the film #635642, which spans the years 1873–1877, and I would fill out a film order form for this microfilm. When it arrived in three to six weeks, I would look for my

```
************************************************************************************
MEXICO, TAMAULIPAS, XICOTÉNCATL - CHURCH RECORDS
                                                                     +-------------+
Iglesia Católica. Dulce Nombre de Jesús (Xicoténcatl,                |LATIN AMERICA|
      Tamaulipas).                                                   |FILM AREA    |
    Registros parroquiales, 1755-1934. -- Salt Lake City : Filmado   +-------------+
      por la Sociedad Genealógica de Utah, 1964, 1992. -- 12
      carretes de microfilme ; 35 mm.

    Microfilme de manuscritos en Xicoténcatl.
    Estos registros incluyen partidas de las parroquias de Aldama, Gómez
       Farías, Magiscatzin (ahora González), Llera (ahora Llera de Canales
       y de ranchos y haciendas en los municipios de los mismos.
       Magiscatzin cambió nombre oficial a González en 1938. La cabecera
       del municipio de Llera cambió nombre oficial a Llera de Canales en
       1934.
    Parish registers of baptisms, confirmations, marriages and deaths.

    Bautismos     1755-1803,1835-1844 ----------------------------- 0639913
       (incluye matrimonios y defunciones)                          item 1-3.
    Bautismos     1804-1835 --------------------------------------- 0639914
    Bautismos     1844-1858 --------------------------------------- 0639915
    Bautismos     1858-1874 --------------------------------------- 0639916
    Bautismos     1879-1902 --------------------------------------- 0639917
    Bautismos     1888-1899 --------------------------------------- 0639918
    Confirmaciones 1855 ------------------------------------------- 0639919
    Matrimonios   1810-1853,1876-1878,1882-1920,1923- ------------- 0639920
       1934
    Defunciones   1775-1832 --------------------------------------- 0639921

    Defunciones   1883-1860,1878-1918 ----------------------------- 0639922
    Bautismos           1902-1918 --------------------------------- 1835101
    Bautismos           1919-1926 --------------------------------- 1835102

************************************************************************************
MEXICO, TAMAULIPAS, XICOTÉNCATL - CIVIL REGISTRATION
                                                                     +-------------+
Xicoténcatl (Tamaulipas). Registro Civil.                            |LATIN AMERICA|
    Registros parroquiales, 1860-1930. -- Salt Lake City : Filmado   |FILM AREA    |
      por la Sociedad Genealógica de Utah, 1975. -- 21 rollos de     +-------------+
      microfilm ; 35 mm.

    Microfilm de manuscritos en el archivo del Registro Civil en Ciudad
       Victoria.
    Algunos tomos incluyen su propio índice.

    Nacimientos   1860-1861,1863-1864,1866-1874 (1860 ------------- 1106792
       incluye mat., con 1863 hay nac. de 1873 y hojas
       sueltas de 1876-1877)
    Nacimientos   1875-1886 --------------------------------------- 1106793
    Nacimientos   1887-1898 --------------------------------------- 1106794
    Nacimientos   1899-1905 --------------------------------------- 1106795
    Nacimientos   1906-1913 --------------------------------------- 1106796
    Nacimientos   1914-1916,1918-1920,1922-1927 ------------------- 1106797
    Nacimientos   1928-1930 --------------------------------------- 1106798
    Matrimonios   1860-1861 --------------------------------------- 1107604
    Matrimonios   1863,1866-1871 ---------------------------------- 1107605
    Matrimonios   1875-1885 --------------------------------------- 1107606
    Matrimonios   1886-1892 (1890-1892 incluye mat. --------------- 1107607
       1894-1895 y def. 1880)
    Matrimonios   1894-1901 --------------------------------------- 1107608
    Matrimonios   1902-1906 --------------------------------------- 1107609
    Matrimonios   1907-1915 --------------------------------------- 1107610
    Matrimonios   1916,1918-1920,1922-1930 ------------------------ 1107611
    Defunciones   1863-1864,1866-1875 (1868 incluye --------------- 1107612
       matrimonios)
    Defunciones   1876,1879-1888 (1876 incluyen mat. -------------- 1107613
       1868,1876-1877 y def. 1868,1877)
    Defunciones   1889-1899 (1895 fuera de orden) ----------------- 1106799
    Defunciones   1900-1906 --------------------------------------- 1106800
    Defunciones   1907-1915 --------------------------------------- 1106801
    Defunciones   1916,1918-1920,1922-1930 ------------------------ 1106802

************************************************************************************
MEXICO, TAMAULIPAS, XICOTENCATL (MUNICIPIO) - CENSUS
                                                                     +-------------+
México. Dirección General de Estadística.                            |LATIN AMERICA|
    Censo de población del municipio de Xicotencatl, Tamaulipas,     |FILM AREA    |
      1930. -- Salt Lake City : Filmado por la Sociedad              +-------------+
      Genealógica de Utah, 1988. -- en 1 carrete de microfilme ;
      35 mm.
```

Figure 4-7 FHLC records for Xicoténcatl, Tamaulipas, Mexico (1993 edition)

ancestor's baptism on it. (I would have first searched the IGI and the Parish and Vital Records List to see if my ancestor's name might have been extracted.)

Once I had found my ancestor's birth and/or baptism record in 1875, I might decide to search for the marriage of his parents. Their places of birth are likely to have been listed on the baptism record. If they were from the town of Rincon de Romos, they were likely to have been married there. If the mother was from a different town, they were likely to have been married in that town. Since they have a child born in 1875, they are likely to have been married somewhere between 1860 and 1875. Film #635733, Matrimonios 1859–1872, and Film #635744, Matrimonios 1872–1888, both cover that time period, and I would order both films. If I found their marriage record, I might also want to find their *información matrimonial*. A complete discussion of the process for utilizing parish records, which explains the process from this point on, is contained in chapters 9 and 10.

The same approach could have been used with the civil registration records listed for Rincon de Romos. Civil registration records are frequently more complete than parish records. They are definitely worth searching in the time period for which they are available, which is generally after 1861 in Mexico. (See chapter 8 for details on other Hispanic countries.)

When your pedigree chart and family group sheets have been updated as far as possible through a complete search of the available parish records, you will want to consult other available records. These can be located by checking the Locality section under the state "General" section, as well as under the principal regional towns and the smaller locality.

It is important to check under the names of the state or provincial capital, and the city of the diocese to which the location belongs. Marriage dispensations, censuses, Inquisition records, notarial records, and other broad regional records, as well as general court and governmental records, may appear under those city names. Thus, if you are interested in records in the state of Jalisco, you would check under Guadalajara, which is both the diocesan and political capital. To determine the possible locations of records, it is important to recognize the changes that have taken place in various political and ecclesiastical units. For example, the municipal and parish archives in Hidalgo de Parral, Chihuahua, have information for large portions of Chihuahua, as Hidalgo de Parral served as the informal political capital of Chihuahua for an extensive period. Diocesan records for Chihuahua would be found under Durango, where the Bishop of the diocese that included Chihuahua resided.

There is no better way for the researcher to learn to use the Family History Library Catalog than by looking for an actual parish. You should not be afraid to seek assistance from the librarians or to consult the excellent instructional materials entitled "How to Use the Family History Library

Catalog on Microfiche" and "How to Use the Family History Library Catalog on CD ROM." A wealth of original records and excellent secondary source material is readily available to you on a local level through this important catalog.

Family History Catalog on CD ROM[5]

The Locality Search in the FHLC on CD ROM allows you to search at each of the three levels discussed for the microfiche FHLC — national, state or provincial, and local town. For any locality you can request a Topics Search of all topics or of a specific topic. The result of a search for all topics in Mexico is reproduced in figure 4-6. You should, however, always initiate your search at the smallest geographical level that you know. It is at the parish and municipality level where church parish records and government civil records will be found.

One major advantage of the CD ROM is that it will search for a part of the name. For example, if you ask it to search for Santa Maria de Cambados and it does not find one, it will then search for Cambados and Santa Maria. In the author's experience, there has been only one time when this was a detriment. Not finding "San Claudio" or "Claudio," the program listed (several minutes later) all 1,256 place names in the catalog beginning with "San"!

When you want to see all of the localities in a given region, start with Locality Browse under that region. The Computer FHLC Catalog will also do a Surname Search, but does not have an Author/Title Search or Subject Search.

SUMMARY

The Hispanic researcher will almost certainly find the keys to beginning and extending his research in the local LDS family history center. This article should be viewed only as an introduction to the many valuable materials available. By using this introduction, you should be able to begin your research, identify the reference materials available, and successfully pursue your personal Hispanic research.

---

1. *FamilySearch: Using Ancestral File* (Salt Lake City: The Church of Jesus Christ of Latter-day Saints, 1994); *FamilySearch: Contributing Information to Ancestral File* (Salt Lake City: The Church of Jesus Christ of Latter-day Saints, 1992); *FamilySearch: Correcting Information in Ancestral File* (Salt Lake City: The Church of Jesus Christ of Latter-day Saints, 1992).

2. Elizabeth Nichols, "The International Genealogical Index," *New England Historical and Genealogical Register* CXXXVII (July 1983): 193–217.

[3] *FamilySearch: International Genealogical Index (on compact disc)* (Salt Lake City: The Church of Jesus Christ of Latter-day Saints, 1993); *FamilySearch: International Genealogical Index (on microfiche)* (Salt Lake City: The Church of Jesus Christ of Latter-day Saints, 1992); *FamilySearch: Finding an IGI Source* (Salt Lake City: The Church of Jesus Christ of Latter-day Saints, 1992).

[4] For more information see *Family History Library Catalog (on microfiche)* (Salt Lake City: The Church of Jesus Christ of Latter-day Saints, 1993).

[5] For further details see *Family History Library Catalog (on compact disc)* (Salt Lake City: The Church of Jesus Christ of Latter-day Saints, 1990)

CHAPTER 5

Tracing the Hispanic Immigrant in United States Records

The first established European colonists in the area now called the United States were Spaniards who came from Cuba to Saint Augustine, Florida in 1565 and Spaniards who came from northern Mexico to Santa Fe, New Mexico in 1598.[1] Since that time millions of Hispanics from all over Latin America, Spain, Portugal, and the Philippines have immigrated to the United States.[2] While we have recently heard much about the illegal immigration of Hispanics, especially Mexicans, to this country, in reality the vast majority of Hispanic immigrants have come legally, seeking work and better opportunities for their families. In addition, several hundred thousand were citizens of Mexico in 1848 when the northern third of Mexican territory was seized by the United States in the war that we call the Mexican War and Mexicans refer to as the North American Invasion.[3] There are many records available for identifying the place of origin of the immigrant ancestor in all time periods, but especially for the great waves of immigration that came to the United States during the twentieth century.

U.S. RECORD SOURCES

The emphasis of this chapter will be on United States record sources that are most likely to provide the place of origin of the Hispanic immigrant ancestor. It will not be uncommon for many who read this book to find that they have one or more lines that extend several generations in the United States. Their research should concentrate primarily on American sources, using books such as *The Source* (2nd ed.), edited by Loretto Szucs and Sandra Luebking; *The Researcher's Guide to American Genealogy* by Val Greenwood; or *Preserving Your American Heritage* by Norman Wright.[4] In addition, excellent publications on Anglo-American sources are the research outlines for the United States published by The Church of Jesus Christ of Latter-day Saints. Of particular interest from that series are *Tracing Immigrant Origins*, which deals with immigration records in the United States, and the *Latin American Research Outline*. In addition, those whose ancestors can be traced back into the Spanish colonial period in what is now the United States will find the descriptions of records in the other chapters of this book of value, since the record systems adopted by Spanish colonials in areas that are now the United States parallel those in other parts of the Spanish-speaking world.

Civil Vital Records

The records of births, marriages, and deaths maintained by various city, county, and state political jurisdictions in the United States should be checked for clues as to the specific place of origin in Mexico, Spain, or other Hispanic countries. Generally, United States vital records are considerably less detailed than those in the Hispanic countries and will only give the country of origin. There are numerous exceptions, especially when dealing with marriage applications or delayed birth registration, where a specific city of origin may be given. The places to write for these are generally the county or the state where the event took place. A check of the *Handy Book for Genealogists,*[5] *Ancestry's Red Book,*[6] or the *International Vital Records Handbook*[7] will indicate the appropriate place for each specific state or county where you should write for those records. Prior to writing, you should check the Family History Library Catalog, as many vital records as well as statewide indexes in the United States have been microfilmed.

Church Records

In this author's experience church records often are the best source of information about the specific place of origin of the immigrant ancestor. Most Hispanics were Catholic and initially attended church in a Spanish-speaking parish of the Catholic Church. These parishes were staffed by priests who often wrote in Spanish and were generally familiar with the geography of the countries of origin. They also were more oriented towards thinking about specific parishes or dioceses in those countries. For all these reasons, as well as the more detailed nature of Catholic Church records compared with the United States civil vital records, this is often a good place to search. As illustrated in figures 5-1a and 5-1b, it is important to request a photocopy or literal copy of the original entry: The extract forms often used for English Catholic records do not always provide the detailed information found in a Spanish-language entry.

U.S. Census Records

Since 1790 the United States has taken a federal census every ten years. These records, particularly those after 1850, provide detailed information. While they almost never give more than a country of origin, they can still be valuable in determining facts about immigration and in locating immigration records, particularly beginning with the 1900 Census. Figure 5-2 is a page from the United States federal census for Arizona Territory, Pinell County, Florence Township. Note that relationships are given regarding

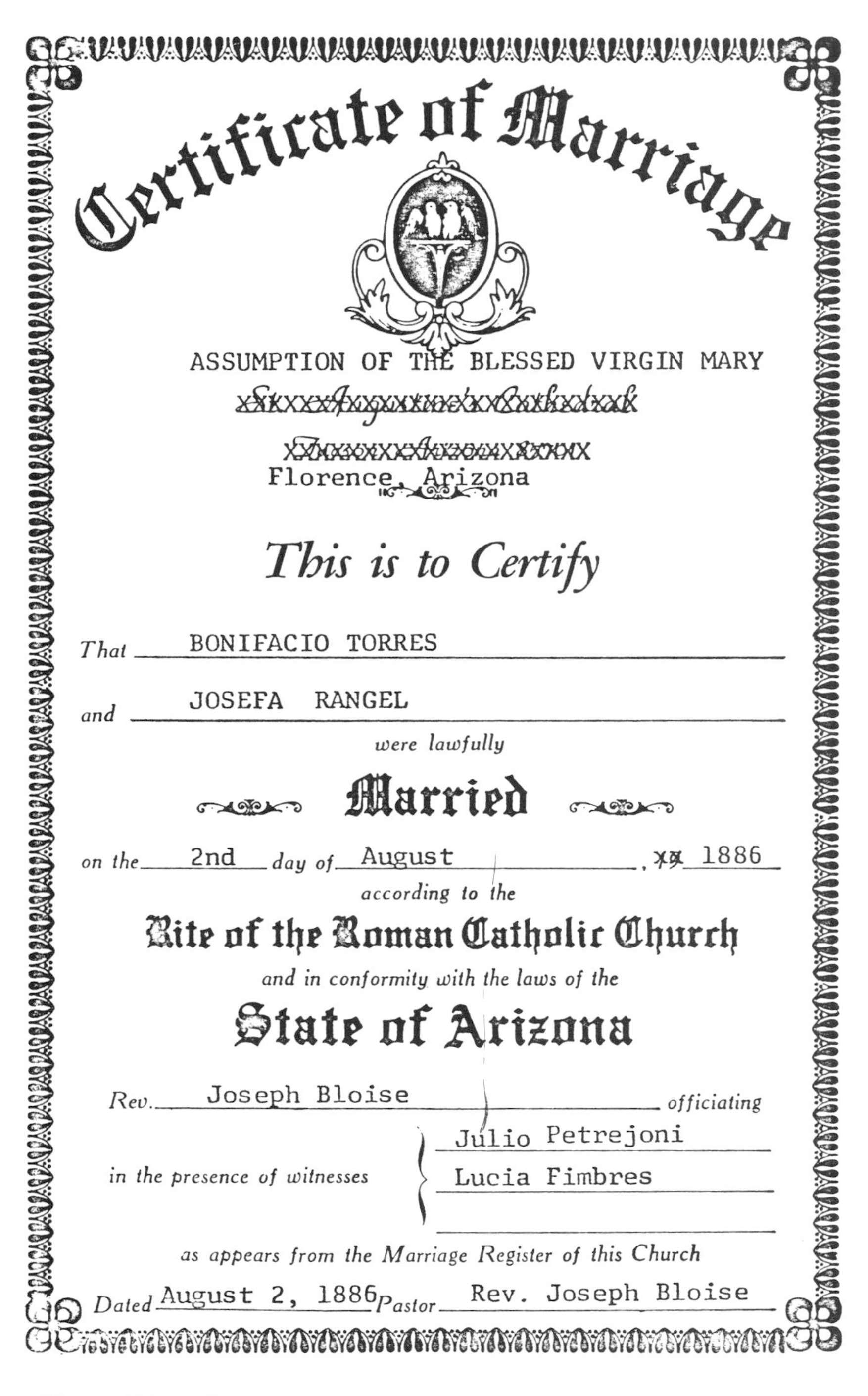
Certificate of Marriage

ASSUMPTION OF THE BLESSED VIRGIN MARY

Florence, Arizona

This is to Certify

That BONIFACIO TORRES

and JOSEFA RANGEL

were lawfully

Married

on the 2nd day of August , 1886

according to the

Rite of the Roman Catholic Church

and in conformity with the laws of the

State of Arizona

Rev. Joseph Bloise officiating

in the presence of witnesses Julio Petrejoni
Lucia Fimbres

as appears from the Marriage Register of this Church

Dated August 2, 1886 Pastor Rev. Joseph Bloise

Figure 5-1a Marriage certificate from Catholic church, Florence, Arizona (author's copy)

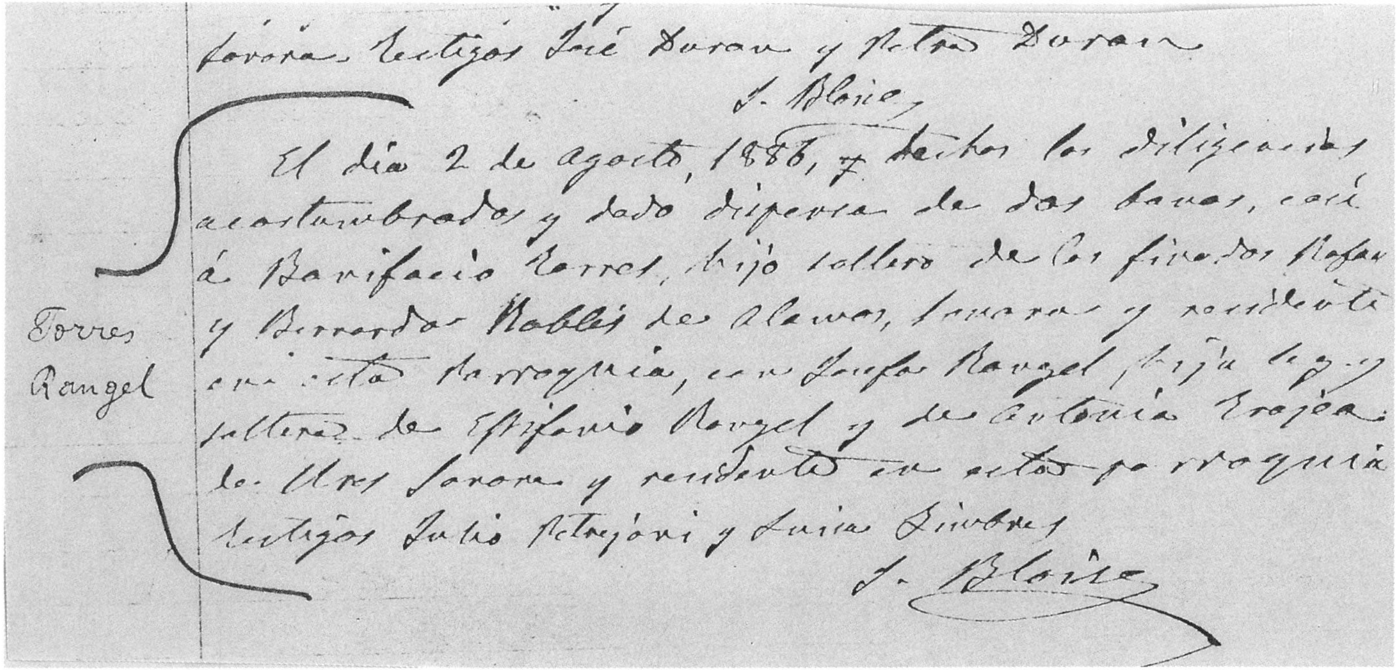
Sonora. testigos José Duran y Petra Duran
J. Blanc,
El día 2 de agosto, 1886, y hechas las diligencias
acostumbradas y dado dispensa de dos banas, casé
á Bonifacio Torres, hijo soltero de los finados Rafael
y Bernarda Robles de Alamos, Sonora y residente
en esta parroquia, con Josefa Rangel hija leg.
soltera de Epifanio Rangel y de Antonia Trejo
de Ures Sonora y residente en esta parroquia
testigos Julio Petrajani y Lucia Jimenez
J. Blanc

Torres
Rangel

Figure 5-1b Original marriage entry (literal copy), parish records, Florence, Arizona (author's copy)

TWELFTH CENSUS OF THE UNITED STATES. 202

SCHEDULE No. 1.—POPULATION.

State Arizona Territory
County Pinal
Township or other division of county Florence Township
Name of incorporated city, town, or village, within the above-named division,
Enumerated by me on the 1st day of June, 1900, John J. Pool, Enumerator.

Supervisor's District No. 11
Enumeration District No. 55
Name of Institution X
Ward of city,

Line	Dwelling No.	Family No.	Name	Relation	Color	Sex	Month	Year	Age	Marital	Yrs married	Mother of how many	Living	Birthplace	Father's birthplace	Mother's birthplace	Yr immigration	Yrs in U.S.	Naturalization	Occupation	Months not employed	Attended school (months)	Can read / write / speak English
1	1	1	Victory, Curly E.	Head	W	M	Jan	1833	67	Wd				[illegible]	England	England				Stock raiser	0		yes yes yes
2			Martinez, Ignacio	Servant	In	M	May	1825	75	S				Mexico	Mexico	Mexico	1870	30	al	[illegible]	0		no no no
3	2	2	Summers, [illegible]	Head	W	F	Feb	1839	61	Wd		2	2	Pennsylvania	Pennsylvania	Pennsylvania				Teacher School	5		yes [illegible]
4			Bierzyda, June	Daughter	W	F	June	1864	35	M	13	2	2	California	Kentucky	Pennsylvania							
5			— Joy S.	Granddaughter	W	F	Apr	1888	12	S				Arizona Ty	Iowa	California							yes yes yes
6			— Donald A.	Grandson	W	M	Jan	1896	4	S				Arizona Ty	Iowa	California				At school		7	yes yes yes
7	3	3	Bustamante, Rufina	Head	W	F	Dec	1821	79	Wd		9	2	Mexico	Mexico	Mexico	1880	20					
8			Ureia, Manuela	Lodger	W	F	June	1861	38	M	15	0	0	California	Mexico	Mexico							no no no
9			— Roman	Lodger	W	M	Jan	1856	44	M	15			Mexico	Mexico	Mexico							no no no
10			Urtiaga, Antonia	Lodger	W	F	July	1888	11	S				Arizona Ty	California	California	1874	26	al	Day laborer	6		yes yes no
11			— Rafiel	Lodger	W	M	June	1889	10	S				Arizona Ty	California	California				At school		7	yes yes yes
12	4	4	Rangel, Antonia	Head	W	F	Mar	1830	70	Wd		14	8	Mexico	Mexico	Mexico	1880	20		At school		7	yes yes yes
13			— Elias	Son	W	M	May	1869	31	S				Mexico	Mexico	Mexico							no no no
14			— Angelita	Daughter	W	F	Feb	1875	25	S				Mexico	Mexico	Mexico	1880	20	na	Day laborer	5		yes yes yes
15	5	5	Soto, Fernando	Head	W	M	May	1860	40	S				Mexico	Mexico	Mexico	1880	20		House Keeper	10		no no no
16	6	6	Torres, Josefita	Head	W	F	July	1869	30	M	14	7	6	Mexico	Mexico	Mexico	1878	22	al	Day laborer	3		no no no
17			— Antonia	Daughter	W	F	May	1887	13	S				Arizona Ty	Mexico	Mexico	1880	20					no no no
18			— Paula	Daughter	W	F	Jan	1888	12	S				Arizona Ty	Mexico	Mexico				At school		7	yes yes yes
19			— Eloisa	Daughter	W	F	May	1890	10	S				Arizona Ty	Mexico	Mexico				At school		7	yes yes yes
20			— Carmelita	Daughter	W	F	Jan	1891	9	S				Arizona Ty	Mexico	Mexico				At school		7	yes yes yes
21			— [illegible]	Son	W	M	Feb	1893	7	S				Arizona Ty	Mexico	Mexico				At school		7	yes yes
22			— Alfredo	Son	W	M	Feb	1898	2	S				Arizona Ty	Mexico	Mexico				At school		7	
23	7	7	Stanley, Charles W.	Head	W	M	Apr	1865	35	M	7			Ohio	Michigan	Ohio				Saloon keeper	0		
24			— Elizabeth C.	Wife	W	F	April	1875	25	M	7	4	4	Arizona	Ireland	Mexico							

Figure 5-2 Page from 1900 U.S. federal census, Florence, Arizona, p. 202

the parties, as well as their ages and birth dates; marital status; the number of years married; the number of children the mother has given birth to, as well as the number of children living; the birth country of the individual and that person's mother and father; the year of immigration to the United States; the number of years lived in the United States; and whether the individual has been naturalized (shown by marking AL if they are an alien and NA if they are naturalized).

Look at Family 6 on figure 5-2 and you will find the mother, Josefita Torres, listed as the head of household with her six living children. She immigrated in 1880, which would have been twenty years before the census was taken, meaning that she had already immigrated here when she was married in 1886. This fact is further supported by documentation that the birth of her first child was in Arizona, not Mexico. This would mean that a search for her marriage record could be made in Arizona. A search was made in the 1886 Florence, Arizona marriage records, and the record appearing as figures 5-1a and 5-1b is the result of that search. There is no indication in this record that she is an alien, since usually only adult males were identified as to citizenship, and females during this time period took on their husband's nationality. Clues in a census record that could give you further sources to search for crucial immigration records would be the date of immigration and an indication that an application for citizenship (pa) was filed or that citizenship was granted (na).

Newspapers

Local newspapers should be checked in the areas where your ancestors resided. There is often a belief that because many Hispanics were agricultural laborers they did not appear in local newspapers. However, this author has encountered several obituaries and other articles about Hispanics, even those who were humble workers in the orange groves. Figure 5-3 shows a portion of a page from the December 14, 1934 *San Jose Mercury Herald* (San Jose, California) which mentions a number of Mexicans, Italians, and Portuguese; included is the obituary of Maria L. Oliver, which identifies her place of birth as Topo in the Azores Islands. Many newspapers are available through inter-library loan on microfilm or microfiche. Check with your local library for their availability.

Miscellaneous Local Records

Remember to check in all United States records of a local nature. You can never be certain when a specific reference to a place of origin or the time and place of immigration or naturalization might appear. An example of this is figure 5-4, showing a page from the Placer County Great Register of Voters for the year 1892, which lists Jacinta Acuña, states he is a native of Chile, and gives the specific date and place where he was naturalized. As is the case in any genealogical search, thoroughness in check-

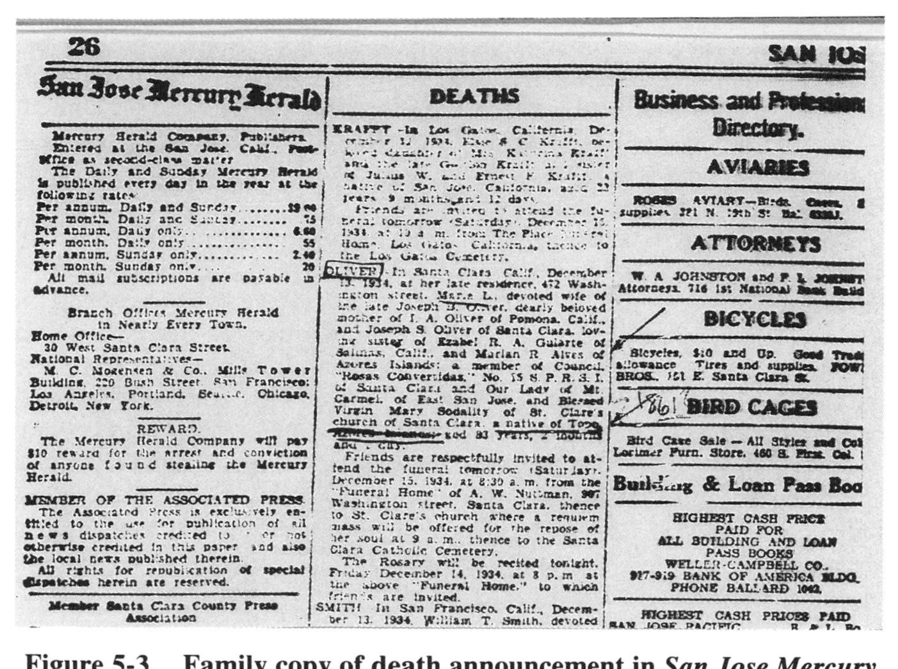

26

SAN JOS[illegible]

San Jose Mercury Herald

Mercury Herald Company, Publishers.
Entered at the San Jose, Calif., Postoffice as second-class matter.
The Daily and Sunday Mercury Herald is published every day in the year at the following rates:

Per annum, Daily and Sunday	$9.00
Per month, Daily and Sunday	75
Per annum, Daily only	6.60
Per month, Daily only	55
Per annum, Sunday only	2.40
Per month, Sunday only	20

All mail subscriptions are payable in advance.

Branch Offices Mercury Herald in Nearly Every Town.
Home Office—
30 West Santa Clara Street.
National Representatives—
M. C. Mogensen & Co., Mills Tower Building, 220 Bush Street, San Francisco; Los Angeles, Portland, Seattle, Chicago, Detroit, New York.

REWARD.
The Mercury Herald Company will pay $10 reward for the arrest and conviction of anyone found stealing the Mercury Herald.

MEMBER OF THE ASSOCIATED PRESS.
The Associated Press is exclusively entitled to the use for publication of all news dispatches credited to it or not otherwise credited in this paper and also the local news published therein.
All rights for republication of special dispatches herein are reserved.

Member Santa Clara County Press Association

DEATHS

KRAFFT—In Los Gatos, California, December 12, 1934, Elsie S. C. Krafft, beloved daughter of Mrs. K[illegible] Krafft and the late G[illegible] Krafft, and sister of Julius W. and Ernest F. Krafft, a native of San Jose, California, aged 22 years, 9 months and 12 days.
Friends are invited to attend the funeral tomorrow (Saturday), December 15, 1934, at 10 a. m. from The Place [illegible] Home, Los Gatos, California, thence to the Los Gatos Cemetery.

OLIVER—In Santa Clara, Calif., December 13, 1934, at her late residence, 472 Washington street, Maria L., devoted wife of the late Joseph B. Oliver, dearly beloved mother of I. A. Oliver of Pomona, Calif., and Joseph S. Oliver of Santa Clara, loving sister of Ezabel R. A. Guiarte of Salinas, Calif., and Marian R. Alves of Azores Islands; a member of Council "Rosas Convertidas," No. 55 S. P. R. S. I. of Santa Clara and Our Lady of Mt. Carmel, of East San Jose, and Blessed Virgin Mary Sodality of St. Clare's church of Santa Clara, a native of To[illegible] [illegible] aged 83 years, 2 months and [illegible] days.
Friends are respectfully invited to attend the funeral tomorrow (Saturday), December 15, 1934, at 8:30 a. m. from the "Funeral Home" of A. W. Nuttman, 907 Washington street, Santa Clara, thence to St. Clare's church where a requiem mass will be offered for the repose of her soul at 9 a. m., thence to the Santa Clara Catholic Cemetery.
The Rosary will be recited tonight, Friday, December 14, 1934, at 8 p. m. at the above "Funeral Home," to which friends are invited.

SMITH—In San Francisco, Calif., December 13, 1934, William T. Smith, devoted

Business and Profession[illegible] Directory.

AVIARIES

ROSES AVIARY—Birds, Cages, [illegible] supplies. 321 N. 19th St. Bal. [illegible]

ATTORNEYS

W. A. JOHNSTON and F. L. JOHNST[illegible] Attorneys. 716 1st National Bank Build[illegible]

BICYCLES

Bicycles, $10 and Up. Good Trade allowance. Tires and supplies. FOW[illegible] BROS. 151 E. Santa Clara St.

1861

BIRD CAGES

Bird Cage Sale — All Styles and Col[illegible] Lorimer Furn. Store, 460 S. First. Cal. [illegible]

Building & Loan Pass Boo[illegible]

HIGHEST CASH PRICE PAID FOR ALL BUILDING AND LOAN PASS BOOKS
WELLER-CAMPBELL CO.,
917-919 BANK OF AMERICA BLDG.
PHONE BALLARD 1042.

HIGHEST CASH PRICES PAID
SAN JOSE PACIFIC [illegible]

Figure 5-3 Family copy of death announcement in *San Jose Mercury Herald*, San Jose, California, December 1934, p. 26 (author's copy)

ing all record sources for a specific locality is equally important whether you are searching in United States records or those of a foreign country.

Passenger Lists and Border Crossing Records

Without doubt, the most informative United States records concerning the place of immigration are passenger lists and their border-crossing manifest counterparts. Figure 5-5 reproduces the two parts of a page from the passenger list for the S.S. *Chalmette*, which arrived in New Orleans from Havana on 14 October 1916. Note the number of Spaniards reaching the United States from Cuba. The information given includes the age, sex, occupation, and marital status of the individual. The individual also indicates whether he or she is able to read and write. (It is interesting to note that, on this page, the vast majority of immigrants could do both.) It also gives the country of origin, the passenger's race, and the country and city of the last permanent residence, as well as the name and address of the nearest relative or friend in the country from which the alien came. In some cases this will give a place of long-term residence in an interim country such as Cuba, and in others it will give information concerning a specific relative; for example, Jesus Colminares, who appears on line 11, gives the name of Marcelino Colminares, his father, and his father's address in Santander. The final destination of the passenger, whether he has a ticket for that destination, who paid the passage, and whether the passenger has

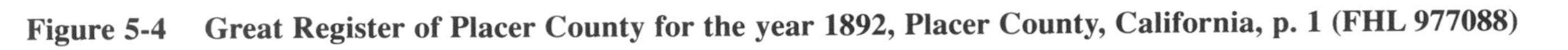

Great Register of Placer County for the Year 1892.

Voted	No.	NAME.	Age.	Height. ft.	in.	Complexion.	Color of Eyes.	Color of Hair.	Visible marks or scars, if any, and their locality.	Occupation.	Country of Nativity.	Precinct.	P.O. Address.	Where and when Naturalized.	[illegible]
		A													
	1	Aagaard, Marcus	42	5	11	Light	Blue	Dark	Mole on forehead	Wheelwright	Denmark	Auburn No. 1	Auburn	Mch. 20, '86, Placer co., Cal., Su. Ct.	Aug. 15
	2	Abbott, Azro George	53	5	9¾	Light	Blue	Gray	Right eye lost	Liveryman	New Hampshire	Newcastle	Newcastle		Aug. 23
	3	Abbott, Guy Elmer	21	5	10½	Light	Hazel	Light	Scar on right wrist	Wheelwright	Lodi, Wisconsin	Newcastle	Newcastle		Aug. 31
	4	Abbott, Frank Lawrence	41	5	7½	Dark	Brown	Brown		Constable	Portsmouth, N. H.	Newcastle	Newcastle		Aug. 15
	5	Abram, James	62	5	5	Light	Blue	Gray	Coal mark on nose	Miner	England	Mich. Bluff	Mich. Bluff	Sept. 7, '57, Luzerne co., Pa., Co. Ct.	Aug. 20
	6	Abram, John	40	5	7	Medi'm	Blue	Brown		Merchant	England	Auburn No. 2	Auburn	By virtue of father's naturalization	Aug. 12
	7	Abram, Albert James	23	5	9¾	Medi'm	Blue	Brown	Scar on left thumb	Miner	Placer co., Cal	Mich. Bluff	Mich. Bluff		Aug. 20
	8	Ackerman, Truman	72	5	10	Light	Blue	Gray		Farmer	Jefferson co., N. Y.	Junction	Auburn		Sept. 9
	9	Ackerman, Francis Marion	34	5	9½	Light	Blue	Brown		Exp. Agent	Maine	Colfax	Colfax		Aug. 1
	10	Ackerman, John Quincy	36	5	8½	Light	Gray	Brown		Miner	Lowell, Mass	Iowa Hill	Iowa City		Aug. 27
	11	Acuna, Jacinto	55	5	9	Dark	Black	Black		Miner	Chile	Forest Hill	Forest Hill	Sept. 8, '77, Placer co., Cal., Co. Ct.	Aug. 25
	12	Adams, Calvin Tracy	60	6	½	Medi'm	Hazel	Dark	End of left thumb off	Farmer	Delaware co., O.	Newcastle	Newcastle		Aug. 6
	13	Adams, Charles Henry	38	5	11	Medi'm	Blue	Dark	Right index finger crooked	Sp. Mess'nger	Colesburg, Iowa	Auburn No. 1	Auburn		July 30
	14	Adams, Eugene Edward	22	6		Light	Blue	Light		Rancher	Plumas co., Cal	Auburn No. 1	Auburn		Sept. 8
	15	Adams, Frank Drew	42	5	11	Medi'm	Blue	Dk Br'wn		Real Es. Agt.	Middlesex co., Mass	Auburn No. 1	Auburn		Aug. 2
	16	Adams, George Washington	61	5	9¾	Medi'm	Blue	Dark	Left little finger crooked	Miner	Worcester co., Mass	Mayflower	Forest Hill		Aug. 20
	17	Adams, George Washington	31	5	10	Dark	Dk Br'wn	Black		Laborer	Nevada co., Cal	Lincoln No. 1	Lincoln		Aug. 30
	18	Adams, Harry Francis	48	5	9	Medi'm	Blue	Dark		Miner	Lamoille co., Vt	Yankee Jims	Yankee Jims		Aug. 20
	19	Adams, Henry	40	5	10½	Medi'm	Blue	IronGray		Laborer	England	Clipper Gap	Clipper Gap	July 22, '76, Placer co., Cal., Co. Ct.	July 30
	20	Adams, John	51	5	8½	Fair	Brown	Dark		Farmer	Delaware co., O.	Auburn No. 1	Auburn		Aug. 1
	21	Adams, Joseph Carter	44	5	9½	Dark	Brown	Dark	Right eye blind	Carpenter	Warwick co., Ind	Auburn No. 1	Auburn		July 30
	22	Adams, Luman Boyden	54	5	7	Dark	Blue	Brown		Farmer	Lamoille co., Vt	Central	Lincoln		Aug. 27
	23	Adams, Lorenzo Dow	46	5	8	Medi'm	Gray	Brown	Tattoo marks on left wrist	Merchant	Rock co., Wis	Lincoln No. 1	Lincoln		Aug. 27
	24	Adams, Norman Claude	23	5	5¾	Light	Gray	Blonde	Scar over left eye	Farmer	Adamsville, Mich	Clipper Gap	Clipper Gap		July 30
	25	Adams, Veranes Augustus	56	5	7	Medi'm	Hazel	IronGray		Miner	Lunenburgh, Mass	Yankee Jims	Yankee Jims		Aug. 20
	26	Adams, William Perry	40	5	7	Light	Blue	Dk Br'wn		Butcher	Wisconsin co., Ill	Sheridan	Sheridan		Sept. 1
	27	Adge, Frederic Isadore	39	5	7½	Medi'm	Hazel	Dark		Miner	New Orleans, La	Iowa Hill	Iowa City		Aug. 24
	28	Ahart, Peter	60	5	8	Dark	Brown	IronGray		Farmer	Germany	Manzanita	Lincoln	By virtue of father's naturalization	Aug. 27
	29	Ahart, George W.	25	5	9	Light	Gray	Brown	Scar on right wrist	Rancher	Lincoln, Cal	Manzanita	Lincoln		Aug. 27
	30	Ahart, William Edgar	23	5	9	Dark	Dark	Black	Scar on right second finger	Rancher	Lincoln, Cal	Manzanita	Lincoln		Aug. 27
	31	Ahart, George Phillip	21	5	9	Light	Blue	Brown		Rancher	Placer co., Cal	Manzanita	Lincoln		Aug. 31
	32	Ahrberg, William A. P.	64	5	11½	Light	Gray	Gray	Blind in left eye	Miner	Hanover	Weimar	Weimar	By virtue of annexation of Texas	Sept. 8
	33	Akers, Isaac	61	6		Dark	Blue	Dark		Farmer	Kentucky	Rocklin No. 2	Rocklin		Aug. 6
	34	Akers, Jesse	57	5	10½	Light	Gray	Gray		Laborer	Russell co., Ky	Roseville	Rosevillee		Sept. 7
	35	Albee, Henry Freeman	62	5	10¾	Light	Blue	Gray	Scar on left thumb	Merchant	New Brunswick	Penryn	Penryn	Born of American parents	Sept. 7
	36	Albee, Henry Daniel	31	5	9½	Light	Hazel	Dark		Clerk	California	Penryn	Penryn		Sept. 7
	37	Albee, Elmer H	53	5	7¾	Light	Gray	Gray	Scar on forehead	Clerk	New Brunswick	Penryn	Penryn	By virtue of father's naturalization	Sept. 24
	38	Albnos, Facundo Gorgonia	31	5	6	Dark	Brown	Black		Blacksmith	El Dorado co., Cal	Forest Hill	Forest Hill		Aug. 19
	39	Albrecht, Charles	58	5	8	Med'im	Brown	Black	Right thumb stiff	Merchant	Germany	Forest Hill	Forest Hill	June 20, '67, Placer co., Cal., Dist. Ct.	Aug. 19
	40	Albright, Richard James	53	5	10½	Medi'm	Blue	Gray	Scar on left middle finger	Fruitgrower	Syracuse, N. Y.	Long Valley	Auburn		Sept. 22
	41	Alexander, Abraham	60	5	6	Medi'm	Brown	Gray	Right thumb nail split	Merchant	Germany	Auburn No. 1	Auburn	Aug. 27, '58, Sac. co. Cal., Co. Ct.	Aug. 12
	42	Alexander, Abraham Jr	28	5	7½	Dark	Brown	Black		Merchant	Sacramento co., Cal.	Auburn No. 1	Auburn		Sept. 8
	43	Alford, William Clinton	64	5	8	Light	Lt Blue	Brown		Farmer	Upson county, Ga	Allens	Roseville		Sept. 11
	44	Alford, Erastus	43	5	11	Light	Blue	Black		Laborer	Iowa	Roseville	Roseville		Aug. 28
	45	Alfoncia, Alexander	34	6		Dark	Brown	Dark		Laborer	Cape de Verde Isles	Newcastle	Newcastle	July 16, '88, Placer co., Cal., Su. Ct.	Sept. 7
	46	Allen, Benjamin	24	6		Florid	Blue	Light		Laborer	Placer co., Cal	Mt. Pleasant	Lincoln		Aug. 29
	47	Allen, Charles Edgar	67	5	10	Dark	Black	Gray		Jus. of Peace	Clark co., Ky	Lincoln No. 2	Lincoln		Aug. 27
	48	Allen, Charles Edwin	40	5	7	Dark	Dk Br'wn	Black		Potter	Putnam co., Ind	Lincoln No. 2	Lincoln		Aug. 30
	49	Allen, Darwin Luther	61	5	6¾	Medi'm	Blue	Dark	Scar on left little finger	Farmer	Plainfield, N. H.	Allens	Roseville		Aug. 6
	50	Allen, Erskine	45	5	7	Medi'm	Hazel	Black	Scar on left cheek	Carpenter	Scotland	Bath	Bath	By virtue of father's naturalization	Aug. 20
	51	Allen, Elihu Gartrell	25	5	9½	Medi'm	Brown	Brown		Peddler	Adams co., Ill	Lincoln No. 1	Lincoln		Aug. 30
	52	Allen, George Aldrich	21	5	9	Dark	Black	Dark	Mole under left eye	Rancher	Placer co., Cal	Manzanita	Lincoln		Sept. 20
	53	Allen, George	35	5	11	Dark	Brown	Dark	Scar on right temple	Wag'nmaker	Marshall co., Ill	Auburn No. 2	Auburn		Sept. 7
	54	Allen, George	34	5	11½	Light	Blue	Dk Br'wn		Rancher	Placer co., Cal	Mt. Pleasant	Lincoln		Aug. 30
	55	Allen, Harry Goodno	23	6		Dark	Black	Black	Right index finger crooked	Rancher	Quincy, Illinois	Manzanita	Lincoln		Aug. 18
	56	Allen, Ira Philbrook	41	5	8	Fair	Blue	Brown		Stonecutter	Washington co., Me.	Rocklin No. 1	Rocklin		Aug. 31
	57	Allen, James Douglas	37	5	11	Dark	Brown	Black	Mole on chin	Carpenter	Lucas co., Ia	Lincoln No. 2	Lincoln		Aug. 28
	58	Allen, Otis Briggs	63	5	11	Light	Gray	Gray		Rancher	Erie co., Pa	Manzanita	Lincoln		Sept. 24
	59	Allen, Robert Grant	28	5	9	Dark	Dk Brw'n	Black		Clerk	Iowa	Lincoln No. 2	Lincoln		Aug. 31
	60	Allen, Samuel Lorenzo	71	5	6½	Medi'm	Hazel	IronGray		Carpenter	Oswego, N. Y.	Auburn No. 2	Auburn		Sept. 17
	61	Allen, William Silas	43	5	7½	Dark	Brown	Dark		Carpenter	Putnam co., Ind	Lincoln No. 2	Lincoln		Aug. 30
	62	Allen, William Henry	23	5	10	Light	Blue	Brown		Teamster	Marshall co., Ind	Auburn No. 1	Auburn		Sept. 17
	63	Allen, Walter	27	5	11	Dark	Gray	Brown		Rancher	Placer co., Cal	Mt. Pleasant	Lincoln		Sept. 18
	64	Allen, William	39	5	8	Light	Gray	Light		Laborer	Placer co., Cal	Mt. Pleasant	Lincoln		Sept. 26

CALIFORNIA STATE

Figure 5-4 Great Register of Placer County for the year 1892, Placer County, California, p. 1 (FHL 977088)

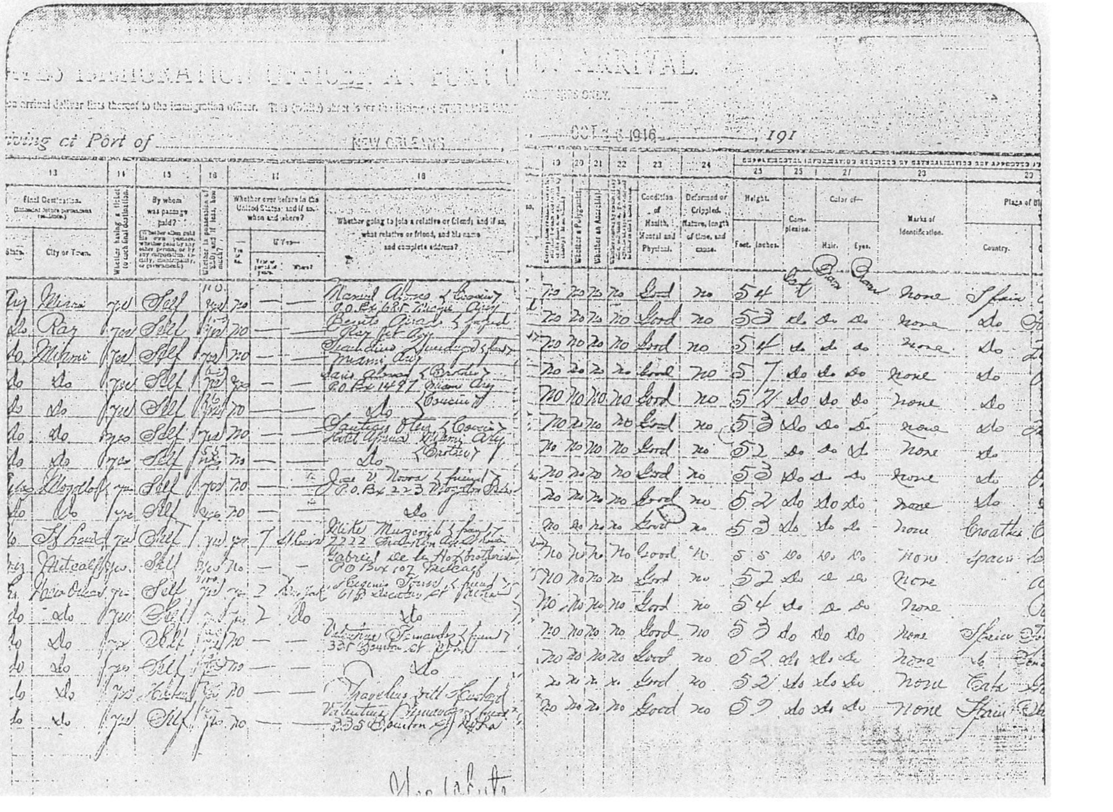

Figure 5-5 Page from the passenger list for the Port of New Orleans for the S.S. *Chalmette*, October 16, 1916 (author's copy)

been in the United States before all offer information concerning the origin of the person and indicate what other records might be available.

In addition to the above information, passenger lists give the name of a relative or friend with whom the immigrant will be living. Often this individual is a relative who has previously arrived in the United States. It may be that in searching this person's passenger list or other records you will find clues not given in the direct-line immigrant's records as to the place of origin. Beyond the specific items relating to the immigrant's place of origin, passenger lists can provide considerable detail and information concerning your ancestor. Note in the last column (29) that the place of birth includes not just the country but the city or town as well.

Passenger lists dating from 1820 have been microfilmed in most instances and are available through the family history centers. A check should also be made in the Family History Library Catalog for lists since many, although not the majority, have also been indexed.

If your ancestor arrived in America by crossing the border between Mexico and the United States after 1903, a similar collection of records is available. At the border, cards or manifests were completed for each person. In some cases these individuals were identified as permanent immigrants and in others as temporary visitors. The records themselves were microfilmed a number of years ago by the National Archives and the original records destroyed. These films were located in 1994 by Immigration and Naturalization Service historians, and the National Archives is currently cataloging them. When completed, the records will be available at the National Archives in Washington, D.C. and possibly at regional archival facilities in Laguna Niguel, California or El Paso, Texas as well.

You will find the introduction to the new catalog helpful in understanding these records. The entire collection is arranged by port of entry and alphabetically therein. There are cross-referencing indexes between various records within the collection, as well as to Immigration and Naturalization Service files. In addition to information concerning border crossings, the records often list accompanying family members, family members in the United States, and the specific city or town of origin in Mexico or other Hispanic country of origin. Figure 5-6 shows a typical manifest card.

Naturalization Records

Even though current studies indicate that a majority of Hispanic immigrants did not seek citizenship, naturalization records should still be searched since there were significant numbers of immigrants who did seek citizenship.[8] After 1906 these files were prepared by the Immigration and Naturalization Service. For a fee they will search for specific immigration files. The recommendation made by their personnel is to first write to the local regional office in the locality you are searching, although a request may be sent to the national office at the following address: U.S. Depart-

Ldo.# 6708 RECORD OF LAWFUL ENTRY Ldo. File No.
(As of Date of Arrival) 978/3546
NAME (Then) BAUTISTA, LUIS Age 2
(Now) BAUTISTA, LUIS Age 22
Sex M Occupation NONE Race WHITE
Last residence before entry SALTILLO, COAH., MEXICO
Date of arrival in U.S. 2-4-1922 Port Laredo, Texas
(As of Present Date)
Now resides 1903½ Main Ave, Laredo, Tex.
Occupation BAKER Description 5' 8", Drk. Com;
Br. Eyes, blk. Hr; 2 Sm.pocks L. side of cheek
Place of birth Saltillo, Coah., Mexico
C.O. No. R-219934 Approved by C.O. (date) 11-19-42
Rec'd. Laredo (date) 12-4-42
Certificate of Lawful Entry No. 214034

Figure 5-6 Mexican Border Manifest Card, 1942 (author's copy)

ment of Justice, Immigration and Naturalization Service, 425 I Street NW, Washington, DC 20536.

The process of securing citizenship was two-fold. First, the immigrant prepared a Declaration of Intention to become a U.S. citizen. Then, after a prescribed number of years (usually at least two), the Petition for Naturalization was filed (see figure 5-7). Often, both of these records will provide a specific place of birth in the country of origin.

Prior to 1906 naturalization was handled by the local court. This local court file may provide detail similar to that in the Petition for Naturalization, but generally these records are much more limited in the information that they provide. Nevertheless, as illustrated by the 1877 naturalization of Jacinta Acuña in Placer County, California (figure 5-8), they sometimes provide a specific place of origin.

Social Security Records

Social security is the first of three federally mandated records that might assist you in locating immigrants during the late nineteenth and twentieth centuries. Many individuals who did not become citizens of the United States still registered with the Social Security Administration and paid social security taxes. If these individuals registered, they filed an application known as an SS-5. Figure 5-9 reproduces a copy of the SS-5, which can be obtained by writing to: Freedom of Information Officer, 4-H-8 Annex Building, 6401 Security Boulevard, Baltimore, MD 21235. You should request a full copy of the SS-5 of the deceased person, giving the applicant's name and his/her social security number, if you know it. If you

Form 2214—Salt Lake City

IMPORTANT NOTICE TO APPLICANT.—It is VERY IMPORTANT that this Form be CAREFULLY AND COMPLETELY FILLED IN. Then take or mail it and your "FIRST PAPER" to the NATURALIZATION EXAMINER'S ADDRESS given below.

PRELIMINARY FORM FOR PETITION FOR NATURALIZATION

NOT TO BE FILLED IN BY ALIEN
For use of officials searching immigration records
RECORDS EXAMINED.
Card index ....
Index books ....
Manifests ....
Name ....
Date .... SS ....
Line .... Clerk ....

U.S. DEPARTMENT OF LABOR
NATURALIZATION SERVICE

This form is NOT a petition, but is used to obtain essential information, which must be furnished by the applicant BEFORE a petition may be filed.

NOTE FOR CLERK.—Hand this form to the alien so he may fill it at his leisure.

TO THE ALIEN: Fill in all the blanks in this form. Be sure the information is correct. When completed, take or mail it to the Naturalization Examiner and he will furnish you instructions. Send your Declaration of Intention with this form.

Take or mail this to—

DISTRICT DIRECTOR OF NATURALIZATION,
Federal Building,
Salt Lake City, Utah

I desire to petition for naturalization in the Third District Court, at Kemmerer (City.) Lincoln (County.) Wyoming (State.) The following information is furnished that you may arrange for my preliminary examination, and that the necessary papers may be sent to the Clerk of Court:

My full, true, and correct name is {Mr. Mrs. Miss} Daniel Castano

I have not used another name (If you have ever used any other name write that name here.)

I used that name because ....

The name on my steamship ticket was Daniel Castano (Give name in full.)

My mother's maiden name was Felisa Castano

1. My present residence is Sublet Wyoming
My post office address is (Number and street.) Sublet (City or town.) Wyo. (State.)
2. My present occupation is Miner
3. I was born on May (Month.) 19 (Day.) 1896 (Year.) at [illegible] (City or town.) [illegible] Spain (Country.)
4. (a) The place where I took the ship or train which landed me in the United States was Havana Cuba on Sept. or October 16, 1916
(b) I landed in the United States at New Orleans on Sept. or October (Month.) (Day.) 1916 (Year.)
(c) The name of the ship or railroad on which I came was Don't Know
(d) If by ship: Name of steamship line was Don't Know I came by {1st cabin, 2d cabin, steerage}
(e) I arrived as (passenger, stowaway, deserting seaman, or otherwise) Passenger
(f) The person in the United States I was coming to was None (Give name in full.)
(g) The place in the United States I was going to was Miami Arizona
(h) The names of some of the persons or passengers I traveled with were [illegible]
(i) I purchased the ticket on which I came to this country at Havana Cuba
It was purchased by My Self Daniel Castano

If you came from or through Canada or Mexico, also fill in lines (A) to (F), inclusive:

(A) The place in Canada where I landed was .... on .... (Month.) (Day.) (Year.)
(B) The place in {Canada, Mexico} from which I entered the United States was ....
(C) On .... (Month.) (Day.) (Year.)
(D) The place where I was examined for admission into the United States was ....
(E) If not examined, state why, and give the circumstances of your entry ....
(F) The place in {Canada, Mexico} where I bought my railroad ticket to come to the United States was ....

(If you came to the United States on visit, not to stay, please so state, and give facts.)

5. (a) The date of my Declaration (first paper) is Sept (Month.) 16 (Day.) 1925 (Year.)
(b) It was made in the Third Dist (Title of court.) Court, located at Kemmerer (City or town.) Lincoln (County.) Wyo (State.)
6. (a) I am Yes married. My {wife's} name is Mary Castano
(b) {She} was born Nov. (Month.) 3 (Day.) 1898 (Year.) at Heber City (City or town.) Utah Wasatch (Country.)
(c) And now resides at Sublet (Number and street.) (City or town.) Wyoming (State.)
(d) We were married on January (Month.) 16 (Day.) 1922 (Year.)
(e) I have 5 children. (In the following blanks write name, date and place of birth, and residence of each child.)
Minerva born April day of 19, 1920 at Park City resides at Sublet
Genevie born Sep day of 8, 1921 at Park City resides at Sublet
[illegible] born Sept day of 29, 1923 at Sublet resides at Sublet
Frank born March day of 16, 1925 at Sublet resides at Sublet
Ruby born Sept day of 3, 1927 at Sublet resides at Sublet
(f) If not now, have you ever been married? .... Are you divorced? ....
7. The foreign country of which I am now a subject or citizen is Spain
8. I can [illegible] speak English.
9. (a) I have resided *continuously* in the United States since Sept Oct (Month.) 16 (Day.) 1916 (Year.)
(b) I have resided *continuously* in the State where I now live since August (Month.) (Day.) 1922 (Year.)
10. I have not previously made petition for naturalization (second paper). If so, it was made in the .... (Title of court.) Court of .... (City or town.) (State.) on .... (Month.) (Day.) (Year.), and was not granted because ....
11. If you wish to have your name changed, give *full name* you desire ....
12. Give names, occupations, and addresses of the two citizens you expect to use as witnesses. (If either witness is foreign-born, he must bring proof of citizenship.) These witnesses must have personal knowledge of your residence in the State at least, and of your good character, and must appear with you for examination.
(1st) Earnest A. Hepner (Name.) County Commissioner (Occupation.) Kemmerer (Residence address.)
(2d) Frank [illegible] (Name.) [illegible] (Occupation.) Kemmerer (Residence address.)

If applicant is a married woman, answer the following:

My husband was .... naturalized on .... (Month.) (Day.) (Year.) at .... (City or town.) (State.)

Figure 5-7 Preliminary Form for Petition for Naturalization, Immigration and Naturalization Service, 1927 (author's copy)

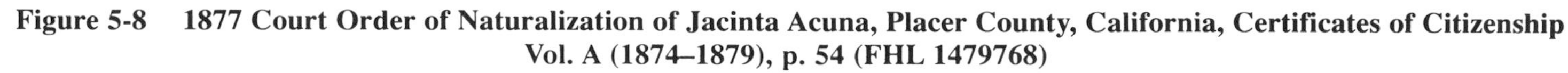

No. 64

[illegible] County Court of the County of Placer,

State of California.

Present: Hon. J. Ives Fitch ....Judge.

In the matter of the Application of

Jacinta Acunia

An Alein ......

To become a Citizen of the United States of America.

IN OPEN COURT

Sept ....Term, A. D., 1877

this First ......day of October

A. D. 1877, as yet of said Term.

It appearing to the satisfaction of this Court by the oaths of ......Wm B. McGuire &

and John Romero ....citizens of the United States of America, witnesses for that purpose, first duly sworn and examined, that......

Jacinta Acunia

a native of .... Valparaso Chili ......

has resided within the limits and under the jurisdiction of the United States five years at least last past, and within the State of California for one year last past; and that during all of said five years' time he has behaved as a man of good moral character, attached to the principles of the Constitution of the United States, and well disposed to the good order and happiness of the same; and it also appearing to the Court, by competent evidence, that the said applicant has heretofore, and more than two years since, and in due form of law, declared his intention to become a citizen of the United States; and having now here, before this Court taken an oath that he will support the Constitution of the United States of America, and that he doth absolutely and entirely renounce and abjure all allegiance and fidelity to every foreign Prince, Potentate, State or Sovereignty whatever, and particularly to The Republic of Chili

It is therefore ordered, adjudged and decreed that said ...... Jacinta Acunia ......

be, and he is hereby admitted and declared to be a Citizen of the United States of America.

......................Judge.

SIGNATURE: ...... Jacito Acuna ......

Figure 5-8 **1877 Court Order of Naturalization of Jacinta Acuna, Placer County, California, Certificates of Citizenship Vol. A (1874–1879), p. 54 (FHL 1479768)**

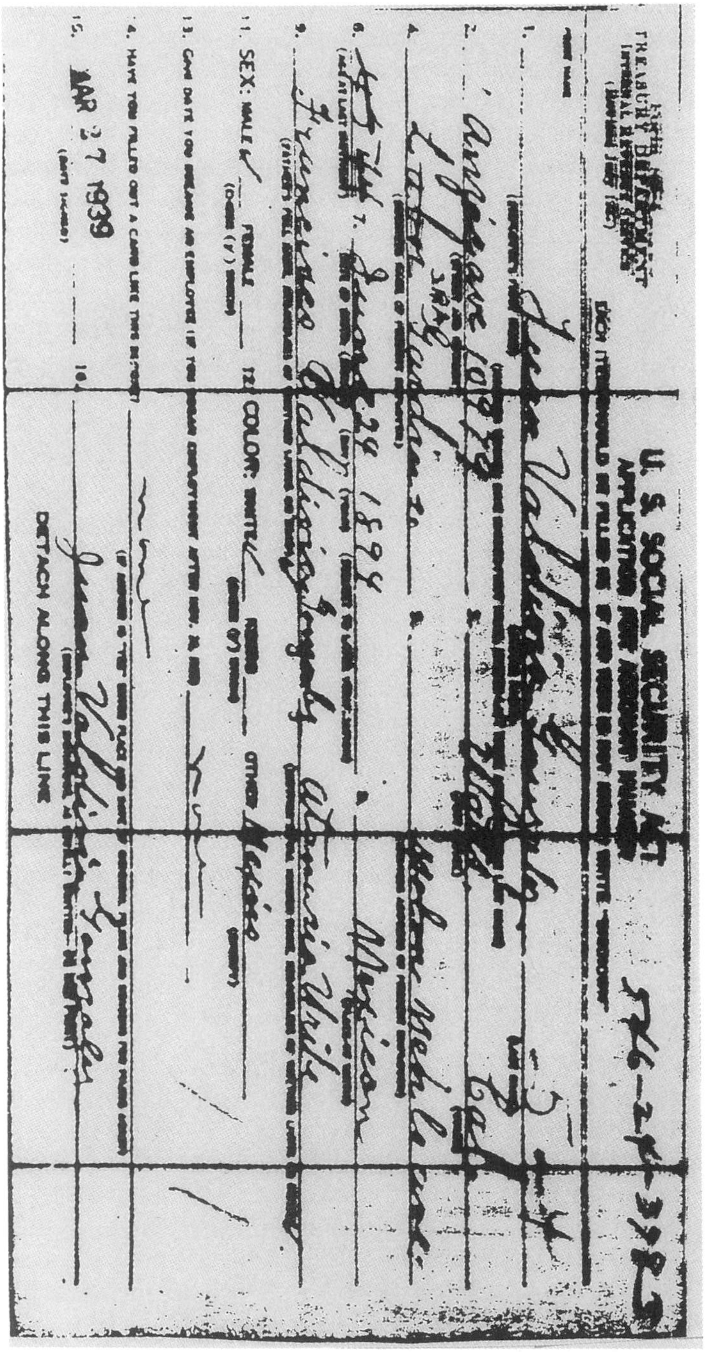

TREASURY DEPARTMENT
INTERNAL REVENUE SERVICE

U. S. SOCIAL SECURITY ACT
APPLICATION FOR ACCOUNT NUMBER

11. SEX: MALE FEMALE
12. COLOR: WHITE NEGRO OTHER Mexican

15. MAR 27 1939

DETACH ALONG THIS LINE

Figure 5-9 U.S. Social Security SS-5 Application (author's copy)

know the social security number, the cost for the search (at the time of publication) is $7.00. If you do not, the cost is $16.50.

The individual's social security number will appear on a variety of local forms, including his death certificate if he died in the United States. If he died while receiving social security benefits, a check should be made of the Social Security Death Index, which is found both as a part of the FamilySearch programs at the local LDS family history centers and on the social security disks produced by the Banner Blue Division of Brøderbund Software and others. The latter have about 4 million additional names, primarily railroad pensioners. The personnel at the family history center or at the library where you are consulting either of these indexes will be able to assist you in doing the computer search for the individual.

Alien Registration

In 1940, as the United States government recognized the approaching World War, the Alien Immigration Registration Act was adopted, requiring the registration of all non-citizens. In compliance with that act, non-citizens filed an Alien Registration form with the government of the type reproduced in figure 5-10. That sheet provides much of the same information that would have been available on a Petition for Naturalization, including the city of birth and the last arrival date and place in the United States as well as the ship's name. All non-citizens had to register, no matter how long they had been in the country. The individual appearing in figure 5-10 had arrived thirty-four years earlier in 1906 at the age of sixteen.

These records can be obtained by writing to the Immigration and Naturalization Service at their regional offices or the national office at the address given above. Be sure to include as much of the following information as possible: birth date, death date, spouse's name, year immigrated, and social security number.

Draft Registration Records — 1917

In preparation for the war effort of the United States in World War I, a registration was required for all males ages seventeen to forty-five. Local draft boards were organized for every 30,000 citizens. The draft boards handled the registration of all males, often even those over the age of forty-five. These registration records were filed with the Selective Service and have now been filmed and are available through the family history centers. You should search in the FHLC under United States-Military Records-World War I for these records. They are arranged by local draft boards, so you will need to know where the individual resided in 1917 and to which draft board he would have reported.

FORM AR-2
OFFICE USE 1935934

UNITED STATES DEPARTMENT OF JUSTICE
IMMIGRATION AND NATURALIZATION SERVICE

ALIEN REGISTRATION FORM

1.☆(a) My name is ANTONIO (FIRST NAME) FRAGA (MIDDLE NAME) SILVA (LAST NAME)

☆(b) I entered the United States under the name of ANTONIO FRAGA DA-SILVEIRA

☆(c) I have also been known by the following names ANTONIO FRAGA DA SILVEIRA (include maiden name if a married woman, professional names, nicknames, and aliases):

2.☆(a) I live at GEN DEL (STREET ADDRESS OR RURAL ROUTE) GUSTINE (CITY) MERCED (COUNTY) CALIFORNIA (STATE)

☆(b) My post-office address is GEN DEL (POST OFFICE) GUSTINE CALIFORNIA (STATE)

3.☆(a) I was born on October (MONTH) 6 (DAY) 1890 (YEAR)

☆(b) I was born in (or near) Cedros (CITY) Azores Islands (PROVINCE) Portugal (COUNTRY)

4.☆ I am a citizen or subject of Portugal (COUNTRY)

5.☆(a) I am a (check one): Male [X] Female [ ]
☆(b) My marital status is (check one): Single [ ] Married [ ] Widowed [X] Divorced [ ]
☆(c) My race is (check one): White [X] Negro [ ] Japanese [ ] Chinese [ ] Other

6. I am 5 feet, 6 inches in height, weigh 155 pounds, have Black (COLOR) hair and Brown (COLOR) eyes.

7.☆(a) I last arrived in the United States at Providence, R. I. (PORT OR PLACE OF ENTRY) on May (unk) 1912 (MONTH, DAY, AND YEAR)

☆(b) I came in by S S Roma (NAME OF VESSEL, STEAMSHIP COMPANY, OR OTHER MEANS OF TRANSPORTATION)

☆(c) I came as a (check one): Passenger [X] Crew member [ ] Stowaway [ ] Other

☆(d) I entered the United States as a (check one): Permanent resident [X] Visitor [ ] Student [ ] Treaty merchant [ ] Seaman [ ] Official of a foreign government [ ] Employee of a foreign government official [ ] Other

☆(e) I first arrived in the United States on October (MONTH) 10 (DAY) 1906 (YEAR)

8.☆(a) I have lived in the United States a total of Thirty Three years.

☆(b) I expect to remain in the United States Permanently (PERMANENTLY, OR DURATION OF EXPECTED STAY)

9. (a) My usual occupation is Dairymen (b) My present occupation is Dairymen

☆(c) My employer (or registering parent or guardian) is Self (NAME)

whose address is (STREET ADDRESS OR RURAL ROUTE) (CITY) (STATE)

and whose business is

All items must be answered by persons 14 years of age, or older. For children under 14 years of age, only the items marked with a star (☆) must be answered by the parent or guardian. All answers must be accurate and complete.

10. I am, or have been within the past 5 years, or intend to be engaged in the following activities:
In addition to other information, list memberships or activities in clubs, organizations, or societies
East West Dairymens Union
Western Cooperative Dairymens Union

11. My military or naval service has been None (COUNTRY) (BRANCH OF SERVICE) From (DATE) to (DATE)

12.☆I Have not (HAVE, HAVE NOT) applied for first citizenship papers in the United States. Date of application
First citizenship papers received (DATE) (NUMBER) (CITY) (STATE)
Filed petition for naturalization (DATE) (CITY) (STATE)

13.☆I have the following specified relatives living in the United States:
Parent(s) none (NONE, OR ONE, OR BOTH) Husband or wife no (YES OR NO) Children two (NUMBER)

14. I have not (HAVE, HAVE NOT) been arrested or indicted for, or convicted of any offense (or offenses). These offenses are:

Nature of offense	Date of arrest	Place of arrest	Disposition of case

15. Within the past 5 years I have not (HAVE, HAVE NOT) been affiliated with or active in (a member of, official of, a worker for) organizations, devoted in whole or in part to influencing or furthering the political activities, public relations, or public policy of a foreign government.

RIGHT INDEX FINGER

AFFIDAVIT FOR PERSONS 14 YEARS OF AGE AND OLDER

I have read or have had read to me the above statements, and do hereby swear (or affirm) that these statements are true and complete to the best of my knowledge and belief.

Antonio F Silva (SIGNATURE OF REGISTRANT)

Subscribed and sworn to (or affirmed) before me at the place and on the date here designated by the official post-office stamp below.

William R. Woods (REGISTERING OFFICIAL)

AFFIDAVIT FOR PARENT OR GUARDIAN ONLY

I am the (PARENT OF, OR GUARDIAN OF, OR PERSON RESPONSIBLE FOR) the above-named alien, who is (UNDER 14 YEARS OF AGE, OR INSANE) and have made the above allegations for him (or her). I have read or have had the same read to me, and do hereby swear (or affirm) that they are true and complete to the best of my knowledge, information, and belief.

PRINT NAME, ADDRESS, AND BUSINESS OF PERSON SIGNING THIS AFFIDAVIT IN 9(c), ABOVE.

Subscribed and sworn to (or affirmed) before me at the place and on the date here designated by the official post-office stamp at the right.

(SIGNATURE OF PARENT OR GUARDIAN OR PERSON RESPONSIBLE FOR THE ALIEN) (REGISTERING OFFICIAL)

GUSTINE, CAL. SEP 16 1940 M. O. B.

Figure 5-10 Alien Registration Form by United States Department of Justice-Immigration and Naturalization Service, 1940 (author's copy)

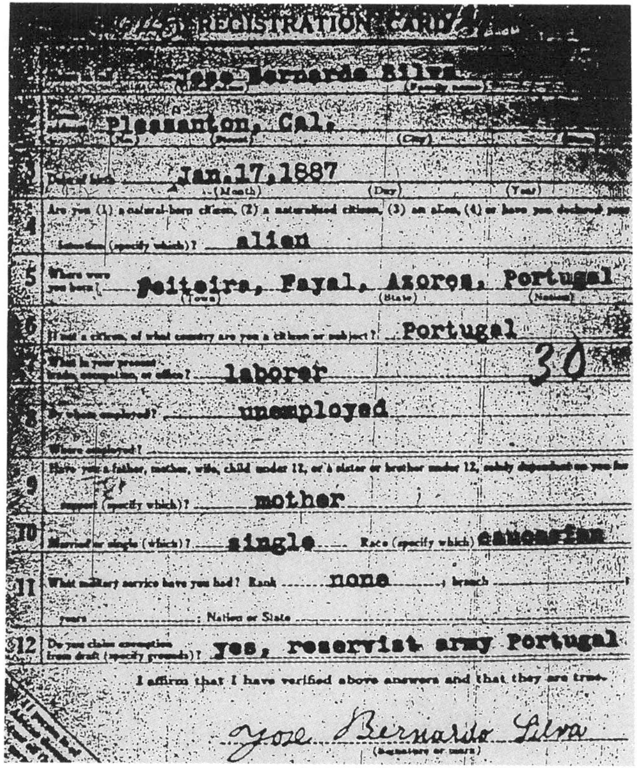

REGISTRATION CARD

1 Jose Bernardo Silva

2 Pleasanton, Cal.

3 Date of birth Jan. 17, 1887 (Month) (Day) (Year)

4 Are you (1) a natural-born citizen, (2) a naturalized citizen, (3) an alien, (4) or have you declared your intention (specify which)? alien

5 Where were you born? Feiteira, Fayal, Azores, Portugal (Town) (State) (Nation)

6 If not a citizen, of what country are you a citizen or subject? Portugal

7 What is your present trade, occupation, or office? laborer 30

8 By whom employed? unemployed

Where employed?

9 Have you a father, mother, wife, child under 12, or a sister or brother under 12, solely dependent on you for support (specify which)? mother

10 Married or single (which)? single Race (specify which) caucasian

11 What military service have you had? Rank none ; branch
years ; Nation or State

12 Do you claim exemption from draft (specify grounds)? yes, reservist army Portugal

I affirm that I have verified above answers and that they are true.

Jose Bernardo Silva
(Signature or mark)

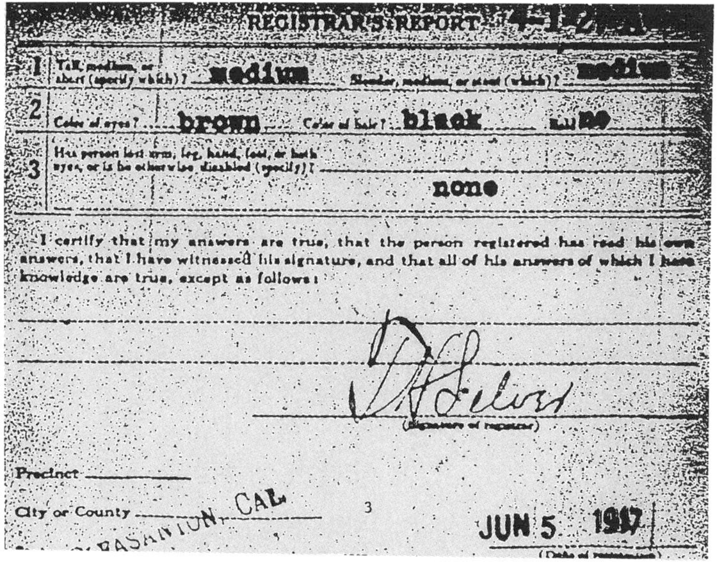

REGISTRAR'S REPORT 4-1-2

1 Tall, medium, or short (specify which)? medium Slender, medium, or stout (which)? medium

2 Color of eyes? brown Color of hair? black Bald? no

3 Has person lost arm, leg, hand, foot, or both eyes, or is he otherwise disabled (specify)? none

I certify that my answers are true, that the person registered has read his own answers, that I have witnessed his signature, and that all of his answers of which I have knowledge are true, except as follows:

D. H. Silva
(Signature of registrar)

Precinct

City or County PLEASANTON, CAL 3

JUN 5 1917
(Date of registration)

Figure 5-11 World War I Draft Registration Card, Pleasanton, Alameda County, California (FHL 1530653)

In a separate catalog entry in the Family History Library Catalog are maps of the various draft boards, especially those of large cities such as Los Angeles, Chicago, and New York. Figure 5-11 illustrates the type of information found on draft registration cards. Most significant is that they include the specific town of birth as well as a statement as to whether or not the individual had served in the military previously, which would have constituted an exemption. Such was the case with the individual registering in figure 5-11.

SUMMARY

There are extensive records available for finding your Hispanic immigrant ancestor. Once again, the records discussed here are those which would most commonly provide you with information concerning the place of origin of the immigrant ancestor. If the place of origin for your immigrant ancestor is not found in one of these types of records, check all local records. It is entirely possible that local records, such as those for organizations like the Knights of Columbus, school records for elementary or high school students, or employment records on a sugar plantation in Hawaii or a large farm in California may have the place of origin listed.

---

1. David J. Weber, *The Spanish Frontier in North America* (New Haven: Yale University Press, 1992), 60–91.

2. Roger Daniels, *Coming to America* (Princeton: Harper Perennial, 1991), 96, 307–327, and 371–384.

3. Ibid., 97.

4. Loretto Szucs and Sandra Luebking, eds., *The Source*. 2nd ed. (Salt Lake City: Ancestry Publishing Company, 1996); Val D. Greenwood, *The Researcher's Guide to American Genealogy*. 2d ed. (Baltimore: Genealogical Publishing Company, 1990); Norman E. Wright, *Preserving Your American Heritage* (Provo, Utah: Brigham Young University Press, 1981).

5. George B. Everton, Sr., ed., *Handy Book for Genealogists*. 8th ed. (Logan, Utah: Everton Publishers, 1991).

6. Alice Eichholz, ed. *Ancestry's Red Book. rev. ed.* (Salt Lake City: Ancestry, 1992).

7. Thomas J. Kemp, *International Vital Records Handbook*. 3d ed. (Baltimore: Genealogical Publishing Co., 1994).

8. George J. Sanchez, *Becoming Mexican American* (New York: Oxford University Press, 1993), 275.

CHAPTER 6

General Spanish Research Techniques

Successful research involves learning how to read and understand records and identify the individuals found in them, as well as skill in writing letters. This chapter discusses the basics of language and handwriting, naming systems, and correspondence techniques in Spanish.

SECTION A: Language and Handwriting

One of the major challenges facing family historians in any language is learning to use and understand older language forms and handwriting styles. Through a discussion of the common areas of difficulty encountered by researchers, this chapter will help the reader, whether a Spanish-speaking native or a novice, to understand older Spanish records.

A basic familiarity with the language is essential in doing Spanish family history research. Anybody with two or three semesters of university-level Spanish, plus enthusiasm, should be able to handle any challenges he might encounter. Many researchers with less Spanish than this have been able to do excellent work in Spanish and Latin American archives.

You can compensate for any deficiency in formal Spanish instruction by study, patience, and a determination to understand the records. Consulting a good beginning grammar book and always having a dictionary at hand will also be helpful. Of course, the more Spanish language training you have, the easier the work will be; but no one should be discouraged from doing his own research by a lack of formal training in the Spanish language.

While reading this discussion, do not panic if you are just beginning to do research. The ability to read early records develops slowly and can only be learned through actual experience. Rather than trying to absorb in a single reading all of the material in the following sections, keep this information handy to refer to as you need it. With this in mind, the following sections have been arranged for easy accessibility rather than smooth reading style. Also, no attempt has been made to translate the Spanish words used as examples in this chapter.

SPANISH PALEOGRAPHY

A Brief History of Spanish Handwriting

Paleography, the study of ancient handwriting, is well developed in Spain and Latin America, and several excellent treatises on handwriting are designed to help both the beginner and the advanced researcher to more readily understand and read early handwriting forms. Since most of the records you will be using do not antedate the fifteenth century, this discussion of handwriting begins with that time period.

In the fifteenth century there were five different types of handwriting found in Spain: *itálica*, *redonda*, *cortesana*, *alemana*, and *procesal*. The examples in figure 6-1 will help you see the differences in each of these handwriting styles.

By the sixteenth century the *redonda* and the *alemana* styles were no longer in use. During the seventeenth and eighteenth centuries there was even further transition, and by the end of the seventeenth century nearly all records were written in *itálica*. Nevertheless, as you work in different parishes you will most likely run into examples of *cortesana*, *itálica*, and *procesal* handwriting throughout the sixteenth, seventeenth, and eighteenth centuries.

Fortunately, the most difficult of these to read, the *procesal* and its derivative *escritura cadena*, or "chain script," only appear in the very earliest of parish records, and never after 1600. When this style of handwriting is encountered, or if you want to become familiar with such handwriting before actually encountering it in your research, consult any or all of the following books: *Paleografía diplomática española y sus peculiaridades en América* by Jorge A. Garces (Quito, Ecuador, 1949); *Album de paleografía Hispano-americana de los siglos XVI y XVII* by Agustin Millares Carlo, 3 vols. (Mexico, 1955); and *Tratado de Paleografía Española* by Agustin Millares Carlo, 3 vols. (Madrid: España Calpe, 1983).

Handwriting Analysis

With practice, reading old handwriting can be mastered by anyone. The following seven guidelines offer some general, practical suggestions about how to work with a new handwriting style.

1. Study a new hand carefully. It is important to work carefully and slowly when beginning a new handwriting style, so as to develop a familiarity with the personal writing style of the priest or recorder and the type of writing he is using. Also, notice any idiosyncrasies, such as unique forms of particular letters, the use of certain abbreviations, or peculiar syntactical approaches. If you work slowly at first, your reading ability and speed will soon increase dramatically.

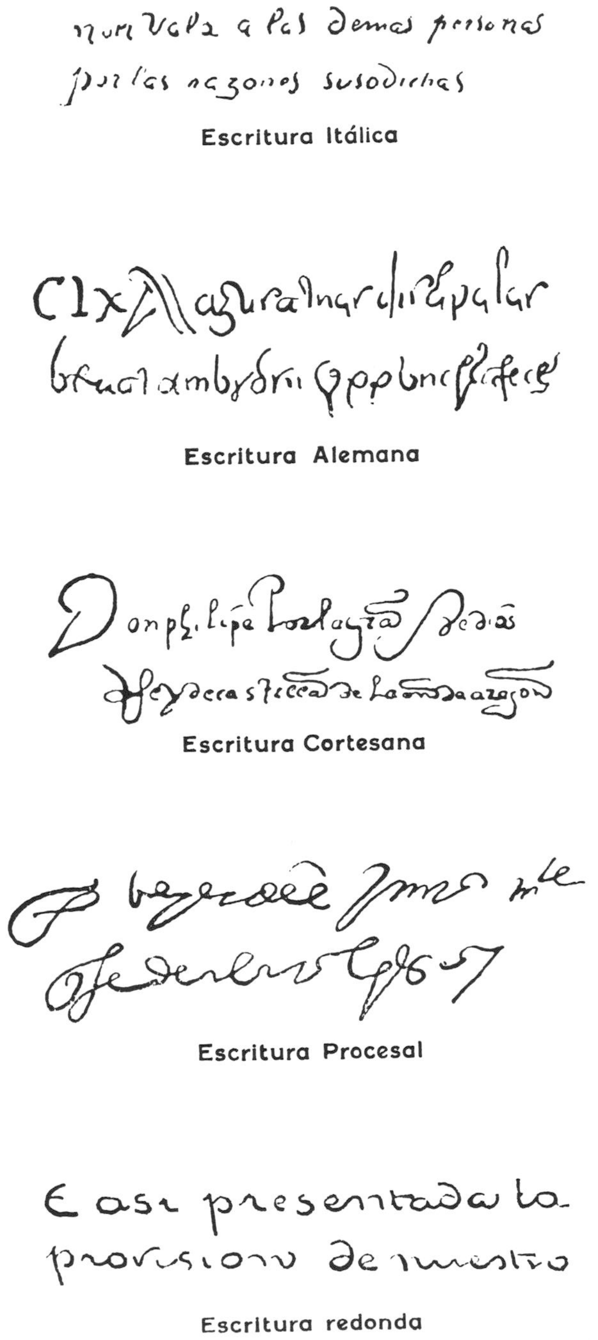

Escritura Itálica

Escritura Alemana

Escritura Cortesana

Escritura Procesal

Escritura redonda

Figure 6-1 Example of Spanish handwriting styles, 1100–1500 A.D. (author's copy)

2. Begin with those portions of the record that are familiar. Repeated phrases, dates, and names which you already know can help familiarize you with a new handwriting style. For example, when working with baptismal records in Spanish-language parishes such phrases as *bautizé solemnemente*, *yo, el infrascrito cura, hija legítima de*, and *por la linea paterna* can all help familiarize you with a particular style. You can also identify, in surnames and given names already encountered in other records, specific letter styles used by the writer. Dates are also a valuable source, since the number of alternatives that a date can be is limited to twelve months and thirty-one numbers, as well as the numbers for the years, all of which can be compared with preceding or succeeding entries.

3. Use the surrounding text as a guide. Generally, the text you are working with can help you find the meaning of a difficult word or passage. The following three suggestions should assist you in using the surrounding text:

a. *Compare the letters in unknown words or names with those of known words or names.* In this way you can make good use of the familiar dates, phrases, and known names discussed above.

b. *Read the word in the context in which it was written.* This can be especially helpful where the information in the records is in complete sentences, or where you are already familiar with the basic concept that is being developed.

c. *Look for the same word or name elsewhere.* This can be especially helpful where there are marginal notes, or where the same surname is repeated several times in a single document. The name written in the other place may not be abbreviated or may be more clearly written, or in many cases, the writer may have chosen completely different letter styles the second time he wrote the name.

4. Remember that a great deal of variety in handwriting can be found in a single document. It is common to find various styles of the same letter within a given document, and frequently within the same word. The same word may also be written two different ways. There can also be various spellings of the same name. A variation in spelling is even common in the same manuscript.

5. Compare the unknown letters with those on the alphabet chart. Frequently, you can get a general idea of what a particularly difficult letter is by comparing it with those letters on the alphabet chart in figure 6-2.[1] However, it should be recognized that handwriting varies drastically from person to person, as well as from time period to time period, and a particular letter in a document may not be found on the alphabet chart.

6. Consult an outside source, especially where a name is involved. The following sources, or ones similar to them, can be of great assistance in figuring out a name:

a. *Priests or archives personnel.* Local people, particularly priests in the parish, are familiar with the different surnames found in the area, as

	Secretary	Secretary	Italic	Italic		Secretary	Secretary	Italic	Italic
A					**a**				
B					**b**				
C					**c**				
Ch		-			**ch**				
D					**d**				
E					**e**				
F					**f**				
G					**g**				
H					**h**				
I		-			**i**				
J					**j**				
K	-	-			**k**	-	-		
L					**l**				
Ll	-	-			**ll**				
M					**m**				

	Secretary	Secretary	Italic	Italic		Secretary	Secretary	Italic	Italic
N					**n**				
Ñ	-	-	-		**ñ**				
O					**o**				
P					**p**				
Qu		-			**qu**				
R					**r**				
RR	-	-	-		**rr**				
S					**s**				
T					**t**				
U					**u**				
V					**v**				
W	-	-			**w**		-		
X					**x**				
Y					**y**				
Z					**z**				

Figure 6-2 Alphabet chart, reprinted from *Spanish Handwriting* (Salt Lake City, 1979)

well as with the surrounding places, towns, and villages. They may also be somewhat familiar with earlier handwriting styles. Generally, priests and archives personnel are more than willing to help in deciphering a particularly difficult name or confirming a name with which the researcher is unfamiliar. In a parish archives such questions may also serve the function of focusing the conversation on the work that you are doing.

b. *A list of saints' names and a list of surnames like that published by The Church of Jesus Christ of Latter-day Saints for use in its Name Extraction Program.* While these are by no means all-inclusive, they may be a guide in identifying a difficult name or in finding a correct spelling.

c. *Gazetteers and geographical dictionaries.* These contain alphabetical lists of place names, which can be used to compare spellings. Many, especially those published in the last half of the 1800s, can be helpful in determining the existence of a parish listed in an old record, or in confirming the spelling of a difficult place name.

Place names may also have changed as a result of shortening or combining two words into one. For example, a town which today is known as *Riodeva* was known in early records as *Rio de Eva*. Another example is a place known today as *Aldea Real*, which a century and a half ago was known as *Aldea el Rey*. Using care and a little bit of creativity in the spelling and combining of words, it is usually possible to determine the parish that is being named. Naturally, final confirmation can only come from checking the parish records for that particular parish.

d. *Maps*. Generally, most of an ancestral family within a single generation or two will come from a relatively limited geographical area. A detailed map of that area will be useful in identifying those *lugares* or *caseríos* (small places) that make up a parish. A map can supplement gazetteers and geographical dictionaries by allowing you to see the physical relationship between the parish or locality in which you are currently working and that of the newly encountered parish, town, or locality.

7. Don't spend too much time on a particularly difficult letter or name. If you cannot decipher a name or word after reasonable efforts, trace or copy it on a piece of paper. Write down your best guess or guesses as to what the word may be, and then go on. The word, especially if it is a name, will most likely appear again. When it does, it may be much clearer the second time, or you may be better able to decipher it in the new context. If it does not appear a second time, you can go back and look again at the word, having had more experience with less difficult words in that same individual's handwriting.

Beyond these suggestions and the following discussion about language in the old records and certain handwriting problem areas, practical experience is what is needed most to be able to understand early Spanish handwriting. If you want more practice before going into the archives, refer to the books on paleography mentioned earlier in the chapter. All of these offer a wide variety of documents in several handwriting styles, which can provide practice for you as you read and compare them with the transcriptions given.

THE LANGUAGE OF OLD SPANISH RECORDS

In working with the language in early Spanish records, the most important point to keep in mind is that Spanish is basically phonetic; it is written the way it sounds. This is the result of the activities of the thirteenth-century scribes in Toledo who concentrated on developing a simple system of writing the Castilian language, which at that time was just beginning to take modern forms. The *Real Academia de la Lengua Española** has worked even further toward this development and simplification. As a result, with a basic knowledge of Spanish pronunciation and an understanding of some language changes that have taken place, you can usually understand the words of an original document by merely reading them out loud.

Interchangeable Letters

i–y

Even in modern Spanish, these two letters represent a single sound. Until less than 100 years ago they were used interchangeably, whether the letter was found at the beginning, the middle, or the end of a word. It was not until after the establishment of the Real Academia that any effort was even made to give order to the varied use of these two letters. As a result you will frequently find that words which today only appear with an *i* or with a *y* may appear in older documents using either letter. Words such as *ayer, ya*, *Isabel*, *habia*, and *iglesia* may be written *aier*, *ia*, *Ysabel*, *habya*, *yglesya*. This can make initial recognition of the word difficult, but as with many other problems in this section, as you pronounce the word it will become evident what the original was. Remember the interchangeability of these two letters when consulting an index, since the names *Isabel* or *Ibarra* might be found either under *i* or *y*. In fact, in many indexes the capital *Y* will be found in the position now held by *I* in the alphabetization system.

b–v

In Spanish the *b* and the *v* stand for the same phonetic sound. Even today, it is not at all uncommon to find words such as *habia* and *venia* spelled *havia* and *benia*. The ultimate decision to use a *v* and not a *b*, or

* Created over 200 years ago, the Royal Academy of the Spanish Language is a board of scholars that supervises and promulgates rules governing spelling and grammar usage in Spanish. Its opinions are generally followed by educated Spanish-speaking persons all over the world.

vice versa as dictated by the Real Academia, is based entirely upon etymological principles and has nothing to do with the pronunciation of the word. In early documents words such as *Vicente*, *Vasques*, *nueve*, *habiendo*, *vecinos*, or *Oliveiro* might be seen as *Bicente*, *Basques*, *nuebe*, *haviendo*, *becinos*, or *Olibeiro*, respectively.

The difficulty with the *b* and the *v* is further complicated by the fact that the written *v*, which in Spain today is still called the "u–b," did not become clearly distinguishable from the *u* until a very late date. The *v* is frequently found written as a *u*, so that words which would normally have a *b* in them, such as *habia*, *habiendo*, and *abad*, might be found as *hauia*, *hauiendo*, and *auad*, respectively.

j, x, g

By 1550 the symbols for *j*, *x*, and *g* (when used before the letters *e* and *i*) had all come to express the same sound — that generally expressed by the letter *j* in modern Spanish. It was not until 1850 that the Real Academia condemned the use of *x* in works employing this sound. An excellent example of this is the fact that Mexico is spelled with an *x*, unless you are consulting a Spanish map, where it will be spelled with a *j* in accordance with the rules of the Real Academia. The *x*, *j*, and the *g* before *i* and *e* appear interchangeably, for example:

mujer	muger	muxer
viaje	viage	viaxe
dijo	dixo	
Jimenez	Gimenez	Ximenez
Javier		Xavier
jornalero		xornalero

c, s, z, ss, ç

Until the seventeenth century several sounds existed that later either merged with other sounds or completely dropped out of the Spanish language. For example, there was once a sound represented by the English *sh*, written with the letter *x*. Other sounds represented by linguists with the phonemes /tz/, /ds/, /z/, /x/, and /s/ were all found in Spanish during the sixteenth century either throughout Spain or in some of its regions and colonies. As the language developed and crystallized in the latter part of the sixteenth century, these sounds were all reduced, or in some cases lost their voicing and became soft. In the area of Castile, these sounds were reduced to two: the modern Spanish *s* and the modern Spanish *zeta,* where the *z* is pronounced somewhat like the *th* in English.

For the researcher, the practical importance of knowing this is to recognize that where in modern Spanish words one might find a *c*, *z*, or an *s*, in early manuscripts one might find *c*, *z*, *s*, *ss*, *ç*, or *x*. Even for a contemporary Spanish speaker living in Andalucia or throughout the Americas where the *zeta* sound is no longer found, the *c*, *z*, and *s* are frequently interchanged. There are many examples of this phenomenon:

once	onze	moza	moça
diciembre	diziembre	trece	treze
asi	assi	vecinos	vezinos
cosa	cossa	coza	
certifico	zertifico	ese	esse
zapatero	çapatero	Garcia	Garsia
Rodriguez	Rodrigues	consejos	concejos

i–e, a–o, a–u, o–u

The above-listed vowel combinations were frequently interchangeable as the Spanish language developed. Even today, in some regions of Spain and South America, several of these vowel interchanges can be heard. Probably the most common of these is the *i–e* interchange. For example, words such as *mismo* and *recibir* can appear as *mesmo* and *receber*. While examples of the other interchanges are not as extensive, you may find a word such as *trajo* spelled *trujo*, or *Juan* spelled *Joan*.

ch–ll

Those who are familiar with other Romance languages such as Italian will recognize the relationship between Italian words such as *chiave* and *chiamo* and Spanish words such as *llave* and *llamo*. These developed from words in Latin beginning with *cl*. That initial *cl* has been preserved in Catalan and French. For example, the French word for key is *clef* and the Spanish word is *llave*. In some early records where the development of the *ll* was incomplete, it is possible to find words such as *llamar* or the name *Llaves* written *chamar* and *Chaves*. In fact, the more common form of the latter has retained the *ch* sound at the beginning. This slight tendency is heightened in Catalonia and Galicia, where the original spoken language still uses *ch* or *cl* in lieu of *ll*.

The Letter *h*

The letter *h* became silent relatively early in the development of the Spanish language and can present difficulties because it is often omitted or added arbitrarily, or replaced by either *g* or *f* (the result of the continued sounding of the letter *h*).

The finding of an *f* in a word that would now be written with an *h* — for example, *facer* for *hacer* — is not uncommon where the original Latin word like *fare* had begun with an *f*. Due in part to the learned tendency discussed above, the *f* persisted into the sixteenth and seventeenth centuries, especially among notaries and other legally oriented people. Therefore, such words as *fijo* and *fallar* may be found where today they would be spelled *hijo* and *hallar*. Thus, in many early records the surnames

Fernandez and Hernandez become interchangeable. The sounding of the *h* may also result in its being replaced by a *g*, as in *Guerta* and *Huerta*, or *agora* and *ahora*.

Since the *h* is silent, it was frequently misplaced, omitted, or needlessly added without regularity or reason. For example, the name *Catalina* might also be found written as *Cathalina*, *Chatalina*, or *Catalhina*. Other examples are as follows:

Enero	Henero	Oyos	Hoyos
oy	hoy	Tomas	Thomas
abia	habia		

The best way to get around the placing of the *h* where it does not belong, or the omission of the *h* where it should be, is once again to pronounce the words out loud, and since the *h* is silent, the meaning rapidly becomes clear.

Latin Influence

Since the Spanish language is a direct descendant of Latin, these languages have many common words and cognates. As a result, Latin frequently influenced Spanish spelling and pronunciation. These natural tendencies were further heightened by the fact that the educated classes nearly all spoke Latin as well as Spanish; therefore, many words which today have a definite pronunciation or spelling are found in older manuscripts in a Latin version. This is particularly noticeable in reading parish or other ecclesiastical records, since all of the priests were familiar with Latin.

c–q

In modern Spanish the Latin *qu* has been replaced by *cu*, having the same pronunciation. It was not until the time of the Real Academia that the use of modern Spanish forms such as *cuanto*, *cuatro,* or *cuando,* instead of the Latin forms of *quanto*, *quatro,* or *quando* were actually specified as correct. Even in the early nineteenth century, it was still possible to find words in many legal documents where the Latin spelling with a *q* instead of a *c* was retained.

f–ph

The *ph* was introduced into Spanish from Latin, where it was used primarily to express the sound in words of Greek origin such as *philosophía* (*filosofía*) and *Phelipe* (*Felipe*). It was always pronounced with the *f* sound in common speech, and would probably have been entirely replaced by the *f* were it not for the tendency of the educated, who were familiar with Latin, to spell the words using *ph*.

Insertion of Letters

In many cases the original Latin spelling of a word is followed more closely in writing and results in the insertion of additional letters. For example, *santo* may be found written as *sancto*, or *bautizar* is found as *baptizar*.

Impure s

In the development of Castilian, when the *s* sound occurred at the beginning of a word and was followed immediately by another consonant, it proved difficult for the early Spanish speaker to pronounce. As a result, at first an *i* and later an *e* were added to the beginning of these words. This natural tendency of the language was counteracted at times by the familiarity that the priests and scribes had with Latin, resulting in words such as *espíritu*, *espiritual*, and *escritura* being written *spíritu*, *spiritual*, and *scritura*, respectively. Generally, these words will be ecclesiastical and/or learned terms.

AREAS OF SPECIAL HANDWRITING PROBLEMS

Confusing Letters

f, i, j, s, t

These letters, especially as they appear in upper-case form, are often very difficult to distinguish. There was, in fact, no linguistic distinction made between *i* and *j* until after the fifteenth century, and it was not totally defined for two more centuries. The examples of these letters in figure 6-3, all taken from the same handwritten manuscript, show the confusion that can arise.

There is no easy way to always distinguish any one of these letters from the others. All you can do is try sounding out the word to see if it makes sense with an *f*, *j*, *s*, *i*, or *t*. The real difficulty comes when a new name appears. Write down your best estimate with a notation that you are unsure. After seeing the surname again, you should be able to decide what it is. You might also check surname dictionaries or lists of surnames, or consult with the parish priest to confirm more unique surnames.

a, o, v, c

All of these letters, especially in their lower-case forms, can be confused with one another and with other lower-case letters. This is particularly true in recently encountered names, where the *u* could have been an *n* or a *v*, and the *a* could have been an *o*.

a.

o.

c.

v.

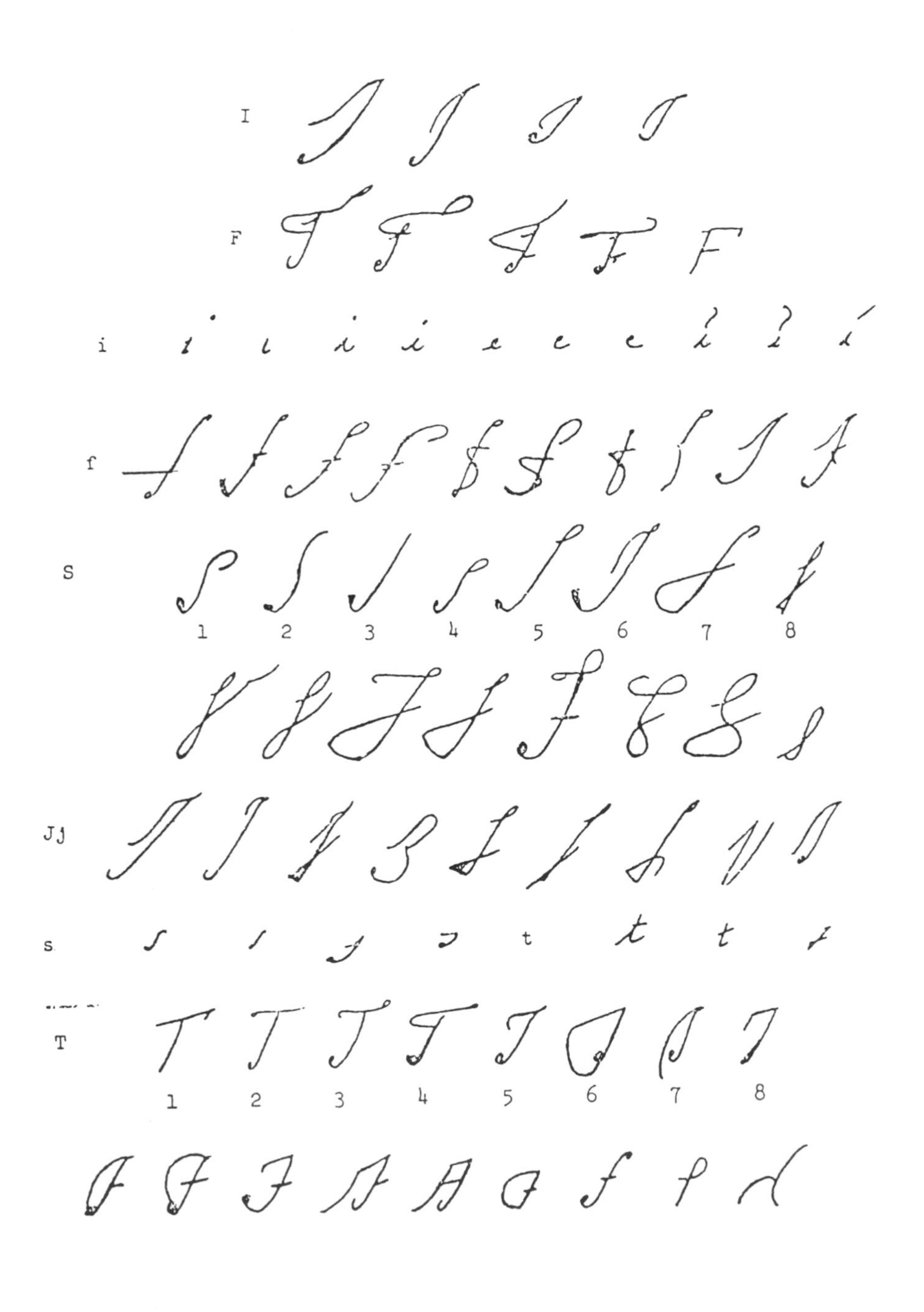

Figure 6-3 Examples of confusing letters *f, i, j, s,* and *t* (author's copy)

r, x

Very common in most manuscripts, even as late as the 1850s, is the use of the symbol " " for *r*. This is usually easily distinguished from the symbols for *x*: . The beginner needs to be careful with these at first, but will soon find that he reads *r*, not *x*, and wonders why he ever had any difficulty.

s

Although previously discussed, the letter *s* deserves special mention because of its many varieties, which frequently look like several other letters in the alphabet. While the following examples will help familiarize you with some of the various forms the letter *s* may take, you will undoubtedly find that you need to carefully work though each new word or name.

t

Like the *s*, the *t* is found in a wide variety of styles which often resemble many letters other than a *t*. The *t* frequently appears more like a connection between two letters, and varies according to its position within the word.

Double Letters

In old manuscripts it is possible to find double letter combinations not found in modern Spanish. Usually these had no linguistic significance, or they represented a sound that was in the process of being merged with the sound now symbolized by the single letter. Two exceptions to this are the *nn* and the *rr*. The *nn* and *gn* were used prior to the seventeenth century to represent the modern *ñ*. The word *peña*, then, may be found as *penna* or *pegna*. The *rr* was used when the writer wished to indicate that the trill *r* sound was present. Therefore, *Manrique* might have been written as *Manrrique*, or *Rodriquez* as *Rrodriguez*. Also a special symbol " " was often employed to represent the *rr* sound, as in (*Herrero*).

You will need to be aware of the presence of double letters to avoid inadvertently converting one of the letters into another letter, especially where each of the letters in a double letter pair is written in a different style. Take for example, . Knowing that a double *s* is common, one reads *cossa*, not *cosia* or *cosja*. The *f*, *t*, *s*, *m*, *r*, and *x* all frequently appear double.

There is one other use of double letters, which should not be confused with that just discussed. In certain abbreviations double letters are used to indicate plurality. *PP* is *padres*; *SS* symbolizes *santos*; and *EE UU* is

Estados Unidos. Unlike those discussed above, such double letters are significant in determining the meaning and should be carefully noted.

The Linking of Letters

Perhaps one of the most difficult aspects of reading older Spanish manuscripts is the linking of letters. Letters within a single word may or may not be linked together. Letters from the end of one word may also be linked with those at the beginning of the next. This can be particularly difficult when an abbreviation is involved. The result is that word division may not be clear upon the first reading. Reading the words out loud, and slightly run together, will frequently help suggest the correct alternative.

Flourishes

As if all of the above does not make reading the old handwriting challenging enough, the writers frequently decorated their letters and words with flourishes. Such embellishments come most frequently at the end of the word, but can also come at the beginning, or on any letter in the middle. Generally, a letter with a flourish will not be linked with the next. Flourishes are usually meaningless embellishments, but be mindful that what appears to be a flourish may in reality have a purpose, such as serving as the tilde over the *n*. It may also indicate an abbreviation, either of the word itself or of the next word in the sentence.

Suppression of the *e*

In written Spanish the *e* frequently appears and disappears at the end of words. *Ausente* may also be written *ausent*, and the names *De Arcos* and *De Hoyos* may be written as *D'arcos* and *Doyos*, respectively.

Alternate Spellings

Several different spellings of the same word may occur in a single document, and even in the same sentence. There will be no regularity as to the use of a particular spelling. This is due to the number of interchangeable letters and the variety of writing styles for the various letters. Always keep this in mind when studying a document.

CAPITALIZATION AND PUNCTUATION

There are no definite patterns for the use of upper-case or capital letters. Such letters may appear at the beginning, in the middle, or at the end of a word. Sentences usually begin with one, but need not do so. Names can be found capitalized at one point in the document and not in another.

Some letters, most notably the *L* and the *J*, had no lower-case forms distinguishable from the upper-case ones, and therefore all examples of these letters appear to be capitals. The *Z* also had only one form, and the only difference between the upper and lower case of that letter was its size.

One definite difficulty the researcher will encounter is that capital letters found in the middle of a word will frequently not be linked with the letter before it. The word, therefore, will appear as if it were two different words. Once again, the best way to handle these is to read with care and pronounce the words out loud and slightly run together.

As with capitalization, punctuation did not follow any set rules. All of the following punctuation symbols will be found in documents. Usually, some type of pause will be indicated by the use of most of these. Beyond that, little real help can be given that would prove consistent.

Period: •
Comma:
Question Mark:
Exclamation Point:
Equal Marks:
Colon:
Semicolon:
Cross:

Perhaps as significant as the inconsistent use of punctuation is the non-use of punctuation in places where modern usage demands it. Sentences, phrases, and even questions may not be set off with any punctuation. Of particular difficulty for the beginner is the total absence of any type of punctuation where today one finds a hyphen when a word is split at the end of a line and continues on the next line. To understand such words, the documents should be read as if there were no lines.

ABBREVIATIONS

One real challenge in your research will be the frequent use of abbreviations, common in older manuscripts. It is extremely rare to consult any type of Spanish document, including parish records, and not find at least two or three abbreviations. Even at the time these records were being written, it was recognized that abbreviations made understanding of documents difficult. Many attempts were made by civil and ecclesiastical authorities to limit or prohibit their use. For example, in the 1500s Phillip II prohibited the use of abbreviations in all documents throughout his kingdoms coming out of the Royal Chancellery. It was to no avail, and the use of abbreviations continued without any order or regulation, frequently without any general rules to guide either the writer or the reader.

Any word may be abbreviated. The first time the author encountered *Res* in a parish record in Galicia, he was surprised that it would be a Spanish surname. Not until three or four entries later when the same surname was spelled out did it became clear that *Res* was in reality an abbreviation for *Rodrígues*. Being aware of possible abbreviations is very important. They will frequently be noted by a period at the end of the word, just as with modern abbreviations, or by a slash or tilde over the abbreviated word. However, the absence of a period or any other type of punctuation mark is not infrequent, and it is best not to rely on the presence of such marks as a means of spotting them.

Abbreviations in older Spanish documents are divided into six categories:[2]

1. Contractions. These were formed by dropping out the middle letter or letters of the word, leaving at least the first and last letters, and frequently one or more of the letters in the middle of the word. For example, *natural* is abbreviated *ntl.*, *nrl.*, or *ntrl.* The word *real* is abbreviated *rl.*, *apostol* is abbreviated *apol.*, and *Herrera* is abbreviated *Herra.*

2. Superpositions. This might actually be considered a subcategory of contractions. The first few letters of a word are written on the base line in the same size as other letters in the manuscript, and the last one or two letters of the word are written in smaller letters above the base line. For example, *Francisco* would be written *Fran*^{co}, *real* would be *r*^{l}, *vecino* would be *v*^{zo}, or *Rodrígues* would be *R*^{es}. These are usually the easiest of the abbreviations to spot because the letters are raised, and when you look at the word you will rapidly recognize that it is abbreviated.

3. Suspensions. Here, the first letters of the word are written out and the last part of the word is eliminated. For example, *Herrera* would be written *Herr.*, *vezino* would be *vez.*, and *legítimo* would be *leg.*

4. Siglas. These can be considered a type of suspension where a single letter, usually the first letter in the word, has come through practice to stand for the entire word. Common examples are *N.S.*, which stands for *Nuestro Señor*; *P.* for *Pedro* or *J.* for *Juan*; and *F.* for *Francisco*. Sometimes these will contain a second or even a third letter. For example, *Dr.* for *doctor*; *Ga.* for *Garcia*; *Ma.* for *Maria*; or *Ldo.* for *licenciado*. Frequently, such *siglas* are doubled to indicate plurality or superlativeness. For example, *NN* for *Nuestros*; *PP* for *padres*; *HH* for *hermanos*; or *SS* for *santísimo*.

5. Interwoven. This form, usually found only in *procesal* or chain-script handwriting, is where the letters of a word are superimposed upon each other to form a single unit. For example, *escribano público* may be written .[3]

6. Conventionalism. Frequently found in the older Latin documents and in some Spanish documents, these were symbols used for entire words.

The most common is the use of *X* or the *Xpo* for *Christo*. Therefore, a word such as *Jesucristo* would be written *Jesuxpo*, or *Christobal* would be written *Xpobal*. Jorge A. Garces provides a list of the more common ones on page 80 of *Paleografia diplomática española y sus peculiaridades en América* (Quito, Equador, 1949).

ACCENT MARKS

The use of the accent mark has undergone extensive development in Spanish. During the early periods, all three types of accent marks, ´ and ` and ^, might have been employed interchangeably, as in *hablô*, *hablò*, and *habló*. Only the first of these has been retained in modern Spanish. Probably the most significant point to note about the accent mark is its absence in the majority of cases in the older Spanish manuscripts. The modern use of the accent mark was not set down by the Real Academia until a century after it was organized, and as recently as 1911 significant changes were made in its usage. As a result, you should not expect accent marks in older documents, and when they are found they might have a different form or might be placed where they would not be found today.

NUMBERS

In Spanish records two basic types of numbers are found. The first of these is arabic numbers, which as the chart indicates are similar to those used today. Care must be taken in distinguishing the 1, 3, 5, and the 7, which are at times similar in appearance and can be confused. Except for this, and the fact that the numbers are sometimes joined as in the number 10, they can be easily read.

1: 6:
2: 7:
3: 8:
4: 9:
5: 0:

The second type of numbers found in Spanish records is a gothic script variation of roman numerals. In these, the I, V, X, L, C, D, and M equal 1, 5, 10, 50, 100, 500, and 1,000, respectively. Unlike the more common forms of roman numerals, these were frequently indicated with lower-case letters as the following examples indicate. In this numeral system, a line above the numbers indicates that they have a value 1,000 times greater than that of the number alone.

i 1	xii 12	xxiii . . . 23	lxx 70	dcccc . . . 900
ii 2	xiii 13	xxiiii . . . 24	lxxx 80	[illegible] . . 1000
iii 3	xiiii 14	xxv 25	lxxxx . . 90	[illegible] . 1000
iiii 4	xv 15	xxvi . . . 26	c 100	[illegible] 2000
v 5	xvi 16	xxvii . . . 27	cc 200	[illegible] 3000
vi 6	xvii . . . 17	xxviii . . 28	ccc . . 300	[illegible] . . . 4000
vii 7	xviii . . . 18	xxviiii . 29	cccc . . 400	[illegible] 5000
viii 8	xviiii . . 19	xxx . . . 30	d D . . 500	[illegible] . . 10000
viiii . . . 9	xx 20	xl . . . 40	dc . . . 600	[illegible] . 40000
x . . 10	xxi 21	l . . . 50	dcc . . . 700	[illegible] . . 90000
xi 11	xxii . . . 22	lx . . 60	dccc . . 800	[illegible] . . . 100000

A variation of the gothic numeral system appeared during the thirteenth and fourteenth centuries. In this variation the following symbol was placed on the base line: U . The numerals, which appeared to the right and on the base line, signified the numbers below 1,000. If those same numerals appeared to the left of the symbol and slightly below the base line level, they represented multiples of 1,000. Numbers appearing to the left with a line above them were multiples of 10,000.

SECTION B: Naming Systems

Names, places, and dates are the fundamental building blocks upon which you as the family historian create a family history. When the most significant of these names, places, and dates are assembled on a pedigree chart, they form the framework for family history research. It is easy to see why the ability to understand and use the Hispanic naming systems used by your ancestors is crucial.

Each person today has a name made up of two parts, which taken together identify him and generally distinguish him from any other person. While in English we refer to both of these as his name, in Spanish they are clearly differentiated. The first is the *nombre* or *nombre de pila* (given name, Christian name, or first name), and the second is the *apellido* (surname). *Nombre de pila*, that given at the baptismal font (*pila*), identifies the person as a distinct and unique individual. The *apellido*, a direct descendant of the Roman *nomen gentilitium* (family name), identifies the individual as a member of a particular family.

SURNAMES (*APELLIDOS*)

In many societies the Roman pattern of a family name was not followed. Instead, a patronymic system was used. Vestiges of such a system in Spain can be found in the many Spanish *apellidos* ending in -ez, -es, or -iz. These endings signified "son of"; therefore, names such as Sanchez, Rodriguez, Fernandez, Gonzales, and Garcez were originally son of Sancho, son of Rodrigo, son of Fernando, son of Gonzalo, and son of Garcia.

While the patronymic system can be found in the genealogies of the early kings of Asturias and Castile, it had completely died out by the end of the Middle Ages. Most of the common people throughout the Middle Ages were known by a *nombre* (given name) and some type of *apodo* (nickname), usually relating to their work, physical attributes, or family characteristics. At the end of the Middle Ages, and therefore before the beginning of most parish records, the use of *apellidos* as a means of identifying particular families became nearly universal. (However, for Indians in colonial areas the use of only given names was common into the nineteenth century.) This near-universality makes the tracing of Spanish lines easier than in those countries where the patronymic was used. It does not, however, eliminate variety and flexibility in such usage.

The use of *apellidos* (surnames) in Spain and those countries inheriting the Spanish surname system is distinguished from that of other countries by two features: First, each individual, at least since the middle of the nineteenth century, uses two surnames rather than one; and second, upon marrying, a woman does not take the surname of her husband, but retains the "maiden name" by which she has been known since birth and will be known until the time of her death. While both of these approaches may be confusing to the person who is oriented to the surname system used in the English-speaking world, they are of great value to the family historian.

In the Spanish double surname system, each double surname is a miniature genealogical tree giving the mother's as well as the father's family name, thereby more uniquely identifying the individual by identifying both families from which he descends. The first surname a person has is that of his father, the one that English-speaking people commonly use as their surname. The second surname is his mother's surname, called her "maiden name" in English. For example, in the case of Faustino Lopez Ramirez, Faustino is his *nombre* or *nombre de pila*, given to him in the Catholic Church. Lopez is the surname of his father (*apellido paterno*), and Ramirez is the surname of his mother (*apellido materno*). Faustino married a girl named Maria del Aguilar Gines. Aguilar is the surname of her father and Gines is that of her mother. Faustino and Maria have a child whose name is Daniel Lopez Aguilar. Daniel is his *nombre* or *nombre de pila*; Lopez is his *apellido paterno* (the surname of his father); and Aguilar is his *apellido materno* (the surname of his mother).

The double surname system originated in sixteenth-century Castile among the upper classes. It became universal throughout Spain by the middle part of the nineteenth century. (Prior to the nineteenth century most records for the common people did not use more than the paternal surname.) This double surname system was carried over to most of Latin America, although in Argentina the use of a single surname system dominates.

In many cases, when Spanish-speaking immigrants brought their dual surnames to the United States, confusion resulted. Frequently they were called by their mothers' surnames instead of their fathers'. In order to adjust to the English surname system, many Hispanics have reversed the order of their surnames and list the maternal surname first, treating it as a middle name as it is sometimes used in the English naming system. This pattern frequently persists even among children and grandchildren of the original immigrant, if Spanish continues to be spoken.

While the upper and middle classes in the Spanish colonies used the dual surname system, the indigenous populations generally did not. In Mexico, for example, throughout the nineteenth century *Indios* (Indians) frequently appear in the parish records identified only by their Christian given names, making the tracing of family lines more difficult.

The second unique characteristic of the Spanish approach to surnames is the treatment of a woman's surname. Women in most Hispanic countries retain throughout their lives the surname or surnames that they receive at birth. A woman's subsequent marriage has no effect on that surname. The only change might be the addition of her husband's surname at the time of marriage. For example, if Faustino Lopez Ramirez and Chelo Aguilar Gines have a female child whose name is Maria, she will then be Maria Lopez Aguilar. If Maria later marries Juan Gomez Carpintero, her name on the marriage document, the birth records of their children, all legal documents, her personal mail, and even her mailbox will still appear as Maria Lopez Aguilar. She may at times add "de (of) Gomez" or "esposa de (wife of) Juan Gomez," or, if he should die, she might add "viuda de (widow of) Gomez." In all cases, however, her name at birth, Maria Lopez Aguilar, will continue to be used, not only in all official documents but in daily personal activities.

The value of this system to the family historian rapidly becomes apparent. One of the difficulties in working with earlier records in most countries is trying to find the maiden name of the wife where a marriage record has not been located. Under the Spanish approach to surnames this is rarely a problem, since the surname recorded for a woman in all documents is the same surname she received at her birth. Even on a death record, the surname given is the one she was given at birth.

Prior to the universal adoption of the upper-class Castilian double surname system, great flexibility was common in the use of surnames. A family's surname in the eighteenth century or earlier could come from several different sources. The most common was the use of the father's surname. However, surnames often changed, not only from one generation to another but even within a generation. In many cases the individual adopted the surname of the mother or a grandparent because it came from a more prominent side of the family, or was a means of identifying and distinguishing his branch of the family. This was frequently a conscious decision, sometimes even required as an inheritance qualification by a prominent rich relative, or implemented during the time of the Inquisition to hide Jewish ancestry.

Another practice was to modify the inherited surname by the addition of a second surname or title, distinguishing that individual from others with the same surname and, in some cases, even the same given name. In most small towns extensive intermarrying resulted in there being only a small number of *apellidos*. To distinguish these, an additional surname was added to the first surname: It could be the name of an attribute, e.g., Garcia Hermoso; the given name of a father or grandfather, e.g., Gonzales de Andres; the surname of a renowned ancestor, e.g., Gonzalez Trejo; or an occupation, e.g., Gomez Carpintero. At first this was usually done informally among the people of the village. Then, after a generation or more of use, it became the only surname by which that person was known and began to appear in official records. For example, a priest in a parish of Caceres, Spain, recorded the birth of Francisco Moreno de Alnarte and added in the margin the note that the father, also Francisco Moreno de Alnarte, was more commonly known as Francisco Moreno de Tome. In this case Tome was the surname of the maternal grandfather. A generation later all members of the family appear only as Moreno de Tome. Such flexibility calls for great care and a certain amount of creative investigation. Watch for inconsistencies in the use of a surname and be careful not to miss important data about the family due to surname changes.

The additional name in composite surnames frequently became the one most commonly used and the original family surname disappeared, especially if it was a common one such as Garcia, Gomez, Sanchez, or Gonzalez. In such cases you will need to be careful to look for the appearance of the original surname as you follow a line back. For example, the ancestors of Carmen Vigo were named Vigo for four generations. The initial search for her fourth great-grandfather proved fruitless. A more careful search showed her fourth great-grandfather using the *apellido* Garcia Vigo. In the later generations Garcia disappeared. The appearance and disappearance of the more common name, Garcia, as well as the more unique one, Vigo, could be seen even within that single generation.

The case of the ancestry of Francisco Reyes exhibited another slightly different pattern of surname variances. The records over the 100-year period from 1700 to 1800 recorded the family name as Garcia de los Reyes, Garcia del Rey, Rey, Reyes, and de los Reyes. Careful study and documentation showed that all of the individuals appearing under these various surnames were, in fact, from the same family.

There are also certain regional differences of which the researcher must be aware. The regions of Spain near Portugal are the most notable of these. In Galicia, prior to about 1760, and in Extremadura, prior to about 1820, a different approach was used for surnames. At that time most individuals throughout Spain (other than the Castilian upper class) used only a single surname, usually the paternal. In Galicia and Extremadura, however, women generally took the surname of their mother instead of the surname of their father. For example, Maria, the daughter of Alonso Gonzales and Josefa Zarza, would be known throughout her life as Maria Zarza. Her brothers would be known by the surname Gonzalez. This results in the repetition of a surname along a line of female ancestors in the same way you would normally find for male ancestors.

For the family historian searching in these areas, the impact of this unique surname system is immense. If you are unaware of its existence, the first time you encounter it you can lose track of many of the family lines you are attempting to follow. When searching in these areas for marriages of the brothers and sisters of your direct-line ancestor, be careful to search for children with either the paternal or maternal surname of the earlier generation, since the sisters of a male direct-line ancestor will have the mother's surname, and the brothers of the direct-line female ancestor will have a different surname than their sisters. Special care must also be taken during the years of transition, from about 1780 to 1840 in Extremadura and from 1730 to 1800 in Galicia, when the Castilian system becomes dominant and women can be found listed in records under either the paternal or the maternal surname, or both.

Another regional difference in Spain constitutes the only exception to the system of a woman keeping the same surname throughout her life, whether or not she marries. In Catalonia, prior to the increase of the Castilian influence at the end of the eighteenth century, the Catalans used a surname system similar to that of most European nations, whereby the wife took her husband's surname upon marriage. There is also a transition period when both surnames can be found. For example, the daughter of Anton Palao and Maria Gabarro, born in 1740, was named Mariangeles Palao. Following her marriage to Ramon Tapiol, she appears on the birth records of their children as Mariangeles Tapiol or Mariangeles Tapiol y Palao. Note that the double surname in this case is not composed of maternal and paternal surnames, but rather her married and then her maiden (paternal) surname. Upon the death of Ramon Tapiol and her subsequent remarriage to Magi Foquet, she appears as Mariangeles Tapiol. In the birth records of the children from this marriage, she is listed as Mariangeles Foquet y Palao or as Mariangeles Foquet y Tapiol. In her death record she is recorded as Mariangeles Foquet. This is strictly a Catalan exception; in all other areas of Spain you can be sure the surname given for a woman is hers and not her husband's.

In Latin America several additional variables can occur in the surname system. In families with greater social mobility, surname changes are more frequent and more difficult to trace. A change in surname by the immigrant ancestor is common. Non-Spaniards did not always adopt the Spanish double surname system, and in some places the foreign influence, such as the German and British in Argentina, totally eliminated the use of that system. As previously mentioned, the Indian population frequently did not use surnames, and when they did the surnames came from a variety of sources, such as birthplace, residence, the owner of the ranch where they worked or were indentured, or a respected *español* whose patronage they enjoyed. In some regions where the Indian population was in the majority, indigenous family names were also used.

A family historian must take care to look at all possible combinations for surname variations. This is especially true when you are using an index where the information given may not reflect the various surnames that will appear in the actual documents. Individuals may be known by several surnames during the course of their lives, and depending on who was doing the writing and giving the information, any one of several surnames could be used.

GIVEN NAMES (*NOMBRES, NOMBRES DE PILA*)

Unlike the flexibility (and therefore the difficulties) in the use of *apellidos*, *nombres de pila* are nearly always used consistently throughout the life of the individual. In some places only one name will be given at the time of birth and baptism; in many other places, two, three, or even more names are given. As can be seen in the baptismal certificate in figure 9-5, even six given names are not impossible. Both the number and choice of names generally followed regional or local patterns. For example, Gumersindo and Cosme are used only in Galicia, Spain; and in the parish of Los Angeles in Cabra, Andalucia, Spain, all of the children for nearly the last century and a half have received a given name such as Juan Jorge and to this has been added "de la Santísima Trinidad."

Nombres were nearly always saints' names drawn from the liturgical calendar. Some combinations may seem somewhat strange to the English-speaking person. For example, Jesus is a very common first name. Jose Maria is a common name for a male and Maria Jose is common for a female. Given names are frequently chosen for the saint's day on which the child was born. Most likely, if a child's *nombre* is Maria Reyes or Melchor Gaspar Baltasar, she or he was born on or near the sixth of January—*Dia de los Reyes* (Day of the Wise Men). You can never, however, assume a birth date because of the name of the child, since many parents did not follow that pattern. Equally common, but by no means universal, was the practice of naming children after their godparents or their deceased siblings.

The most common variation found in given names over a person's lifetime is where that person is given more than one *nombre* at the time of his birth, but all of the given names are not repeated at the time of his marriage or at the birth of his children. A person often decided in later life not to use the first in the series of given names that he received at birth. For example, it is quite common to find three given names at birth, with the second or third more frequently used in later life—a person born Joan Manoel Magi Montserrat might have gone through life as Manoel Montserrat on all records except the birth record.

Another variation is that the birth record might list a child as Juan Antonio Jorge Garcia, but for many of his adult years he might appear in records only as Juan Garcia; then, later in his life, he might begin appearing as Juan Antonio Garcia. Such changes can most frequently be explained by a second Juan Garcia either moving in or, more likely, becoming of age, so that Antonio Garcia is added to distinguish one Juan Garcia from the other. This type of circumstance can also lead to changes in surnames, or to the addition of titles such as *mayor* (elder), *menor* (younger), *hijo* (junior), *el mozo* (the young), or *el viejo* (the old). It is important to notice in the use of such titles that the persons having the same name — for example, Juan Gomez, *mayor* and Juan Gomez, *menor* — need not be father and son. They could also be uncle and nephew, or grandson and grandfather. It is even possible, when terms such as *el mozo* and *el viejo* are used, that the individuals being referred to are not even directly related, but merely residing in the town at the same time.

In Latin America an Indian, when baptized, was given a Christian saint's name. In nearly all records that is the only name that appears, and no mention is made of his original Indian name.

TITLES

Certain titles may appear along with the *nombre de pila* and *apellidos*. These are frequently related to a particular status the individual has inherited or attained. We are all aware of titles of nobility such as *conde* (count), *duque* (duke), or *marques* (marquis). More common than these, however, is the use of *Don* or *Doña*, uniquely Spanish titles of respect that only the nobility could use prior to the year 1832. Such titles were used by both the titled and untitled nobility, and appear from the moment of birth onward. During the colonial period the use of *Don* and *Doña* was so consistent that if in all other documents the person was referred to as *Don*, its absence indicates that the individual in the new document is probably not the same as the one who had *Don* before his name.

Unlike titles that show inherited status, other titles indicating status achieved during the lifetime of the individual can appear and may vary from record to record. For example, *licenciado* and *bachiller* indicate master's and bachelor's degrees of education, respectively; *escribano* indicates a position as a notary; *alcalde* (mayor) and *secretario* indicate a political or administrative position. Such titles usually appear consistently in all records referring to the individual following the achievement of the particular status.

The appearance of any of these titles should automatically alert you to the potential of further sources of information about the family or individual. The use of *Don* or *Doña* is indicative of a social position involving many privileges, such as officer status in the military, exemption from paying certain taxes, ability to join certain military and civil orders (if other requirements were met), and many others. While not synonymous with wealth, those whose noble status allowed them to use *Don* or *Doña* are more commonly found to have drawn up wills, marriage contracts, property sales, and other legal transactions.

Special titles of nobility such as *conde* or *duque* should trigger a search for information about such things as the grant of nobility, the *casa solar* (ancestral home) of the family, the coat of arms, and any published or manuscript genealogies of the family. Military titles suggest searching military records. *Licenciado* or *bachiller* should suggest a search of nearby university records or, if the individual was a priest, the local seminary. A search of regional notary lists would be recommended when a person is described as an *escribano*, since such a search might provide information about any other places the family resided.

SECTION C: Doing Research by Correspondence

Although there are many Hispanic records in microfilm and published formats in the United States, most are found in repositories in their respective countries of origin. This means that nearly every researcher will need to do part of his research by correspondence. This section is designed to help you successfully write letters in Spanish.

GENERAL SUGGESTIONS

The following suggestions are offered to guide the researcher in preparing letters requesting genealogical information from Hispanic countries.

1. Write in Spanish. There are many individuals in Hispanic countries who do not speak English well enough to understand a letter, and this is especially true in small towns. There is nothing sadder than the case of a parish priest who receives a well-written letter in English and is unable to understand or answer it. If you do not speak much Spanish, prepare each letter using the models on pages 154 and 185 and then ask a friend who speaks Spanish to review it. If you do not know anyone personally who speaks Spanish, it may even be necessary to go to a local high school and/or college and ask a Spanish teacher to review the letter.

2. Keep it short. This is a cardinal rule in any type of letter writing where you are asking for information. Letters should rarely, if ever, exceed one page. Make it easy for the individual to review your letter and understand what he needs to do. Do not add excess information that is not essential to the reply you are requesting.

3. Make all requests specific and positive. The wandering kind of letter, such as one asking for a complete history of the family, or for the parish priest to fill out a complete pedigree and mail all available certificates, will most likely not be answered or be answered with a short letter indicating that the person does not have the time to do the work requested. Always sound positive as to the information given. Even when you are in doubt that the person came from that particular town or was born in that particular year, do not express that doubt in the letter. People tend to be more willing to search for things that they think they are going to find.

4. Carefully proofread your letter. Anyone can make mistakes, even in his own language. If you do not understand Spanish, carefully compare the finished letter you have typed against the model to be sure you have not inadvertently changed or left out a word. It is also helpful to set the letter aside for a day or two and then review it before mailing. Careful proofreading will eliminate errors.

5. Make the letter look neat. The physical appearance of a letter frequently determines the initial reaction and subsequent response to it. The following suggestions will give it a neat, positive appearance.

a. Type if possible. This is especially important in Spanish. Handwritten letters, especially by a beginning Spanish speaker, are more difficult for the person receiving the letter to understand. The styles of handwriting in the United States are very different from those in Hispanic countries and may be difficult to read. One area of possible confusion is between the number 1 and the number 7. A Spanish-speaking native writes his number 1 like this (7) and the number 7 is distinguished by the small slash across it like this (7). It is likely that a written 7 could be confused for a 1 in an address or a date. In addition to being more readable, a typewritten letter is also much cleaner looking.

b. Leave adequate margins. Wider margins make a letter look neater and also tend to help the writer keep it short.

c. Use proper letter form. The model letters have been adapted somewhat to meet the needs of the family history researcher, but are basically in the proper form for Spanish letters and therefore will be well received. It is important to follow the formalities of written Spanish that appear in these letters, especially in the opening and closing parts of the letter. One common mistake is translating the English phrase "Dear Sir" into "*Querido Señor*," which actually means "Most Beloved Sir." Spanish is by nature a more flowery and formal language than English. As a result, letters have phrases that appear comical and, in some cases, nonsensical when translated into English.

6. Be willing to pay for both time and materials. You are writing someone asking a favor, and none of the people to whom you will write are paid to look up genealogical information. Since you are asking for work to be done, you should be willing to pay for the time the individual spends, and of course cover any costs for photocopies or other expenses he may incur.

7. Limit your requests. Your letter is most likely to be answered if it requests only one, two, or at most three documents or pieces of specific information. Even the most cooperative person will be overwhelmed by a request for a complete pedigree. In one case a researcher sent a letter to a parish priest asking for a pedigree chart of the direct-line ancestors of her great-grandfather who was born in that parish. Included in the letter was a twenty-dollar bill. The priest in all sincerity began the research, and three years later, when a paid professional genealogist arrived to try to do the work for the family, the priest apologetically handed him the pedigree chart with four complete generations that he had searched out from his parish books. He had not yet answered because he had not found time to finish all seven generations that the pedigree chart called for. During those three years, the priest would most likely have answered a dozen or more requests for two or three documents at a time, and the researcher would have avoided frustration in not knowing what had happened to her letter, and might even have avoided the expense of the paid genealogist.

8. Always include your return address. There is nothing more tragically comical than a request for information that contains no return address. The return address should also be written inside the letter because often the envelope is destroyed. It is preferable to type it, as this is clearer to read.

9. Make a copy of every letter for your files. Comparing the answer you receive with the letter you sent helps in knowing if everything you asked for has been included and, when there are omissions, if the errors were in your original letter and you need to write again.

CORRESPONDENCE LOG

Each researcher should keep a correspondence log with notations of the research letters that he writes. At a minimum, it should contain columns for the following information:

a. The date of the outgoing letter.
b. The name and address of the person to whom the letter is sent.
c. The purpose of the letter.
d. The date a reply is received.
e. A file number for any documents received with the reply.

All of the letters should be kept in a central correspondence file, or in separate correspondence sections within the surname or individual files discussed in chapter 3. Recording a file number in the correspondence log of any documents received with the reply makes it unnecessary to keep the documents with the letter. An alternative to this would be to keep photocopies of the reply in the files of the various individuals or families to whom the letter referred.

BASIC ELEMENTS IN A GENEALOGICAL RESEARCH LETTER

There are certain basic elements that a good genealogical research letter should contain. All of the elements listed below are found in figure 9-9, a model letter to a parish priest, and figure 8-5, a model letter to a civil register. These model letters can be used by anybody who does not write well in Spanish by merely substituting information about his ancestor for that of the person in the model letter.

1. Date and place the letter was written. This item, appearing in the upper right-hand corner of the letter, is placed there according to the standard Spanish letter format. It indicates to the reader the time and place the letter was written.

2. Name, title, and address of the person to whom the letter is directed.

3. Salutation. In choosing a salutation, remember the more formal nature of Spanish. For those who are not fluent in Spanish, it is recommended that they use only those salutations appearing in the model letters.

4. Give a brief statement of why you are writing. The stated purpose should never exceed more than a sentence or two. It is merely to explain the purpose for your inquiry and assure the reader that you are searching for details about your own family because of personal interest and not for any public, monetary, or legal purpose.

5. Ask briefly and specifically for what you want. The more specific your request, the more likely you are to receive a clear answer, either in the form of the documents or material you have requested, or a definite statement that either they do not exist or at least are not in the possession of the person to whom you are writing.

6. Refer to payment enclosed or offer to pay for any work done. Family history research is enjoyable, exciting, and fascinating, but it is still work. When writing a letter, you are asking a person who does not necessarily share your enthusiasm or concern about your family to spend his time and energy on your behalf. It is certainly appropriate to expect to pay something for his services. Due to past abuse, many Catholic dioceses throughout the world have established certain minimum fees for each certificate a priest copies from his parish books. It is wise to include money in your letter where possible, with an offer to send more if necessary. Money should be sent in U.S. currency (bills only) if in small quantities, and if in larger quantities, by cashier's check (New York Bank Draft) in U.S. currency or in the currency of the country to which you are sending it. The foreign currency can be purchased at most large banks.

7. Express gratitude for the anticipated assistance. Gratitude is appreciated in any culture, but especially so in Hispanic cultures. Remember the people who answer correspondence are donating their time and knowledge, usually in exchange for relatively little remuneration. An expression of gratitude is clearly appropriate and deserved.

8. Include your return address in the body of the letter. This can be done most clearly by placing it either at the top of the letter as is the custom in American business letters, or, more in keeping with Spanish practice, by placing it below the signature on the letter.

---

[1] The chart in figure 6-2 is reprinted from *Spanish Handwriting* (Salt Lake City: Genealogical Department of The Church of Jesus Christ of Latter-day Saints, 1978), 5–6.

[2] Jorge A. Garces, *Paleografía diplomática española y sus peculiaridades en América* (Quito, Ecuador, 1949), 62.

[3] An extensive list of abbreviations in facsimile can be found in Garces, *Paleografía diplomática española* (see note 2 above), 86–88. Angel Riesco Terrero, *Diccionario de abreviaturas hispanas de los siglos XII al XVIII* (Salamanca: Varona, 1983) is an entire book of abbreviations. One or both of these should be consulted when you encounter documents in chain-script handwriting.

CHAPTER 7

Determining Objectives and Starting Work in Original Sources

Before beginning the dual process of determining objectives and starting work in original source materials, recall the theme of the introductory chapter: the family historian seeks to find out all he can about a specific group of people — his Hispanic ancestors — and recreate their lives as much as possible from original records. In doing this the researcher should remember these are people who lived, loved, toiled, and died in much the same way that we do now. With this in mind, the researcher should strive to create a family history that is fleshed out with additional details beyond mere dates and places. By consulting a broader variety of original and secondary sources, a richer, more meaningful family history can be compiled.

As in any endeavor, success in compiling a family history is based on establishing objectives and following through to accomplish them. The process of determining objectives in family history research will be divided into three types of analysis: People Analysis, Locality Analysis, and Records Analysis.

PEOPLE ANALYSIS

The goal of a People Analysis is to come to know each ancestor as an individual person. In order to accomplish this, take the pedigree chart you have filled out with the information found in your preliminary survey, and for each of the ancestors appearing on this chart, ask — and where possible, answer — a long series of questions. The questions, and answers where available, should be written down. This analysis will determine the objectives for your research and show you where to begin.

All of the following questions should be asked for each ancestor, along with any others that might relate to his specific life circumstances. Begin with basic questions: When did he live? Who were his parents? Where did he live? What was his occupation? To these can be added a wide variety of more specific questions: Did he serve in the military? If so, when? Did he join any particular social group? What was the social class from which he came? Whom did he marry? Did he marry more than once? Did he travel far from his place of birth? What kind of education did he pursue? Did he own land? Did he have a trade which he would have learned by apprenticeship? All of these questions, and many more, can be asked about the life of each of your ancestors. The frame of mind with which you approach these questions is very important. Remember that these ancestors were real people and ask the kinds of questions you would like to ask if you could talk to each one personally.

Questions should also be asked about your ancestor's brothers and sisters. Perhaps a brother or sister did something exceptional that makes that member of the family stand out more than the direct-line ancestor. For example, in some cases a brother might have become a priest and, due to greater mobility within the church structure, might have achieved at least regional renown.

Beyond these specific questions about the individual and his immediate family, take a look at the broad historical context in which your ancestor lived. Was there any event such as a war, drought, revolution, or social upheaval which might have had a particular impact upon the ancestor's life? To be able to answer this last question, you may need to acquire a better understanding of the history of the country from which your ancestor came. This can be gained by reading some of the many histories available in local libraries concerning Hispanic countries and their regional areas. Such broad reading should be supplemented with local or specific time-period histories, where available.

Once you have done this, write down each of these People Analysis questions with the answers, where possible, and then keep this written list handy as you continue with the analyses outlined below. Eventually you will want to place a copy in the permanent file you have created for that particular ancestor or ancestral family, as a guide for future research. As new information is obtained, you may also ask additional questions and/or answer questions already asked.

LOCALITY ANALYSIS

A Locality Analysis plays an essential part in determining your objectives for family history research. The Locality Analysis involves two processes. The first is to locate the exact place or places from which your ancestors came and determine the various jurisdictions to which that place belonged. (This is, in effect, an answer to one of the initial questions asked in the People Analysis: Where did the ancestor live?) The second goal of a Locality Analysis is to learn as much about that particular place as you can to better understand the life of your ancestor. This includes not only a knowledge of the physical location and geographical features of the place but also of its history and physical appearance.

There are seven major categories of books that can be valuable in completing a Locality Analysis. The bibliography at the end of this chapter lists, for each Hispanic country, examples of books available from all but the last category.

1. Atlases and Maps. Individual atlases that exist for most Hispanic countries can help locate ancestral towns and establish the proximity of ancestral towns to other towns found during your research. Typical of these is the one for Mexico, *Nuevo Atlas Porrúa de la Republica Mexicana,*[1] available in many local libraries. This small volume contains maps of each state, historical maps, and a general countrywide index, as well as various geographical entity lists. Maps in these should be in a scale of at least 1:250,000.

Another useful geographical tool for the Latin American genealogist is the *Index to the Map of Hispanic America*, published by the American Geographical Society.[2] Because this is an index to a collection of maps, scale 1:1,000,000, it will generally only be found in a large public or university library. It is a valuable source, since it covers all Latin American countries in good detail.

Also of value for locating especially small hamlets and for recreating geographical details of local life are the *United States Army Map Service Select Series* and topographical maps produced for all of these countries. Any place, no matter how small, will appear on these detailed maps (scale 1:50,000). Unfortunately they have no direct index, and locating places can only be accomplished by using latitude and longitude references in the gazetteers such as those published by the U.S. Office of Geography. (See the following section on gazetteers.)

Maps and atlases are being digitalized for computer storage at an incredible rate. As that process continues, these will become increasingly available on CD ROM and on the Internet and World Wide Web. Currently, for example, at the University of Texas in the Austin Perry Castañeda Library, there is a map collection which has placed many atlases and maps from the CIA on the Internet. Check with that library for its Internet address and the countries for which maps are available.

2. Gazetteers. Gazetteers are long lists of place names with a minimal amount of information to identify and locate each particular place. Since many of these gazetteers list geographical subdivisions smaller than the parish or municipality, and other features such as rivers and mountains, they can be of great help when the particular place to be located does not appear in the atlases or geographical dictionaries available to the researcher. Many countries also publish postal guides and political divisions guides.

Gazetteers, such as the *United States Board on Geographical Names Gazetteer*, prepared by the Office of Geography of the Department of the Interior, are frequently more readily obtained in the United States than are local geographical dictionaries or detailed atlases of Hispanic countries.[3] For a number of Hispanic countries there are updated versions of these gazetteers published by the Defense Mapping Agency (DMA). These are listed under each country's name in the last section of this chapter. These gazetteers have now been placed by the DMA (in collaboration with the U.S. Board of Geographic Names) on the computer Internet under the title GEOnet Names Server.

3. Geographical dictionaries. These vary in size, from one- and two-volume dictionaries to large series containing sixteen to twenty volumes. In the United States those covering Hispanic countries are generally found in the Family History Library Catalog or in large public or university libraries that have map collections. Some of the large countries such as Mexico even have state or regional geographic dictionaries. Whether national or regional, these are most helpful in locating a particular town or other geographical unit, especially in identifying the larger geographical unit (where records would usually be found) in instances where the only name known is of a smaller area. Figure 7-1, a page from Volume I of the *Diccionario geográfico del Salvador*, is an example of this, showing the *caseríos* of such small geographical units. These dictionaries often provide written descriptions useful in developing the history of your ancestral locality as a background to your family history. Encyclopedias from various Latin American countries and Spain often provide similar information to that found in geographical dictionaries, although often with less detail. These are listed separately in the bibliography at the end of this chapter.

4. Ecclesiastical Directories. Many Catholic dioceses publish directories listing the various parishes, seminaries, and conventos that make up the diocese. These directories always include the names of local parishes and the priests who serve there. They also may contain maps and other aids, and interesting and pertinent information about local history, including even local jurisdictional changes. Many of these are available through the LDS family history centers and in libraries having the CIDOC[4] collection of Latin American church documents on microfilm. For at least four countries — Spain, Puerto Rico, Mexico, and Argentina — guides exist that also indicate the earliest date records are available for parish registers in nearly every parish in the country.

5. Historical Atlases, Maps, and Materials. In the bibliography in the last section of this chapter, a special category has been created for geographic reference tools that were printed before 1900 but are still widely available, or were written to deal with geography during a historical time period, most often the colonial period. The use and format of these materials parallels that of their contemporary counterparts described in other sections above.

6. Encyclopedias. Many countries have national encyclopedias that contain articles on geographical entities as small as municipalities and parishes. These can often provide information and maps as found in atlases, gazetteers, and geographical dictionaries. They also might contain interesting background data on a variety of subjects, such as military ranks, local racial designations, national political leaders and events, etc.

7. Local histories. As the name implies, these are histories that deal entirely with a particular town or region, found either as books or as articles in periodicals. Scholarly historical journals such as *The Americas*

G

GALES POINT, o Manatee, pueblo en el distrito (mun.) de Belice, territorio guatemalteco del mismo nombre. Aprox. a 45 km. de Belice por la vía fluvial.

GALIZ, quebrada en jurisd. mun. Petapa, Gua. Surte de agua potable a la aldea Santa Inés Petapa.

GALLEGOS, caserío de la aldea Tierra Blanca, mun. Morazán, Pro. 38 hab.

GALLUSER, estación del ferrocarril, de bandera, en jurisd. mun. Los Amates, Iza. A 67.4 millas por vía férrea de Puerto Barrios (Iza.) y 130.7 millas de la capital. 282 pies SNM; cota F. I. de C. A.

GALÓN, paraje en jurisd. mun. San Benito, Pet.

GÁLVEZ, aldea del mun. Flores Costa Cuca, Que. 356 hab.

GANCHO DE FIERRO, caserío del núcleo poblado El Porvenir, mun. La Libertad, Pet.

GANCHO DE FIERRO, caserío de la aldea San Juan Acul, mun. Sayaxché, Pet.

GARAY, antes Garay Viejo, caserío de la aldea Morazán, mun. Monjas, Jal. Aprox. a 3 km. de la cab.

GARAY, riachuelo en jurisd. mun. Monjas, Jal. Corre de Oeste a Este y desagua en el río Güirila.

GARCÍA, caserío de la aldea Barbasco, mun. Gualán, Za. 21 hab.

GARIBALDI, caserío de la aldea El Caulote, mun. San José del Golfo, Gua. 79 hab. Aprox. a 3 km. de la cab.

GARIBALDI, barrio de la cab. deptal. y mun. Quezaltenango, Que.

GARITA CHAPINA, aldea del mun. Moyuta, Jut. 115 hab. Tiene los caseríos

Las Champas
La Blanca

GARITA VIEJA, caserío de la aldea Chocabaj, mun. Sibinal, S. M.

GASCHOCOLÁ, caserío de la aldea Sumal, mun. Nebaj, Qui.

GELNÁ, núcleo poblado del mun. Soloma, Hue. 125 hab. Según indica la municipalidad es aldea; no existe Acdo. Gub. al respecto. Tiene los caseríos

Quec
Becajuich
Chil

GEMÁ, aldea del mun. Soloma, Hue. 225 hab. Tiene los caseríos

Moclil
Yinjom
Pajaj
Xochilá

GEMÁ, riachuelo en jurisd. mun. Soloma, Hue.

GÉNOVA, municipio del departamento de Quezaltenango; municipalidad de 2ª categoría.

Colinda al Norte con Colomba y Flores Costa Cuca (Que.); al Este con El Asintal (Reu.) y Colomba; al Sur con Retalhuleu (Reu.); al Oeste con Coatepeque y Flores Costa Cuca (Que.). El límite entre Flores Costa Cuca y Génova, es el río El Rosario, parcialmente.

Sobre la Ruta Nacional 13, conocida también por Ruta Justo Rufino Barrios, Génova está a unos 5 km. de Flores Costa Cuca y 12 km. de Coatepeque, donde entronca con la Ruta Nacional 6-W y la Carretera Internacional del Pacífico, CA-2. Cuenta asimismo, con carreteras municipales, veredas y caminos de herradura que unen la cabecera con sus poblados y municipios vecinos. El ferrocarril atraviesa parcialmente el municipio.

Figure 7-1 Page from *Diccionario geográfico del Salvador*, volume 1

and *Hispanic American Historical Review* are particularly valuable. While these do not help in locating exact places, they can be extremely valuable in helping to understand the history of a specific locality, and especially to trace its jurisdictional changes.

There are several types of local histories. While the most traditional form is the history of a specific town or region, you will also want to look for ethnic histories and for histories of families whose stories may be deeply entwined with a particular town or region.[5] Even local entities, such as clubs and churches, may have published local histories.[6]

A visit or a letter to the local library in the area where you are searching may yield one of these treasures of information. A broad search for these sources can also be made by computer on the Internet. For books, search computer library catalog systems such as RLIN and WORLDCAT. For periodical articles, check Hispanic American Index (HAPI) and Latin American Studies Handbook. In any of these, do a Key Word Search under the name(s) of the town, province, and/or region of your ancestral locality.

Locality Report

After doing your Locality Analysis, you will want to do a summary, or report, of each ancestral locality you have searched. Your initial report can be brief, but should include a short description of the locality, including its history and major crops and industries. A map showing nearby towns and geographical features such as rivers and mountains should be included. Because records are found in a variety of archives, at a minimum the following jurisdictions to which the locality belonged should be determined and listed:

Political: *municipio* and *estado* or *provincia*

Ecclesiastical: *parroquia* and *diocesis*

In larger cities municipalities are often divided into districts for civil registration and judicial purposes. In some countries there is a political unit between municipality and state, similar to the county in the United States. (See the chart in figure 7-2.) A few also have an ecclesiastical administrative unit between the parish and the diocese called the *arciprestazgo* or *vicariato* under which *parroquias* are listed in the ecclesiastical directories.

While preparing this report, watch for indications of political and ecclesiastical divisions to which the ancestral locality belonged. For example, Saltillo, Mexico is today one of the Mexican dioceses of the Catholic Church. The Saltillo diocese was created in 1891. Prior to that time, Saltillo was a part of the diocese of Linares/Monterrey. That diocese was created from the diocese of Guadalajara in 1777. Diocesan records relating to Saltillo will be found in Guadalajara for the period 1580 to 1777, in

Divisiones Politicas

Argentina	Provincia, Departamento (Distrito Federal, Partido)
Bolivia	Departamento, Provincia, Canton
Brazil	Estado, Municipio
Chile	Region, Provincia, Comuna
Colombia	Departamento (Intendencia o Comisaria), Municipio
Costa Rica	Provincia, Canton, Distrito
Cuba	Provincia, Municipio
Dominican Republic	Provincia, Municipio, Distrito Municipio (Early: Provincia, Distrito, Canton)
Ecuador	Provincia, Municipio
El Salvador	Departamento, Municipio
Guatemala	Departamento, Municipio
Honduras	Departamento, Municipio
México	Estado, Municipio
Nicaragua	Departamento, Municipio
Panama	Provincia, Distrito, Corregimiento
Paraguay	Departamento, Distrito
Perú	Departamento, Provincia, Distrito
Portugal	Distrito, Provincia, Concelho
Puerto Rico	Municipio, Barrio
Spain	Provincia, Ayuntamiento or Municipalidad
Uruguay	Departamento, Localidad or Seción Judicial
Venezuela	Estado, Seción, Distrito or Municipalidad (Before 1863=Provincia, Canton, Parroquia)

Figure 7-2 Political divisions of Latin America, Spain, and Portugal

Monterrey from 1777 to 1891, and in Saltillo from 1891 to the present. Similar changes have occurred in the political divisions for Saltillo. From 1580 to 1787, Saltillo was part of Nueva Vizcaya with the capital in Durango. In 1787 it became part of the province of Coahuila (Nueva Extremadura) where it remained until the end of the colonial period. Knowing such ecclesiastical and jurisdictional changes for the locality of your ancestors will prove helpful in knowing where records are found.

RECORDS ANALYSIS

The Records Analysis is a two-step process that brings the People and Locality analyses into focus and points out the future directions you will want to take. Step one answers the following question:

What records might this ancestor have generated?

Look again at the many questions that you asked in the People Analysis. Each of these questions may indicate some type of record in which your ancestor possibly appeared.You may find it helpful to review chapters in this book on specific record types in order to become familiar with the types of records that exist.[7] Then review the list of questions and answers from the People Analysis and write down what type of record each activity may have generated. For example, was the ancestor baptized in the Catholic Church? If the answer is yes, there should be a baptismal record. What was his occupation? Perhaps there were special licenses necessary for his occupation. If he was a carpenter, there could be records indicating that he had done work for the local parish or the city hall or some other important building in the town. Did he work as a government civil servant? If he was a member of a local *cofradía* (church social unit), his name might appear in the membership lists, and he might have also been an officer. If he attended a university, that university's records should be examined. Did he serve in the military? In that case a military archives should be searched.

As you review the materials on record types, you will undoubtedly think of new questions to ask in your People Analysis, and of more records that may be worth checking. If your ancestor lived during the last half of the nineteenth century, he is almost certain to appear in the civil registers, which began in most Hispanic countries between 1860 and 1880. These registers are usually contained in the municipal archives. Did he own land, make a will, or become involved in some type of legal process? If so, there might be notarial records available. Would he have lived in the United States between 1850 and 1910 when the censuses — for which state and regional indexes are available — were taken? Did he live in a Mexican frontier area? If so, he might appear in military records or a census from the Spanish colonial period and even later. He might also appear in municipal or state census records. Did he live in Spain or one of her colonies before 1832? If so, he might appear in Inquisition records. If your ancester was a member of the nobility, there is an even greater selection of records to consult.

Diocesan archives also prompt a wide variety of potential questions. Was the person your ancestor married related to him within the fourth degree of consanguinity? (In other words, were they more closely related than third cousins?) Were there any other unusual circumstances about his marriage that might have required special permission to marry? Did he pay any special taxes to the Church, or make special grants in his will? Was his brother a priest or his sister a nun? If so, there might be records in a diocesan archives recording these events.

Did your ancestor travel? Did he take out a passport? Was he on a ship that went to another country? Why did he emigrate? He may have been recruited or conscripted to colonize, as were many others, not only from Spain to the American colonies but also from older settled regions to frontier areas within each colony. Questions like these will come to mind as the researcher reviews the chapters on record types, does his People and Records analyses, and continues to do his research. The process of asking questions will lead you to a wide variety of record types that may contain information about your ancestor and/or the ancestral locality.

The second part of a Records Analysis answers the question: What records are available for a particular locality?

After following the above procedure, you will have made a list of potential records to search. The next step is to determine whether any or all of these records are available for the locality from which your ancestor came? Records for many localities are available on microfilm at your local LDS family history center. Consult the Family History Library Catalog under the name of the locality, as well as the names of the political and ecclesiatical divisions to which the locality belonged. In some cases the availability of records can only be determined by actually going, or at least writing, to the local archives in a particular area. There are, however, certain research tools that can assist the researcher in determining what types of records are available for a particular locality.

Locating Catholic Church Records

A critical question for any Hispanic researcher is whether there are Catholic parish records available for his ancestor's locality. You may find that you are able to spend all of your available research time and resources for a long period of time solely making use of these records. The process of locating parish records and Catholic diocesan records is described in detail in chapter 9.

Locating Other Records

The chart in figure 7-3 lists the principal types of records found in Hispanic countries and the archives where they most often are found. Some collections in state and national archives — such as notarial records, government reports, and censuses — may contain detailed local information and be extremely helpful in doing research in your ancestral locality.

Una Guia Genealógico-Histórica de Latino América by Lyman Platt[8] offers both general descriptions and specific identification of records existing in a particular locality, depending upon the type of record and the Latin American country involved. The Church of Jesus Christ of Latter-day Saints published a series of resource papers on each Hispanic country except Brazil, Cuba, Portugal, and Spain, which also offer overviews of records in specific countries. The periodicals *The Spanish American Genealogist* and *Revista del Instituto de Genealogía e Historia Latinoamericana*, as well as the periodicals published by the various Hispanic genealogical societies listed in the Appendix, are also continually growing sources of information on non-parish records.

Record Type	Where Found
Burial Records	Municipal Archives, Parish Church Archives
Catholic Church — Parish Records	Local Parish Archives, Diocesan Archives, State or National Archives
Cemetery Records	Municipal Archives, Parish Church Archives, State or Provincial Archives
Census Records	National Archives, Parish Archives, Diocesan Archives
City Council Minutes	Municipal Archives
Civil Register (Births, Marriages, and Deaths)	Local Civil Register Office, Municipal Archives
Court Records — Ecclesiastical	Diocesan Archives
Court Records — Civil	Municipal Archives, State or Provincial Archives, National Archives
Hospital Records	Municipal Archives
Immigration Records	National Archives
Inquisition Records	National Archives
Land Records	Municipal Archives, State or Provincial Archives, National Archives
Marriage Conflicts and Disputes	Diocesan Archives, Municipal Archives
Marriage Dispensations	Diocesan Archives
Marriage Information	Parish Archives, Diocesan Archives, National Archives
Military and Census Militia Lists	Municipal Archives, National Archives
Military Draft Lists	Municipal Archives, State or Provincial Archives
Military Service Records	National Archives
Naturalization Records	Local Civil Register Archives, National Archives
Nobility Records	Municipal Archives, National Archives
Notarial Records — Contracts, Testaments	Municipal Archives, State or Provincial Archives, National Archives
Passenger Lists	National Archives, State or Municipal Archives
Passports	National Archives, State or Provincial Archives
Pensions	National Archives, Military Archives
Priesthood Ordination Records	Diocesan Archives
Probate Records	Municipal Archives, State or Provincial Archives, National Archives
Public Employment Records	Municipal Archives, State or Provincial Archives, National Archives
Purity of Blood Records	National Archives
Tax Records	Municipal Archives, State or Provincial Archives, National Archives
University Records	University Archives, State or Provincial Archives, National Archives
Voting Lists	Municipal Archives

Figure 7-3 Principal types of records and where they can be found

Guides to specific archives and/or individual countries exist for many Hispanic countries and archives. Many archives, such as the Archivo General de la Nación in Mexico City, publish broad guides in book or periodical form, as well as indexes to specific sections of their archives. There may be general guides to all archives in a country or state. For example, *Guia de archivos municipales de Tamaulipas*[9] describes the records of all of the municipal archives in the Mexican state of Tamaulipas. The information contained in these volumes is valuable for those archives that are listed. Unfortunately the list may be incomplete for many localities, so that the absence of an archives listing for a political unit does not necessarily mean that there is no archives. Many of these catalogs will be listed in the Family History Library Catalog. It is also possible to identify others in libraries throughout the world by searching RLIN, WORLDCAT or other library catalogs on the Internet, World Wide Web, or through a local library computer. Use a Key Word Search under "Archivo" or "Archives" and the name(s) of the ancestral locality as well as the political and ecclesiastical divisions to which it belongs or belonged. Also check under the names of the pertinent state and national capital cities.

Figure 7-4 shows information taken from page 680 of the *Censo-Guía de Archivos Españoles*,[10] a national archives guide, showing the variety of records that can be found for a single locality. A researcher interested in Coín, Málaga, Spain, would review this list as part of the Records Analysis to identify the types of records that are available in Coín. For example, the early civil registers from 1841 to 1865 may be the only source for birth or marriage records, as many Spanish parish archives were destroyed in that area during the Civil War. (Note that the 1960 *Guía de la Iglesia* indicates there are four parishes in Coín, so the list of archives on page 680 of the *Censo-Guía* is incomplete.)

If it is known from the People Analysis that the ancestor served in the military, the first item under the *ayuntamiento* (City Hall) archives, *expedientes de quinta*, will be significant since these are military draft records that will contain individual names of those going into military service, along with other information of genealogical import. The local neighborhood census (*padrón vecinal*) would also be of great interest. The Archivo Histórico and the Archivo Notarial are repositories for notarial records, and depending on the status of the family, there could be a wide variety of valuable genealogical materials in these two archives. Also of interest would be court records and various tax records contained in these local archives.

In cases where no information is found about archives or records for a locality, you will need to correspond with the various archives in the area, or visit them in an attempt to ascertain what types of records are available. In some cases, in small localities where there are no trained archivists, even corresponding with the archives will not produce satisfactory results as to what types of records exist, and a trip made either by you or a

	L.	E.	CoL	Málaga (680 F.
COIN				
Ayuntamiento				
Expedientes de quintas			22	1817–1965
Correspondencia			65	1889– "
Actas capitulares	56		34	1604– "
Padrones de ristica y urbana			12	1901–1965
Documentos varios			10	S.XVI–XIX
Registro matrimonios			1	1841–1865
" nacimientos			3	1845–1869
" defunciones			2	1841–1869
Padrón vecinal			11	1858–1965
Klecciones de concejales			1	1851–1905
Arrendamiento de arbitrios			2	1866–1965
Repartimiento de utilidades			7	1924–1944
Matrícula industrial			1	1893–1965
Nombramientos de guardas			2	1907–1935
Expedientes de sanidad y beneficencia			1	
Contabilidad, intervención, y depositaría	120		101	1916–1965
Archivo Histórico				
Fondos generales			550	1504–1865
Archivo Notariales				
Fondos generales			397	1866–1965
Juzgado Municipial (Registro civil)				
Nacimientos			96	1871–1965
Matrimonios			39	1871– "
Defunciones			75	1871– "
Juicios de faltas			80	1933– "
Asuntos civiles y gubernativos			40	1931– "
Registro civil			38	1931– "
Registro de panados	4		1	1945– "
Juzgado de 1ª Instancia e Instrucción				
Asuntos civiles	3		37	1940–1965
" criminales	5		36	1944– "
" gubernativos	2		15	1940– "
Parroquia de San Juan				
Bautismos	60			1571–1965

Figure 7-4 Page from *Censo-Guía de Archivos Españoles*

paid professional genealogist will be necessary to ascertain what records are available.

In addition to the records that appear in local archives, you should be aware that many local records have been transferred to central provincial archives. In the case of Coín referred to in figure 7-4, the parish records have now all been transferred to a central diocesan archives in the capital city of Málaga. You will always want to search state, provincial and regional archives for information of a local nature. When searching for these in the Family History Library Catalog, look under both the state or province and its capital city.

The major national archives of the country where you are researching should also be checked, since it may have materials relating to your particular ancestor or his locality. For example, there will be no Inquisition records available in a town such as Tuéjar in Valencia, Spain, or even in the regional archives in Valencia. There is, however, information about members and victims of the Inquisition who lived in Tuéjar in the Archivo Histórico Nacional in Madrid, Spain. The same would be true for national census records, for most military records, for records of military fraternal orders, and for any other type of national organization where the records would have been centralized. Many local census records are to be found filed in regional or national archives. For example, early military census records for Tucson, Arizona are found in the Archives of the Indies in Seville, Spain and in the Franciscan Archives housed in the *Biblioteca Nacional* in Mexico City. Early California censuses and descriptions of early colonizing expeditions are to be found in the Archivo General de la Nación in Mexico City. These examples show that consulting a national archives for both your ancestral surname and locality may yield additional information about your family. Many indexes to national collections of records will be arranged with both name and locality indexes, so the process of searching in the indexes of national archives may be the beginning point of your research process.

For records dealing with a particular locality or family, you should also check libraries and archives in the United States, especially those in the southwest — such as the University of Texas, the University of Arizona, and the Bancroft Library at the University of California in Berkeley — where there is great interest in Hispanic culture. In addition, other libraries connected with universities in California, Arizona, Texas, and Florida have also filmed original Hispanic records. A review of periodicals and bibliographies concerning your particular country or locality of research should yield important information about sources for copies of original records.

LOCALITY AND RECORDS ANALYSES SAMPLE

Situation: George Gonzalez was born and raised in California, but whenever he talked with his parents about their birth place, his father always jokingly referred to it as "a peach of a place" in Guatemala, referring to the name of the place as *El Durazno*. His mother always insisted she was from Jalapa. After his parents' death he wrote to an aunt in Florida who replied that she and her sister (George's mother), were born in Mataquesquinla. She also indicated that, while she did not have any birth records, she knew she was born in Mataquesquinla and remembered visiting her father's mother's home in a place called La Laguneta just before they left for the United States.

Analysis: George began his search at the local university library, where he located a copy of the *Index of the Map of Hispanic America*. In the sections on Guatemala on page 202 of that index, he found no entry for El Durazno or La Laguneta, but did find one for Jalapa as a major *departamento* and as a *municipio*. He also found a separate *municipio* named Mataquesquinla in the *departamento* of Jalapa. He then obtained a copy of the *Diccionario geográfico de Guatemala*, a multi-volume geographical dictionary published in Guatemala in 1961. In that book he looked under El Durazno and found the long list of entries listed for that name on page 219 of Volume 1, as reproduced in Figure 7-5. In reviewing the list he initially despaired at how many places there were with that name. Upon careful examination, however, he noted an El Durazno which was an *aldea* in the *municipio* of Jalapa and had a *caserío* in it called La Laguneta.The correlation of both El Durazno and La Laguneta led him to believe that he had probably located the correct *municipio*. He guessed that his mother was probably from the *municipio* of Mataquesquinla in the *departamento* of Jalapa, and his father was from the *municipio* of Jalapa. He further surmised that his father had lived within that *municipio* (Jalapa) in the *aldea* of El Durazno, and that the house was located within that *aldea* in the *caserío* of La Laguneta. He then consulted the Family History Library Catalog in his hometown LDS family history center and found that there were civil register films for both the municipality of Mataquesquinla in the *departamento* of Jalapa, and also for the *municipio* of Jalapa in that same *departamento*. In addition, he found parish registers for Mataquesquinla running back to 1688. He was then able to order the civil register films and locate the birth records of his parents in the late 1870s, his mother in Mataquesquinla, and his father in Jalapa.

BEGINNING RESEARCH IN ORIGINAL SOURCES

The list of what records are available that you develop in preparing the Records Analysis will bring you to the point of consulting original records.You will have accumulated all of the information you can from home and family sources, and have checked for research done by others both in printed sources and in LDS Church genealogical records. In addi-

EL DUENDE, paraje en jurisd. mun. Dolores, Pet.
EL DULCE NOMBRE, antes La Culebra, aldea del mun. Palencia, Gua. 88 hab.
EL DULCE NOMBRE, caserío de la cab. mun. San José, Esc.
EL DURAZNITO, caserío de la aldea El Durazno, mun. Jalapa, Jal.
EL DURAZNO, aldea del mun. Amatitlán, Gua. 303 hab. *(Amygdalus persica.)* Aprox. a 6 km. de la cab. Tiene el caserío

Chajil

EL DURAZNO, aldea del mun. Villa Canales, Gua. 254 hab. Aprox. a 3 km. de la cab. Tiene el caserío

Colmenitas

EL DURAZNO, aldea del mun. Chiquimula, Chiq. 338 hab. Tiene los caseríos

Limar
Pinalón
Limón

EL DURAZNO, aldea del mun. San Pedro Pinula, Jal. 252 hab. Aprox. a 17 km. de la cab.
EL DURAZNO, aldea del mun. Río Blanco, S. M. 325 hab. Tiene el caserío
Patzeque
EL DURAZNO, aldea del mun. San Jerónimo, B. V. 63 hab. Aprox. a 10 km. de la cab.
EL DURAZNO, aldea del mun. Chinautla, Gua. 668 hab. Tiene los caseríos

El Guayabo
Los Altos
La Laguneta

EL DURAZNO, aldea del mun. Jalapa, Jal. 562 hab. Aprox. a 28 km. de la cab. Tiene los caseríos

La Laguneta
Urayansapo
Lagunita
El Duraznito

EL DURAZNO, caserío de la aldea El Jícaro, mun. San Jerónimo, B. V. 14 fam.
EL DURAZNO, caserío de la aldea El Trapichillo, mun. La Libertad, Hue.
EL DURAZNO, caserío de la aldea Raxjut, mun. Rabinal, B. V. 25 fam. Aprox. a 4 km. de la cab.
EL DURAZNO, caserío del mun. Chinique, Qui.
EL DURAZNO, caserío de la aldea Chiquililá, mun. Ixtahuacán, Hue. 24 hab.
EL DURAZNO, caserío de la aldea Soledad Colorado, mun. Mataquescuintla, Jal. Aprox. a 18 km. de la cab.
EL DURAZNO, caserío de la aldea San Miguel, mun. Mataquescuintla, Jal. Aprox. a 13 km. de la cab.
EL DURAZNO, caserío de la aldea Escaleras, mun. San Agustín Acasaguastlán, Pro. 30 hab.
EL DURAZNO, sitio arqueológico en mun. San Pedro Jalapa, Jal.
EL DURAZNO, montaña en jurisd. mun. Concepción Las Minas, Chiq.
EL DURAZNO, loma al Este de la cab. mun. Chimaltenango, Chim.
EL DURAZNO, río en jurisd. mun. Zacualpa, Qui.
EL DURAZNO, riachuelo en jurisd. mun. La Libertad, Hue.
EL DURAZNO, riachuelo en jurisd. mun. Mataquescuintla, Jal.
EL DURAZNO, arroyo en jurisd. mun. Malacatancito, Hue.
EL DURAZNO, quebrada en jurisd. mun. Rabinal, B. V.
EL DURAZNO, quebrada en jurisd. mun. Jalapa, Jal.
EL EDÉN, aldea del mun. Palestina de los Altos, Que. 2,920 mts. SNM. Latitud 14°57′10″, longitud 91°39′32″. 1,086 hab. Tiene el caserío
La Cumbre
EL EMBARCADERO, caserío de la aldea El Paraíso, mun. Moyuta, Jut.
EL ENCANTO, caserío de la aldea Chisiram, mun. San Cristóbal Verapaz, A. V. 50 hab.
EL ENCANTO, cerro en jurisd. aldea Puerta Abajo, mun. Zaragoza, Chim.
EL ENCANTO, río en jurisd. mun. San Bernardino, Such.
EL ENCINAL, aldea del mun. Huité, Za. 147 hab.
EL ENCINAL, caserío de la cab. mun. San Antonio La Paz, Pro. 31 hab.

Figure 7-5 Page from *Diccionario geográfico de Guatemala*

tion, you will have completed the analyses discussed in this chapter. These analyses will have indicated to you a series of records, which can now be consulted to see if they do in fact contain information about the particular ancestor or ancestral family for which you are searching.

Initially, many readers may not need to go beyond working with parish and civil registers, as these records, when preserved, can be very extensive. However, for a good family history other records will eventually have to be used. The remaining chapters in this book about records are designed to help you become familiar with the variety, nature, and use of certain other Hispanic records. As your research expands beyond the parish and civil register, or in the case where no such registers exist or you are not sure from which parish your ancestor came, you will need to carefully review those chapters.

Research Calendar

As you actually begin your research, you will want to make use of the systems discussed in chapter 3 for organizing and evaluating the information you find, and also for determining further objectives in your search. To assist in this effort, a calendar or log should be kept of all of the research that you do. In this way, you can rapidly review what sources have or have not been checked, when they were checked, and if it is necessary to review them again. This research log can be a simple affair similar to figure 7-6. The form should indicate the place of research, a description of the source examined including any identifying library reference numbers, the date of the search, and a reference as to the place where the results of the search are filed. Generally, it is convenient to number all documents in a particular file, whether this be a family surname file, an individual file, or a records type of file, enabling the researcher to rapidly find information from any particular search.

The research calendar should be kept on a continual basis as you do research. When each new record source is checked, an entry should be made at that time on the research log. The value of a log that records all research done will be lost if an attempt is made to reconstruct the events several days, weeks, or months after the fact.

Research Reports and Notetaking

In addition to keeping a research calendar, you should write periodic research reports, just as a professional genealogist writes for the family who pays for his research. These reports form an on-going record of the research being done. They also include information relating to the analysis and thought processes involved in reviewing the various documents. This research report not only benefits other members of the family, but it can be of great value for you as well. In instances where you have not worked with the family line for an extended period of time, the research

RESEARCH LOG

ANCESTOR ______________________ RESEARCHER ______________________

JURISDICTION ____

PLACE OF RESEARCH	DESCRIPTION OF SOURCE including call no.	DATE OF SEARCH	FILE REFERENCE

GENEALOGICAL RESEARCH SUPPLY, P. O. BOX 1534, SALT LAKE CITY, UTAH 84110 5-75

Figure 7-6 Sample research log

report can refresh your memory as to steps that were taken in determining objectives, and can help you know where to proceed.

After having worked for an extended period of time on a particular line, you will find your time well spent to sit down and make a report of your activities in researching that family line. Val D. Greenwood suggests that six elements should make up this research report:[11]

1. A brief explanation of the problem.
2. A notation of the records you have searched.
3. A statement of your reasons for searching those records.
4. Your findings therein.
5. Your interpretation and evaluation of these findings as they relate to the problem (in whatever detail is required).
6. An outline of the problem as it now stands and suggestions on what needs to be done next.

The above points need not be discussed in numbered order, but each of them should be covered in the process of writing the report. Where a report covers several goals or problems in working on a particular family line, each of the above points must be covered for each problem that the researcher is working on. Covering all the points is especially crucial where the research involves complex connections between generations. Being able to remember the sources checked, and the reasoning behind particular connections recorded in a permanent record, will prove invaluable in the future for reviewing research already completed and determining the next steps to be taken.

You will want to make sure in taking notes that they are clear and legible. It is recommended that notes be taken in ink and that they be recorded in a permanent form to be filed in the appropriate file. In referring to any books or other types of records or sources, always indicate either a library reference number or a description of the location of the book so that any researcher in years to come can find the original source. Notes of a temporary nature, such as "need to check death records for the death date of Juan Gomez," should be discarded when the particular temporary instruction has been fulfilled and a permanent record has been made. (In this example, the permanent record must state that a search was made for the death record of Juan Gomez, and it can be found on page 215 of Death Book 10 in the parish of Solana.) By eliminating all temporary research instructions after they have been followed, confusion as to what has been done and what needs to be done can be greatly reduced.

SELECTED BIBLIOGRAPHY of Hispanic Locality Reference Works by Country

The reference works that follow may be located in public and university libraries throughout the United States. In many cases they can also be ordered on microform at the local LDS family history centers. After each entry appears one or more references where the author has located a copy. BYU indicates the work is found in the Harold B. Lee Library at Brigham Young University, Provo, Utah. FHL followed by a film number, indicates it may be ordered on microform at one of the LDS family history centers near. FHL standing alone indicates that it is available in book form at the Family History Library in Salt Lake City, Utah. Where not available at one of these locations, a specific university is named and a library call number given. Most can also be located through library catalogs on the Internet and ordered to your local library through inter-library loan.

ARGENTINA

Modern Atlases and Maps

Atlas de la República Argentina. Buenos Aires: Instituto Geográfico Militar, 1972. (BYU G 1755 .A72 1965) (2nd ed. 1972 FHL)

Kleiner, Alberto. *Atlas de los territorios de la Jewish Colonization Association en Argentina y Brasil, 1913–1941.* Buenos Aires: Poligono, 1983. (BYU G 1756 .E27 K54x 1983)

Gazetteers

Guia de la secretaría de estado y comunicaciones. Buenos Aires: La Secretaría, 1949. (FHL film no. 1162430 item 3)

Marazzo, Javier. *Nuevo diccionario geográfico histórico de la República Argentina.* Buenos Aires: Talleres Randaelli, 1921. (FHL film no. 1162484 item 10)

Geographical Dictionaries

Marrazzo, Javier. *Ciudades, pueblos y colonias de la República Argentina.* 2nd ed. Buenos Aires: Talleres Gráficos "Optimus," 1910. (FHL film 0845238 item 2)

Marrazzo, Javier. *Nuevo diccionario geográfico historico de la República Argentina.* Buenos Aires: Talleres Randaelli, 1921. (FHL film 1162484 item 10)

Historical Atlases, Maps, and Materials (pre-1900)

Indice de Nombres geográficos y etnográficos del Virreinato del Rio de la Plata: y regiones limitrofes con la nomina de los treinta pueblos del las misiones guaraniticas. Salt Lake City: filmado por la Sociedad Genealogica de Utah, 1989. (FHL film 1614821 item 4)

Latzin, Francisco. *Diccionario geográfico Argentino: con amplicaciones enciclopedias rioplatenses.* Buenos Aires: Jacobo Peuser, 1899. (FHL film 08966818 item 1)

Navamuel, Ercilia. *Atlas histórico de Salta.* Limache, Salta, República Argentina: Araoz Anzoategui Impresores, 1986. (BYU Maps G 1758 .S2 N38x 1986)

Paz Soldán, Mariano Felipe, *Diccionario geográfico estadístico nacional argentino.* Buenos Aires: Félix Lajouane, 1885. (FHL film 0873667 item 2)

Ecclesiastical Directories

Anuario eclesiástico de la República Argentina. Buenos Aires: Instituto Bibliotecologia del Arzobispado de Buenos Aires, 1961. (CIDOC Collection no. 21040) (FHL film 0249924)

Guía eclesiástica de la República Argentina. Editada por la Revista Eclesiastíca del Arzobispado de Buenos Aires, 1946. (CIDOC Collection no.1366/1)

BOLIVIA

Modern Atlases and Maps

Atlas censal de Bolivia. La Paz, Bolivia: Instituto Nacional de Estadística, 1982. (BYU Maps G 1746 E2 A8x 1982)

Camacho Lara, Rene R. *Atlas de Bolivia.* La Paz: R.R. Camacho Lara, 1958. (BYU Maps G 1745 .C356x)

Gazetteers

División política de Bolivia. La Paz: Instituto Geográfico Militar, 1968. (FHL film 1102977 item 5)

Historical Atlases, Maps, and Materials

Indice de nombres geográficos y etnográficos del virreinato del Rio de la Plata: y regiones limitrofes con la nomina de los treinta pueblos del las misiones guaraniticas. Salt Lake City: filmado por la Sociedad Genealógica de Utah, 1989. (FHL film 1614821 item 4)

Pozo Cano, Raul del. *Paraguay-Bolivia, la real cedula de 1743 a la luz de la geografía de la epoca.* Asunción: Imprenta Nacional, 1935. (BYU G 1771 .F2 P68x)

Ecclesiastical Directories

Anuario eclesiástico de Bolivia, ano 1964. (CIDOC Collection 21,064/1) (FHL)

Lopez Menendez, Felipe. *Anuario eclesiástico de Bolivia, 1953.* (CIDOC Collection no. 1651/1)

BRAZIL

Modern Atlases and Maps

Atlas do Brasil Globo. Pôrto Alegre: Editôra Globo, 1960. (FHL)

Quadro dos municípios brasileiros vigorante no. Rio de Janeiro: Impresa Nacional, 1939. (FHL)

Gazetteers

Guía postal (geogrâphico) da República dos Estados Unidos do Brasil. Rio de Janeiro: Directoria Geral dos Correios, 1930–31. (FHL film 1102988)

Supplement to Brazil Gazetteer. Washington, D.C.: Defense Mapping Agency, 1992. (BYU F 2504 .S87 1992)

VIII recenseamento geral do Brasil, 1970: código de municípios. Rio de Janeiro: Instituto Brasileiro de Estatística, 1970. (FHL)

Geographical Dictionaries

Dicionário da terra e da gente do Brasil. Sao Paulo: Companhia Editora Nacional, 1961. (FHL film 0908537 item 1)

Dicionário geográfico Brasileiro Porto Alegre, Brazil: Editora Globo, 1966, 1972. (1st ed. BYU F 2504 .D5; 2nd ed. BYU F2504 .D524x 1972) (FHL)

Ecclesiastical Directories

Anuario católico do Brasil. 3rd ed. Petropolis, Rio de Janeiro: Editora Vozes Limitadas, 1966. (CIDOC Collection no. 21017) (2nd ed. FHL film 0962910)

Rossi, Agnolo. *Diretorio protestante no Brasil.* Campinas: Tip. Paulista, 1939. (CIDOC Collection no. 970/1)

Encyclopedias

Grande Enciclopédia Portuguesa e Brasileira. Lisboa, Rio de Janeiro: Editorial Enciclopédia, limitada, 1936–60. (BYU AE 37 .G7)

CHILE

Modern Atlases and Maps

Atlas geográfico de Chile para la educación. 2nd ed. Santiago: Instituto Geográfico Militar, 1988. (BYU G 1750 .I54x 1988)

Gazetteers

Supplement to Chile Gazetteer. Washington, D.C.: Defense Mapping Agency, 1992. (BYU Maps F 3054 .S87 1992)

Geographical Dictionaries

Diccionario jeográfico de Chile. Salt Lake City: Filmado por la Sociedad Genealógico de Utah, 1973. (FHL film 0897925 item 1)

Solano Asta-Buruaga y Cienfuegos, Francisco. *Diccionario geográfico de la República de Chile.* Santiago: n.p., 1899. (FHL film 0496805 item 2) (1867 ed. FHL film 0897024 item 1)

Historical Atlases, Maps, and Materials

Atlas cartográfico del Reino de Chile, siglos XVII – XIX. Santiago: Instituto Geográfico Militar, 1981. (BYU Maps G 1750 I48 1981)

Relaciones Chileno-Argentinas: la controversia del Canal Beagle. Geneve: Imprenta Atar, 1979. (BYU Maps G 1751 .F2 R4 1979)

Silva G., Osvaldo. *Atlas de historia de Chile.* Santiago: Editorial Universitaria, 1984. (BYU G 1750 .S 54x 1984)

Ecclesiastical Directories

Díaz Vial, Raul. *Revista de estudios históricos.* "Situación de los libros parroquiales." No. 10 (1960/1961) (FHL)

Guía de la Iglesia en Chile, 1976. Santiago: Ediciones Mundo, 1976. (FHL film 1149536 item 2)

Guía eclesiástica de Chile. Santiago: Arzobispado de Santiago de Chile, 1956. (CIDOC Collection no. 21071) (1964 ed. FHL film 1162496 item 10)

Guía eclesiástica de Chile. Santiago: Estadística de la Acción Católica Chilena, 1944. (CIDOC Collection no. 1649/1)

Guía eclesiástica y parroquial de Chile. Santiago: Arzobispado de Santiago, 1972. (FHL film 0908643 item 3)

Guía parroquial de Chile, 1959. Santiago: Talleres "Claret," 1959. (FHL)

Parroquias de la arquidiócesis de Santiago, 1840–1925. 1980. Santiago: Arzobispado de Santiago, 1980. (FHL) (CIDOC Collection no. 1648/1)

Parroquias de la arquidiócesis de Santiago de Chile en 1929. Santiago: Imprenta Arturo Prat, 1929. (FHL film 1162481 item 6)

COLOMBIA

Modern Atlases and Maps

Atlas de Colombia. Bogotá: Instituto Geográfico Agustín Codazzi, 1977. (3rd ed. BYU Maps G 1730 .C65 1977) (2nd ed. FHL)

Atlas Básico de Colombia. Bogotá: Instituto Geográfico Agustín Codazzi, 1989. (BYU G 1730 .I53 1989)

Gazetteers

Gazetteer of Colombia. 3rd ed. Washington, D.C.: Defense Mapping Agency, 1988. (BYU F2254 .G39 1988)

Geographical Dictionaries

Codazzi, Agustín. *Diccionario geográfico de Colombia.* Bogotá: La Subdirección, 1980. (BYU F 2254 .D53 1980 2 vol) (1971 ed. FHL)

Colombia división político administrativa, 1992. Bogotá: DANE, 1992. (FHL)

Esquerra Ortiz, Joaquin. *Diccionario geográfico de los Estados Unidos de Colombia.* Bogotá: J.B. Gaitán, 1879. (FHL film 0599568 item 2)

Gómez, Eugenio J. *Diccionario geográfico de Colombia.* Bogotá: Banco de la República, 1953. (FHL)

Rojas Morales, Ernesto. *División político administrativa de Colombia.* Bogotá: Departmento Administrativo Nacional de Estadística, 1970. (FHL film 1102977 item 4)

Historical Atlases, Maps, and Materials

Atlas de Cartografía Histórica de Colombia. Bogota: Instituto Geográfico Agustín Codazzi, 1985. (BYU G 1730 .A84x 1985)

Atlas de mapas antiguos de Colombia, siglos XVI a XIX. Bogotá: Litografía Arco, 19 — . (FHL film 0873924 item 1)

Blanco, Augustin. *Atlas histórico geográfico de Colombia.* Archivo General de la Nación, 1992. (BYU Maps G 1730 .B63 1992)

Ecclesiastical Directories

Anuario de la Iglesia Católica en Colombia, 1961. Bogotá: Centro de Investigaciones Sociales, 1961. (CIDOC Collection no. 21020) (FHL)

Anuario de la Iglesia Católica en Colombia, 1953. Bogotá: Editorial "El Catolicismo," 1953. (CIDOC Collection no. 21090)

Parroquias de Colombia, según jurisdicciones: directorio. Bogotá: n.p., 1974. (FHL)

COSTA RICA

Modern Atlases and Maps

Chinchilla Valenciano, Eduardo. *Atlas cantonal de Costa Rica.* San José, Costa Rica: Instituto de Fomento y Asesoria Municipal, 1987. (BYU G 1580 .C54x 1987)

Gazetteers

Gazetteer of Costa Rica, 2nd ed. Washington: Defense Mapping Agency, 1983. (BYU F1542 .G39x 1983)

Geografía ilustrada de Costa Rica. Salt Lake City: filmado por la Sociedad Genealógico de Utah, 1973. (FHL film 0897927 item 2)

Geographical Dictionaries

Costa Rica: analisis regional de recursos fisicos Centroamerica y Panama. Washington: Aid Resources Inventory Center, U.S. Army, 1965. (BYU G 1580 .U52 1965)

Noriega, Felix F. *Diccionario geográfico de Costa Rica*. 2nd ed. San José, Costa Rica: Imprenta nacional, 1923. (BYU F1542 .N 842 1923)

Historical Atlases, Maps, and Materials

Hernandez, Hermogenes. *Costa Rica: evolución territorial y principales censos de población, 1502–1984*. San José, Costa Rica: Editorial Universidad Estatal a Distancia, 1985. (BYU Maps G 1581 .E25 H4 1985)

Ecclesiastical Directories

Anuario eclesiástico, 1990. San José, Costa Rica: Secretariado Conferencia Episcopal, 1990. (FHL)

Estado del clero de la Provincia de Costa Rica 1966. San José, Costa Rica: Imp. Metropolitana, 1966. (FHL)

CUBA

Modern Atlases and Maps

Atlas de Cuba. La Habana: Instituto Cubano de Geodesia y Cartografía, 1978. (BYU G 1605 .I5 1978) (FHL film 1162487 item 2)

Nuevo atlas nacional de Cuba. La Habana: Instituto de Geografía de la Academia de Ciencias de Cuba, 1989. (BYU Maps G 1605 .N83x 1989)

Gazetteers

Gazetteer of Cuba, Vol I & II. 3rd ed. Washington, D.C.: Defense Mapping Agency, 1991. (BYU F 1754 .G39 1991)

Sánchez-Johnson, Mayra F. *Locality Guide for Cuba*. Salt Lake City: Cuban Genealogical Society, 1992. (FHL)

Historical Atlases, Maps, and Materials

Atlas of Ports, Cities, and Localities of the Island of Cuba. Washington, D.C.: Norris Peters Co., 1898. (BYU G 1605 .U5 1898)

Atlas geográfico de España, islas adyacentes y posesiones españoles de ultramar. Madrid: Gaspar y Roig, 1864. (FHL film 0897114 item 1)

Ecclesiastical Directories

Martin Leisaca, Juan. *Apuntes para la historia eclesiástica de Cuba*. Habana: Talleres Tipográficas de Carana, 1938. (U. of Florida 282.72 L532)

Encyclopedias

Báez, Vicente, ed. *La Enciclopedia de Cuba*. Madrid: Playor, S.A., 1973.

DOMINICAN REPUBLIC

Geographical Dictionaries

Chauvet, Robert and Henri. *Grande géographie de l'île d'Haiti*. Paris: Imprimerie Goupy, G. Maurin, successeur, 1896. (FHL film 1102984 item 2, 1976 and 1149536 item 1, 1978)

Ecclesiastical Directories

Directorio del personal eclesiástico en la República Dominicana, 1981–1982. Santo Domingo: Secretaría del INP, 1981. (FHL)

Encyclopedias

Enciclopedia Dominicana, Tomo I. Santo Domingo, R.D.: Enciclopédica Dominicana, S.A., 1986–1988. (BYU F 1932 .E52 1986)

ECUADOR

Modern Atlases and Maps

Atlas geográfico de la República del Ecuador. Quito: El Instituto, 1977. (BYU G 1735.E3 1977)

Atlas geográfico del Ecuador. Quito: Gráficas Claridad, 1975–1976. (BYU G 1735.S2 1979)

División territorial de la República de Ecuador. Quito: Junta naciional de Planificación y Coordinación, 1968. (FHL)

Gomez E., Nelson. *Atlas del Ecuador: geografía y economía.* Quito: Editorial Ediguias, 1990. (BYU G 1735 .G65x 1990)

Mapa especial, carreteras principales del Ecuador. Quito: Ministerio de Obras Públicas, 1966. (FHL)

Gazetteers

División política territorial. Quito: M. Jaramillo, 1967. (FHL)

Historical Atlases, Maps, and Materials

Atlas histórico-geográfico del Ecuador. Quito: Instituto geográfico militar, 1990. (G 1735 .S36x 1990)

Ecclesiastical Directories

Directorio de la Iglesia en el Ecuador. Quito: 1963. (CIDOC Collection no. 21045)

La Iglesia en el Ecuador, 1949. Quito: Editorial franciscana “Fray Jadoco Ricke,” 1949. (FHL film 0873924 item 3)

EL SALVADOR

Modern Atlases and Maps

Atlas censal de El Salvador. San Salvador: n.p., 1955. (BYU G 1570 .S3 1955)

Gazetteers

Gazetteer of El Salvador. Washington, D.C.: Defense Mapping Agency, 1982. (BYU F1482 .S9)

Geographical Dictionaries

Diccionario geográfico de El Salvador, tomo I & II. San Salvador: Instituto Geográfico Nacional, 1971. (BYU F1482 .D53 1971)

Ecclesiastical Directories

Anuario eclesiástico de El Salvador, 1963. San Salvador: Secretaría Social Interdiocesano Arzobispado, 1963. (CIDOC Collection no. 21013)

GUATEMALA

Gazetteers

Gazetteer of Guatemala. 2nd ed. Washington, D.C.: Defense Mapping Agency, 1984.

Morales Urrutia, Mateo. *La división política y administrativa de la República de Guatemala con sus datos históricos y de legislación*. 2 vols. Guatemala: Editorial Iberia-Gutenburg, 1961. (FHL film vol. 1, 0924656 and vol. 2, 0924657)

Prado Ponce, Eduardo. *Comunidades de Guatemala*. Guatemala: AGAYC, 1984, c1985. (FHL)

Geographical Dictionaries

El libro de las geonimias de Guatemala: diccionario entimológico. Guatemala: Editorial "José de Pineda Ibarra," 1973. (FHL)

Gall, Francis, ed. *Diccionario geográfico de Guatemala*. Guatemala, C.A.: Instituto Geográfico Nacional, 1976. 4 vols. (BYU F1462 .D53 1976) (1961–1964 ed., 2 vols. FHL film 0873808)

Mejía, José Victor. *Geografía de la República de Guatemala*. Salt Lake City: Filmado por la Sociedad Genealógico de Utah, 1973. Microreproducíon de publicación original: 2nd ed. Guatemala: Tipografía Nacional, 1927. (FHL film 1090481 item 3)

Suplemento del diccionario geográfico de Guatemala, 1961–1964. Guatemala: Tipográfia Nacional, 1968. (FHL film 1149534 item 5–6)

Historical Atlases, Maps, and Materials

Juarros, Domingo. *A Statistical and Commercial History of the Kingdom of Guatemala in Spanish America*. New York: AMS Press, 1971. (FHL)

Ecclesiastical Directories

Guia de la Iglesia en Guatemala. Guatemala: Imprenta "Santa Isabel," 1967. (FHL film 0873807 item 1)

HONDURAS

Modern Atlases and Maps

Atlas de Honduras y el mundo. Tegucigalpa: Ediciones Ramses, 1991. (BYU G 1565 .A85x 1991)

Castellanos Garcia, J. E. *Atlas geográfico de Honduras*. Tegucigalpa: ServiCopiax, 1980. (BYU G 1565 .C3 1980a)

Guia para investigadores de Honduras. Tegucigalpa: Instituto Geográfico Nacional, 1986. (BYU G 1565 .I47 1986)

Gazetteers

División político territorial. Washington. D.C.: Filmado por Library of Congress, Photoduplication Service, 1970. (FHL film 0847710)

Gazetteer of Honduras. 2nd ed. Washington, D.C.: Defense Mapping Agency, 1983. (BYU F1502 .G39x 1983)

Geographical Dictionaries

Diccionario geográfico de Honduras. Tegucigalpa: Ministerio de Comunicaciones, Obras Públicas y Transporte, Instituto Geográfico Nacional, 1976. (FHL)

Ecclesiastical Directories

Anuario Eclesiástico de Honduras. 1964. (CIDOC Collection no. 21032)

Anuario de la Iglesia de Honduras, 1973. [Tegucigalpa]: Impreso en la Compañía Editora Nacional, 1973. (FHL)

Instituto Geográfico Nacional. *Nombres geográficos de Honduras.* Comayaguela: El Instituto, 1976. (FHL)

MEXICO

Modern Atlases and Maps

Atlas de los estados de la república Mexicana y planos urbanos de las principales ciudades. México, D.F.: HFET, S.A. de C.V., 1993. (BYU Maps G 1545 .H33x 1993)

Enciclopedia de los municipios de México. México, D.F.: Imprenta Nacional, 1990.

García de Miranda, Enriqueta y Zaida Falcón de Gyves. *Nuevo atlas Porrúa de la república mexicana.* México, D.F. : Edit. Porrúa, 1989. (FHL)

Gazetteers

Gazetteer of México, Vols. I & II. 3rd ed. Washington, D.C.: Defense Mapping Agency, 1992. (BYU F 1204 .G38 1992 3 vols)

División municipal de las entidades federativas. México: Dirección General de Estadística, 1938. (FHL film 1102985 item 1–4, 0896970 item 3)

Hinton, Rosie Marie B. *Places of México.* Salt Lake City: Instituto Genealógico e Histórico Latinoamericano, 1987. (FHL)

Localidades de la República por entidades federativas y municipios (del) VIII censo general de población, 1960. México: Talleres Gráficos de la Nación, 1963. (FHL film 0873575)

Peñafiel, Antonio. *División municipal de la república mexicana.* México: Ministerio de Fomento, 1896. (FHL 0896837 item 4)

Geographical Dictionaries

Diccionario porrúa de história, biografía y geografía de México. México, D.F.: Editorial Porrua, 1976. (BYU F 1204 .D56 1976 2 vols)

Diccionario universal de história y de geografía. 4 vols. México, D.F.: Típografía de Rafael, 1853. (FHL film v. 1–2 0599332, v. 3 1162477 item 10, v. 4 0599333)

Garcia Cubas, Antonio. *Diccionario geográfico, histórico y biográfico de los estados unidos Méxicanos.* México, D.F.: Antigua Impr. de Murguia, 1888–91. (BYU F 1204 .G2 5 vols) (FHL film 1102587 vol 1–3, 1102588 vol 4–5)

Historical Atlases, Maps, and Materials

Burrus, Ernest J. *La obra cartográfica de la provincia Mexicana de la Companía de Jesús (1567–1967).* Madrid: José Porrúa Turanzas, 1967. (FHL)

Gerhard, Peter. *Geografía histórica de la Nueva España, 1519–1821.* México, D.F.: Universidad Nacional Autónoma de México, 1986.

Gerhard, Peter. *The North Frontier of New Spain.* Norman, OK: University of Oklahoma Press, 1982. (BYU F 1229 .G47)

Gerhard, Peter. *The Southeast Frontier of New Spain.* Norman, OK: Univ. of Oklahoma Press, 1993. (BYU F 1231 .G42 1993)

A Guide to the Historical Geography of New Spain. Cambridge, [U.K.]: Cambridge Univ. Press, 1972. (FHL)

Ecclesiastical Directories

Directorio de la Iglesia en México. México, D.F.: Buena Prensa, 1952. (CIDOC Collection no. 21014)

Directorio eclesiástico. México: Arzobispado de México, 1968. (FHL)

Galindo Mendoza, Alfredo. *Apuntes geográficos y estadísticos de la iglesia católica en México*. México, D.H.: Administración de la revista La Cruz, 1945. (FHL)

Galindo Mendoza, P. Alfredo. *Apuntes geográficos y estadísticos de la Iglesia Católica en México*. México: Administración de la Revista "La Cruz," 1945. (CIDOC Collection no. 21076)

Platt, Lyman D. *México: guía general: divisiones eclesiásticas*. Salt Lake City: Instituto Genealógico e Histórico Latinoamericano, 1989. (FHL)

Romero Ortigozo, José Antonio. *Directorio de la iglesia en México*. México: Buena Prensa, 1952. (FHL film 1224501 item 3)

Encyclopedias

Alvarez, Josée Rogelio. *Enciclopedia de México*. México, D.F.: Secretaría de Educación Pública, 1987. (BYU F 1204 .E5x 1987)

NICARAGUA

Gazetteers

Gazetteer of Nicaragua. 3rd ed. Washington, D.C.: Defense Mapping Agency, 1985. (BYU F 1522 .G39x 1985)

Geographical Dictionaries

Guerrero, Julián N., y Lola Soriano de Guerrero. *Diccionario nicaragüense geográfico e histórico*. Managua, Nicaragua: Editorial Somarriba, 1985. (FHL)

Ecclesiastical Directories

Anuario eclesiástico de Nicaragua. [León, Nicaragua: Editorial Hispicio], 1967. (FHL)

PANAMA

Modern Atlases and Maps

Atlas de Panamá. Panamá: n.p., 1965. (BYU Maps G 1585 .P3 1965)

Gazetteers

Gazetteer of Panamá. 3rd ed. Washington, D.C.: Defense Mapping Agency, 1990. (BYU F1562 .G39 1990)

Geographical Dictionaries

Diccionario geográfico de Panamá. Panamá: Editorial Universitaria, 1972–1974. 2 vols. (FHL film 1162497 item 2–3)

Jaen Suarez, Omar. *Geografía de Panamá, Tomo I*. Panamá: Biblioteca de la Cultura Panamena, 1985.

Historical Atlases, Maps, and Materials

Jaen Suarez, Omar. *La Población del Istmo de Panamá del siglo XVI al siglo XX*. Panamá, 1978.

Ecclesiastical Directories

Anuario Eclesiástico de Panamá, 1965. Panamá: [n.p., 1965]. (CIDOC Collection no. 21099) (FHL film 1162495 item 2)

Castillero R., Ernesto J. *Breve historia de la iglesia panameña: episcopologios de la diócesis de Panamá*. Panamá: Impresora Panamá, 1965. (FHL)

PARAGUAY

Modern Atlases and Maps

da Ponte, Alberto. *Atlas de la República del Paraguay por departamentos*. Asunción: Instituto Geográfico Militar, 1945. (BYU Maps G 1770 .P6 1945) (FHL)

Emategui, Federico. *Atlas hermes, compendio geográfico del Paraguay*. [Asunción?]: Hermes Editorial Pedagogica, 1977. (BYU Maps G 1770 .E4 1977)

Historical Atlases, Maps, and Materials

Carvallo, Casiano N. *Historia Cartográfica de Misiones*. Posadas, Misiones, Argentina: Ediciones Montoya, 1983. (BYU Maps G 1758 .M5 S1 C37x 1983)

Indice de nombres geográficos y etnográficos del Virreinato del Rio de la Plata: y regiones limitrofes con la nomina de los treinta pueblos del las misiones guaraniticas. Salt Lake City: filmado por la Sociedad Genealógica de Utah, 1989. (FHL film 1614821 item 4)

Manchuca Martinez, Marcelino. *Mapas históricos del Paraguay gigante*. Asunción: [n.p.], 1951. (FHL)

Pozo Cano, Raul del. *Paraguay-Bolivia, La Real Cedula de 1743 a la Luz de la Geografía de la Epoca*. Imprenta Nacional Asunción, 1935. (BYU G 1771 .F2 P68x)

Ecclesiastical Directories

Anuario Eclesiástico del Paraguay. [Asunción?]: Conferencia Episcopal Paraguaya, 1963. (CIDOC Collection no, 21008)

Anuario Eclesiástico del Paraguay. [Asunción?]: Conferencia Episcopal Paraguaya, 1972. (FHL film 1102978 item 2)

PERU

Modern Atlases and Maps

Atlas del Perú Lima: Guia Lascano, 1967. (BYU G 1740 .A85x 1967)

del Aguila, Carlos P., ed. *Atlas del Perú*. Lima: El Instituto, 1989. (BYU G 1740 .I59x 1989)

Nuevo atlas geográfico del Perú. (BYU G 1740 .R64x)

Gazetteers

Cortázar, Pedro Felipe. *Documental del Perú*. Lima, Perú: Imformación Opinión, Publicidad y Encuestas, 19— . (FHL)

Demarcación política del Perú. Lima: Instituto Geográfico Militar, 1983. (FHL)

Demarcación política del Perú por departamento, provincia y distritos. Syracuse, N.Y.: D.J. Robinson, 1989. (FHL film 1224501 item 5)

Geographical Dictionaries

Diccionario geográfico del Perú. Lima: Torres Aguirre, 1922. (BYU F 3404 .S85x 1922) (FHL film 0845239)

Historical Atlases, Maps, and Materials

Alishky, Marvin. *Historical Dictionary of Perú*. Metuchen, N.J.: Scarecrow, 1979. (FHL)

Ecclesiastical Directories

Anuario eclesiástico del Perú. Lima : Arzobispado de Lima, 1947. (FHL fiche 6030554)

Jordán Rodriguez, Jesús. *Pueblos y parroquias de el Perú.* Lima: [Imprenta Pasaje Piura 18], 1950. (FHL film 1162495 item 4)

Encyclopedias

Tauro, Alberto. *Diccionario Enciclopédico del Perú.* Lima: Editorial Juan Mejía Baca, 1966. (FHL film 1162476 item 1–3)

PORTUGAL

Modern Atlases and Maps

Carta de Portugal. Lisboa: Instituto Geográfico e Cadastral, 1935. (FHL)

Gazetteers

Archivo Histórico de Portugal. Lisboa: Typographia Lealdade, 1890. (FHL Film 0973147 item 2–3)

Táboas topográficas e estatísticas, 1801. [Lisboa?: n.p., 1948?] (FHL)

Geographical Dictionaries

Portugal: dicionário histórico, chorográphico, heráldico, biográphico, bibliográphico, numismático e artístico. 7 vols. Lisboa: Joao Romano Torres, 1904–1915. (7 vols. FHL films 0496796, 0496797, 0496799, 0496800, 0496803, 0496804, 0496805 item 1)

Dicionário chorográphico de Portugal, continental e insular. 12 vols. [Porto, Portugal: n.p.], 1929–1949. (FHL fiche 6053542 through 6053553)

Historical Atlases, Maps, and Materials

Os Portuguezes em Africa, Asia, América e Occeania: obra clássica. Lisboa: Borges, 1849–1850. (FHL film 0924833)

Ecclesiastical Directories

Anuario católico de Portugal. [Lisboa?]: O Secretariado, 1931. (FHL)

Encyclopedias

Grande Enciclopédia Portuguesa e Brasileira. Lisboa, Rio de Janeiro: Editorial Enciclopedia, limitada, 1936–60. (BYU AE 37 .G7)

PUERTO RICO

Gazetteers

Geographic Names Information System: Puerto Rico: alphabetical listing, July 1990. Reston, Va.: U.S.2 Geological Survey, National Mapping Division, Office of Geographic Research, 1990. (BYU E 155 .U58 P83x 1990)

Omni Gazetteer of the United States of America. Detroit: Omnigraphics, Inc., 1991. (BYU E 154 .O45 1991) (FHL)

Geographical Dictionaries

Arana-Soto, S. *Diccionario geográfico de Puerto Rico.* San José, P.R.: [n.p.], 1978. (FHL)

Ecclesiastical Directories

Directorio arquidiocesano, San Juan, P.R.: Sección II; parroquias capillas, personal encargado. San Juan, P.R.: La Arquidiócesis, 1980. (FHL film 1162471 item 5)

Estampas de nuestra iglesia. San Germán, P.R.: Editora Corripio, C.,1989. (FHL)

Registros parroquiales de Puerto Rico. Puerto Rico: La Sociedad, 1973. (FHL film 0924733 item 7)

Rodríguez León, Mario A. *Los registros parroquiales y la microhistoria demográfia en Puerto Rico.* San Juan, P.R.: Centro de Estudios Avanzados de Puerto Rico y el Caribe, 1990. (FHL)

Encyclopedias

Báez, Vicente, ed. *La Gran Enciclopedia de Puerto Rico, Tomo I Historia.* Madrid: C. Corredera, 1976.

SPAIN

Modern Atlases and Maps

Atlas geográfico de España. Barcelona: Edit. Alberto Martín, 1953. (FHL Film 0599863 item 1)

Atlas nacional de España. Madrid: Instituto Geográfico y Catastral, 1965. (FHL)

Gran Atlas de España. Pamplona: Salvat, S.A. de eds., 1991. (FHL)

Gazetteers

Nomenclator de las ciudades, villas, lugares, aldeas y demás entidades de población de España. 5 vols. Madrid: Sucesores de Rivadeneyra, 1954. (FHL film 1573122, 1183646 item 6)

Nomenclatura geográfica de España. Barcelona: Ediciones El Albir, 1978. (FHL)

Historical Geographical Dictionaries, Atlases, Maps, and Materials

Atlas geográfico de España, islas adyacentes y posesiones españolas de ultramar. Madrid: Gaspar y Roig, 1864. (FHL film 0897114 item 1)

Bleiberg, Germán. *Diccionario de historia de España.* 2nd ed. Madrid: Revista de Occidente, 1968. (FHL)

González Ponce, Andrés. *Diccionario geográfico de correos de España, con sus posesiones de ultramar.* Madrid: Manuel Morales y Rodríguez, 1856. (FHL film 0599363)

Historical Dictionary of Modern Spain, 1700–1988. Westport, Conn.: Greenwood Press, 1990. (FHL)

Madoz, Pascual. *Diccionario geográfico-estadístico-histórico de España y sus posesiones de ultramar.* Madrid, 1849–1854. (16 vols. FHL film 0897114 item 2 through 0897123) Reprint, Almendralejo (Madrid): Biblioteca Santa Ana, 1989. (BYU DP 12 .M33x 1989)

Menéndez Pidal, Antonio. *Atlas histórico Español.* Barcelona: Editora Nacional, 1941. (FHL Film 0896767 item 3)

Muñoz y Romero, Tomás. *Diccionario bibliográfico-histórico de los antiguos reinos, provincias, ciudades, villas, iglesias y santuarios de Epaña.* Madrid: M. Rivadeneyra, 1858. (FHL film 1181875 item 5)

Ubieto Arteta, Antonio. *Atlas histórico: como se formó España.* Valencia : [n.p.], 1970. (FHL)

Ecclesiastical Directories

Guía de la Iglesia en España. Madrid: Secretariado del Episcopado Español, 1954. Suplementos: 1955, 1956 and 1957. (FHL film 1162424 item 1–4, 0924464 item 1)

Encyclopedias

Gran enciclopedia universal ilustrada Espasa-Calpe. 88 vols. Madrid: Editorial Espasa-Calpe, 1923. (BYU)

URUGUAY

Modern Atlases and Maps

Atlas geográfico de la república oriental del Uruguay. Montevideo: Mosca Hnos., 1980. (BYU G 1765 .P37x 1930)

Daroczi, Isabel. *Atlas para la república oriental del Uruguay.* Montevideo: Ediciones Montevideo S.R.L., 1983. (FHL)

Geographical Dictionaries

Diccionario geográfico del Uruguay. Montevideo: Imprenta Artistica de Dornaleche y Reyes, 1900. (BYU F 2704 .A72x 1900) (FHL film 0599355)

Historical Atlases, Maps, and Materials

Indice de Nombres geográficos y etnográficos del Virreinato del Rio de la Plata: y regiones limitrofes con la nomina de los treinta pueblos del las misiones guaraniticas. Salt Lake City: filmado por la Sociedad Genealógica de Utah, 1989. (FHL film 1614821 item 4)

Ecclesiastical Directories

Anuario Católico, 1949. Montevideo: Acción Católica del Uruguay, 1949. (CIDOC Collection no. 1429/1)

VENEZUELA

Modern Atlases and Maps

Atlas de Venezuela y del mundo. Caracas: Ministerio de Obras Públicas, Dirección de Cartografía Nacional, 1969. (BYU G 1725 .V4 1969)

Geographical Dictionaries

Martinez, Francisco A. *Diccionario geográfico del Estado Tachira.* Merida, Venezuela: Universidad de los Andes <1962>. (BYU F2331 .T2 M3)

Historical Atlases, Maps, and Materials

Cartografía histórica de Venezuela, 1635–1946. Caracas: Comisión Preparatoria de la IV Asamblea General del Instituto Panamericano de Geografía e Historia, 1946. (BYU Maps G 1725 .S1 C37x 1946)

Geográfia de Venezuela y geográfia física universal. Salt Lake City: filmado por la Sociedad Genealógica de Utah, 1973. (FHL film 0897925 item 3)

MacPherson, Telasco A. *Diccionario histórico, geográfico, estadístico y biográfico del estado Miranda (República de Venezuela).* Caracas: Imp. "El Correro de Caracas," 1891. (BYU F 2331 .L3 M2)

Ecclesiastical Directories

Anuario Católico de Venezuela, 1962. Caracas: Libreria Editorial Salesiana, 1962. (CIDOC Collection no. 21019)

Anuario de la Iglesia Católica en Venezuela. Caracas: Centro de Investigaciones Sociales y Socio-religiosas, 1969. (FHL film 0908534 item 1)

Directorio de la Iglesia Católica Venezuela, 1980–81. Caracas: Ediciones SPEV., 1980. (CIDOC Collection no. 21087)

Directorio de la Iglesia Católica en Venezuela, 1977. Caracas: Servicio Estadística de la Iglesia, 1977. (CIDOC no. 21093)

Directorio de la Iglesia Católica en Venezuela, 1975. Caracas: Ediciones SPEV, 1975. (FHL film 1102983 item 1)

---

1. *Nuevo Atlas Porrúa de la Republica Mexicana* (Editorial Porrua: Mexico, D.F., 1980).

2. *Index to the Map of Hispanic America* (Washington: American Geographical Society, 1945).

3. The Hispanic countries covered by the U.S. Board on Geographical Names series, and their numbers in that series, are: Argentina, 103; Bolivia, 4; Brazil, 71; Chile, 6; Costa Rica, 7; Cuba, 30; Dominican Republic, 33; Ecuador, 36; El Salvador, 26; Guatemala, 94; Honduras, 27; Mexico, 15; Nicaragua, 10; Panama, 110; Paraguay, 35; Puerto Rico, 38; Spain and Andorra, 51; Spanish Sahara, 108; Uruguay, 21; Venezuela, 56.

4. The CIDOC Collection, subtitled "Religiosity in Latin America," is a microfiche collection of documents relating primarily to the Catholic Church. Filmed in a library in Mexico that contains the most extensive collection of such materials in Latin America, the hundreds of titles in the collection are divided into ten categories, including pastoral letters, doctrinal works, church periodicals, histories and ecclesiastical directories. This last category is of particular interest as nearly every Latin American country is represented with at least one directory identifying all dioceses and parishes in the country with details such as size, location, titular name, date of creation and/or even date of the earliest parish records existing. In larger countries directories for specific dioceses are found, and the categories — which include diocesan bulletins and histories, many published in the 19th century — represent an as yet unevaluated source of information for the family historian.Also included are several directories of Protestant churches in Latin America, that could be very valuable if the ancestors you seek were among that very small minority of Protestants in Latin America.

   Published by Inter Documentation Company of Zug, Switzerland, the CIDOC Collection numbers several thousand microfiche and is most likely to be found in major university and public libraries. Many of the national ecclesiastical directories are identified by collection reference numbers in the list at the end of this chapter. A computerized catalog of the collection is available from the company and therefore individual works may be found through the regular library card catalogs as well as in sales brochures/catalogs that accompany the collection. Requests to purchase specific microfiche can be addressed to Inter Documentation Company, Post Strasse 14, 6300 Zug, Switzerland.

5. One excellent example of this is Albert Stagg's *The Almedas and Alamos, 1783–1867* (Tucson: University of Arizona Press), which traces the history of Alamos, Sonora, Mexico. Two good examples of the many ethnic local histories resulting from recent interest in ethnic studies are *Fresno's Hispanic Heritage* by Alex M. Zaragoza (Fresno: San Diego Federal Savings and Loan, 1980) and *Nuestras Raices, the Mexican Community in the Central San Joaquin Valley* by Lea Ybarra (Fresno: La Raza Studies Teach Project, C.C.U.F., 1980). Both deal in detail with the history of the Hispanic community in Fresno, California.

6. For example, *The Story of a Parish* (Anaheim, Calif.: St. Boniface Parish, 1961) is the history of St. Boniface parish in Anaheim, California, telling the history of both the parish and Anaheim.

7. It may also prove helpful to review the more detailed discussions on types of records in *Tracing your Hispanic Heritage* by George R. Ryskamp (Riverside, Calif.: His-

panic Family History Research, 1984) or *Fuentes principales* Series H papers published by the LDS Church.

8. Lyman Platt, *Una Guia Genealógico-Histórica de Latino América* (Ramona, Calif.: Acoma Books, 1978). This is also available in an English language edition (Detroit, Mich.: Gale Publishing Co., 1978).

9. *Guia de archivos municipales de Tamaulipas* (Mexico, D.F.: Archivo General de la Nación, 1989).

10. *Censo-Guía de Archivos Españoles* (Spain: Ministerio de Educación y Ciencia, Dirreción General de Archivos, 1972).

11. Val D. Greenwood, *The Researcher's Guide to American Genealogy.* 2nd ed. (Baltimore: Genealogical Publishing Co., Inc., 1990), 110.

CHAPTER 8

Civil Registers

The concept of civil registration became central to European and world record-keeping following the French Revolution. During the first half of the nineteenth century, movements for civil registration arose in Spain and other Hispanic countries, but were effectively blocked by the conservative elements of society which were dominated by the Catholic Church. These elements feared that civil registration would result in a further secularization of society and a reduction of the control that the Church had over the people. The earliest national civil registration law in a Hispanic country was adopted in Mexico in 1859. The last Hispanic country to adopt a civil registration law was Ecuador in 1901.

Civil registers may be found in local *juzgados* (courts), *oficinas municipales* (city offices), or *oficinas del Registro Civil* (offices of the Civil Register) in each district or municipality in Hispanic countries. Larger cities may have several such civil register districts. In rural areas not every small town has a civil register; instead, districts are drawn. Several small towns belong to the same district, usually located in, and carrying the name of, the major town in the area.

Several Latin American countries maintain separate national repositories for copies of all their civil register entries. The chart in figure 8-1 shows the location of civil registers in each Hispanic country, the year such registers commence, and comments on what has been microfilmed and where copies are located.

THE RECORDS

The books of a civil register are organized into three separate sections: births, marriages, and deaths. There is generally one volume or more for each year, although in some cases during the early years where district populations were small, a volume may cover more than one year. Often, each volume and/or each year will be indexed.

In the civil register the format of the entries and the information they contain are similar to those found in parish registers. There is, however, a much greater uniformity among civil register books within a given country and time period than among parish books, due to the fact that the material contained in the civil register is dictated by national law, and the national governments have often provided printed civil register books. The

Country	Starting Year	Comments
Argentina	1881	Copies in provincial archives.
Bolivia	1940	The laws required those born before 1940 to register; marriages between 1898 and 1940 were registered by notaries.
Chile	1885	Copies in Santiago. Many microfilmed by the Genealogical Society of Utah (hereinafter GSU).
Colombia	1865	Many registers contain entries back to 1800; National Index 1865 to 1888.
Costa Rica	1888	Copies of all registers located in San José, arranged by provinces. All provinces have been microfilmed by the GSU.
Cuba	1885	See *Guide to Cuban Genealogical Research* by Peter Carr (Chicago: Adams Press, 1991), 31–32.
Dominican Republic	1828	Many have been microfilmed by the GSU.
Ecuador	1900	Copies located in Quito.
El Salvador	1859	Many have been microfilmed by the GSU, including records for San Salvador which are indexed.
Guatemala	1877	Many microfilmed by the GSU; many copies are found in Guatemala City.
Honduras	1881	Located in the National Archives in Tegucigalpa; many microfilmed by the GSU.
México	1857	Many microfilmed by the GSU; copies also in state archives.
Nicaragua	1879	
Panama	1914	National law required those born before 1914 to register, so that in many cases there are entries for events running back well into the nineteenth century.
Paraguay	1880	
Perú	1886	Note that the law has changed several times since 1886; current law dates from 1936. The extent of compliance, as well as the requirements of the law, have varied at times from 1886 to 1936.
Puerto Rico	1885	Copies of many registers have been centralized in national archives and an index exists which has been microfilmed by the GSU. Civil registration of marriages and deaths dating back to 1778 for some municipalities have been microfilmed by the GSU.
Uruguay	1879	Birth records for the province of Artigas have been microfilmed by GSU.
Venezuela	1873	

Figure 8-1 National Civil Registers of Latin America

information given in a civil register entry also tends to be much more complete than that in early parish entries, and even superior to parish entries of the later nineteenth and early twentieth centuries.

The following paragraphs discuss the content of the three types of entries found in Spain. Civil registers in Spain are the most complete; the completeness of the content of civil registers in other countries varies over time and place, but generally provides the major part of the information found in those of Spain. All have in common the procedure in which a declarant, often the parent or other relative, appeared before the judge or secretary of the civil register and reported the event recorded. The first person described — often with his marital status, age and/or place of birth and/or residence — will be that declarant.

Births

In Spain each civil birth entry contains the following information: the given names and surname(s) of the newborn; the hour, day, month, and year of birth; the town (distinguishable from the municipality or judicial district of the birth); and the street address of the house or the hospital in which the birth took place. Extensive information is also given about each parent, including place of birth, marital status, age, domicile, profession, and in some cases, date of birth. Also recorded in each entry are the given names and surnames, birthplaces, and marital status of the maternal and paternal grandparents and, in some cases, their professions and/or if they have died. The entry usually ends with the names of those witnesses who were present for the act of recording the birth, and their signatures. However, they are not necessarily witnesses of the birth itself.

In addition to all of the above information, each entry begins with a section indicating the person who appeared before the secretary and/or judge of the district to record the birth. The record will give the given names and surnames, place of birth, profession, domicile, and relationship to the baby, if any, of that person. Since in most cases the person doing the reporting is the father, the information about the father will appear in the first section, and in the place where the father's name would normally appear, it will merely state that the father is the *informante* (that is, the person who given the information). Until you become accustomed to this format, which is similar for births, marriages, and deaths, it can be somewhat confusing.

Figure 8-2, a literal certification of the type that should be requested when writing to a civil register, is translated below. Note the extensive detail of the entry. Remember that the first section of the entry is a description of the person who appears before the judge and secretary to report the birth. In this entry, as was most frequently the case, that person is the father of the child.

MINISTERIO DE JUSTICIA
Registros Civiles

CERTIFICACION LITERAL DE INSCRIPCION DE NACIMIENTO - - - (1)

Sección PRIMERA
Tomo 21 - - -
Pág. - - - -
Folio (2) 72 - -

REGISTRO CIVIL DE MONTELLANO - - - - - - - - - - -
Provincia de Sevilla - - - - - - - - - - - - - - - -

El asiento al margen reseñado literalmente dice así: En la villa de Montellano a las ocho de la noche del día primero de Agosto de mil ochocientos ochenta y ocho, ante Don -- Rafael Ruiz Ruiz, Juez Municipal y Don Francisco Bengoechea Tapia, Secretario, compareció Bartolomé Moreno Moreno, natural de esta villa, termino municipal de iden, provincia de Sevilla, de treinta y dos años de edad, casado, del campo, domiciliado en esta villa, calle Utrera, presentado con el objeto de que se inscriba en el Registro Civil una niña; y al efecto como padre de la misma, declaró: Que dicha niña nació en la casa del declarante el día treinta y uno - del anterior, a las tres de la madrugada. Que es hija legítima del declarante y de su mujer Dolores Escobar Romero, natural de esta villa, de veintidos -- años de edad, casada, dedicada alas ocupaciones propias de su sexo, y domiciliada con su marido. Que es nieta por linea paterna de Manuel Moreno Garcia, natural de esta villa, mayor de edad, viudo, y de Juliana Moreno Rodríguez, natural de esta villa, ya -- difunta, y por la linea materna de José Escobar Garcia, natural de esta villa, ya difunto, y de Concepción Romero Colago, natural de esta villa, ya difunta. Y que a la expresada niña se la habia puesto el nombre de CONCEPCION. Todo lo cual presenciaron como testigos Don Juan Garcia Crúz, natural de esta villa, - mayor de edad, casado, empleado, domiciliado en esta villa, y Don Jośe Romero Romero, natural de esta villa, mayor de edad, soltero, empleado y domiciliado en esta villa. Leida integramente este acta, e invitadas las personas que deben suscribirla a que la leyeran porsímismas si así lo creian conveniente, se estampó en ella el Sellor del Juzgado Municipal y la firmaron el Sr. Juez y los testigos presenciales y por el declarante que no sabe, lo hace Don - José de la Rocha, de esta vecindad, y de todo ello como Secretario certifico.- Rafael Ruiz.- José Romero.- J. Garcia.- José de la Rocha.- F. Bengoechea.-

Figure 8-2 Certificate of birth from the Civil Register of Montellano, Savilla, Spain, 1880 (author's copy)

Literal Certification of Inscription of Birth
Civil Register of Montellano
Province of Sevilla

In the town of Montellano at the eighth hour of the night of the first day of August of one thousand eight hundred eighty and eight, before Don Rafael Ruiz, Municipal Judge and Don Francisco Bengoechea Tapia, Secretary, appeared Bartolome Moreno, native of this town, district of the same [name], province of Sevilla, of thirty and two years of age, married, farm worker, citizen of his town, [living on the] street Utrera, is present for the purpose of inscribing in the Civil Register a little girl; and as father of the same [little girl] he declared: that said female child was born in the house of the informant [the father] the thirty-first day of the previous month, at the third hour of the break of dawn. That she is the legitimate daughter of the informant and of his wife Dolores Escobar Romero, native of this town, of twenty-two years of age, married, dedicated to the occupations of her sex, and living with her husband. That she [the newborn] is the granddaughter through paternal lineage of Manuel Moreno Garcia, native of this town, greater in age, widower, and of Juliana Moreno Rodriguez, native of this town, now deceased, and through maternal lineage of Jose Escobar Garcia, native of this town, now deceased, and of Concepcion Romero Colago, native of this town, now deceased. And that the above named female child has been given the name of CONCEPCION. The following presented as witnesses of the above: Don Juan Garcia Cruz, native of this town, adult, married, employed, resident in this town, and Don Jose Romero, native of this town, adult, bachelor, employed and resident of this town. This act was read in its entirety and the persons who should sign were invited to read for themselves if thus they believed it good. It [the document] was stamped with the Seal of the Municipal Judge, and the Judge and the present witnesses they signed and for the informant who does not know how [to write], Don Jose de la Rocha of this [the] locality, signs it and of all this Secretary certifies. — Rafael Ruiz. — Jose Romero. — J. Garcia. — Jose de la Rocha. — F. Bengoechea.

The civil registers often used a marginal note system similar to that of the parish records. Notes as to both marriage and death appear in the margin of the birth record, giving the name of the civil register, and the volume and page numbers of the record of the later event.

Certain transactions involving changing the legal status of the individual were not legally valid until they had been entered into the margin of the birth record. The *legitimación de hijos naturales* (legitimization of illegitimate children) was accomplished by noting in the margin of the birth certificate the date and place of marriage of the parents and frequently, with that notation, the name of the father and of the paternal grandparents. Similar to this, but not requiring the marriage of the parents, was the recognition by the father of the illegitimate child. Such recognition involved a court order, and the details of that order had to be recorded in the margin of the birth certificate before the child could be considered legally recognized by the father. Also, before a legal change in name or surname could be made, there had to be a court order to that effect, and it was recorded in the margin of the birth certificate.

Large numbers of civil registers throughout Spain and Latin America have been destroyed by war and other disasters. In many cases where this has happened, a process has been outlined for the reconstruction (re-inscription) of civil registers. Any person desiring to have a record of his birth or of his parents' births can have a new record made upon presentation of authentic documentation proving the facts that are being reinscribed (for example, a baptismal certificate, certification from a foreign register, a cemetery book, a census record, or a copy of the record to be reinscribed written prior to the destruction of the civil register). If no such documentation exists, the testimony of two witnesses to the veracity of what is being reinscribed is sufficient. Although they might be of recent date, the genealogist should not ignore such reconstituted records.

In one case where a researcher sought out her ancestors, she found that the civil register had been destroyed, but a great-aunt had come in just prior to her death in 1940 and reinscribed her own birth date as well as the birth dates of her parents and one grandfather, who was born in the year 1820. Of course, all records have not been reconstituted. Only those people who have needed some type of legal evidence for a particular purpose, such as filing retirement papers, contesting a will, or claiming a piece of property, have gone to the trouble of reinscribing.

Marriages

A Spanish marriage entry contains the given names and surnames of the bride and groom, with an indication of their marital status, domicile, nationality, age, and place of birth. In some cases the date of birth is also given. The given names and surnames of the parents of both bride and groom, and the *naturaleza* (birthplace) of those parents, are given. The entire act is dated and signed by the witnesses named in the entry. As illustrated by the entry labeled "Numero 17" in figure 8-3, the Mexican civil registration of marriage is often equally complete.

In some civil registers there will also appear a supporting document called *informacion* or *diligencia matrimonial*, giving parental consent to the marriage, indicating there were no impediments and/or providing copies of baptismal certificates. The following translation of figure 8-4 from the civil records of Mitalaguia, Mexico, shows another approach to such documents.

> In the town of Mitalaguia on the eighteenth day of April of the year one thousand eight hundred and four, before me, Juan de la Cruz Peres, Municipal Judge of this area and in charge of the Civil Register, came C. [Citizen] Celedonio Reyes and Miss Ventura Estrada, the first being twenty years of age, single, day laborer and a native and resident of this municipality, the second age thirteen years, single, native and resident of the same town, both contracting parties stated a desire to unite in civil matrimony, for which today they presented themselves. The mothers of both petitioners were present, being that they were orphaned as to their fathers, [and] stated their approval for said marriage.

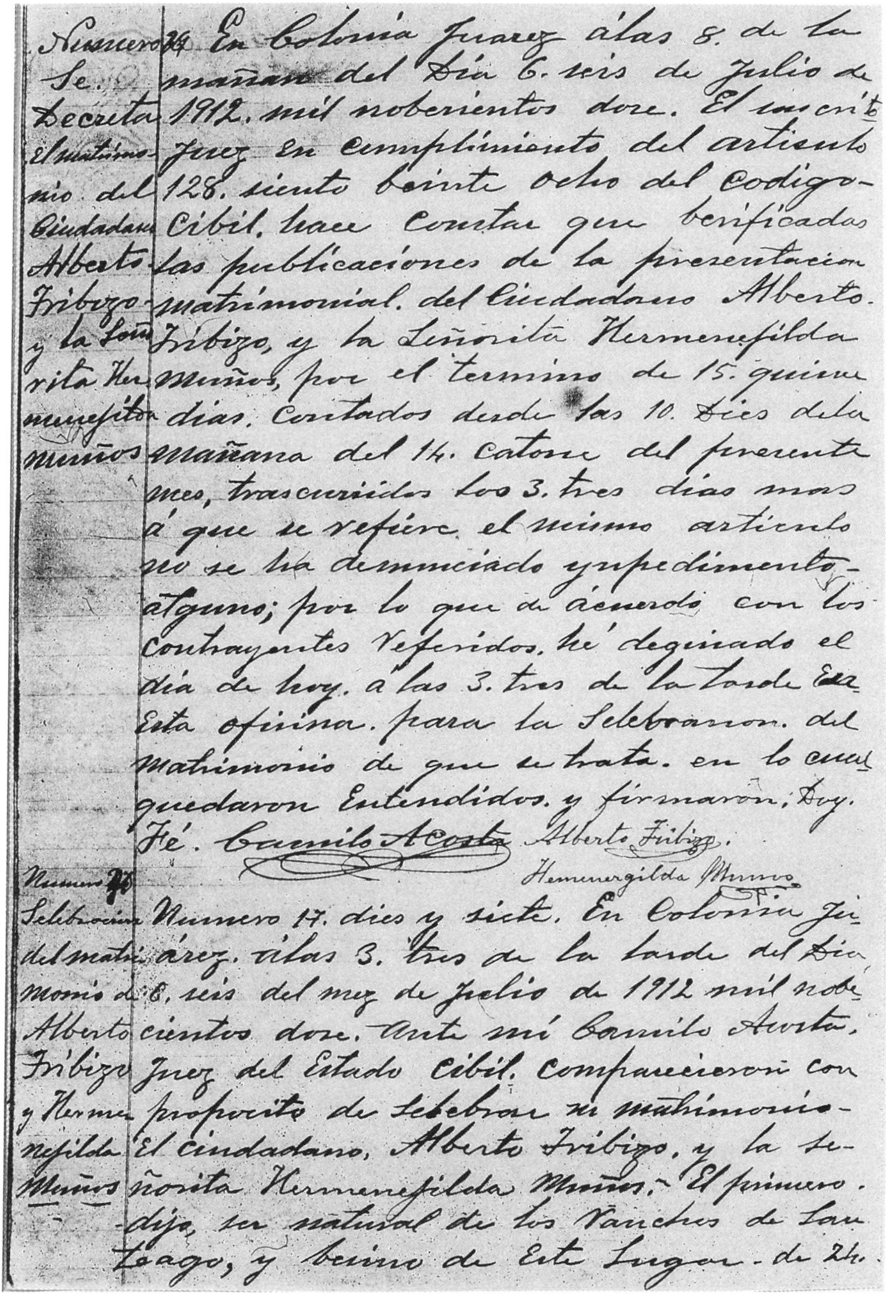

Numero 24 Se. Decreta el matrimonio del Ciudadano Alberto Fribizo y la Señorita Hermenefilda Muños

Numero 24 En Colonia Juarez álas 8. de la mañana del Día 6. seis de Julio de 1912. mil nobecientos dose. El inscrito Juez en cumplimiento del articulo 128. siento beinte ocho del Codigo Cibil. hace constar que berificadas las publicaciones de la presentacion matrimonial. del Ciudadano Alberto Fribizo, y la Señorita Hermenefilda Muños, por el termino de 15. quince dias. Contados desde las 10. dies dela mañana del 14. catorce del presente mes, trascurridos los 3. tres dias mas á que se refiere el mismo articulo no se ha denunciado ympedimento alguno; por lo que de ácuerdo con los contrayentes referidos, he degnado el dia de hoy. á las 3. tres de la tarde en Esta oficina. para la Selebracion. del matrimonio de que se trata. en lo cual quedaron Entendidos. y firmaron; Doy. Fé. Camilo Acosta Alberto Fribizo. Hemenergilda Munos

Numero 25 Selebracion del matrimonio de Alberto Fribizo y Hermenefilda Muños

Numero 17. dies y siete. En Colonia Juárez. álas 3. tres de la tarde del Día 6. seis del mez de Julio de 1912 mil nobecientos dose. Ante mí Camilo Acosta. Juez del Estado Cibil. comparecieron con proposito de Selebrar su matrimonio El ciudadano, Alberto Fribizo, y la señorita Hermenefilda Muños. El primero dijo ser natural de los Ranchos de Santiago, y becino de Este Lugar. de 24.

Figure 8-3 Pages of Marriage Civil Register Colonia Juarez, Chihuahua, Mexico, 1912 (FHL 773944)

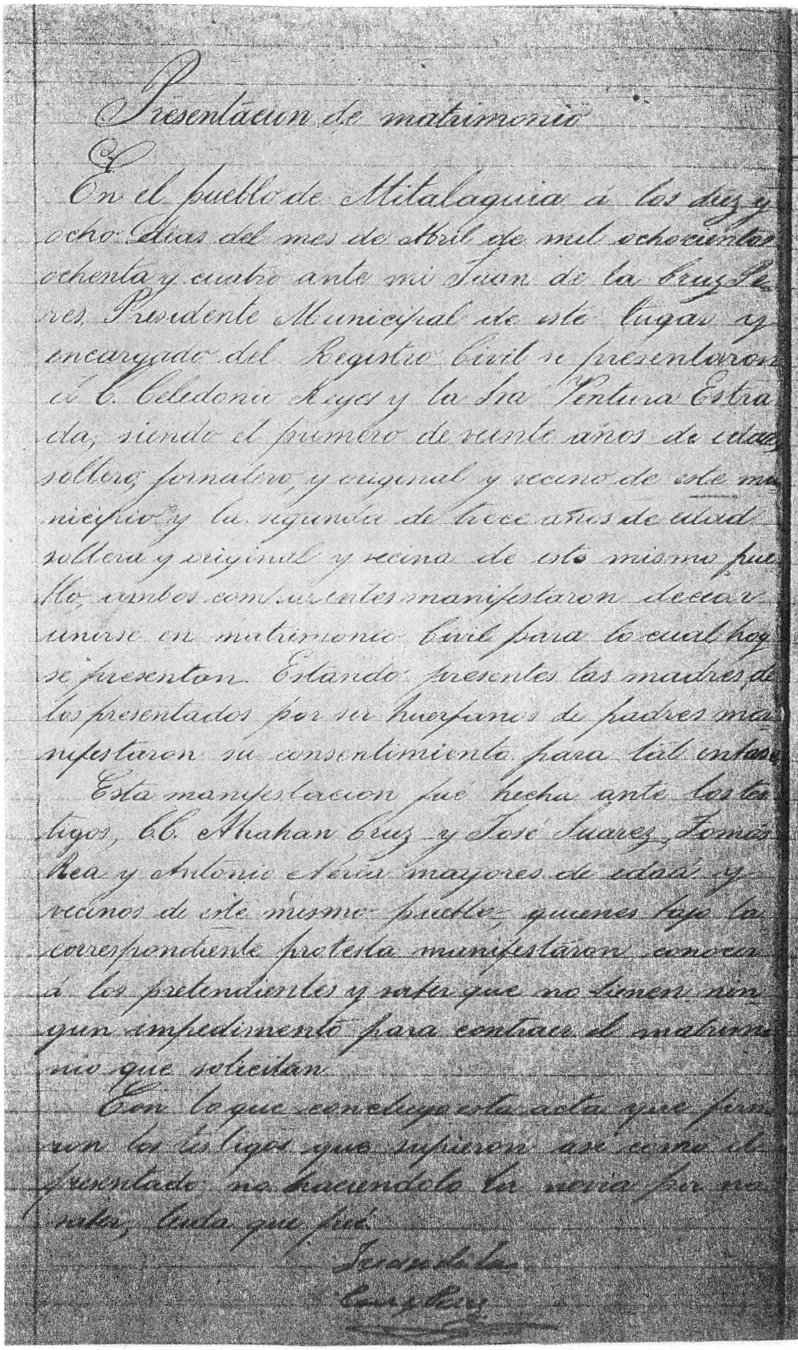

Presentación de matrimonio

En el pueblo de Atitalaquia á los diez y ocho dias del mes de Abril de mil ochocientos ochenta y cuatro ante mi Juan de la Cruz Pérez, Presidente Municipal de este lugar y encargado del Registro Civil se presentaron el C. Celedonio Reyes y la Sra Ventura Estrada, siendo el primero de veinte años de edad soltero, jornalero, y originario y vecino de este municipio y la segunda de trece años de edad soltera y originaria y vecina de este mismo pueblo, ambos contrayentes manifestaron desear unirse en matrimonio Civil para lo cual hoy se presentan. Estando presentes las madres de los presentados por ser huerfanos de padres manifestaron su consentimiento para tal enlace.

Esta manifestacion fué hecha ante los testigos, CC. Abrahan Cruz y José Juarez, Tomás Rea y Antonio Nava mayores de edad y vecinos de este mismo pueblo quienes bajo la correspondiente protesta manifestaron conocer á los pretendientes y saber que no tienen ningun impedimento para contraer el matrimonio que solicitan.

Con lo que concluyo esta acta que firmaron los testigos que supieron asi como el presentado no haciendolo la novia por no saber, Conste que fué.

[illegible]

Figure 8-4 Supporting marriage information, Civil Register, Atitalaquia, Mexico (FHL 657687)

This statement was made before the witnesses, C.C. Miahan Cruz and Jose Suarez Tomas Rea and Antonia Neria, adults, residents of this same town, who under the appropriate oath stated to know the petitioners and to know of no reason to impede them from contracting the marriage that they request.

With which I end this act, that [is] signed [by] the witnesses who know how as well as by the petitioner, not doing so the bride for not knowing [how to write] but read to her. Juan de la Cruz Perez.

Deaths

The death certificate (*certificado de defunción*) contains the given name, both surnames, marital status, nationality, profession, and place of birth of the deceased, as well as the names and surnames of the parents of the deceased. In addition, it frequently contains the date of birth and, in some cases, the cause of death and the cemetery in which the deceased was buried. If the deceased was married, the death certificate will give the name of the spouse, indicating whether the spouse is dead or alive, and the names of the children of the deceased, if any. Deaths from the early years of civil registration should be searched with special care, since they may give more detailed information than the parish records about people born in the eighteenth century. Such records are especially important where parish records have been destroyed.

Libro de familia (Family Book)

In many Hispanic countries the *libro de familia* system is administered by the civil register. Each family, beginning at the time the parents are married, is issued a *libro de familia*. In this book are listed the names of the parents with the date and place of their births and marriage. At the birth of each child, a parent, usually the father, takes the *libro de familia* to the civil register, where the information from the birth entry in the civil register is copied onto the appropriate page for each child and is signed and sealed, making it an officially recognized document. Unfortunately, no record or copy of these books is kept in the civil register. Since such *libros de familia* are many years newer than the civil register system itself, they are most likely to be found among the family effects of those who have left a Spanish-speaking country within the last generation.

CONSULTING CIVIL REGISTERS

Depending upon the country, civil registers are accessible on microfilm, by personal visit, and/or by correspondence. As indicated in figure 8-1, civil registers in nearly half of all Hispanic countries have been microfilmed by the Genealogical Society of Utah (GSU). These records can be found through a locality search in the FHLC under the name of the *municipio* (municipality) or, in cases such as Costa Rica, under the name of the province. (See the section on Locality Analysis in chapter 7 for the way to identify the *municipios* or provinces.)

Figure 8-5 is a sample letter to a civil register. The underlined portions may be changed to reflect the information about the individual(s) you are seeking. While valuable for requesting one, two, or three specific certificates, correspondence is usually not effective for detailed searches. In this case, if records are not filmed, a personal visit will be necessary.

In a larger civil register, it will frequently be difficult to gain permission to use the registers personally. As is common in Hispanic countries, knowing someone in town or having a positive reference from someone who knows the local officials can be a real advantage. Even with such

Ajo, Arizona
15 de mayo 1996

Director
Registro Civil
Los Mochis, Sinaloa
Mexico

Estimado Señor Director:

Estoy preparando una historia de mi familia para la cual necesito copias de las siguientes partidas:

1. Partida de defunción de mi bisabuela Maria Melchora Sanchez quien murió en Los Mochis en el año 1938.
2. Partida de nacimiento de mi bisabuelo Juan Lopez, hijo de Jose Maria Lopez y Manuela Botello, quien nació en Los Mochis en el año 1898.
3. Partida de matrimonio de mis bisabuelos Maria Melchora Sanchez y Juan Lopez, hijo de Jose Maria Lopez y Manuela Botello, quienes se casaron en Los Mochis en el año 1923.

Incluyo con esta carta cinco dólares para los costos de copias literales. Si no es suficiente, indíqueme la cantidad adicional que debo enviarle para las copias literales de esos certificados.

Con anticipación de su amable servicio, le doy las gracias.

Su servidor,

David J. Lopez
211 First Street
Ajo, Arizona

Figure 8-5 Letter to the Secretary of the Civil Register (*Secretario del Registro Civil*)

help, access may still be denied. This inaccessibility of civil records is usually justified on the ground that the oldest civil registers are only slightly over 100 years old, and therefore relate to people who are living or to their parents.

If a personal visit is made, you will want to proceed with caution when making a request for access to civil register records. Generally, in a very large civil register you should ask to speak directly with the *Secretario del Registro Civil* (Secretary of the Civil Register), and explain to him the nature and purpose of your work, assuring him of the limited amount of research you wish to do. In small civil registers it would be best to first suggest to the employee who dispatches the records that you want to do research on a particular family line, and that you had thought it would be best to speak with the *secretario* or *juez* (secretary or judge). Either of them can give you authorization to work with the registers, and once you have such authorization, the other employees will generally be quite helpful. Beginning to do research with only the permission of the employee who dispatches the records can result in the kind of situation one researcher encountered in a small civil register. He worked for an entire day without difficulty and returned the next day to find out that he had been prohibited from using the records by the *secretario*, whose pride had been offended because the researcher had not sought his permission first.

CHAPTER 9

Catholic Church Records

In Spain there is a saying that "El español es más católico que el Papa," meaning "The Spaniard is more Catholic than the Pope." Truly it can be said that Catholicism has contributed more to the shaping of Hispanic life and society than any single factor, possibly more than all others combined. It, therefore, should come as no surprise that its institutionalized form, the Catholic Church, is the first and primary source for family history material at both the diocesan and parish levels. This chapter focuses on the registers that originated on a nearly daily basis in the ecclesiastical unit closest to the people — the parish. It addition, it acquaints the reader with the existence of diocesan records.

Hispanic parishes were not only the principal units of ecclesiastical organization but also the main social unit for much of the rural life in Hispanic countries. Because of the intimate daily role the parish played and in many areas still plays, its registers usually provide the most extensive and accurate glimpse into the lives of your Spanish ancestors. For centuries the registers of Hispanic parishes have documented the lives of even the poorest laborers in tiny villages throughout Spain and Latin America. Births, marriages, deaths, local occurrences and, even occasionally, national events can all be found in those registers.

Parish records can be divided into two major categories — sacramental and non-sacramental. Sacramental parish records include baptisms, marriages, death or burial records, and confirmations. Non-sacramental parish records include fraternal order books, account books, censuses, individual documents, and local history materials.

ORGANIZATION OF PARISH SACRAMENTAL RECORDS

Sacramental records in the Hispanic Catholic parish are generally divided among three books, or sets of books: one for baptisms, another for marriages, and a third for deaths. Confirmations were frequently recorded in the baptismal books, although during some periods, and especially in larger parishes, a separate book for confirmations might have been maintained. In smaller parishes and in earlier years, all three of these record types were kept in the same book. For example, the first hundred pages might have been dedicated to baptisms, the second hundred to marriages, and the third hundred to deaths. When all records appear in a single book, the baptismal portion frequently covers a much shorter period of years than the marriage or death portions, because there are more baptisms than deaths or marriages, and because the baptismal entries tend to be longer.

The size of a parish book generally tends to be slightly larger than an American 8½- by 11-inch, three-ring notebook (see figure 9-1). In many parishes the earliest books in the archives will be of a different size, either quite a bit smaller (approximately the size of a stenographer's notebook) or long and thin, being about four inches wide and twelve inches tall.

Indexes

When consulting archival materials, either in person or using microfilm, check first for indexes. They will usually be found at the beginning of the volume, the end of the volume, or in some cases in a separate book. The latter may be a collection of indexes for individual volumes bound together, or a single index covering several volumes.

Indexes might have originated in three different ways: (1) those written by the original priest as he compiled the entries, (2) those written upon termination of the volume, and (3) those written or typed years later. In the first type the priest, upon completing an entry for the baptism of Juan Gomez, for example, would then turn to the *J*'s in the index at the back of the book and record, under the last entry he had made, the name of Juan Gomez and the folio number of the page on which the baptism record ap-

Figure 9-1 Parish sacramental register (author's copy)

pears. Although mistakes are found, this index is usually the most reliable, since the priest is certain of the entry he has just entered, and there are no difficulties caused by reading another handwriting. In the second type, the priest who finishes a book then goes back through it and makes an index. Because he will have little or no difficulty reading the writing, whether his or that of a former priest, this index is also usually fairly accurate.

The third type of index is written or typed years later by an interested priest or some outsider whom the priest asks to index the parish books. This types of index should be treated with great care. Frequently, the person writing the index may not understand the handwriting or may, in his long and laborious task, omit certain individuals from the list.

Since many parishes are not indexed, the researcher who encounters a well-indexed parish should be extremely grateful. In large parishes, where a single 200-page sacramental book will cover only four or five years, indexes are essential to a reasonably efficient use of the archives. When marriage records are indexed, you can rapidly encounter marriages for the direct-line ancestors without an initial page-by-page search.

There are several hints that can help in understanding indexes. Perhaps the most important is to recognize that a Spanish index will more frequently be arranged by *nombres de pila* (given or Christian names) than by *apellidos* (surnames). Note in the example earlier that the baptism of Juan Gomez will be found under *J* for Juan and not *G* for Gomez. In the list with his name will appear all those whose given names begin with *J*: Juan, Jose, Julia, Josefa, etc. Such lists are generally not alphabetized within each letter, and the names merely appear in the order in which they are recorded in the register. In some large parishes separate indexes were kept for male and female baptisms.

Certain letters are more common for *nombres de pila* than others. Particularly common are names beginning with *A*, *F*, *J*, and *M*. Occasionally you will find that the parish priest had allowed only a certain number of pages for each letter in the index, and the number of entries, for example for the letter *M*, may exceed the space allowed in those pages. When this happens, the last part of the *M*'s will be included elsewhere in the index, perhaps following the letter *Q* or *P* or another letter that has relatively few names. This manner of continuing the list on another page is easily detected. For example, if the book has 400 pages and the index entries under the letter *M* go only to page 321, there must almost certainly be other *M*'s included elsewhere in the book.

GENERAL PROCEDURE IN PARISH RESEARCH

Whether working with the records of a parish on film or using actual records in an archives, the first thing to do is make an inventory of what books are available. This inventory should indicate the book numbers and/

or corresponding film and item numbers, the type of entries found in the books, the years the book covers, whether the book is indexed, if the index is in the book itself, and any other comments as to condition, type of handwriting, and unique problems that may be found in using that book. In cases where such free access to all parish books is not allowed by the priest, or not possible due to unavailability of one or more films, record the information on each book as it becomes available. When working with microfilms, you will find that the card catalog will give at least part of the inventory information, although it generally does not give the volume numbers of the book, and there may be errors in years covered and other information.

Making an inventory is worthwhile for several reasons. Because many parishes do not have their books neatly stacked and organized, or because when working with library films there may be errors in the card catalog, making an inventory forces you to organize your material. As work continues your inventory will provide a guide as to what book is needed next and how the books are numbered.

As your research progresses you will find that the inventory continues to be a valuable help. After your research is finished and the findings are being compiled, you may discover that a book, film, or item number has been omitted in your notes, or you may want to know if a certain date would have been found in a particular book. You may also want to know what other books exist in order to plan future research in that particular parish. Also, after researching in other parishes you may find lines coming back to the original parish, in which case you can check the inventory to find out what records are available for the earlier time period.

Extract Forms

Extract forms, used for recording information found in parish records, have several advantages. First, they provide a uniform and easily understandable way of maintaining a file of your research notes. In addition, the extract form will guide you through the research, reminding you of pertinent information that might be contained in the records and making it easy to ascertain if important details were not inadvertently omitted. If you are physically present in the parish, professional extract forms increase the confidence of the priest in your ability to do quality research.

The parish research forms reproduced in figures 9-2, 9-3, and 9-4 are designed to be used in both parish and in civil registers. Because these records vary so much, the forms have spaces for more information than normally would be found in any single record from a parish or a civil register. Many spaces therefore will be left empty when filling in these forms, especially when working with early parish records.

In copying material from a record to these forms, remember that you are doing an extract, or copying the important parts of the original record

☐ P ☐ RC FECHA DE LA BUSCA ____________ PERSONA QUE BUSCA ____________

PARROQUIA ____________ OBISPADO ____________ PUEBLO ____________ Provincia/Estado ____________

Fecha de Bautismo	Fecha de nacimiento	Hora	Libro Folio Cart.
Primer Apellido y Segundo Apellido	Parentesco	¿Partida de defunción?	
Nombre de pila	M F	Leg. ileg.	Comentarios sobre el matrimonio de los padres
Padre	Natural de Vecino de		Raza
Madre	Natural de Vecino de		Raza
Abuelo paterno	Natural de Vecino de	¿difunto?	Raza
Abuela paterna	Natural de Vecino de	¿difunta?	Raza
Abuelo materno	Natural de Vecino de	¿difunto?	Raza
Abuela materna	Natural de Vecino de	¿difunta?	Raza
Padrinos			
Inscripciones marginales u otros comentarios:			

Figure 9-2 Extract form, Civil Register/Parish, Birth/Baptism

☐ P ☐ RC FECHA DE LA BUSCA ____________ PERSONA QUE BUSCA ____________

PARROQUIA ____________ OBISPADO ____________ PUEBLO ____________ Provincia/Estado ____________

Fecha de casamiento	Libro Folio Cert.	Parentesco	¿Partida de defunción? Esposo: Esposa:	
Esposo: Nombre de pila y apellidos	Edad y/o Estado		Natural de Vecino de	Raza
Padre del esposo			Natural de Vecino de	Raza
Madre del esposo			Natural de Vecino de	Raza
Esposa: Nombre de pila y apellidos	Edad y/o Estado		Natural de Vecino de	Raza
Padre de la esposa			Natural de Vecino de	Raza
Madre de la esposa			Natural de Vecino de	Raza
Comentarios:				

Figure 9-3 Extract form, Civil Register/Parish, Marriage

☐ P ☐ RC FECHA DE LA BUSCA ____________ PERSONA QUE BUSCA ____________

PARROQUIA ____________ OBISPADO ____________ PUEBLO ____________ Provincia/Estado ____________

Fecha de Entierro	Fecha de Defunción		Libro Folio Cart.
Nombres y Apellidos del difunto/ difunta	Natural de Vecino de	Raza	Edad
Esposo/a del Viudo/a de	Esposo/a: Natural de Vecino de		
Hijo/a de	Padres: Naturales de Vecinos de		
¿Hizo testamento?	Fecha del testamento y ante quién se hizo		Causa de muerte
Hijos del difunto/a			Lugar de entierro
Comentarios:			

Figure 9-4 Extract form, Civil Register/Parish, Death/Burial

as they are written. Be careful not to place on your extract form any information that does not appear in the original document. For example, write both name and surname for a person only when they are given. Many baptismal records do not give the surnames of the child, but merely say "Juan, hijo de Juan Gomez y Lucinda Arguello." In that case do not assume what the surname would be, but only write down the given name, "Juan." Because records vary extensively, leaving blank spaces or drawing a line in the blank space is important, as it shows that this information was omitted on the original record.

Always copy information from the original record onto the extract form first, and then transfer that information to the family group sheet or computer database as part of the organization and evaluation process discussed in chapter 3. It is tempting to want to take notes directly onto family group sheets or straight into the computer database, but this is not a good practice for a number of reasons. First, the family group sheet does not always allow for all the information contained on an original record. For example, there may be no place to put the information about *padrinos* (godparents), and where they are from. The other reason, perhaps more important, is that part of the value of the original records comes in recognizing the relationship between the various items of information given and not given, and the date on which they were entered. It is possible that in the baptism records of eight children in a single family, you may find more than one parish listed as the birthplace of the paternal grandmother. Knowing which of these entries was recorded when the grandmother was still alive may identify which parish is more likely to be correct. Or, the fact that the godparents of the first children in a family all came from a nearby town, while the godparents of the later children came from the town where the family lived, might be a clue as to the origin of the mother or father.

Actual Research with Parish Records

As in all family history research, you should begin parish record research with the information you already know. Generally, you will know either that a particular ancestor was born in a certain parish or that two ancestors were married to each other in a particular parish.

Suppose that your grandmother Maria Mendoza was born in the year 1900 in Chiapulco, Mexico, the daughter of Juan Mendoza and Josefina Lugo. By the time you reach the parish records, you should have already followed the Locality Analysis process outlined in chapter 4. This would have taught you that Chiapulco, a small town in the state of Puebla, had only one parish in 1900. You would have also checked the Family History Library Catalog at your local LDS family history center and found parish records covering the years 1732–1966.

Knowing only that Maria Mendoza was born in or about 1900 in Chiapulco, you would order the Family History Library film number

698,999, which includes the baptismal book for the years around 1900 in that parish. You would then begin the process of reading the baptismal entries from this time period page by page to locate the baptismal record for a Maria Mendoza who is the daughter of Juan Mendoza and Josefina Lugo. (Of course, if there is an index, you would consult this first.)

Don't become discouraged if the entry is not in the exact time period you were led to believe. Frequently, the dates people remember are incorrect. If you were working on our hypothetical case, you would search both before and after the supposed date of birth, say from 1890 to 1910, until you find the birth.

While searching for direct-line ancestors, it is important to watch for their brothers and sisters. You may find one or more siblings before the direct ancestor. Once you locate a baptismal certificate for any member of your direct-line ancestor's family, copy this information onto an extract form. If the birth certificate is that of the direct-line progenitor, proceed as outlined below; if not, continue to look for the direct-line ancestor.

Once your direct-line ancestor has been located, continue backward in time from that point, searching for all his brothers and sisters in the baptismal records. If you found in the hypothetical example that Maria Mendoza, the daughter of Juan Mendoza and Josefina Lugo, had been born 25 November 1900, you would then search backward in time looking for the older brothers and sisters of Maria, checking first in 1899, then in 1898, 1897, etc. Suppose you find that Maria had an older brother Jose born in 1898, an older sister Aurelia born in 1896, and another older brother Juan born in 1893. You would continue to go backward past Juan's birth, searching 1892, 1891, 1890, 1889, etc., for a time period of at least five or six years past the birth of the last child you found for Juan Mendoza and Josefina Lugo.

After having searched back in time five or six years without finding the baptisms of any other children, look at the marriage records beginning with the date on which the oldest child was born. In the hypothetical example, you would begin with the marriages from the year 1893, searching for that of a Juan Mendoza and Josefina Lugo. If both Juan Mendoza and Josefina Lugo were listed as having been born in Chiapulco, you would most likely find their marriage record in that same parish. Since they had no children in the records prior to 1893, you would expect to find that they were married in 1892 or 1891.

The marriage record of Juan Mendoza and Josefina Lugo should contain the names of their parents. At this point you would return to the baptismal records, starting in the last year checked, looking for the baptisms of Juan Mendoza and Josefina Lugo or their brothers and sisters. (Also, do not forget to return to the year of birth for your initial direct-line ancestor and look forward in time to find children who are younger.)

This process should continue until you reach a period where five or six years pass both forward and backward in time in which no baptismal entry is found for either of those families. At that point you will want to return to the marriages, searching for the marriage of the parents of both Juan Mendoza and Josefina Lugo, using the year in which their first child appears in the baptismal records as a guide. This process will generally yield a marriage date several months or more before the birth of the oldest child. However, since some people were married for many years prior to having children, and also since there might be a gap of up to ten or fifteen years between two children, you might have to search through several years prior to the birth date of the apparent oldest child. If there is a period of more than a year between the marriage and the birth of the oldest child, it is wise to recheck that time period for any children that may have been missed.

After you have followed this process for several years' worth of records and found a generation or two of names, consult the marriage index or go page by page through all of the marriage records, looking for the marriages of brothers and sisters of the direct-line ancestors. For example, in the hypothetical example you would want to pick up the marriage records of the brothers and sisters of Maria Mendoza, as well as the brothers and sisters of Maria's parents, Juan Mendoza and Josefina Lugo.

After completing nearly fifty or sixty years of baptismal and marriage records, turn to the death records. In order to recognize the names of possible family members in the death records, it is wise to wait until the pedigree is extended back two to three generations from the point where you began. Death records should be consulted beginning about 80 years after the ancestor was born, if these are available, or about 1980 in the hypothetical case of Maria Mendoza. Then work backward in time, looking for all of the people with the same surnames as the direct-line ancestors, i.e., Mendoza and Lugo in the hypothetical example.

Death records are usually the least complete of all parish registers. It is important therefore to copy the name of any person who may possibly be related. This may mean copying many entries, even though much of what you copy may not ultimately be useful. While this may seem like a waste of time and energy at first, the entries that you find may prove extremely valuable.

Generally, in doing family history research you collect the names of all those people in an area with the same surnames as the family you are searching. An exception may be made in working with certain parish records. When the parish baptismal records give the names of both maternal and paternal grandparents, you can initially copy only the names the individuals who have at least one set of grandparents in common with the people who appear on your direct-line pedigree chart. This saves considerable copying time with little sacrifice, as the information contained in the baptismal record will probably only be of value if the child being baptized has the same grandparents as the direct-line ancestor on one side or the other.

While time is always important, it should be emphasized that there is nothing improper about having to review the same parish book more than once. In some cases it may be necessary to pass over the same pages two or three times, especially as later information is acquired. For example, if you have already done marriages and then find the surname of a wife from an earlier marriage, you may want to go back and search for the marriages of her brothers and sisters. This will be especially important if she happens to be the oldest child, because it would mean that her brothers and sisters would probably have been married after her.

BAUTISMOS (BAPTISMS)

The baptismal records of the Catholic Church are among the most complete in the world. A baptismal entry from most Hispanic countries during the late nineteenth century will contain the following: the given name of the person being baptized (anywhere from one to six names, depending on the naming customs in the area); the surnames (at least the paternal, and frequently the maternal as well); the day, month, and year of the baptism; the names, surnames, residences, and birthplaces of the parents and grandparents; the birth date and birthplace of the person being baptized; whether the child being baptized was legitimate or illegitimate; marital status of the parents; the date the baptismal entry was made (usually, but not necessarily, the date of the baptism); the names of the godparents and sometimes their relationship to the child; residences and/or birthplaces of the godparents; and the name of the officiating priest.

Even a single baptismal certificate can be a valuable find. It will, in effect, point out the next research steps to be taken. The following analysis, accompanied by a completed extract form, identifies and discusses the various parts of an actual baptismal certificate.

Using a Baptismal Extract Form

Before receiving or finding a baptismal certificate, the information known about an ancestor would likely be limited to that which appears on the pedigree chart in figure 9-5. Suppose that you search a parish baptismal register for the period from 1825 to 1830 and find the baptismal entry found in figure 9-5. Your next step would be to transfer the pertinent information from the baptismal certificate onto an abstract form, as in figure 9-6. (Note that the circled numbers in both figures have been added for your convenience in correlating the original entry with the abstract form and the following commentary.)

In making an extract, first record the book and folio numbers. In Spanish a folio is a two-sided page with the front side of the page numbered 1, 2, 3, 4, etc. The back side of the page is not numbered and would be referred to as 1v, 2v, 3v, 4v, etc. For example, 2v would be the back side of

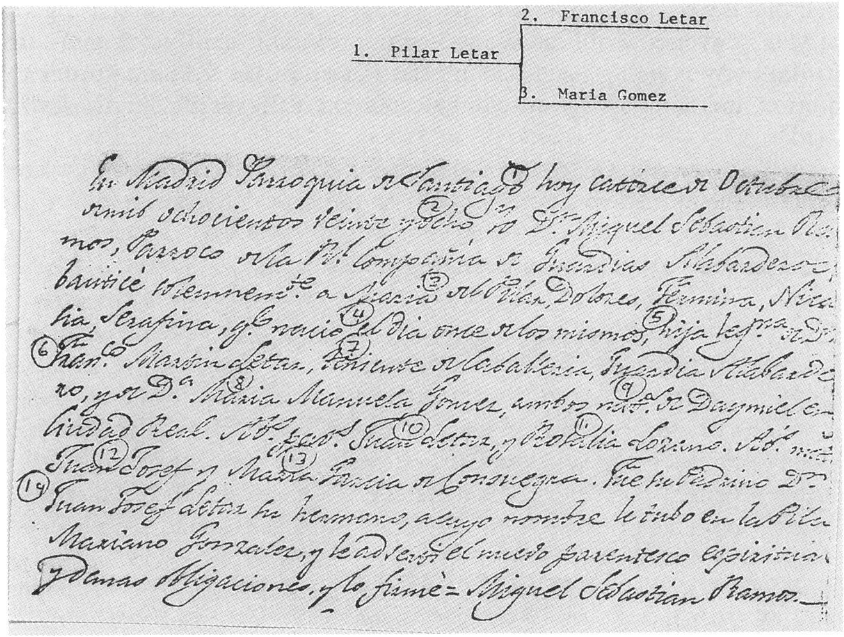

2. Francisco Letar

1. Pilar Letar

3. Maria Gomez

En Madrid Parroquia de Santiago (1) hoy catorce de Octubre de mil ochocientos veinte y ocho (2), yo Dn. Miguel Sebastian Ramos, Parroco de la Rl. Compañia de Guardias Alabarderos, bautice solemnemte. a Maria (3) del Pilar, Dolores, Fermina, Nicasia, Serafina, q. nacio (4) el dia once de los mismos (5), hija legma. de Dn. (6) Franco. Martin Letar, (7) Teniente de Caballeria, Guardia Alabardero, y de Da. (8) Maria Manuela Gomez, ambos nats. (9) de Daymiel en Ciudad Real. Abs. pats. (10) Juan Letar, y (11) Rosalia Lozano. Abs. mats. (12) Juan Josef y (13) Maria Garcia de Consuegra. Fue su Padrino (14) Dn. Juan Josef Letar su hermano, a cuyo nombre le tubo en la Pila Mariano Gonzalez, y le adverti el mucho parentesco espiritual y demas obligaciones, y lo firme = Miguel Sebastian Ramos.

Figure 9-5 Baptismal certificate from Daymiel, Spain copied from *Archivo Histórico Nacional* (Madrid, Spain), Sección de Ordenes Militares (author's copy)

☐ P ☐ RC (1) FECHA DE LA BUSCA 5 May 1983 PERSONA QUE BUSCA G.R.R

PARROQUIA Santiago OBISPADO Alcala PUEBLO Madrid Provincia/Estado Madrid

(2) Fecha de Bautismo: 14 Oct 1828	(4) Fecha de nacimiento: 11 Oct 1828	Hora	Libro Folio Cart.: año 1828 182
Primer Apellido y Segundo Apellido	Parentesco	¿Partida de defunción?	
(3) Nombre de pila: Maria del Pilar Dolores Fermina Nicasia Serafina	M (F)	(Leg) ileg. (5)	Comentarios sobre el matrimonio de los padres
(6) Padre: Dn. Franco Martin Letar	(Natural de) Vecino de: Daymiel, Ciudad Real		Raza
(8) Madre: Da Maria Mariela Gomez	(Natural de) Vecino de: Daymiel, Ciudad Real		Raza
(10) Abuelo paterno: Juan Letar	Natural de Vecino de	¿difunto?	Raza
(11) Abuela paterna: Rosalia Lozano	Natural de Vecino de	¿difunta?	Raza
(12) Abuelo materno: Juan Josef	Natural de Vecino de	¿difunto?	Raza
(13) Abuela materna: Maria Garcia de Consuegra	Natural de Vecino de	¿difunta?	Raza
(14) Padrinos: Dn Juan Josef Letar, su hermano*			
Inscripciones marginales u otros comentarios: (7) Padre es teniente de Caballeria Guardia Alabardero			
* a cuyo nombre le tuvo en la Pila Marieno Gonzalez			

Figure 9-6 Extraction of baptism in figure 9-5

page 2, the *v* referring to *vuelto* (reverse). If no volume number is given, the years covered in the book (and/or the film and item number if a microfilm copy is being used) are placed in lieu of the volume number. In addition, the name of the researcher and date of research should also be noted.

The following numbered paragraphs correspond to the circled numbers found on the extract in figure 9-6 and on the original certificate in figure 9-5.

1. *Lugar de nacimiento* (birthplace): *parroquia de* Santiago, Madrid, *obispado* of Alcala, *provincia* of Madrid. It is important to include the *obispado* (the diocese) and the province, because they may determine the places for further searches in ecclesiastical and provincial records. Although not pertinent in the case of Madrid, some towns on the borders of provinces or dioceses in Spain and throughout Latin America have changed, in some cases several times, from one diocese or province to another adjacent one during their history. As discussed in the section on Locality Analysis in chapter 7, knowledge of such changes and an awareness as to which diocese or province the parish belonged during the period in which you are researching is useful in continuing research beyond the initial parish.

No mention is made in the record in figure 9-6 as to where the birth took place. It can generally be assumed that the birth took place within the boundaries of the parish, unless a note to the contrary is included within the entry. Since baptism almost always took place soon after the birth of the child, the baptism of a child in a parish other than that in which he or she was born is somewhat rare, although by no means impossible, especially among the military and nobility, among Indians or among migrant workers, or in rural or frontier areas far removed from a parish church.

2. *Fecha de bautismo* (date of baptism): 14 Oct. 1828.

3. *Nombre de pila* (given or Christian name): Maria del Pilar Dolores Fermina Nicosia Serafina. The name found in the baptismal records is often much longer than in any other record for that person. The individual who has several names could possibly use any one of them in later life. For example, in the marriage records this particular individual could appear as Dolores Fermina, Pilar Dolores, or even simply Maria.

Note that the surnames (*primer apellido y segundo apellido*) have not been entered, because the original record does not list surnames for the child. It is a good practice not to write anything on the abstract form that does not appear in the original record, so that this becomes an exact extract of the original. When referring back to this certificate, you would then know the use, or the non-use, of the various surnames and their interrelation at the particular moment the religious act took place. Since in some areas of the country surnames had a changing pattern of use, it is helpful to know what surnames are or are not used, and when they are used.

4. *Fecha de nacimiento* (date of birth): 11 Oct. 1828. When the date of birth itself is specified, the day is most commonly recorded as an integral part of the entry, but the month and year may be summarized as a phrase like *de los mismos* (of the same) or *de los corrientes* (of the current), meaning of the same month and year as the entry date. In entries prior to 1800, many parishes will not include the date of birth, and this space would then be left blank.

5. Female and legitimate: The record almost always states that the child is an *hijo legítimo* (legitimate child). In peninsular Spanish records, where the child is illegitimate, he will usually be referred to as an *hijo natural*. In Latin America this term only applies to a child whose parents could be married in the church but have not been, and *hijo ilegítimo* is used to describe those whose parents could not be married under canon law.

While the entry does not state the sex of the child as a separate category, the use in Spanish of the masculine *hijo* or the feminine *hija* will indicate the child's sex. In some records it is difficult to distinguish the *o* from the *a*. Fortunately, in many such cases the record will read differently than that which we see in figure 9-6. It might read, "*bauticé solemnemente a un niño*" ("baptized solemnly a child"). Since *un niño* (boy) is clearly distinguishable from *una niña* (a girl), the sex can readily be determined from the record itself. Names such as Fermina and Serafina are also indications that the child is a girl, since they would be Fermín and Serafín, respectively, in the case of a boy. It should be noted, however, that the Spanish use Maria and Jose as male and female names. Jose Maria is a common male name, and Maria Jose is a common female name.

6. *Padre* (father): D^{n} Fran$^{co.}$ Martín Letar. Once again, note that an exact abstract is made, including the various spellings. Although in this case Francisco is clearly abbreviated, some abbreviations can be confusing and might stand for two or more different surnames or names. For example, the abbreviation Gez could represent Gomez or Gonzalez. By not making a supposition at the moment of copying the record, you can then later check the abstract if you find that your initial assumption appears to be incorrect.

The title "*Don*" is also included in the abstract for records originating prior to independence in Latin America and to the elimination of the traditional nobility privileges in Spain in the 1830s. Before that time the use of *Don* or *Doña* was indicative of noble status. Since records on noble families generally are more complete and available than those for other families, the use of *Don* is significant and should be noted.

7. *Oficio del padre* (occupation of father): *teniente de caballería, guardia alabardero* (lieutenant of the cavalry, Queen's guard). This information is recorded under *otros commentarios* (other commentaries). The recording of the father's occupation is not a standard procedure in most entries, but it is found in some areas and time periods. This information can be of great assistance in establishing identity and extending research beyond the original parish. In this case check to see if the person has a military service file, as discussed in chapter 12. It might also be a clue that this might be an exception to the rule that the marriage always took place in the bride's parish. It is possible that the father, when he was a groom, was stationed in another town and the mother (his bride) joined him there to be married.

As well as confirming identity and offering a possible point of departure for further research, the knowledge of the father's occupation can provide particularly interesting insights into the life of your ancestor. In this case the *Guardia Alabardero* was the special royal guard whose function was to guard the royal palace, and in which only sons of nobles were allowed to serve. Even today, as one takes a tour of the *palacio real* (royal palace) in Madrid, the first room one enters in the private quarters of the king and queen is called the room of the *guardia alabardero*, since this was the point where the guards had their station.

8. *Madre* (mother): D^{n} Maria Manuela Gomez.

9. *Naturaleza* or *lugares de nacimiento de los padres* (birthplace of parents): Daymiel, Ciudad Real. This information is extremely important, since it indicates in what parishes to continue research. In this case the parents are both from the same city (Daymiel), which is different from that of the parish in which the certificate was issued (Madrid); therefore, most of your research will continue in the newly identified city, Daymiel. The birthplace of the mother can be especially significant, since it is also most likely the place where the marriage of the parents took place. The parents' marriage record is very important — especially prior to the time when grandparents' names were included in baptismal records — since it will give the names of the parents of the bride and groom, i.e., the grandfather and the grandmother in the baptismal certificate.

10. *Abuelo paterno* (paternal grandfather): Juan Letar. As mentioned earlier, records in most areas of Spain and Latin America throughout much of the nineteenth century, and in some areas as early as 1750, included the names of both paternal and maternal grandparents. Although this record makes no mention of it, many records specify where the grandparents were then residing (*vecinos de*) and/or where they were born (*naturales de*). In addition, the record may indicate if they were then deceased. This information, while it is secondary and not primary source information, can be of value in indicating where the research should be continued. For example, if the birthplaces of the grandparents had been listed in this record and had been cities other than Daymiel, Ciudad Real, you would then know that there were additional parishes in which you would need to do research.

11. *Abuela paterna* (paternal grandmother): Rosalia Lozano.

12. *Abuelo materno* (maternal grandfather): Juan Josef. Note again that since the record does not specify the surname of this grandfather, we record no surname. In making entries on the pedigree chart or in the computer database, the assumption is made that the surname is Gomez, that of the mother.

13. *Abuela materna* (maternal grandmother): Maria Garcia de Consuegra.

14. *Padrinos* (godparents): D^{n} Juan Josef Letar, *su hermano* (her brother). The copying of the godparents' names can be very important. During early time periods when the birthplace of the mother was not included, the residences and/or birthplaces of the godparents are frequently still included in the record. An entry recording the godparents as coming from another town, especially when they have the same surname as the mother, can be a clue as to the location of the mother's birth and perhaps marriage. The entry for godparents may also include a relationship with the family.

15. Race or caste: In Latin American parishes this space is used to indicate any references as to race or caste. During the colonial period most records stated a race, but this may reflect only the priest's assumptions as to the race based on color or social position of the parents, not on actual racial background.

16. *Otros Commentarios* (other commentaries): These can be used to include information about the *padrinos* where there is not enough room in the given section, or to include any other information (i.e., marginal notations, commentaries as to the condition of the record, or any special circumstances relating to this particular entry). In this case it is significant that the child was not held in arms at the time of the baptism by the godfather, but rather by an individual named Mario Gonzales. This indicates one of two things — either the brother was too small to hold the child for the baptism, or he was not present in Madrid at the time the baptism took place. Either one of these is a possibility, depending on the age of the parents and, therefore, the possible age of the brother.

Once you have read and analyzed the entire record and made an abstract of it, transfer this information from the extract form to the computer database or the paper pedigree charts and family group sheets you are using. At this point, make your assumptions as to surnames, full name spellings, etc. Also, determine the additional places where records should be checked: in this case the parish at Daymiel, the records of the Guardia Alabardero, and the military service records kept at the archives in Segovia, Spain. In searching for the ancestors of Maria del Pilar Dolores Fermina Nicasia Serafina, you will want to remember the importance of searching for her brothers and sisters in the parish records of Santiago in Madrid, and possibly in other parishes if her father was involved in military service outside Madrid.

Sample Baptismal Entries

Obviously not every baptismal entry is going to be as complete and detailed as the example above. However, the vast majority of this information will be found in most Hispanic parish baptismal entries during the nineteenth century. The following is a literal transcription and translation of a baptismal certificate from the parish of Santa Catalina, Jujuy, Argentina, in the year 1872, and is typical of the entries to be found in many Latin American parishes:

> En esta Iglesia Parroquial de Santa Catalina a los viente y un dias del mes de enero // Del año Del Señor mil ochocientos setenta y dos, yo el Cura Provisorio de esta Parroquia // Bautizé solemnemente y puse oleo y Crisma a un Párvulo de quinze dias de edad, hijo // legítimo de Saturnino Vasquez y de Patrona Chayli, vecinos de San Leon de este Cu // rato, al cual puse por Nom bre Remigio, y fue su Madrina Juana Vasquez her // mana del padre del Bautizado y vecina del mismo Lugar: a quien instruí del // parentesco espiritual con el Bautizado, y con los Padres de este, y De las demas obliga // ciones, que como tal Madrina ha contraida: y para que conste lo firmo.
>
> Pedro V. Moreno

> In this parish church of Santa Catalina on the twenty-first day of the month of January // of the year of the Lord one thousand seventy and two, I the Provisional Priest of the parish // baptized solemnly and placed the oil and chrisma on a small [male] child of fifteen days of age, legitimate son // of Saturnino Vasquez and of Petrona Chayli, residents of San Leon of this par // ish, to whom I gave the name Remigio, and his godmother was Juana Vasquez, sis // ter of the father of the baptized and resident of the same place: whom I instructed in // the spiritual relationship with the baptized and with the parents of the same, and of the other obliga // tions, that as such godmother she has contracted: and that it so be I sign,
>
> Pedro V. Moreno

Note that while no grandparents' names are given, the relationship of the godmother is noted. Also, the parents' residence is identified as a place within the *curato*, a Latin American term for "parish." Other such terms include *doctrina*, *freguesia*, and *anteiglesia*.

The completeness of the above information gradually decreases in working backward throughout the centuries. The use of the grandparents' names in each entry began in some areas of Spain — for example, in the Basque dioceses — as early as the year 1720. In other areas, such as the diocese of Barcelona, the use of the grandparents' names will not appear until about the year 1800. In some dioceses in Latin America, the grandparents' names were not recorded until the twentieth century.

Common Baptismal Phrases

The baptismal entries above contain many of the phrases commonly found in parish records. Knowing what these phrases mean can be an aid in understanding the entries and also in deciphering handwriting. Examples of such phrases are: *Nació el dia ocho de los corrientes* (was born on the eighth day of the current [month and year]); *Yo el licenciado cura teniente de este lugar* (I the licensed assistant priest of this place); *Yo el infrascrito cura, les advertí las obligaciones espirituales* (I the below named priest advised them of the spiritual obligations); *bauticé solemnemente* (I baptized solemnly); *bapticé y puse los santos oleos* (I baptized and placed holy oil); *bapticé segun el rito del Santo Concilio de Trenta* (I baptized according to the rite of the Holy Council of Trent); *baptice el siete del mismo* (I baptized [on] the seventh of the same [month]); *fue su padrino* (was his [her] godparent). The manual *Spanish Records Extraction* offers excellent discussion and examples of such phrases.[1]

Occasionally you will find a baptismal entry where the child was baptized *en caso de necesidad* (in case of need). Since it is Catholic Church doctrine that small babies who die without being baptized go to a special place in purgatory called "limbo," there was real concern that a baby be baptized before dying. Because infant mortality was relatively high and the priest would frequently be several kilometers away, it was quite common for a lay person to baptize the child by sprinkling him with a little water and giving him a name. The Church recognized such baptisms and prescribed the manner in which they were to be performed, as well as the ritual that was to be followed by the priest in repeating the baptism if the child lived. You may find this wording in up to 25 percent of the baptismal entries you read in some parishes during certain years. While they often read as the above does, *en caso de necesidad echó agua*, or similarly, *bautizó bajo necesidad* (baptized under necessity), the Latin phrase for this circumstance was also used: *bautizó sub conditione* (baptized under condition). In all of these cases it is worth noting who performed that baptism, since it might have been a close relative or the *comadre* (midwife).

Another interesting common writing practice, found not only in baptismal entries but in all sacramental entries, is the means used to correct mistakes. One frequent way is the use of the word *digo*, just as it is used today in spoken Spanish. For example, the priest may write "*hijo de Juan Gómez, digo, Juan Fernández*." This indicates that he has made a mistake in writing the surname as "Gómez" and in actuality it should be "Fernandez." Another way to correct would be to scratch out the mistaken word and write in the correction above the part that was marked out (*parte tachada*). Also, a little mark such as (^) or an asterisk might be written above the word, with the correct name recorded in the margin next to a similar mark. In any of these cases, the priest usually indicated at the end of the entry that he had made the corrections himself. For example, he would write "*vale la palabra Fernández*" (the word Fernandez is valid) or "*no vale la parte tachada*" (the marked-out portion is not valid). At the end of an entry, the use of the *por verdad lo firmo* (for the truth of it I sign), or *firmé* (I signed), or *ut supra* (as above), or a combination of these was the means of indicating that this was a legally complete entry.

Illegitimate and Abandoned Children

The common practice for illegitimate children was for the entry to state *hijo natural de*, that is, "the natural" or "illegitimate son of." An entry for an illegitimate child may or may not contain the names of both parents. Note that in some countries, such as El Salvador, the illegitimacy rate can run as high as 80 percent.

Such entries reflect both the humor and the pathos of your ancestors' lives. In one entry from a small parish in Asturias, Spain, the priest wrote that he had asked the young girl three times who the father of the child was, and each time she had insisted that she did not know. He indicated at the end of the entry that he was still trying to find out who the father was and the mother was still insisting she would not tell him, but he was certain it was that soldier who had passed through town nine months earlier.

At other times the entry not only names the father, but indicates that the mother has taken legal action to have him recognized as the father of the child. Due in part to the legal consequences of illegitimacy (for example, inability to become a priest), the status of the child was carefully noted. One entry in a Galician parish recorded the name of the mother followed by "*esposa de Pedro Gomez, hace ya dos años que está ausente en el reino de Portugal*" (the wife of Pedro Gomez who has, for the past two years, been absent in the kingdom of Portugal), and the father was recorded as "*incógnito*" (unknown). Most commonly, the entry merely states that the father was "*no conocido*" or "*desconocido*" (unknown).

Perhaps some of the saddest baptismal entries are those for abandoned children. Usually the circumstances of the child being abandoned on a doorstep or left exposed to the elements were recorded. Many entries for abandoned children offer no further clues, but if the child was abandoned in an orphanage and later brought by someone to the parish, the orphanage from which the child was brought might be indicated. Such entries may offer a fascinating glimpse into the early years of a direct ancestor.

There are several surnames that were frequently given to such orphans. One of these was Iglesia, obviously referring to the fact that the child was left on the church steps. Another was Exposito, the technical term for orphan or foundling. The surnames Gines and Jimenez were also commonly given to orphans. There is nothing to be ashamed of in finding among your direct-line ancestors either an illegitimate or an abandoned child.

Marginal Notes

Marginal notes may be found on any of the sacramental entries, but they are more frequent and of greater interest in the baptismal records. They can be of several types, the most common being corrections or additions of the nature previously discussed. In such cases the priest makes a mistake in the body of the entry and corrects it by placing a note in the margin. Of greater interest are additions and corrections made at a later date by legal or canonical actions, such as a change of surname or the addition of the father's name in the case of an illegitimate birth that is later legitimized by the marriage of the parents or recognized by legal action involving the father. Marginal notes may also record later sacraments such as marriages and last rites. If the sacrament referred to was performed in the same parish, in many cases the priest will list the volume and folio number where the later record can be found.

One additional notation commonly used in reference to later sacraments is the annotation *murió* (died) or *murió párvulo* (died as a small child). The comment *murió* is no indication as to the age of the person when he died. In one case this notation was added beside the birth record, although the person's death certificate indicated that he had died at the age of seventy-two years! The phrase *murió párvulo*, however, indicates the death of a child usually younger than five or six. The author has never encountered a case where the child was older than seven. The word *párvulo* in Spanish literally means "small," "tiny child," or "tot."

MATRIMONIOS (MARRIAGE RECORDS)

Due to the importance of marriage records in family history research and the number of different record types involved in the marriage process, these records are discussed at length in chapter 10.

DEFUNCIONES, COLECTURÍAS O ENTIERROS (DEATH, COLLECTION, OR BURIAL RECORDS)

Of the three types of sacramental books, death records are the least consistent as to the date in which they begin, the types of information they contain, and the extensiveness of the individual entries. In some parishes death or burial records will be limited to one or two lines, while in others they will be fairly extensive. Unlike baptismal and marriage records, kept specifically to record those sacraments, death or burial records had a wide variety of functions. The variance in the records themselves reflects this. Some burial records indicate the date of death and burial. Others may simply give the date of death, with no mention made as to the burial. The style and information given in death records differs not only from one parish to another but also within books of the same parish.

Parish death registers frequently served not only as a place for recording burials and/or deaths but also as an account book for the masses for the dead, called *colecturías*. In most cases at least one *misa* (mass), usually a *misa del cuerpo presente* (funeral mass with the body present), was ordered for the dead person either in his will or by direction of his descendants. Also, many times additional masses were ordered either in the will of the deceased or by order of close family members. Each mass had a different price and involved a different amount of work for the priest.

As nearly everyone ordered masses, the number of masses given is less indicative of the piety of the individual involved than of his economic status. Further evidence of the account-book nature of some death records is the use in the adult death entries of the phrases *como todo mas largamente consta de la hijuela que se me exhibio* and *que entregué al colector* ("as is all more fully contained in the obligation which was shown to me," and "I gave to the collector"). The will written by the deceased, or the obligation drawn up by the heirs in the case where there was no will, was turned over to a person whose job it was to collect the money according to set fees for religious services.

The importance of death records should not be overlooked in your research. Some family historians feel that death records are expendable, since they do not usually assist in the rapid tracing of a family line. However, death records are important for several reasons. First, they can verify information that has already been collected. They can confirm marriages and confirm relationships of parents to children. They can also verify assumptions you have made — for example, that a second marriage took place or that a particular child died prior to the date of the father's death.

Another reason to search death records is that they frequently fill in the gaps in information that has been collected on a family up to that point in the research. For example, a death record may indicate the name of a child whose name has not appeared before. Or perhaps the death of a spouse from an earlier or later marriage than that of the direct-line ancestor may be noted, since death records frequently give the names of spouses both living and dead.

In one case the death record of a man listed all of his living children, including two children whose baptismal records had not yet been found. The family group sheet as then compiled indicated a gap from 1823 to 1837 between the births of two children, and the assumption was made that the missing siblings could have been born during this time period. The occupation of the father as a notary was also recorded in the death certificate. This led to a search in notarial records, which stated that he was the *escribano* (notary) of a nearby town from 1824 until 1840. The baptismal records of that neighboring parish were checked, and the two "missing" children were found, as well as the record of a child who had died at a very young age.

Another function served by searching death records is to close some avenues of research in a particular family; for example, indication that a child died at an age of six or seven years eliminates the need to search for further record of that child. Also, if a father or mother dies it is certain that there is no need to search more than nine months after the death date for the births of further children from that marriage.

Another common occurrence is when a researcher looking in the baptismal records for the children of a particular marriage suddenly finds children born to a father of the same name, but with a different woman given as the mother. If there are no more records found for the mother of the family being searched, but more birth records of a later date listing the father with this second woman as the mother continue to show up, the researcher's first reaction is to search for a marriage record. However, since most marriages take place in the wife's parish, and she may be from a different parish than the one being searched, the marriage record may not appear. In this case a death record for the first wife could verify the assumption that the husband had remarried. The occurrence of the mother's death between the birth of her last child and the birth of the first child by the second woman confirms the possibility that a second marriage has taken place, and gives a strong impetus to check for clues as to where.

The final reason why death records are important is that they frequently give information that will lead to other sources. One of the most crucial examples of this is if a will (*hizo testamento*) was made. If this is the case you will want to write down all the information given, especially the name of the notary, and use this to lead you into the exciting and more personalized world of notarial documents (see chapter 13).

Using The Death Record Abstract Form

Figure 9-7 illustrates abstract forms completed for the entries in figure 9-8 and is indicative of what may be found on death certificates generally. The spaces for information on that form are:

1. *Fecha de entierro* (date of burial). In addition to recording the date of burial, the entry may also record the place of burial. Prior to the late 1800s, nearly all burials took place within the church itself. These were usually done without any visible marker unless the family made a large donation to the church for the placing of one. The record will usually make a statement such as *se enterró en el tercer nave a la derecha del altar mayor* (buried in the third niche to the right of the high altar).

2. *Fecha de defunción* (date of death). Since most records are records of burial, this date will appear, if at all, later in the body of the text. If the record is of a death, the first date given is usually the death date.

3. *Libro, Folio, Cert.* (book, page, certificate number).

4. *Nombres y apellidos del difunto/a* (given names and surnames of the deceased).

5. *Natural de* (native of). Ordinarily, *lugar de nacimiento* (birthplace of the deceased) is indicated by stating that the deceased is *natural de*, followed by the name of the town. In some cases this information will not be given, and the entry will merely state that the deceased is a *vecino* or *residente de* (neighbor or resident of), and name the town of current residence.

6. *Edad* (age). This is generally found only in records from the nineteenth century; however, its appearance depends entirely upon the information that the priest either chose to write or was ordered to write by his presiding authorities.

7. *Esposo/a de* or *viudo/a de* (spouse of or widower/widow of). The death record nearly always indicates the marital status of the deceased, and in cases where the deceased was married the name of the spouse will often follow the indication of that marital status.

Note that the record also indicates the sex of the deceased by the use of the masculine or feminine ending, or by the use of the masculine word *marido.* The record will always indicate whether the spouse of the deceased has died earlier, because it will state that the deceased was either an *esposo/a* or *marido* (spouse), or *viudo/a* (widow or widower). Marital status frequently also indicates that the deceased was married more than once. In such cases it may state: *Juan Gómez esposo que era de Juana Lopez y vuido en primeras nupcias de Josefa Salgado y en segundas de Maria Mata* (Juan Gomez spouse of Juana Lopez and widower from his first marriage to Josefa Salgado and from his second to Maria Mata). In such a case the death record may be the only clue in those particular parish books that the deceased was married more than once.

8. *Esposo/a Natural de* (spouse native of). The record will frequently indicate where the spouse was residing and, in some cases, where the spouse was born by stating that the spouse is a *vecino de* or *natural de.*

9. *Hijo/a* (son/daughter of). Names of the parents of the deceased, *nombres y apellidos de los padres del difunto,* are rarely given in earlier records. However, in nearly all time periods the names of the parents of small children, and those adults who have remained single all of their lives, are given.

10. *Padres Naturales de* (parents natives of). When the names of the parents are stated, it is also quite common to indicate their place of residence and/or birth, and if either indicates another parish, the search can then be continued there.

11. *Hizo testamento?* (wrote will?). Many death records will indicate whether the deceased made a last will and testament. This is usually answered in the negative by statements such as *no hizo testamento, por no tener de que* (she made no testament because she did not have anything), *no testó por ser pobre* (did not testate, being poor), or *por haber muerto de repente* or *porque murió repentinamente* (because he died suddenly).

12. *Fecha del testamento y ante quién se hizo* (date of will and before whom it was made). There were generally two ways in which a deceased could have left a will and testament: (1) by dictation to the parish priest, who then wrote up the will or stated its terms in the death record; (2) by dictation to a notary who would then have drawn up the original and left it in his permanent files. Where a notary was involved, the death record may give the name of the notary (*notario* or *escribano*) and, in many cases, the date the will was executed. Collection death records frequently give at least some of the details contained in the will, such as *albaceas* or *testamentarios* (executors), *herederos* (heirs), and *mandas y donaciones* (directives and donations given to the church) including masses. While the latter are generally nothing more than a record of masses to be said, this part of the death record should be read carefully, since it may contain the name of a deceased spouse or, on rare occasions, the names of parents, parents-in-law, or some other relative.

13. *Causa de muerte* (cause of death). Many death records give the cause of death. More than any other source, death records help us appreciate the progress of modern life. There is nothing sadder than to watch an

☒ P ☐ RC FECHA DE LA BUSCA 2/15/94 PERSONA QUE BUSCA PR

PARROQUIA San Mateo OBISPADO Plasencia PUEBLO Logrosan Provincia/Estado Caceres

Fecha de Entierro	Fecha de Defunción	Libro/Folio Cart.
6 Dec 1788		3/228

Nombres y Apellidos del difunto/ difunta	Natural de / Vecino de	Raza	Edad
Juana Garcia *	(Vecino de) "este pueblo"		

Esposo/a del Viudo/a de	Esposo/a: Natural de / Vecino de
Juan Delgado de Andres	(Vecino de) "este pueblo"

Hijo/a de	Padres: Naturales de / Vecinos de

¿Hizo testamento?	Fecha del testamento y ante quién se hizo	Causa de muerte
no		

Hijos del difunto/a	Lugar de entierro
Juan, Ana y Thomas Delgado	

Comentarios: * "fue su muerte tan prompta que apenas pudo recibir la extrema uncion."

☐ P ☐ RC FECHA DE LA BUSCA 2/15/94 PERSONA QUE BUSCA PR

PARROQUIA San Mateo OBISPADO Plasencia PUEBLO Logrosan Provincia/Estado Caceres

Fecha de Entierro	Fecha de Defunción	Libro Folio Cart.
13 Dec 1788		3/228

Nombres y Apellidos del difunto/ difunta	Natural de / Vecino de	Raza	Edad
Dn Alonso Gonzalez Diaz Trejo	(Vecino de) este pueblo		

Esposo/a del Viudo/a de	Esposo/a: Natural de / Vecino de
Juana Shēz Ximz	(Vecino de) este pueblo

Hijo/a de	Padres: Naturales de / Vecinos de

¿Hizo testamento?	Fecha del testamento y ante quién se hizo	Causa de muerte
si	14 Sep 1788 Diego Naranjo Bravo, Essno	

Hijos del difunto/a	Lugar de entierro
Dn Alonso (escribano de Cañamero), Matheo, Luis, Miguel, Barthme Gonzalez Diaz Trejo,	

Comentarios: Alonso Mariano su yerno
Hija = Juana Gonzalez Diaz Trejo – los cinco hijos son de el y de su dicha mujer.

☐ P ☐ RC FECHA DE LA BUSCA 2/15/94 PERSONA QUE BUSCA PR

PARROQUIA Sn Mateo OBISPADO Plasencia PUEBLO Logrosan Provincia/Estado Caceres

Fecha de Entierro	Fecha de Defunción	Libro Folio Cart.
13 Dec 1788		3/228v

Nombres y Apellidos del difunto/ difunta	Natural de / Vecino de	Raza	Edad
Catha			parvula

Esposo/a del Viudo/a de	Esposo/a: Natural de / Vecino de

Hija de	Padres: Naturales de / Vecinos de
Lucas Barbas y Ana Vaez	(Vecinos de) este pueblo

¿Hizo testamento?	Fecha del testamento y ante quién se hizo	Causa de muerte

Hijos del difunto/a	Lugar de entierro

Comentarios:

Figure 9-7 Extractions of death entries from figure 9-8

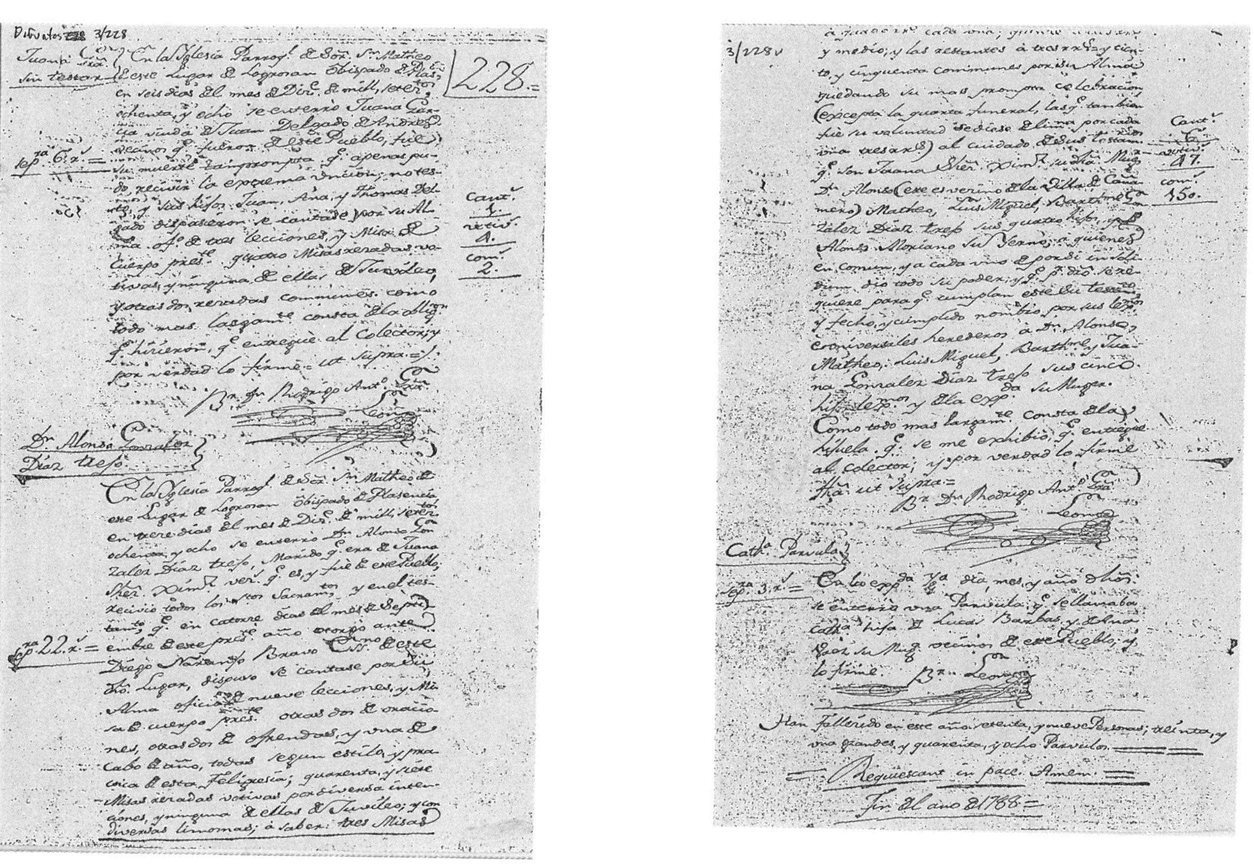

Figure 9-8 Pages of Death Register 1788, Logrosan, Caceres, Spain (FHL 1458682)

entire family decimated by *viruela* (smallpox) in a matter of a week or two.

14. *Hijos del difunto/a* (children of the deceased). Where a will existed, children may be listed as executors and/or as heirs. In cases where there was no will, one or more of the children may have paid to have certain masses celebrated for their deceased parent. Where the deceased was married more than once, the death record may specify the mother of the children in language such as the following: *Juan y Juana Gómez, hijos del difunto y de su primera esposa Josefa Salgado, y Juana y Gumersindo Gómez, hijos del difunto y su segunda mujer Maria Mata* (Juan and Juana Gómez, children of the deceased and of his first wife, Josefa Salgado and Juana and Gumersindo Gómez, children of the deceased and his second wife Maria Mata). Names of children who have already died as small babies may also appear, either in the section for masses or in the list of children, with some indication of the fact that they are dead.

15. *Comentarios* (comments). On the abstract form, a special section is reserved for comments (*comentarios*). Record here any other information that does not fit into the spaces allotted in the form. Death records can contain items of human interest, as well as surprises for the family historian. One example is the following description of a person's death encountered in a Catalan death record:

> Joan Fontanet, owner of the place called Dalmosas, was buried on September 11, 1682. He died that same day from being shot. Before dying he had time to confess, with great pain from his wounds, and ask forgiveness of his sins. After he took the holy sacrament, and was absolved of his spiritual wounds, he publicly exclaimed to God, in spite of his wounds, in the great act of a true Christian.

Common Phrases in Death Records

As with the other parish sacramental registers, there are certain phrases that appear regularly in death records that can help you in understanding them. Among them are the following: *se dió sepultura al cadaver de* (burial was given to the body of); *se enterró* (was buried); *falleció* and *murió* (died). The name of the person is almost always followed by the marital status: *soltero* (single), *viudo* (widower), *marido* (spouse), *casado con* (married to), or *consorte de* (spouse of). The record will also discuss whether the sacraments were administered, and phrases such as *recibió todos los santos sacramentos* (he received all of the holy sacraments) are very common. Also frequently encountered are cases of sudden death, described with phrases such as *fue su muerte tan pronto que apenas pudo recibir la extrema unción* (his death was so sudden that he was barely able to receive the last rites), or *murió tan de repente y no recibió ningún sacramento* (he died suddenly and received no sacrament). It is quite common to use the word *párvulo* without any name to refer to either a male or a female infant, making it difficult to identify even the sex of the child or to determine which of two or three children born during the previous five or six years the deceased *párvulo* could have been.

Note the third entry on folio 228v in figure 9-8, where Cathalina is listed as a *párvula*. Mortality statistics such as those recorded by the priest at the bottom of figure 9-8 following the third entry are common. During this time the number of infants who died was nearly always greater than the number of adults and/or older children. (The term *párvulos* usually meant between the ages of newborn and six or seven years, while the term *grandes* included not only adults but also older children and teenagers.) In larger parishes the number of infant deaths was so great that there were separate books for recording the deaths of *párvulos*, especially during the nineteenth century. The death records for *párvulos* should be consulted; they will frequently indicate that a brother or sister of the direct-line ancestor died young and need not be checked for in marriage records.

CONFIRMACIONES (CONFIRMATIONS)

Of the seven sacraments, the only one other than the three just discussed that may be recorded in parish books is the confirmation. Unlike the other three, the recording of this sacrament has not been consistently maintained. For particular time periods in some of the larger parishes, a separate book for confirmations will exist; in most parishes the record of confirmations is intermingled with the baptisms, appearing at the chronological point where the confirmation took place. In some dioceses confirmation records were kept only by the bishop and are found in the diocesan archives.

Unlike the sacraments of baptism, marriage, and the last rites, or extreme unction, the confirmation was not performed by the priest. Only a bishop or his authorized representative could perform confirmations, which would take place when he visited the parish. In some cases this was an annual or bi-annual event, but in many smaller parishes, far removed from the cathedral, there would be a wait of at least five years, and in some cases as many as fifteen years. It is not at all uncommon to find situations where a mother and her first child both received their confirmations on the same day.

Confirmation entries tend to be brief. At the top of the entry is basic information relating to the date and the presence of the bishop who performed the confirmation. This will also state the name of the parish in which the confirmation took place. Below this are the names of the godparents at the confirmation. Following this introductory paragraph, each individual entry contains the given name and in some cases the surname of the individual, and frequently the name of his father or those of both parents. If it has been a long period of time since the bishop's last visit, the register of the confirmation ceremony can cover several pages. The godparents assigned at the beginning may have changed after a few pages, and new godparents may be indicated.

As a family historian, you will find the value of confirmation records is primarily to verify the research already done in other parish records. Since several children of a marriage may appear, you will know that you have found all of the children born up to that time. It can also verify doubts as to the identity of a particular individual, or may be used to fill in gaps caused by missing baptismal records.

On some occasions the name given at the confirmation may not agree with the one recorded in the register. Suppose, for example, that you are searching for Alonso Fernandez, the son of Juan Fernandez and Serafina Sanchez. If three children, named Juan, Gonzalo, and Maria, appear in the baptismal records and only three — Juan, Alonso, and Maria — appear in the confirmations, this may suggest that Alonso and Gonzalo are the same individual using different names. In such cases this may be the connecting point between the baptismal record and the name used at the time of the marriage.

Frequently a page will appear, either just before or just after the confirmation, wherein the bishop or his representatives record the *visita pastoral* or *santa visita* (pastoral visit or visit of the bishop). These should not be confused with the confirmation act itself. Pastoral visits were frequently made by representatives of the bishop (for example, his secretary), who came to check the well-being of the parish. The primary purpose of recording the pastoral visits in the parish registers was to indicate that the records had been reviewed and approved as written.

LOCATING PARISH RECORDS

The work of locating parish records will be simplified if a Locality Analysis (see chapter 7) has already been completed. This will tell you to what parish or parishes your ancestors belonged, or may have belonged, during a particular time period. Your next step is to check the Family History Library Catalog under the name of the town. After finding the town and determining that parish records are available, order the microfilms and begin the searching process explained earlier.

If the parish records are not available on film, the next step is to determine if they exist. Again, as described in chapter 4, existing guides to parish records for the diocese, region, or country should be consulted. These guides will often tell you if the parish records exist, what years are covered, and in what archives they are located (parish, diocesan, governmental, or private).

Once existing records have been located, there are three ways to consult the records: writing a letter, making a personal trip to the archives, or hiring a researcher. Whichever of these you ultimately choose, writing a letter is the best way to start. The general process of letter writing is described in chapter 6. A model letter to a parish priest is reproduced in figure 9-9.

13 de Marzo de 1989

Sr. Cura Parroco
Parroquia de Casares
Malaga, Espana

Estimado Senor:

Estoy preparando un arbol genealogico y mi libro familiar para los cuales se me hace imperiso dirigirme a usted a fin de obtener ciertos datos sobre mis abuelos que detello a continuacion:

1. Partida de bautismo de Joaquina Franco Perez, hija de Jose Franco y Juana Perez, que nacio en Casares entre los anos 1878 y 1886.
2. Partida de matrimonio de Jose Franco y Juana Perez, entre los anos 1865 y 1881.

Para esta informacion necesito nombres de los abuelos y de los lugares de donde son naturales, si estos estan en las partidas. Incluyo un billete de 5 dolares para cubrir los gastos de los certificados.

Reconozco lo ocupado que debe estar usted, y por eso le agradeceria mucho lo que pudiera hacer al respecto ya que, de otra manera, mi trabajo quedaria paralizado.

Quedo a la espera de sus noticias y le agradezco de antemano por su ayuda.

Lo saluda,

Jorge R. Ryskamp
4522 Indian Hill Road
Riverside, California, USA
92501

Figure 9-9 Letter to the parish priest

Once you have a response confirming that parish records exist, you can call or write to arrange a personal visit, or to ask if the parish priest knows of someone who can be hired to do research.

Parish Administrative Records

Administrative records of the Church are generated and usually encountered in archives at two principal hierarchical levels: the parish and the diocese. Due to the predominant position of the Catholic Church in Hispanic life, its administrative records offer a wealth of information. More than parish registers, these records can offer the human interest details that as a family historian you are seeking.

The following categories of administrative records can be found in parish archives. The extent of their preservation and their organization vary dramatically from parish to parish. Most of the records are non-sacramental and can be clearly distinguished from the sacramental registers discussed earlier in the chapter. *Expedientes matrimoniales* (marriage petitions) are one major exception because in some parishes, especially in Latin America, these were recorded into, or subsequently bound in, books indistinguishable in appearance from the marriage registers.

Libros de Fábrica, Cuentas e inventarios (Books of Parish Property, Accounts, and Inventories)

Nearly every parish has a large collection of record books and inventories of its property. Unless a direct-line ancestor worked for the parish, or had some type of business or financial transaction with it, there is little possibility that information about your family will appear in these parish financial books. On the other hand, if you are interested in writing local histories or ascertaining the age and origin of parish artwork, these books are of particular interest.

Padrones y Matrículas (Censuses and Enrollments)

For the period after 1900, and in some cases during the late 1800s, the use of parish *matrículas* (enrollment records) was very common, and a family from that time period will be listed with all of its members. In many parishes, however, there are *padrones* (censuses) that are much older.

Individual Documents

In most parishes and dioceses, there will be a varied collection of separate and individual documents. These may be bound into volumes that at first glance may resemble parish sacramental and account books, or may be tied into bundles. Among the various documents you might find in such a collection are the following:

1. *Testamentos* (wills)
2. *Capellanías* (chaplaincies)
3. *Pleitos* (suits)
4. *Expedientes matrimoniales* (marriage petitions)

Libros de Cofradías (Books of the Co-Fraternities)

Cofradías were societies of laymen organized in most parishes to further social activities and assist in organizing religious and charitable events within the parish. Perhaps the most famous of the *cofradías* were those in the city of Seville, Spain, whose members annually paraded through the city during Holy Week, frequently dressed in long flowing robes and hoods, dragging chains or carrying crosses or large religious images. Although not as large and spectacular as those of Seville, the *cofradías* in other cities and towns played important roles and even today organize the various religious processions celebrating important holidays such as Maundy Thursday and Good Friday.

Membership in a *cofradía* was frequently hereditary, passing from a father to his sons. These organizations were presided over by elected officers. An important person in town, such as the mayor, the notary, or a nobleman, might belong to several or even all the *cofradías* in his town.

The books of the *cofradías* rarely follow any particular format. They contain three basic types of material: membership lists, financial accounts, and minutes of meetings. Membership lists will have the greatest interest for the family historian. These vary greatly. Some are taken yearly and represent a complete list of all of the members, which can then serve as an indication as to whether a family was in that town during a particular year. Others are cumulative lists, where the names of individuals are added as they join the *cofradía*. Full membership frequently came only upon marrying, and a person's first appearance on a membership list may fall close to his marriage date. When a person died his name was crossed off the membership list, occasionally with a year written beside it indicating the date of his death.

In smaller towns the *cofradías* were open to both men and women. It is quite common to find a husband and his wife listed together in the membership lists with the notation "*Juan Molina y Maria Fernandez, su mujer*," indicating that they were in fact married at that time.

Local History Materials

This is a class of materials not retained in separate books or composed of a single type of document. Instead, it includes materials that may be found throughout all parish records. The priests often recognized that the sacramental books were documents that would be preserved for centuries and, as a result, made notes about historical moments of particular interest to the parish, or about times and events of national importance. Comments of local interest were occasionally added about such things as the date on which the stonemason laid the first stone for the building of the sacristy in a small parish, or notations about important people who came through the town and activities at the time of their visit.

Local history materials such as these can provide some of the greatest human interest materials. The following is translated from a notation by the parish priest in the small town of Rus in the province of La Coruña, Spain. It exemplifies the types of materials that can be found in parish books, and the insights these materials can give regarding the difficulties, as well as the high points, of your ancestor's life.

> Note for the year of 1769:
> This year of one thousand seven hundred sixty-nine was fatal for the kingdom of Galicia due to the notable scarcity of fruit [of the land] that had its origin in the continual rains which began to fall during May of last year (one thousand seven hundred and sixty-eight). In the entire year we have barely seen eight consecutive days of calm weather without rain, so that the harvest of wheat in said year of sixty-eight was mediocre. Because we were not able to cut and thresh the grain, a large portion of it was lost in the valleys, and in the mountains an even greater part. The corn sown in said year of sixty-eight, for the lack of sun,

> did not produce even seed in the mountains. In the valleys, in irrigated and flat lands, nearly the same occurred. In the areas near the sea and in dry lands, there was produced a mediocre harvest of corn, but this was of very little to help the kingdom; therefore before said year sixty-eight had ended, there began to be felt hunger. The grains had an excessive value; the lowest price for a unit of wheat, at the beginning of the year sixty-nine, was 20 *reales*, and at such high prices poor laborers were unable to purchase, either to eat or to sow. Many left their places in the mountains, leaving them uncultivated, and began begging through the valleys and through the cities. Day by day the value of fruit increased and, if it had not come to have an end, all would have been lost and hunger felt by rich and poor, if it were not for the Providence of God, our Lord, who felt our misery and wanted to help the kingdom by means of shipping. In the beginning of the spring of this year of sixty-nine the merchants of the cities brought grains from outside of the kingdom. From this time until the end of said year, thanks to God, there was grain from abroad in the ports and maritime cities at a moderate price (for that year).

NON-PARISH ADMINISTRATIVE RECORDS

A good source, beyond the local parish records, for adding dimension to your family history is the Catholic Church's ecclesiastical records. Such records fall into three major categories: diocesan records, cathedral records, and records of monasteries and religious orders. If your ancestors lived in a city that was the headquarters for the bishop, you should consult the cathedral records. If your ancestral families had some direct contact with a particular religious order or monastery, you should look at their records as well. Although these record types will not be covered in this book, if somebody in your ancestral family can be identified as a member of one of these institutions, its personnel records should be searched. Always try to determine what records exist for your ancestor's diocese, because when good records are available they can be of great value to you as a family historian.

Both diocesan and cathedral records originated with the institution of the bishop (*obispo*), who presides over a geographical territory known as the diocese (*diócesis* or *obispado*). There were 64 *obispados* in Spain in 1960,[2] and 116 *obispados* in Latin America in 1900.[3] Although the bishop has a power over the religious lives of the subjects of his diocese surpassed in theory only by that of the pope, in the reality of daily life he has a much stronger impact. The diocesan archives is a composite record of various uses and extensions of his power in the judicial, ecclesiastical, and temporal affairs of the people throughout his diocese.

The cathedral is the church or seat of the bishop (the word cathedral originating with the Latin word *catedra,* which means seat). Due to its independent importance and because it was frequently built with special funds donated for that purpose, each cathedral was often administered outside of the regular diocese administration by the *cabildo capitular* (chapter or council of priests and laymen). Usually these served under and responded to the bishop, although at times in their history they exercised a strong amount of independence. As a result, they maintained separate records dealing with the cathedral, its erection, and use.

Diocesan Records

In nearly every diocese, records are found in the diocesan headquarters called the *obispado*, located near or attached to the cathedral. This building usually houses not only the archives but the administrative and judicial institutions responsible for these record collections. The primary administrative institution under the bishop is the *curia* (curate). While the titular head of this *curia* is the bishop, most of the direct administration is carried out by the *vicario general* or *provisor* (vicar general), who is the bishop's chief assistant. He is appointed by the bishop and must resign upon the death of the bishop who appointed him.

The *curia* is divided into various departments, depending upon the needs of the diocese, and deals with a variety of problems such as matrimonial questions, personnel problems, finances, etc. In addition to administrative organization, each diocese has at least one *tribunal,* which hears court cases and rules on matters of canon law. The president of this tribunal is known as the *official*. In larger dioceses, such as those in Mexico City, Lima, Seville, and Barcelona, these tribunals may be divided into *secciones* or *oficios* (sections). In some cases this may be a subject matter jurisdiction division, and in others a geographical division or even a pure lottery system based on workload. Associated with both the judicial and administrative institutions are the *escribanos* or *notarios eclesiásticos* (ecclesiastical notaries), who prepare all the legal documentation for the various transactions and cases involving the church and its courts.

The biggest difficulty in describing diocesan records is the great variety you will encounter in the archives of the various dioceses. Factors accounting for this variety are the power of the particular bishopric as it developed over the centuries, the extensiveness of the control of the bishop, the geographical size of the diocese, the state of preservation of the records, and the order with which the records have been maintained. The records of some dioceses have been microfilmed in their entirety and are available through the LDS family history centers.

The broadest categories of records that may be encountered in an Hispanic diocese are:

1. Marriage dispensations
   - A. Consanguinity or apostolic
   - B. Ordinary
   - C. Secret
2. Financial and administrative records
3. Ecclesiastical personnel records
4. Charitable donations and foundations: *capellanias, beneficios, causas pias,* etc.

5. Judicial materials
   A. Civil
   B. Church building funds
   C. Disputes concerning charitable properties and positions
   D. Cancellation of religious vows
   E. Collections
   F. Fraternal orders and brotherhoods
   G. Proofs of baptism and marriage
   H. Testaments and probate matters
   I. Criminal matters
   J. Excommunication
   K. Divorces
6. Pastoral visits and confirmations
7. Notarial records
8. Others

Every diocesan archives has its own system of categorizing its collections of documents, usually originating from its own administrative structure and variations therein over time. Therefore, the categories above should not be considered as specific categories found in every archives, but as a general description of what you might encounter.[4]

Locating Diocesan Records

To locate the records of a particular diocese you would do the following:

1. Determine to what diocese the particular area or parish in which you are researching belongs. This process was discussed in chapter 7.

2. Determine if the records have been microfilmed. This is done by checking the FHLC under the locality name of the diocese in the town search, or under the province or state name in which the diocese is located. The records topic in the FHLC will usually be the broad topic "church records" or a specific type of records, e.g., "ordinations," "notarial records," or "marriage dispensations." Generally, any church records not identified as parish registers are from the diocese. In many cases even the FHLC descriptions may not accurately describe the material that exists in a diocese's archives.[5]

3. Search computerized library card catalogs on the Internet for guides and catalogs for the diocesan archives, as well as the possibility that other films not made by the LDS Church may exist. This is done most effectively by searching under a key word search using both the name of the diocese and the word *diocese*.

4. Do actual research in the archives. The same concepts discussed above for parishes are applicable, except that a letter or phone call should be made in advance to prearrange the visit, since diocesan archives often have short hours.

Once you have located the diocesan records, you will find they are rarely indexed. Expect to spend long hours reviewing many pages of documents. Your effort will be worth it, however, if you find a marriage dispensation with four generations of your direct-line ancestors, or the ordination of a family member as a priest.

---

1. *Spanish Records Extraction* (Salt Lake City: The Church of Jesus Christ of Latter-day Saints, 1981).

2. "Oficina general de información estadística de la Iglesia en España," *Guía de la Iglesia en España* (Madrid: Sucesores de Rivadeneyra, 1960), 764–766.

3. Lyman Platt, *Una guia genealógico-histórica de Latino-America* (Ramona, Calif.: Acoma Books, 1978), 86–110.

4. These categories have been drawn primarily from experience in the diocesan archival collections of Caceres, Sevilla, Granada, and Barcelona in Spain, and those on film for the archives for the archdioceses of Michoacan and Guadalajara in Mexico. For more detailed information, see chapter 10 of George R. Ryskamp, *Tracing Your Hispanic Heritage* (Riverside, CA: Hispanic Family History Research, 1984) and Jose Sanare, *Los archivos eclesiásticos de la diócesis de Barcelona, volumen uno, el archivo diocesano* (Barcelona, 1947).

5. For a good discussion of this problem, particularly as it relates to the microfilms of archive records available through the LDS family history centers, see G. Douglas Inglis' article "The Morelia Project of Mexico," *Latin American and Iberian Family and Local History, World Conference on Records* (Salt Lake City, 1980), #711. That article will help the researcher understand the problems that confront him when working with poorly organized diocesan records and the potential of a thorough search of these records.

CHAPTER 10

Marriage Records

Marriage records are the most significant records searched by the family historian, since they are often the only place where names of the older generation are provided. They also temporally define the beginning of a new unit that needs to be researched. Fortunately for you as a family historian, the process of marrying in Hispanic societies potentially generated several different records:

1. Pre-marriage investigation (*información*, *diligencia*, or *expediente matrimonial*)
2. Parish marriage register entry (*partida de casamiento*)
3. Marriage dispensation (*dispensa matrimonial*)
4. Church and civil court records relating to marital relations
5. Dowry inventories and pre-nuptial/post-nuptial contracts

The first two record types on the above list relate to the marriage performed by the parish priest. The third refers to the application by a future bride and groom to the bishop, and subsequent investigation to waive an impediment to the proposed marriage. The fourth category refers generally to broken promises to marry — lawsuits and prosecutions relating to marital conflicts and annulments found in the diocesan and civil courts. The last items are contracts defining property contributions to and ultimate property distributions from the marriage, often not only involving the bride and groom but their respective parents as well.

PRE-MARRIAGE INVESTIGATIONS

Parish marriage records reflect the degree to which the Church controlled the institution of marriage. Each marriage record contains a phrase similar to this: *aviendo presedido ynformación de libertad y soltura y no abiendo resultado impedimento alguno, casé y velé* (having preceded the information concerning freedom and single status and there having resulted no impediment, I married and blessed). Prior to performing each marriage, the Catholic parish priest conducted an investigation to ensure that the bride and groom met the church's requirements. Although not extant for all parishes, the written records of these investigations (*informaciones matrimoniales* or *diligencias matrimoniales*) are available in separate books or files from the sacramental registers of marriage in many Latin American parishes. These records are called *expedientes matrimoniales* in Spain, where they tend to only exist for the nineteenth and twentieth centuries.[1]

The pre-marriage investigation included proof of good standing in the Catholic Church (often this proof was the baptismal certificate of the bride and groom), after 1787 the written permission of the parents if the bride or groom were under age (usually the age was set at twenty-five years, although this did vary),[2] and the priest's permission for the marriage to take place. In addition, if the groom was from another parish there would be a statement by his parish priest that the three canonical admonitions (similar to the English banns) had been read or posted in that parish on three consecutive Sundays or holy days. Since the consent of the father was normally required, if he was deceased his death record would also be included in the petition. The marriage petition sometimes also included any special dispensations that would be needed from the bishop or the pope for the marriage to take place. In some parishes such petitions have been conserved and are of particular interest if the groom was from a parish other than the one in which the marriage took place, since the petition may provide a copy of his baptismal certificate.

Both the concept of an investigation and the nature of it have their roots in the Council of Trent, a meeting of Catholic bishops from throughout Europe held in Trent, Italy in the early 1560s. As a major expression of the Counter-Reformation, the council issued orders concerning the sanctity of Catholic church sacraments and practical means of maintaining that sanctity. For the first time, parish registers of sacraments performed, primarily baptisms and marriages and later burials or deaths, were to be universally kept in each parish. The bishops were to keep records of the confirmations and ordinations that they performed and of the dispensations that they granted.

Prior to the Council of Trent, two viewpoints on marriage had contended for dominance in Spanish legal philosophy: (1) the view that marriage was a contract entered into by both parties at the time of betrothal establishing the marital relationship, the contract being ultimately sealed with consummation of the marriage, but potentially made fully binding by the exchange of *prendas*, gifts between the bride and groom or by payment of part of the dowry; and (2) the view that marriage was a sacramental contract, which could only be finalized by the blessing of the union by the priesthood authority of the Church. The first position could and did lead to difficult personal and legal questions about when the contract for marriage was final. Protracted litigation in civil and ecclesiastical courts arose from this ambiguity. Furthermore, as sexual relations often began once the betrothal was final, children born of those unions not blessed at the time of their birth by the Church's sacrament of marriage were considered illegitimate. In addition, the sexual relations themselves were viewed as sinful, which troubled the clergy.

The positions adopted by the Council of Trent were heavily influenced by the philosophies and criticisms of Protestant reformers. The Church's laxity in maintaining the sanctity of the sacraments was criticized by those Protestants who viewed the sacraments as crucial, and was considered proof of the nonessentiality of the sacraments by those who saw no need for the intercession of the Church in the relationship between God and Man. Protestant doctrines such as predestination forced the Church to a strong stand on the significance and necessity of free will, especially as a prerequisite to a valid marriage. The belief in the sacrament of marriage as the binding act in the union of two free wills found practical expression and protection in the procedural controls of the Church over marriage.

In each marriage investigation, whether conducted by the parish priest prior to the marriage or under the direction of the bishop's vicar general in the investigations for a marital dispensation, an effort was made to ascertain that this marriage was an exercise of free will on the part of the parties. In the case of the parish investigation, a declaration of consent by each party was obtained, stating that the party wanted the marriage of his or her own "spontaneous and free will." In the dispensation marriage investigations, the free will of the bride, who was clearly recognized by the language of the document as the weaker party and therefore the one whose free will was more likely to be violated, was further protected by the interviewing officer of the court who asked each of the witnesses the following question under oath:

> If you know, [give testimony] that in order to contract this marriage the proposed bride has not been by artifices nor by fearful torment by the groom nor by any other person in his name, forced or inclined against her will but that she wants to marry him of her own will.

CANONICAL IMPEDIMENTS TO MARRIAGE

The honor of the Church as an institution was maintained by being certain that a full investigation was conducted and the parties were free from (that is, they were not in violation of) the impediments imposed by Catholic canon law. Under canon law there were a number of impediments to marriage, many of which could be dispensed with or forgiven by the bishop. Included in these were two major categories: diriment, which even if discovered after marriage voided the union; and preventative, which only stood as obstacles if discovered before marriage. Typical of the latter would be the objection that one of the parties had made a previous promise to marry another person. The following were the diriment impediments as they had developed by the end of the Middle Ages and the Council of Trent:

I. *Consentimiento* (consent)
  A. *De Los Contrayente* (of the contracting parties)
  B. *Del Padre si el (la) Contrayente no Tenia la Mayoria (Despues de 1787)* (of the father if one of the contracting parties is not of age [after 1787])
II. *Incapacidad* (incapacity)
  A. *Parentesco* (relationship)
    1. *De Consanguinidad* (by blood or consanguinity)
    2. *De Afinidad* (by marriage or affinity)
    3. *Espiritual o de Compadrazgo* (spiritual or by godparentage)
  B. *Impotencia* (impotence)
  C. *Crimenes Como Adulterio o Homicidio* (crimes such as adultery or homicide)
  D. *Honestidad Publica (Relacion Ilicita o Promesa Publica de Casarse)* (public honesty [illicit relation or public promise to marry another])
  E. *Voto Anterior de Castidad* (previous vow of chastity)
  F. *Ordenacion al Sacerdocio* (ordination to the priesthood)
  G. *Otra Esposa Viviente* (another living spouse)
  H. *No Hacer las Amonestaciones* (the banns were not read)
  I. *No Estar aun en Pubertad* (one of the parties had not reached puberty)
  J. *No Ser Catolico* (one party not a Catholic)
  K. *Clandestinidad Frequentemente Abduccion* (clandestine marriage, often initiated by abduction)

MARRIAGE PARISH REGISTER ENTRIES

The Council of Trent imposed several limitations upon the performance of the marriage sacrament and required that each parish priest maintain a register of all marriages performed. A late-nineteenth-century marriage entry in a parish book contains the following: the names and all surnames of the bride and groom with an indication as to their marital status, whether *soltero/a* or *viudo/a* (single or widowed); their profession, residence, birthplace, age at the time of marriage, and in some cases their birth date; the names of their parents; the birthplace or residence of their parents; the date the marriage was performed; the name of the parish; and the name of the priest who performed the marriage.

In addition to the above, the marriage entry records whether there were any special difficulties or circumstances surrounding the event. For example, on some occasions there was an objection or impediment to the marriage, the most common being the need for an apostolic dispensation (see page 202). Additional comments can also provide moments of human interest and even humor, such as in one case in the parish of Cañamero, province of Caceres, Spain, where the priest recorded that the first Sunday the admonitions were read someone had objected on the grounds that the groom had previously been engaged to the sister of the bride and had failed to fulfill the promises made to that sister. The priest, however, recorded that the objections had proved insubstantial because since that time the sister of the bride had become a nun, and she herself had no objection to her sister's marriage.

According to the procedures outlined by the Council of Trent, the names of the parties and their intention to be married had to be read or posted in the church prior to each of the masses on three consecutive holy days or Sundays. However, these admonitions could be suspended upon special permission from the bishop. The record also states whether the three canonical admonitions were published or dispensed with.

Figure 10-1 is a typical example of nineteenth- and early-twentieth-century marriage entries. A literal transcription and translation follow:

> En la ciudad de Cabra provincia // y obispado de Córdoba a veintiocho // de Octubre de mil novecientos diez; // Yo Don Jose Joaquín Aparicio y Gon // gora Pbro. Rector y Cura propio de // la Parroquia de St. Domingo de Guz // man de la misma, autoricé al Coad // jutor de ella Pbr. Licenciado Don // Antonio Ortiz Ordoñez para que des // posara y casara como lo hizo in // facie ecclesiae por palabras de pre // sente que hacen verdadero y legítimo // matrimonio y seguidamente dió las // bendiciones nupciales // de Nuestra San // ta Madre la Iglesia // a Jose Maria Reyes Ortiz de veintiocho años de // edad hijo legitimo de Antonio Re // yes Rodriguez y de Maria Teresa Ortiz // Casa con Maria Josefa Valle // Mo // reno de dieciocho anos de edad // hija natural de Maria Francisca // Valle Moreno, ambos contrayentes // solteros, naturales y vecinos de esta // Ciudad, habiendo sido amonesta // dos y precidido los requisitos de // derecho para la validez y legitimi // dad de este contrato sacramental // siendo testigos Don Julian Luque, Don Jose Pastor y Don Antonio Pe // na ministros de esta Parroquia. Y // para que conste extiendo y firma // mos la presente en Cabra fecha ut // supra
>
> Jose F. Aparicio
Antonio Ortiz
>
> In the city of Cabra, province // and bishopric of Cordoba, on the twenty-eighth // of October of one thousand nine hundred and ten, // I Mr. Jose Joaquin Aparicio and Gon // gora, rector and priest of // the parish of St. Domingo de Guz // man of the same, authorized its assis // tant priest Licenciate // Antonio Ortiz Ordonez to marry // and wed as he did // *in facie ecclesiae* [before the Church] by words in the pre // sent [tense] they complete a true and legitimate // marriage and he soon after gave the nuptial // blessings of our // Holy Mother the Church // to Jose Maria Reyes Ortiz, twenty-eight years of age // legitimate son of Antonia Re // yes Rodriquez and of Maria Teresa Ortiz // Casas, with Maria Josefa Valle Mo // reno, eighteen years old, illegitimate // daughter of Maria Francisa // Valle, both parties // single, natives and residents of this // city, having been admonished, // and [having] completed the requirements // of law for the validity and legiti // macy of this sacramental // contract, being witnesses Mr. Julian Luque, Mr. Jose Pastor, and Mr. Antonio Pe // na minister of this parish. // That it so stands I set forth, and we sign, // the present [certificate] in Cabra date // *ut supra* [as above].
>
> Jose F. Aparicio
Antonio Ortiz

En la ciudad de Cabra provincia
y obispado de Córdoba á veintiocho
de Octubre de mil novecientos diez;
Yo Don José Joaquín Aparicio y Gón-
gora Pbro. Rector y Cura propio de
la Parroquia de Sto. Domingo de Guzmán de la misma, autoricé al Coad-
jutor de dho. Pbro. Licenciado Don
Antonio Ortiz Ordoñez para que des-
posara y casara como lo hizo in
facie ecclesiae por palabras de presente que hacen verdadero y legítimo
matrimonio y seguidamente dió las
bendiciones nupciales de Nuestra Santa Madre la Iglesia á José María
Reyes Ortiz de veintiocho años de
edad, hijo legítimo de Antonio Reyes Rodríguez y de María Teresa Ortiz
Casas, con María Josefa Valle Moreno de dieciocho años de edad
hija natural de María Francisca
Valle Moreno, ambos contrayentes
solteros, naturales y vecinos de esta
Ciudad, habiendo sido amonesta-
dos y precedido los requisitos de
derecho para la validez y legitimi-
dad de este contrato sacramental
siendo testigos Don Julián Luque
Don José Pastor y Don Antonio Peña ministros de esta Parroquia. Y
para que conste extiendo y firma-
mos la presente en Cabra fecha ut
supra. = José J. Aparicio = Antonio
Ortiz =

Figure 10-1 Parish marriage entry, Cabra, Cordoba, Spain, 1910 (author's copy)

The pre-nineteenth-century records are still relatively complete but are missing many of the smaller details, such as the age of the bride and groom and their birthplaces. Nevertheless, the parents' names and places of residence are usually given. This information is especially valuable since it may be the only clue as to the male direct-line ancestor. The bride's birthplace is usually not difficult to locate, since her parents were probably residents of the parish in which the marriage took place. The entry often records if the parents of the groom or bride have died. It can almost always be assumed that if no mention was made of the parents being dead (*difuntos*), they were still alive at the time of the marriage. It is, however, important to note that there is no definite pattern for marriage entries, and there may be quite a variance from one parish to another, and also from one priest to another.

COMMON PHRASES OF MARRIAGE RECORDS

There are several phrases commonly found throughout most marriage records. The following phrases relate to a discussion of the *amonestaciones* or *moniciones*, known in English as the "banns": *habiendo precidido* [sic] *las tres canónicas moniciones que manda el Santa Concilio de Trento y no habiendo resultado impedimento alguno*, or *despues de haber hecho las tres amonestaciones mandadas por el Santo Concilio de Trento y no habiendo impedimento*. Another important and commonly found phrase is *casé y velé* (married and blessed) or *casé, desposé y velé*, (married, wed, and blessed), indicating the two different marriage actions that took place within the Catholic Church. One was the actual marriage ceremony (*casé* or *casé y desposé*). This could take place at any time and was performed by a priest. The second, *velar*, was a special blessing given by the priest upon the marriage. There were two periods during the year when such *velaciones* (blessings) could not be given: the forty days prior to Christmas, known as *adviento* (Advent), and the forty days prior to Easter, known as *cuaresma* (Lent). Records of marriages that took place during one of those two periods frequently have a note in the margin indicating that the *velaciones* were done on a separate date from the marriage ceremony. In such a case, the newly married couple returned to the church at the end of the forty-day period for the special blessings, and the priest then noted in the margin that the blessings had been given.

Sometimes these *velaciones* were not recorded in the margins but rather in natural order within the marriage book or in a separate book called *El Libro de Velados*, which listed all of the *velaciones* — those that were done concurrently with the marriage and those that were done afterward. The recording of *velaciones* and marriages in the same book can be confusing. A *velación* may be found in the marriage book several pages after the record of the marriage. Both entries may be nearly identical, except the

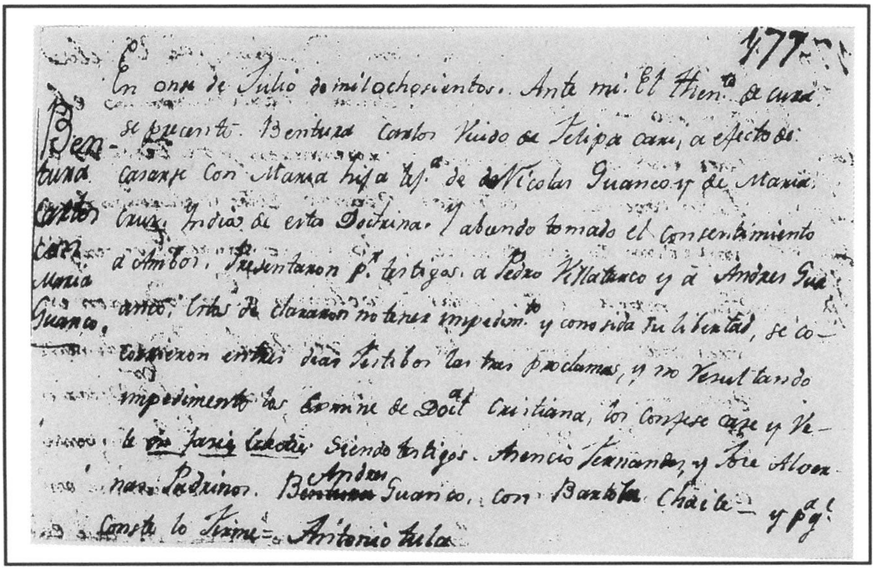

Figure 10–2 Marriage record from Argentina showing racial designators (author's copy)

record of the actual ceremony will say "*casé*." When this happens you should be careful to record the correct marriage date (the earlier of the two). In other cases the marriage might have taken place in the bride's parish, but the *velación* was performed and recorded in the parish of the groom.

Another important phrase is *in facie ecclesia,* "in the face of the church" or "in front of the church," indicating that the marriage was a church marriage, as all such marriages within the parish were. This particular phrase is useful because it helps in rather long marriage entries to spot the point where the name of the groom appears. As you are moving rapidly through a parish book, this can be a particularly helpful means of determining whether an entry will be of interest.

Por palabras de presente indicates that the marriage vows were made at that time and not "in future tense" (a promise to marry in the future). *Habiendo hecho las diligencias acostumbradas* indicates that the marriage investigation was done.

In Latin American parishes, marriage records usually contain annotations as to the race of the bride and groom. The various terms used to describe racial mixtures are found in the Glossary. Figure 10-2 is transcribed below, illustrating a typical entry from Argentina and showing the race of the bride and groom as Indian.

> En onze de Julio de milochosientos. Ante mi El Thente de cura // se presento Bentura Carlos viudo de Felipa Cari a fecto de // casarse con Maria hija leja. de Nicolas Guanco y de Maria // Cruz, indios de esta Doctrina. Y abiendo tomado

el consentimiento // a ambos, Presentaron por testigos a Pedro Villaturco y a Andres Gua // nco Estos declararon no tener impedimto. Y conosida su libertad se co // rrieron en tres dias festibos las tres proclamas y no resultado // impedimento los examine de Docta Christiana, los confese, case y ve // le in fazie [sic] ecclesia siendo testigos Asencio Fernandez y Jose Alver // nos Padrinos: Andres Guanco con Bartola Chaile — y pa. qe // conste lo Firme //
Antonia Tula

On the eleventh of July of eighteen hundred. Before me the assistant priest // came Bentura Carlos widower of Felipa Cari for the purpose of // marrying Maria legitimate daughter of Nicolas Guanco and of Maria // Cruz, Indians of this parish, and having obtained consent // from both, Pedro Villaturco and Andres Gua // nco were presented as witnesses. These declared that there was no impediment and that their liberty [to marry] // was known. The three proclamations were read on three festival days with no impediment resulting // I examined them in Christian doctrine. I confessed, married // and wed them *in facie ecclesia* being witnesses Asencio Fernandez and Jose Al // vernos. Godparents (were) Andres Guanco with Bartola Chaile — and thus be // it so I signed
Antonia Tula

The marriage entry may contain other interesting material for family historians. For example, some records will state the marriage place of the parents of the bride and groom. Others may state that the bride is the *hija legítima de legitimo matrimonio*, which indicates that the parents have been married in the church. Of particular interest is when the record states that the bride or groom is *viuda* or *viudo* (widow or widower). It may also indicate whether a parent of the bride or groom has remarried. For example, the marriage entry may give the bride's name and then describe her as: "*hija legítima de José Gómez García en primeras nupcias con Josefa Luisa Hernán de Herrero*" (legitimate daughter of Jose Gomez Garcia in [his] first marriage to Josefa Luisa Hernan de Herrero).

A parish marriage entry may also contain a phrase such as "*con dispensa de su Santidad en tercero con cuarto grado*" (with dispensation from His Holiness for the third with the fourth degree), or "*dispensa apostólica del cuarto grado de consanguinidad dada por el señor doctor Francisco Olivas y Frances provisor y vicario general despachada ante José Blanco Fernández Montero notario de la audiencia ecclesiástica de la ciudad de Plasencia el ocho de octubre de mil setecientos cuatro*" (apostolic dispensation for the fourth degree of blood relationship given by doctor Francisco Olivas Frances, and vicar general issued before Jose Blanco Fernandez Montero, notary of the ecclesiastical court of the city of Plasencia October 8, 1704). When you are doing parish research, be sure to make a complete copy of that portion of the entry referring to *dispensas apostólicas* so that you have all the information needed to find it in the diocese, as discussed below.

In addition to indicating *dispensas apostólicas* and other formal *dispensas* of a similar nature, marriage entries may offer other interesting information about the bride and groom. For example, if either the bride or groom had lived extensively outside the diocese in which the parish was located, there would be mention of a special *dispensa* or note from the bishopric authorizing the marriage. In some entries there are references to oral statements by the priest of the groom's parish confirming the marital status of the groom, because the written records of his parish had been destroyed. All information of this type should be noted as the parish research is done, since it may provide clues for further research and help uncover some of the human interest involved in these special moments in the lives of your ancestors.

CATHOLIC CHURCH DIOCESAN MARRIAGE DISPENSATIONS

The dioceses or bishoprics of the Catholic Church generated a variety of administrative and canon law documents. The records of the diocesan archives reflect both the variety and the extent of the control of ecclesiastical activities exercised by the bishop.[3] Of particular interest to family historians are the marriage dispensations. Under Catholic canon law, there are a number of impediments to marriage (see page 195) that may be dispensed with or forgiven by the bishop. The most significant and frequent of these are relationships within the fourth degree of consanguinity (blood relationship), or of affinity (relationship by marriage), as well as spiritual relationships such as that of godparent.[4] Also, if an individual was from a residence not within the diocese, a dispensation was required. There are also dispensations that do not relate to marriage records, such as that required for an individual to receive the priesthood.

A marriage dispensation record is made up of the following items:

1. Petition or presentation by applicants. This request for a dispensation, if for consanguinity, will generally outline the relationship of the applicants (proposed bride and groom). Figure 10-3 is an example of such a petition from Mexico. In many cases this relationship extends backward into the third or fourth generation; that is, there is a common great-grandparent named with extensive genealogical data connecting the petitioners with that great-grandparent. (See the chart of relationships to a common ancestor in figure 10-4.) The petition will also provide the names and birthplaces and parentage of those requesting permission to marry. In cases where there is a relationship by affinity with a deceased spouse, that spouse will also be identified and the date of death and burial provided. Where the petition is for a dispensation because the groom was from outside the diocese (*ultramarino*), the year and place of birth will be given as well as information concerning the arrival date in the diocese and even the ship that brought the groom to the New World. There will also be a description of his other places of residence.

2. Receipt of petition. Next comes a document in which the ecclesiastical authority accepts the petition for investigation.

[illegible] En la Villa de S. Tiago del Saltillo en [illegible] de Dizre. de 1701 años ante [illegible] Br. D. [illegible] Sevantes Negrete Cura Benefdo. p. Su Mag. Vic. y Juez ecclco. en ella de [illegible] la presentó el contenido y [illegible] Vis. la hubo p. pres. y mandó [illegible] Lo Rubricó

R. 707

1701

Saltillo —
dispensa de 4o. grado de consang. Joseph Flores de Valdés c. Juana de Abrego

Joseph flores de Valdés español hijo legitimo de Franco. de Valdés, y de Jazinta Menchaca difunta vezinos desta villa de Sntiago del Saltillo ante Vmd. parezco en la mejor forma, i via que a mi derecho convenga, i digo, que para [illegible] servir a Dios nro. Sr. y salvar mi alma tengo tratado, i concertado de contraher matrimonio segun orden de nra. Sta. Madre Iglesia con Juana de Abrego Romero española hija legitima de Nicolas [illegible] de Abrego Romero [illegible] y de Maria de Abrego Romero vezinos desta dha. villa con la qual me hallo ligado en parentesco de sanguinidad de quarto grado en igualdad por causa que mi Abuela Maria de Abrego fue prima hermana carnal de Bernardino de Abrego Abuelo de la susodicha de cuyos troncos procedemos entrambos [illegible] para poder conseguir dispensa de dho. parentesco del Illmo. i Rmo. Señor Obispo deste Obispado, se ha de servir Vmd. de recebirme información que ofresco de dho. parentesco, y de la causa que represento a dho. Señor Illmo. Obispo para poder alcanzar, y conseguir dha. dispensa; la qual [illegible] [illegible] de [illegible] conseguir [illegible] tengo parentesco mas cercano, y [illegible] igual y en calidad a mi, [illegible] [illegible] [illegible] que de no casarme con la dicha, no hallaré otra des[illegible] [illegible] con quien poderlo hazer; i tambien por [illegible] [illegible] [illegible] [illegible] muchos años en una cama sin [illegible] por estar [illegible] [illegible] [illegible] i tambien de como [illegible] [illegible] alguno impedimento no tenemos la susodha., [illegible] [illegible] de dho. impedimento o dirimente para dho. matrimonio [illegible] [illegible] impediente [illegible] lo qual. —

A Vmd. pido i suplico [illegible] [illegible] [illegible] [illegible] [illegible] conforme a derecho; y fecha dha. información [illegible] [illegible] della al Illmo. i Rmo. Señor Obispo deste Obispado [illegible] [illegible] [illegible] [illegible] [illegible] graciosamente [illegible] [illegible] [illegible] [illegible] Vmd. pueda proceder [illegible] de [illegible] dho. parentesco [illegible] de derecho necessarias hasta el efecto de dho. matrimonio, que en hazerlo assi obrara Vmd. con justicia, i [illegible] en debida forma este mi escrito no [illegible] de malicia, y en lo necessario — [illegible]

Joseph flores de Valdés

[illegible] y Villa [illegible] Vis. la hubo p. presentada y para su cumplimiento [illegible] se le de provisión, recibiendo [illegible] declaraciones de [illegible] [illegible] que [illegible] offrese [illegible] [illegible] [illegible] lo que convenga [illegible] de [illegible] Mandolo y firmo en dho. dia diez y siete de dizre. de mil y setecientos y un años —

Br. [illegible] Negrete

Ante mi
[illegible] de Mezena
N. nom.

Figure 10-3 Marriage Dispensation Petition from Guadalajara Diocese, Mexico for parties from Saltillo, 1701 (FHL 168605)

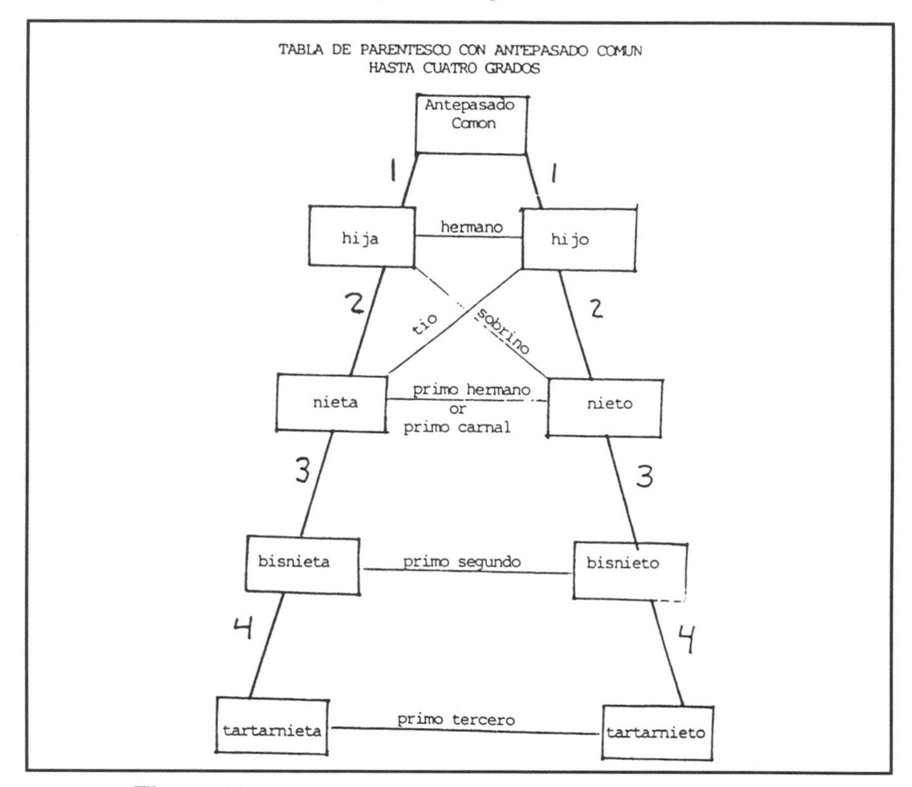

Figure 10-4 Canon Law Blood Relationships Chart

3. Appointment of investigator and direction to take testimony. Either a notary or the local priest is appointed to go to the town(s) of the applicants and take testimony and declarations to be submitted with the application.

4. Testimonies of three or more witnesses. Taken in the form of statements responding to specific questions, the testimonies of witnesses relate facts about the proposed marriage. Questions include whether there has been carnal knowledge between the parties, the nature of the blood relationship of the parties, names and other details about one or more of the related generations as known to the witness, personally or by hearsay, and the standing of the individual in the community relative to the Catholic Church.

5. Declarations of the applicants. The proposed groom gives a statement of the facts as found in the petition for marriage dispensation (number 1, p. 202). A similar declaration by the proposed bride usually includes additional statements that she is not being forced physically or otherwise to request the dispensation and enter into the marriage.

6. Remission of the documents to the bishop. This is a brief statement by the individual who has been authorized to collect the information and submit all of the documentation with a summary to the bishop.

7. The dispensation. This document, usually in Latin and signed by the bishop, waives the impediment to the marriage.

Since the ultimate dispensation was issued by the bishop, these records are found in diocesan archives. Nevertheless, they are records of an intensely local nature. Generally, they deal with families who have resided in a given locality for several generations, not an infrequent occurrence in the small communities of Spain and Latin America as well as in New Mexico, Louisiana, and Florida. Although somewhat difficult to use because of the length and variety of each document, as well as the lack of indexes, the wealth of information that can be found in a single marriage investigation makes the search worthwhile. As indexes are developed for other dioceses, this search will become easier.

Church and Civil Court Records Relating to Marital Relations

Before marriage, disputes sometimes arose over such issues as failure to fulfill what was viewed as a promise to marry, or objections to the planned marriage by the parents of one of the parties.[5] After marriage, disputes arose over such issues as the validity of the marriage or the failure of one of the parties to lead a proper marital life. Until the eighteenth century such disputes were generally heard in the diocesan courts by the bishop or a judge acting under his authority. Depending upon the diocese and the time period, records of such cases can be found in the diocesan records in three different places: mixed with marital dispensations, mixed with other court cases, and/or in a separate section of marital conflict cases. You should check with the diocesan archivist concerning the location of such cases.

During the eighteenth century, jurisdiction over marriage cases was transferred to the civil courts. Marital cases from that time are found mixed with other court cases or, as in the case of Buenos Aires, Argentina, in a separate section for marital conflict cases. Whether civil or ecclesiastical, and whether mixed with other records or in separate sections, these represent a very small percentage of all marriages. Nevertheless, if you find such a case pertaining to your ancestors it can provide extensive information concerning the family and its social status during that time period.

Dowry Inventories and Pre-Nuptial and Post-Nuptial Contracts

In the community property legal system of Spain and her colonies, both men and women maintained rights to separate property either brought to the marriage or received as a gift or inheritance after the ceremony. To clearly define those rights and identify the specific property held as separate, dowry inventories (*inventarios de dote*) or marital contracts (*contratos nupciales o capitulaciones matrimoniales*) were prepared by a notary. The parties to the contract were either the bride and groom or their parents. The document could have been prepared and executed either before the marriage or years after, for example when an inheritance was received upon the death of the husband's or wife's parent. In some regions or countries only the very wealthy wrote marital contracts; in others, like Catalonia in Spain, nearly everyone wrote them.

Marriage contracts can be found in the records of civil and ecclesiastical *notarios*. The procedures for preparing such documents, as well as the process of locating them, are the same as described in chapter 13 for other notarial documents. The only exception is found in dioceses such as Tarragona, in the Catalonian region of Spain, where marriage contracts are in separate sections in the diocesan notarial archives. The sample dowry inventory in chapter 13 reveals the type of detailed descriptions of property transferred to the married couple contained in notarial documents. These provide excellent information concerning the wealth of the families involved, as well as a fascinating glimpse of what daily life was like for the newlyweds.

---

[1] Indicative of the type of information found in those investigations are the conclusions drawn by Ramon Gutierrez in his definitive study on marriage in colonial New Mexico, *When Jesus Came, the Corn Mothers Went Away: Marriage, Sexuality and Power in Colonial New Mexico* (Stanford, Calif.: Stanford University Press, 1991), 291–297. The extensiveness of the information taken from the existing 6000 marriage investigations for New Mexico which he uses as a primary source is typical of the information they contained and indicative of the depth of the investigation.

[2] By Royal Proclamation in 1776 in Spain and in 1787 in the Spanish colonies, Carlos III changed marital law in Spanish dominions to require that parental consent be given before the marriage and made it a crime for a priest to perform a marriage without the previous permission of the father, or if he was deceased, the mother of each of the parties. *Printed manuscript of Royal Decree*, dated 10 May 1776, Archivo Diocesano de Tarragona.

[3] These include, among others, marriage dispensations, court cases, ordinations of priests, and records of visits by bishops to the various parishes. The extensiveness of these records is illustrated by those of the archdiocese of Durango, which consist of 1,120,000 pages. The collection, currently being microfilmed, begins in 1606 with 3 percent of its records from the 1600s, 32 percent from the 1700s, and 59 percent from the 1800s. The records of the dioceses of Durango, Guadalajara, and Michoacan in Mexico, Sao Paulo in Brazil, and Granada, Barcelona, and Gerona in Spain have been microfilmed.

[4] An excellent discussion of those records and detailed analysis of the parts thereof can be found in Raul J. Guerra, Jr., Nadine M. Vasquez and Baldomero Vela, Jr., *Index to the Marriage Investigations of the Dioceses of Guadalajara, Provinces of Coahuila, Nuevo Leon, Nuevo Santander, Texas, Volume 1: 1653–1750* (Edinburg, Tx., 1989), i–v; as well as in the general discussion of diocesan records found in chapter 10 of George R. Ryskamp, *Tracing Your Hispanic Heritage* (Riverside, Calif.: Hispanic Family History Research, 1984).

[5] Patricia Seed in *To Love, Honor, and Obey in Colonial Mexico* (Stanford, Calif.: Stanford University Press, 1988) explores the legal concepts and historical meaning of such cases found as a separate section in the Archives of the Archdiocese of Mexico.

CHAPTER 11

Census Records

The Spanish word *censo* (census or voting list) originated from the ancient Roman word for a tax or tribute paid based upon population.[1] From the time of Roman domination to the present, Spaniards have been taking population counts for purposes of taxation, conscription, and other governmental exactions, both ecclesiastical and civil. In the Royal Chancellery Court Archives at Valladolid, Spain, there is a *Libro de Behetrias* (Book of Property Holders) dating from 1352, which lists all of the property holders in each village in Old Castile. Many villages of Spain have lists of their *Hidalgos* (gentry or lesser nobility) dating back to the sixteenth century and earlier. The practice of using governmental censuses shifted early to the Spanish colonies. The first available census of Lima, Peru is from the year 1535; that of Santa Fe, Argentina from the year 1622; and that of Mexico City, Mexico from 1689.[2]

Census lists in Hispanic archives may appear under any of the following names: *padrones* (local census lists), *censos* (census lists frequently used for taxation or voting, and generally covering a broader geographical area), *matrículas* (register lists showing deaths and other changes in population, which were updated on a regular basis), and *catastros* (registers of the quantities, values, and ownerships of real estate).

THE VALUE OF CENSUS RESEARCH

Census records can be valuable for you as a family historian in a variety of ways. More than any other single record, they provide information about family units. They are generally taken in a form that makes it possible to identify the individual members of the family, which can be particularly valuable where the family was mobile and the children of a single generation were born in several different places. In these situations census records of the *matrícula* variety, indicating annually the residences of the families in a parish and recording the time when they moved, can be of assistance in determining where the family may have gone.

Census records that are national in scope, or from a large municipality, can serve as a locating tool. When you have not been able to locate the exact whereabouts of an ancestor, it is possible to check a broad region in a census record for your ancestor. Census records can also help identify the particular parish or parishes to which your ancestors belonged, especially if they lived in a large city. This is particularly easy where indexes exist. For example, in Madrid, Spain the 1890 municipal census is indexed with a small card appearing for each of the persons enumerated on the census. If a person knew that his ancestor was living in Madrid in 1890, but did not know where he was born, the index card would not only verify in which Madrid parish he lived in 1890 but also give his town of birth.

An amazing wealth of family information can be found in census records. Even in the earlier years of their existence it was common for *padrones* to list information about occupations, marital status, and social status. In addition to fleshing out your own ancestors' lives, these facts can provide valuable demographic information about the ancestral locality.

Census records can also often provide information about possible extended family relations. It was quite common for members of an extended family to live together. When this happened, the census can explain relationships, or at least indicate the presence of a person (often with a different surname) in the appropriate age category to be a brother, sister, niece, nephew, or aged parent of either the head of household or his spouse.

Especially in those areas where parish records have been destroyed by war or natural disaster, census records can provide vital statistics not available elsewhere. For example, many censuses in the late nineteenth and twentieth centuries contain the year and even the exact date of birth, as well as the birthplace.

The census can also be a steppingstone to other types of records. Since censuses were frequently taken for the purpose of taxation, they often identified the property owned by an individual. Evidence of such property may indicate that notarial records should be checked, since the purchase, sale, or inheritance of property was usually validated through the use of a notary. Census records often indicate whether a male had served in the military, as this was one of the ways in which the list for the *quintas* (conscriptions) was derived. If the census record indicates that military service had been completed, it would be appropriate to search military records either at the provincial or the national level. In addition, censuses will almost always indicate whether a person was of the nobility. If this is the case, there will be a variety of records relative to the nobility that can be checked.

LOCAL CENSUSES

Long before national censuses existed, the pattern of taking a local census developed in Spain and other Hispanic countries. The extensive coverage of these local censuses is incredible; there are, for example, thirty-nine rolls of film for censuses of the diocese of Guadalupe, Mexico covering the years 1600–1800. These censuses were generally taken for an ecclesiastical unit such as a parish, or a civil unit such as a municipality. Prior to the nineteenth century, local censuses were generally similar in form to that in figure 11-1, which is a copy of a page from a parish census taken in Saltillo, Mexico in 1777. The basic information listed there includes the name of the head of household, names of persons residing with the head of household, sex and age categories of those persons, and the occupation and age of the head of household, all typical categories for census records taken before the nineteenth century.

Beginning in the nineteenth century, local censuses changed as printed forms were adopted, especially for municipalities. Figure 11-2 is illustrative of the types of municipal censuses taken during the nineteenth and twentieth centuries, showing a page from the large folio-size census records taken in 1907 from the municipality of Valladolid, Spain. Generally, the later in the nineteenth century the census was taken, the more extensive the information is. In addition to these types of censuses, local *matrículas* showing the names of all of the persons in the family, and updating annually whether they were living in the town, became common in some parishes at the end of the nineteenth century.

In addition to the local censuses listing all heads of family and describing family members, either by category or by specific names, there were other types of censuses taken for special purposes. An excellent example of these were the California Mission Censuses, listing the *Neofitas* (Indians who had recently been baptized as Christians). Military censuses were frequently taken of soldiers or related civilian personnel and their families in frontier *presidios* (forts). The earliest census available for Mexico City is also a special purpose census that listed those who were of Spanish origin living in the capital city of Nueva Espana (colonial Mexico) in 1589. In most towns of Spain, censuses were also taken identifying the nobility in the town.

In addition to the censuses themselves, local tax lists, *catastros gremiales* (union or artisan group membership lists), and municipal vital records often exist and are housed in municipal archives where local civil censuses are found.

REGIONAL AND NATIONAL CENSUS RECORDS

The second category of censuses are those that covered a broader region than a locality or city. Colonial censuses covering an entire *audencia* (colony) or *virreinato* (viceroyalty), now forming one or more Latin American nation, exist in some areas from as early as the seventeenth century. Although wide area regional censuses can be found in the archives of Simancas, Spain, the first truly national census in Spain itself was that conducted for the Crown of Castile in the mid-1700s by the Marques de Ensenada. Known as the *Catastro de Ensenada*, this was a house-by-house census listing names, surnames, relationship to the head of household, age, and occupation of all of the persons within the dominions of the Crown of

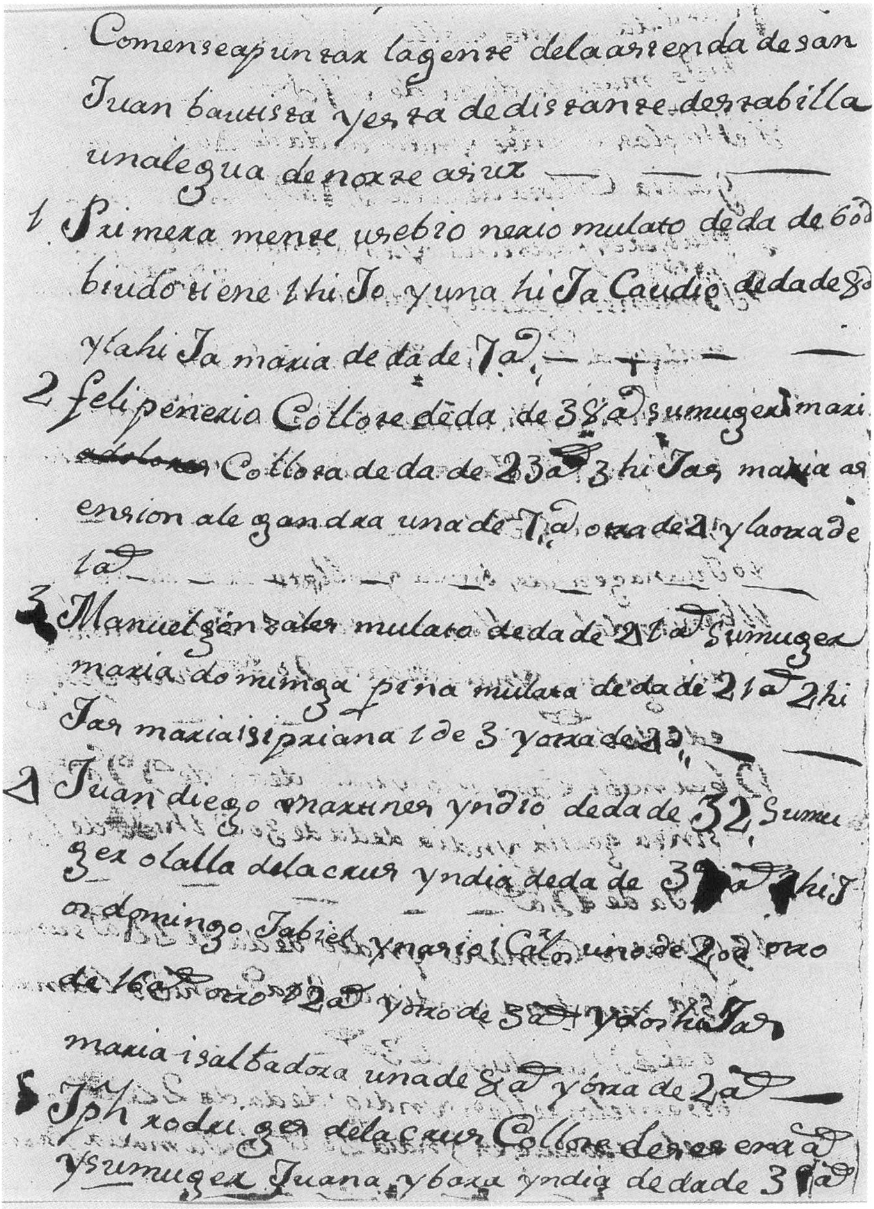

Comensea apuntar la gente dela arienda de san
Juan bautista y esta de distante desta billa
una legua de norte a sur
1 Primera mente urebio negro mulato de edad de 60
biudo tiene 1 hijo y una hija Claudio de edad de 8
y la hija maria de edad de 7 a.
2 felipe nerio Collote de edad de 38 a. su muger maria
~~de dolores~~ Collota de edad de 23 a. 3 hijas maria as
ension alegandra una de 7 a. otra de 4 y la otra de
1 a.
3 Manuel gonzales mulato de edad de 21 a. su muger
maria dominga pina mulata de edad de 21 a. 2 hi
jas maria isipriana 1 de 3 y otra de 2 a.
4 Juan diego martines yndio de edad de 32 su mu
ger olalla dela cruz yndia de edad de 3[illegible] a. hij
os domingo Jabiel y maria Calos una de 2 a. otro
de 16 otro 2 a. y otro de 3 a. y dos hijas
maria isalbadora una de 8 a. y otra de 2 a.
5 Jph rodriguez dela cruz Collote de[illegible] era a.
y su muger Juana ybarra yndia de edad de 3[illegible] a.

Figure 11-1 Page from a colonial census, Saltillo, Coahuila, Mexico, 1777 (Archivo Municipal de Saltillo, Sección Presidencia) (author's copy)

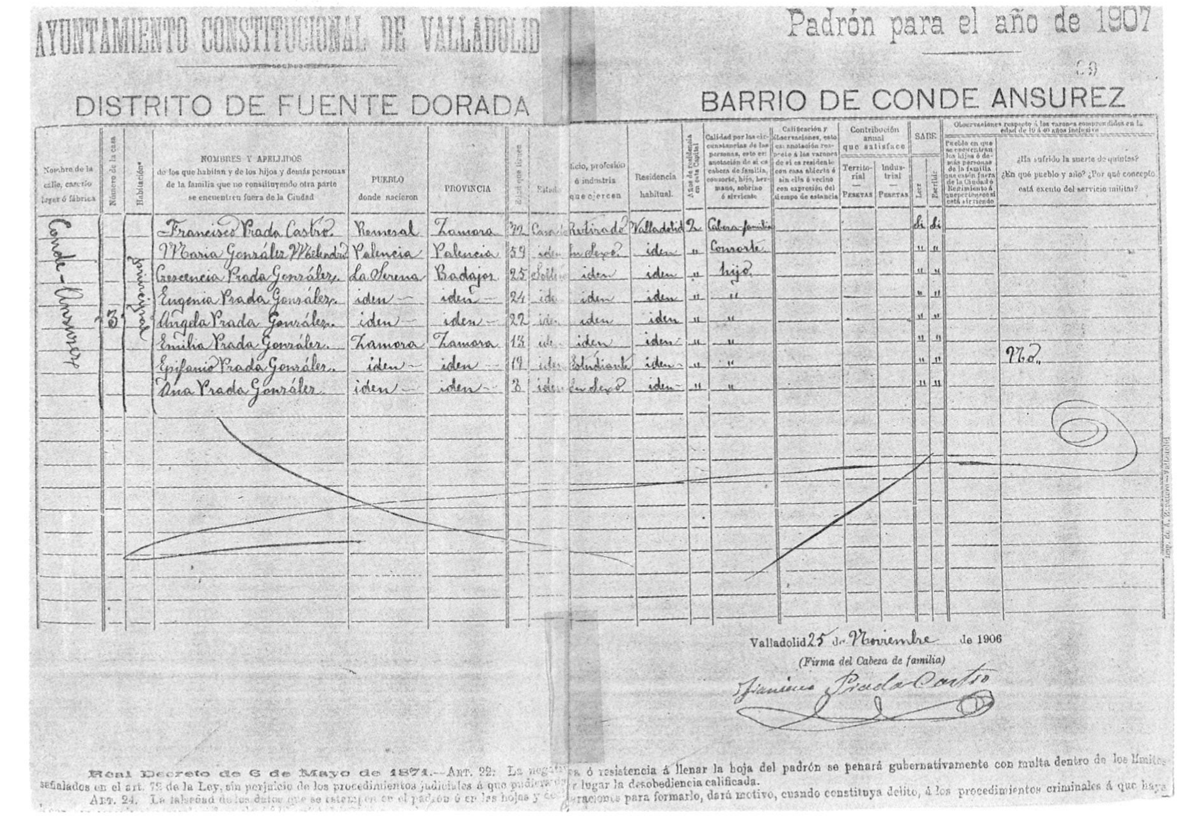
AYUNTAMIENTO CONSTITUCIONAL DE VALLADOLID

Padrón para el año de 1907

DISTRITO DE FUENTE DORADA

BARRIO DE CONDE ANSUREZ

Nombre de la calle, caserío lugar ó fábrica	Número de la casa	Habitación	NOMBRES Y APELLIDOS de los que habitan y de los hijos y demás personas de la familia que no constituyendo otra parte se encuentren fuera de la Ciudad	PUEBLO donde nacieron	PROVINCIA	Edad que tienen	Estado	Oficio, profesión ó industria que ejercen	Residencia habitual.	Años de residencia en esta Capital	Calidad por las circunstancias de las personas, esto es: anotación de si es cabeza de familia, consorte, hijo, hermano, sobrino ó sirviente	Calificación y observaciones, esto es: anotación respecto á los varones de si es residente con casa abierta ó sin ella ó vecino con expresión del tiempo de estancia	Contribución anual que satisface: Territorial — Pesetas	Contribución anual que satisface: Industrial — Pesetas	SABE: Leer	SABE: Escribir	Observaciones respecto á los varones comprendidos en la edad de 19 á 40 años inclusive: Pueblo en que se encuentran los hijos ó demás personas de la familia que estén fuera de la Ciudad ó Regimiento á que pertenecen si está sirviendo	¿Ha sufrido la suerte de quintos? ¿En qué pueblo y año? ¿Por qué concepto está exento del servicio militar?
Conde-Ansurez	3	principal	Francisco Prada Castro	Remesal	Zamora	72	Casado	Retirado	Valladolid	2	Cabeza-familia				Si	Si		
			Maria González Meléndez	Palencia	Palencia	59	iden	Su Sexo	iden	"	Consorte				"	"		
			Crescencia Prada González	La Serena	Badajoz	25	Soltera	iden	iden	"	hijo				"	"		
			Eugenia Prada González	iden	iden	24	iden	iden	iden	"	"				"	"		
			Angela Prada González	iden	iden	22	iden	iden	iden	"	"				"	"		
			Emilia Prada González	Zamora	Zamora	13	iden	iden	iden	"	"				"	"		
			Epifanio Prada González	iden	iden	19	iden	Estudiante	iden	"	"				"	"		No
			Ana Prada González	iden	iden	3	iden	Su Sexo	iden	"	"				"	"		

Valladolid 25 de Noviembre de 1906

(Firma del Cabeza de familia)

Francisco Prada Castro

Real Decreto de 6 de Mayo de 1871.—Art. 22: La negativa ó resistencia á llenar la hoja del padrón se penará gubernativamente con multa dentro de los límites señalados en el art. 78 de la Ley, sin perjuicio de los procedimientos judiciales á que pudiera dar lugar la desobediencia calificada.
Art. 24. La falsedad de los datos que se estampen en el padrón ó en las hojas y declaraciones para formarlo, dará motivo, cuando constituya delito, á los procedimientos criminales á que haya

Imp. de A. Zapatero—Valladolid

Figure 11-2 Page from 1907 Municipal Census Vallodolid, Spain (Archivo Municipal de Vallodolid) (author's copy)

Castile. The census was prepared in triplicate, with one copy remaining in the local municipality, a second being sent to the regional *Delegación de Hacienda* (The Treasury Department, which was responsible for the census, and of which the Marques de Ensenada was the head), and the third to the central government in Madrid. Unfortunately, the complete collection of the copies sent to Madrid was destroyed in 1937 during the Spanish Civil War. The remaining two copies may be found in any well-preserved municipal archives or in provincial or regional historical archives, where they have been sent from the regional *Delegación de Hacienda*.

In nearly every Hispanic country except Spain, at least one national census had been taken by the end of the nineteenth century. During that time period, or in the early twentieth century, the taking of national censuses became a regular governmental activity in most countries. Figure 11-3 reproduces the cover page of the 1869 Argentine national census for the Department of Santa Catalina in the province of Jujuy. Figure 11-4 reproduces an entire page from that census, typical of mid-nineteenth-century censuses. The categories at the top of that census are translated literally as follows:

(1) Inhabitants; (2) surname and name; (3) age by years; (4) sex; (5) civil status; (6) nationality — if he is Argentine, the province of his birth;

LIBRETO DE CENSO

REPÚBLICA ARGENTINA

Provincia de ...

Seccion de ...

Corresponde á poblacion ...

Firma del Empadronador:

Fecha en que se empezó este padron: ...

El empadronador al empezar en sus funciones debe llenar los distintivos de este padron, poniendo primero la provincia, despues la seccion, partido, departamento ó lo que sea; en seguida si la poblacion que vá á empadronar, es *urbana* ó *rural*; y por último, su firma, y fecha en que empieza.

Figure 11-3 Cover page from 1869 Argentine Census (author's copy)

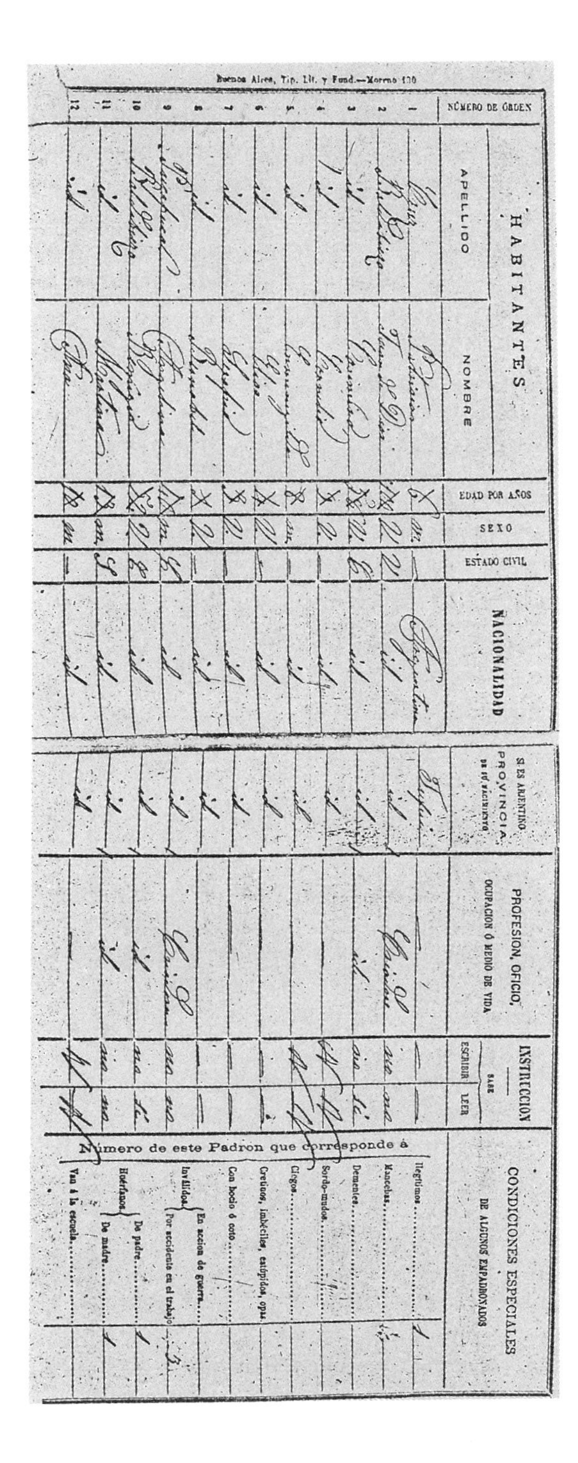

Buenos Aires, Tip. Lit. y Fund.—Moreno 130

NÚMERO DE ÓRDEN	HABITANTES APELLIDO	HABITANTES NOMBRE	EDAD POR AÑOS	SEXO	ESTADO CIVIL	NACIONALIDAD	SI ES ARJENTINO, PROVINCIA DE SU NACIMIENTO	PROFESION, OFICIO, OCUPACION Ó MEDIO DE VIDA	INSTRUCCION ESCRIBIR	INSTRUCCION LEER
1										
2										
3										
4										
5										
6										
7										
8										
9										
10										
11										
12										

CONDICIONES ESPECIALES DE ALGUNOS EMPADRONADOS

Número de este Padron que corresponde á

Ilejítimos
Mancebas
Dementes
Sordo-mudos
Ciegos
Cretinos, imbéciles, estúpidos, opas
Con bocio ó coto
Inválidos: En accion de guerra / Por accidente en el trabajo
Huérfanos: De padre / De madre
Van á la escuela

Figure 11-4 1869 Argentine Census page from Santa Catalina, Jujuy (author's copy)

(7) profession, trade, occupation or means of earning a living; (8) instruction; does the person know how to read or write; (9) the numbers of persons listed on this page with certain special conditions: illegitimate, mistresses, demented, deaf-dumb, blind, imbecile or stupid, those having goiters or who are lame, invalids as result of war service or by accident on the job, orphans without a father or mother, [and] those attending school.

Censuses were usually arranged by family groups. Although no specific relationship to the head of household may be given, it is often possible to hypothesize marital and other family relationships, since marital status and ages are listed together.

The following countries took national censuses in the years indicated.[3] Argentina: 1869, 1895, 1914; Chile: 1813, 1831, 1843, 1854, 1865, 1875, 1885, 1907, 1920, 1930; Colombia: 1812, 1823, 1835, 1843, 1851, 1905, 1912, 1918, 1928, 1938, 1951, 1964; Costa Rica: 1844, 1864, 1875, 1883, 1888, 1892, 1909, 1927, 1950, 1963, 1970; Ecuador: 1861, 1871, 1950, 1962, 1972; Guatemala: 1880, 1893, 1921, 1940, 1950, 1964, 1970; Honduras: 1881, 1887; Mexico: 1895, 1900, 1910, 1921, 1930, and various others to the present; Panama: 1911, 1920, 1930, 1940, 1950, 1960, 1970; Peru: 1836, 1850, 1876, 1940, 1961, 1972; Puerto Rico: 1873, 1877, 1887, 1897, 1898, 1899, 1900, 1920, 1930; Venezuela: 1873, 1881, 1891, 1920, 1926, 1936, 1941, 1950, 1960, 1971.

INDEXES

Indexes for Hispanic censuses, whether local or national, are relatively rare. It will generally be necessary to search the documents page by page to look for a specific ancestor. You will usually find that censuses that cover a large area are divided into geographical units, so the more specific you can be about a locality, the more your search can be narrowed down. There are exceptional cases usually for the colonial period where a local census has been published and, therefore, often indexed, or as in the case already mentioned of the 1890 Madrid census, where a complete index was prepared. It is always wise to inquire whether an index exists when you are using census records.

LOCATING CENSUS RECORDS

The greatest challenge in using Hispanic census records is that they are found in so many different types of archives. Ecclesiastical *padrones* are generally found in local parish archives or the diocesan archives. Local civil censuses, as well as local copies of the information gathered for regional and national censuses, are found in the municipal archives. In large cities these collections may be very extensive. Regional censuses, or those taken on a regional basis by the national government are frequently found in provincial or state archives. Those of national origin, as well as many municipal, provincial, state, or colonial censuses, are frequently found in the country's national archives. Occasionally, census records may also be located in the archives of the Treasury or Interior Department, which had the responsibility for preparing and compiling the census records. For many areas that are former Spanish colonies, including portions of the United States, census records may also be available in the archives of Spain. The national censuses of the United States are available on microfilm in many major libraries, as well as in the regional archives of the National Archives throughout the United States.

As you begin to look for census records for Hispanic countries, first check the Family History Library Catalog. Entire national censuses of some countries, such as those of Argentina for the years 1869 and 1895 and that of Mexico in 1930, have been filmed and may be ordered and viewed in the family history centers. In addition many municipal, parish, and diocesan archives have been microfilmed, and census records from these entities are available through that same source. Also, some early census records, such as those of Florida, Texas, and New Mexico during the Spanish period, have been published in books and periodicals.[4] For some areas, particularly the southwestern United States during the time period when it was still part of the Spanish colonies or part of Mexico, copies of the records are available here in the United States in universities such as the University of California at Berkeley (Bancroft Library), University of Arizona (Documentary Relations of the Southwest), and University of Texas at Austin. Review the computer library catalogs on the Internet to ascertain if such works are available through inter-library loan.

Once a search has been made of the Family History Library Catalog, review the book Latin American Census Records[5] by Lyman Platt for the specific country in which you are interested in order to identify where other specific census records can be found. These same sources will help you to determine whether a census record is, in fact, available in the United States for a particular locality. If the record you want is not available, you will have to either travel to the foreign archives or send someone to do the research for you.

Once census records have been located, you should search them carefully for any mention of the surname you are researching. Write down the names of all persons mentioned with that surname and record the information about them. Frequently, as you proceed to other records beyond census records, you will find relationships between these people and your direct-line ancestor. If you have already copied all the information from the census records, you will not have to search the records again when a new relationship is later established.

[1] The word *censo* not only means census but also refers to the following: (1) A tribute or head tax paid to the crown or titled nobility, (2) an annuity paid by the church to a prelate, and (3) a pledge or contract whereby an estate is pledged to the payment of an annuity without actual transfer of title in the estate to the recipient of that annuity.

[2] Lyman Platt, *Latin American Census Records*. 2nd ed. (St. George, Utah: The Tequayo Press, 1992), 15, 61, and 138.

[3] Ibid, 9, 16, 20, 24, 28, 51, 143, and 148; *Fuentes Principales* (Series H) genealogical research papers published by The Church of Jesus Christ of Latter-day Saints.

[4] 4. William S. Coker and G. Douglas Inglis, *The Spanish Censuses of Pensacola, 1784–1820: A Genealogical Guide to Spanish Pensacola* (Pensacola, Fla.: The Perdido Bay Press, 1980); Donna Rachal Mills, *Florida's First Families: Translated Abstracts of Pre-1821 Spanish Censuses*, (Tuscaloosa, Ala.: 1992); Virginia Langham Olmstead, ed., *Spanish and Mexican Censuses of New Mexico; 1750–1830* (Albuquerque, N.Mex.: New Mexico Genealogical Society, Inc., 1981); Virginia Langham Olmestead, ed., *Spanish and Mexican Colonial Censuses of New Mexico: 1790, 1823, 1845*, 4th ed., (Albuquerque, N.Mex.: New Mexico Genealogical Society, Inc., 1975); The University of Texas, Institute of Texan Cultures, *Residents of Texas: 1782–1836*. 3 vols. (San Antonio, Tex.: The University of Texas, Institute of Texan Cultures, 1984).

[5] Lyman Platt, *Latin American Census Records*. 2nd ed. (St. George, Utah: The Tequayo Press, 1992).

CHAPTER 12

Spanish Military Records

Military records can be a useful source for almost every Hispanic family historian. Even in times of peace a substantial portion of the population of Hispanic countries served in the military, and this number greatly increased in times of war or revolution. In addition to genealogical data such as names of parents and places and dates of birth, military records also frequently give exciting details that tie into the mainstream of national and international history. In many countries military records are brought together in national archives and indexed or arranged alphabetically by surname, which makes them an excellent tool for locating an ancestral place of origin. In Spain military archives contain records of large numbers of soldiers, both American and Spanish born, who served in the American colonies.

As you research in parish, civil, and notarial records, watch for clues that indicate military service. Parish records may indicate at the time of a marriage or birth of a child that either the groom or the father was serving in the military. A notarial record may contain a power of authority given from the person serving in the military to another family member who stayed behind. Home sources also frequently include military records. In nineteenth-century Spain it was necessary to prove discharge or exemption from military service before one could legally emigrate. Nineteenth-century census records frequently indicate if a person had served in the military. When you encounter any mention of military service, a note should be made taking down all the information, especially any indication of the time, place, and/or regiment or other unit of service. These facts may make the difference in being able to locate and identify your ancestor's military records.

It is not uncommon to find that the first contact your immigrant ancestor had with his new country was the result of military service. One American researcher discovered that this was the case for his ancestor Miguel de la Torre Balvontin. The researcher knew only that his ancestor had lived in Matanzas, Cuba, in the late nineteenth century. Due to current difficulties with the Communist regime, research is a greater challenge in Cuba than in other Hispanic countries; therefore, the descendant searched the newspapers for the Cuban cities of Matanzas and Havana, which have been reproduced on microfilm at the National Archives in Washington, D.C. He encountered a newspaper article that mentioned his ancestor's service to Cuba, both in commercial and military spheres. This brief military reference led him to check the index of officers of the *Archivo General Militar de Segovia*[1] on the assumption that since Cuba was one of the few remaining Spanish colonies at that time, service in the Cuban military during the last part of the nineteenth century would probably be recorded in Spain. His search of the officers' index yielded the following entry on page 265 of Volume VIII: *Torre Balbontin, Miguel— voluntario, 1876*. Noting the concordance of the name, surnames, and time period, the descendant then wrote to the Military Archives in Segovia, Spain requesting a copy of his ancestor's military record. The result was a file that included the record reproduced in figure 12-1, which gave the place of origin in Spain. Subsequent research in parish and notarial records, as well as family traditions, verified that this was indeed the family's place of origin.

HISTORICAL ORGANIZATION OF THE SPANISH MILITARY[2]

Although it is not essential to using military records, a basic knowledge of the organization of the Spanish military is helpful. This chapter will outline in broad detail the major historical divisions of peninsular and colonial organization.

Under King Ferdinand and Queen Isabel, the Spanish army was organized into *tercios*, regiments of twelve to fifteen companies of 250 to 300 men each. Originally, each was composed of three groups: pikemen, arquebusiers, and musketeers, although the latter came to dominate in large numbers as the quality of muskets improved. In addition, each *tercio* had one or two units of cavalry attached to it. Due to extensive military operations during the reign of Ferdinand and Isabel, a military policy was proclaimed in which one out of every twelve men between the ages of twelve and forty-five was required to serve in the army and was paid by the Crown. In 1505 the Spanish army consisted of 20 *tercios*, considered at that time to be the most effective fighting force in Europe.

By the middle of the seventeenth century, however, the army had lost its reputation of invincibility. In 1666 Spain's entire regular army was composed of 113 companies of 6,200 men commanded by 600 officers. During that time period the introduction of local militia units began to provide an ever-increasing number of soldiers required to serve in time of war or national crisis. The use of conscripted soldiers ceased, and the army was staffed with a combination of mercenaries and volunteers, many of whom were recruited by the lure of money and shelter available during difficult times. It should be noted that the extensive use of foreign mercenaries throughout Spain and her colonies accounts for many of the non-Spanish surnames found in Spain and the colonies during the period before 1776.

Among the eighteenth-century reforms of the early Bourbon kings was a total reorganization of the military. The army was organized into four

VOLUNTARIOS DE LA ISLA DE CUBA.

Primer Batallon de Matanzas. Pelle. Compañía.

PRIMERA SUBDIVISION.

D. Miguel de la Torre Balbontín nació en Polanco provincia de Santander Capitanía General de C. L. V. el dia 17 de Enero de 1857. es hijo de D. José y Doña María y tiene los méritos y circunstancias que se expresan:

Fecha de los despachos ó nombramientos.			SEGUNDA SUBDIVISION	TIEMPO QUE LOS HA SERVIDO		
DIA	MES	AÑO	EMPLEOS Y GRADOS QUE HA OBTENIDO	AÑOS	MESES	DIAS
4	Julio	1876	Voluntario	14	11	21
25	Junio	1891	1er Teniente		1	6
			Total de servicios efectivos hasta fin de Julio 1891	15	.	27

TERCERA SUBDIVISION AUMENTOS POR ABONOS DE SERVICIOS	AÑOS	MESES	DIAS
Por el doble tiempo servido en las circunstancias que expresa el artículo 121 del Reglamento del Instituto			
Total de servicios inclusos los abonos	15	.	27

Figure 12-1 ***Hoja de Servicio*** **of Miguel de la Torre Balbontin from Archivo General Militar de Segovia (author's copy)**

major divisions: *infantería* (infantry), *caballería* (cavalry), *artillería* (artillery), and *ingenieros* (engineers). Provincial militia units officially originated in 1704. By 1776 these consisted of forty-two regiments with two companies in each regiment.

In 1773 Charles III introduced the *quinta* (fifth), a system in which one out of every five men was selected by lot to serve in the army. This initially met with heavy resistance, and its enforcement was suspended. Nevertheless, it was ultimately instituted. Local municipalities were required to make lists of all male citizens from whom the conscripts were selected by lot.

Each of the regiments in the regular army had a colorful name and its own particular uniforms and banners. In many cases histories of the regiments are available and these, when combined with a knowledge of the dates in which your ancestor served, can give a fairly detailed picture of his actual military service. For Spain, these regimental histories can be obtained in printed form or consulted in manuscript form at the *Servicio Histórico Militar* in Madrid.

In addition to the major regiments of the regular army, there were other units that deserve mention. Throughout this time period there were special regiments of the Guardia Real (Royal Guard) who protected the king and the royal family: the Guardias Españoles (Spanish Guards), the Walones (Waloons Guards), and the Alabarderos (Halberdiers).

The second group of non-regular army units were the *milicias provinciales* (provincial militia). These were recruited from, and served in, each of the local provinces. In some provinces there was only one regiment, and in others there were several. The recruits for these regiments generally came from the area in which they served. Their officers, however, both commissioned and non-commissioned, were frequently drawn from the ranks of the national army. It was possible to shift from active duty in the regular army and transfer to the provincial militia.

Colonial Military History

The Spanish colonies were divided into fourteen *capitanías generales* (general captaincies); these generally corresponded to the thirteen political *audiencias* of Latin America, plus that of the Philippines. Those in existence in 1800 were the following:[3]

1. Buenos Aires
2. Cuba
3. Chile
4. Filipinas
5. Guatemala
6. Nueva España
7. Nueva Granada
8. Perú
9. Puerto Rico
10. Santo Domingo
11. Florida
12. Louisiana
13. Venezuela
14. Yucatán

Before these specific fourteen divisions were created with the reforms of Charles III, the major military division had always been the traditional *virreinatos*. In most cases the civil administrator over the area was also the commander in chief in the region; thus, the viceroy also served as *capitán general*. In those cases where there was more than one *capitanía general* within a *virreinato*, it was usually a provincial governor in the additional *capitanía general* who would be named *capitán general*. Directly under the *capitán general* were the various *tenientes capitanes generales* (lieutenant captain generals), who commanded the various regiments assigned to the viceroyalty. As a practical matter, however, in many of the frontier areas where there was not an assigned regiment of the standing Spanish army, the provincial governor directed military activity.

The colonial army was composed of four categories of troops: (1) veteran Spanish troops assigned to the colony for short durations, (2) veteran Spanish troops assigned permanently to the colony, (3) provincial militia, and (4) urban militia. The first two categories were generally small in number, and constituted the viceregal guards and the major regiments assigned to the capital of the colony. The troops of the provincial militia were drawn from the populace of the colony; however, the officers of these units were generally native-born Spaniards, and most frequently were veterans of the regular Spanish army. The last category tended to originate only in the late eighteenth century and consisted of militias organized in the cities for their defense. The urban militias in most cases never assumed a position of total organization and were comparable to the minutemen of Anglo-American history. The crucial role of the urban and provincial militias came at the time of independence, when with the military training they had received, they made important contributions to the success of the independence movement. For example, it was the presence of these militias assembled in the main square of Buenos Aires on 25 May 1810 that resulted in the toppling of the viceroy and his *cabildo* (council), and the creation of a governing local *junta*.[4]

The number of peninsular troops stationed in a colony, and the extent of the organization of provincial units, varied depending on the time period and the colony. In order to understand your ancestor's military involvement in one of the colonies, it would be wise to search out a military history of that colony.

MILITARY RANKS AND PROMOTIONS

The *grados* (ranks) of the Spanish military during the nineteenth century were as follows:[5]

1. *soldado* (private)
2. *cabo* (corporal)
3. *sargento* (sergeant)
4. *alferez* or *sub-teniente* (second lieutenant)

5. *teniente* (lieutenant)
6. *capitán* (captain)
7. *comandante* (major), also called *sargento mayor*
8. *teniente coronel* (lieutenant colonel)
9. *coronel* (colonel)
10. *comandante general* (major general)
11. *teniente general* (lieutenant general)
12. *general* (general)

There were three ways in which one moved up through the *grados* (ranks) set forth above:

1. *Por elección* (by vote). In the ranks of the non-commissioned officers (*alferez* and below), one was chosen for advancement *por elección* (by vote). The *capitanes* and *tenientes* came together and selected the non-commissioned officers and determined their promotions.

2. *Por gracia general* (by general order). At times of special service, as in a particular battle or at the time of a particular national event such as the coronation of a new monarch, the entire military was given a promotion.

3. *Por antigüedad* (by length of service). During the nineteenth century, the officers of the Spanish army were assigned numbers each year, setting forth their rank in relation to all other officers. As time passed they were given promotions as positions opened up to them.

All of the promotions discussed thus far were for *grados* (ranks), and not the *empleos* (positions of command or responsibility). A position of command or responsibility was generally determined by the need of a particular regiment, as well as by individual merit. It was therefore possible for a person of the *grado* (rank) of *capitán* to be serving in the *empleo* of *teniente* and vice versa, depending upon the circumstances. In addition to military standing, the various *grados* determined the salary level of the individual.

Additionally, it should be noted that prior to the legislation in 1836 that dissolved the distinction of classes, only nobles were allowed to occupy the ranks of the commissioned officers (*teniente* and above). Even after that legislation, the ranks of officers continued to be occupied primarily by those of *hidalgo* status.

RECORD TYPES

There is a wealth of historical and genealogical data contained in military records. The records discussed below have the greatest value to the genealogist, and are likely to be found in most Hispanic military collections.

1. *Hojas de Servicios* (service sheets): These military service records are found in all Hispanic military organizations. Generally, the name of the officer, the date and place of birth, and the names of his parents are set forth at the top of the sheet. The body of the record is a detailed date-by-date list of the various assignments and ranks of his military service. This may cover many pages or be briefly listed on a single page as shown in figure 12-2, a service sheet for a Spanish military officer serving in Mexico in the eighteenth century.

2. *Expedientes Personales* (personal files or petitions): These were generally petitions compiled for officers for a specific purpose, such as to request permission to marry, or to request and prove worthiness for a special promotion or pension. In many archives these *expedientes personales* may be arranged in special sections such as *expedientes de academia* (academy files), *expedientes matrimoniales* (marriage files), or *expedientes de pension* (pension files), or they may be arranged alphabetically with the various petitions for a particular soldier or officer filed together under his name.

3. Military Parish Records: The various units of the Spanish and Latin American armies, being overwhelmingly Catholic, had their own *capellanes* (chaplains). These military priests served under the *vicario general* (chief military chaplain) and performed sacraments for officers, soldiers, and their families, recording those sacraments in special parish registers. A soldier might then have had the option of having the sacraments for himself and his family performed by the military chaplain or the local ecclesiastical authorities, making it possible to find within the same generation some family baptisms, marriages, and last rites performed by local priests and others by military chaplains.

In Spain military parish records are kept by the *vicariato general castrense* in Madrid. If you are planning to use these records, request in advance both military and ecclesiastical permission to do so. Inquiries concerning consultation of these records should be addressed to the Vicario General, Secretaría General del Ejercito, Alcala 9, Madrid, España. This collection covers not only peninsular records, but also those for colonial military units in Cuba, the Philippines, and Puerto Rico.

4. Published Transfers and Promotions: It was a custom in the Spanish army to maintain promotion lists in accordance with tenure as an officer. In addition, the official promotion lists were given at least annually in published form as orders, which were distributed throughout the military. These lists have been bound into books and are available in several of the military archives, including the *Servicio Histórico Militar* in Madrid. Generally, these apply to the nineteenth century and include military officers serving in the colonies, as well as in Spain.

A similar procedure was also followed for transferring officers from one unit to another. Figure 12-3 reproduces an order transferring various soldiers to the overseas armies (*ejércitos de ultramar*) in 1871. This last type of record can be particularly useful, since it allows you to track, year

110

El Cap.[n] de Cavalleria Don Jose de Zuñiga su edad quarenta y cinco años su Pais Quauritlan su calidad Noble su salud Robusta sus servicios y circunstancias los que expresa.

Tiempo en que empezó à servir los Empleos.				Tiempo q há que sirve y quanto en cada Empleo.			
Empleos.	Dias.	Meses.	Años.	Empleos.	Años.	Meses.	Dias.
Soldado Disting.[o]	18	8bre	1772	De Soldado Disting.[o]	5	10	8
2.[o] Alferez	26	Agosto	1778	De 2.[o] Alferez	1	1	8
1.[r] Alf.[z] Volante	4	8bre	1779	De 1.er Alferez volan.[te]	,,	2	17
Ydem de Presidio	21	Dic.[re]	1779	De Yden de Presidio	,,	4	1
Ten.[te] Comand.[te]	21	Abril	1780	De Ten.[te] Com.[te]	11	7	20
Capitan	21	Dic.[re]	1791	De Capitan	9	,,	10
Total hasta fin de Diziembre de 1800					28	2	13

Regimientos y Compañias donde há servido

En el de Dragones de Mexico. En la Comp.[a] del Norte en la 3.[a] Volante, y Pres.[o] de San Carlos. En el de Sn Diego y en el de Sn Agustin del Tucson.

Campañas y acciones de Guerra en que se há hallado

En 9 campañas tres mandadas por si, en la que se apresaron 16 Piezas. Descubrió el Camino del Nuevo Mexico con Comunicacion á la Sonora. En tres Mariscadas en la Creacion y traslacion de los Presidios de la Vizcaya en donde tubo varios encuentros con los Enemigos: En Californias mandó 10 años el Presidio de Sn Diego, perficionando hta. su conclusion la obra del Presidio. Tubo 3 comisiones en dha Provincia teniendo que emprender en la ultima dos viajes a 200 Leguas del Pres.[o] y Pasando con licencia á Mexico fue comisionado p.[r] el Ex.mo Sor Virrey para Aclarar los Ajustes de Quentas de Californias y la terminada quenta del Cap.[n] Moncada que mataron los Enemigos en el Rio colorado, lo que executó reintegrandose la R.[l] Haz.[da] de mas de 70 pesos, y manteniendo los Apaches de Paz con Acomodos concedidos á la R.[l] Haz.[da] y en reconocim.[to] que se han hecho en el tiempo que ha mandado el Pres.[o] del Tucson se han dado muerte á 10 Enemigos. Desde el mes de Junio esta comisionado para correr con el Ramo de Inspeccion de esta Provincia.

Jo. de Zuñiga

Desempeña sus obligaciones.

Valor. Conocido.
Aplicacion. Bastante.
Capacidad. Buena.
Conducta. Arreglada.
Estado. Casado.

Nava

Archivo General de Simancas, Secretaría de Guerra, *Hojas de Servicios de América*, *Legajo* 7279, I, 110.

Figure 12-2 ***Hoja de Servicio*** **de Jose de Zuñiga, Archivo General Militar de Simancas, Secretaria de Guerra, Legajo 7279, 110 (FHL 1156342)**

— 471 —

RELACION QUE SE CITA.

ALTA Y BAJA *ocurrida en las escalas de aspirantes para pasar en su empleo y con ascenso á los diferentes Ejércitos de Ultramar, durante el segundo trimestre del año actual.*

ALTAS.

PROCEDENCIA.	Clases	NOMBRES.	Ejército á que solicitan pasar.	Concepto de su pase.
Reemplazo	T. C.	D. Antonio Jimenez Fajardo.....	Filipinas.	
Idem.....	Com.	D. Benito Gutierrez Gomez......	Id.	En su emp.°
Córdoba 10	Id.	D. Angel Pazos Vela-Hidalgo....	Id.	
Reemplazo	Id.	D. Joaquin Rama Garcia........	Id.	
Navarra 25	Id.	D. Ventura Lopez Nuño.........	Cuba.	Con ascenso
C.ª Mérida	Cap.	D. Joaquin Aymerich Villamil...	Filipinas.	En su emp.°
Bailen 24..	Id.	D. Antonio Nuñez de Prado......	Id.	
Rey 1.....	Id.	D. Luis Lopez García...........	Id.	
A. de Torm	Ten.	D. Diego Bordalonga Ros........	Id.	
Idem.....	Id.	D. Manuel Seco y Shelly.........	Id.	
Iberia 30..	Id.	D. Demetrio Camiñas Garcia....	Id.	
Princesa 4.	Id.	D. Benito Sacz Madruga.........	Id.	Con ascenso
Reemplazo	Id.	D. Rafael Perez Briz............	Id.	
Zaragoza..	Id.	D. Ramon Suarez Rodriguez.....	Fª y Pº Rº	
Bailen 24..	Id.	D. Ricardo Rubalcabar Villareal.	Pto. Rico.	
C.ª Santan.	Id.	D. José Cabello Noguera........	Ultramar	
Castilla 16.	Id.	D. Ricardo Alonso Serrano.......	Cuba.	
Mallorca..	Id.	D. Gaspar Machado Aisa.........	Pto.-Rico	
Reemplazo	Id.	D. Meliton García Trejo Moreno..	Filipinas.	En su emp.°
Idem......	Alf.	D. José Blanco Calvo...........	Id.	
Infante 5..	Id.	D. Gabriel Castro Castro.......	Id.	
Valencia..	Id.	D. Juan Verdié Escalona........	Cuba.	
Castilla 16.	Id.	D. Juan Fraga Silva............	Id.	
Reina 2...	Id.	D. Pedro Rodriguez Sopeña.......	Id.	
Idem......	Id.	D. José Argüelles Cortina.......	Id.	
Reemplazo	Id.	D. Juan Vazquez Pestana.... ...	Id.	
Reemplazo	Id.	D. Juan Zabalinchaurreta Goitia.	Id.	
Caz. Fig..	Id.	D. Antonio Rocel Rocel.........	Pto.-Rico	
Cantábria.	Id.	D. Manuel Rodriguez Gutierrez..	Id.	
Sevilla 33.	Id.	D. Rafael Cerdan Serra..........	Filipinas.	
Idem.....	Id.	D. José Cluet Abadal............	Id.	
Caz. Mad..	Id.	D. Leandro Ciria Roble..........	Id.	
Córdoba 10	Id.	D. Manuel Zamora Veguez.......	Id.	Con ascenso
Caz. Mad..	Id.	D. Agustin Guia Gomez.........	Id.	
Astúrias..	Id.	D. Antonio Perea Lopez.........	Id. ó P.-R.	
Res.ª Mad.	Id.	D. José Gonzalez Huelga........	C.ª ó P.-R.	
Reemplazo	Id.	D. Manuel Mendoza Sainz.......	Filipinas.	
C.ª Santan.	Id.	D. Gerardo Moran Loredo Brana..	Id.	
Caz. Barc.	Sg. 1.°	D. Francisco Madain Celestino...	Cuba.	
Leon 38...	Id.	D. Laureano Alvarez Garcia.....	Id.	
Bon. Prev.	Id.	D. José Alfaro Servan..........	Filipinas.	
Iberia 30..	Id.	D. Luis Pró Trugillo...........	Id.	
Res.ª Bad.	Id.	D. Arturo de la Guardia Baeza...	Cuba.	
Astúrias..	Id.	D. Pedro Valduque Ferrer......	Id.	

Figure 12-3 Published transfer order list from Servicio Histórico Militar, Madrid, Spain (author's copy)

by year, not only the promotions of an individual ancestor but also his transfers from one unit to another.

In countries other than Spain, and in Spain prior to the nineteenth century, similar orders listing various transfers and promotions can be found in archival sections dealing with *empleos* (positions), *gracias* (passes), *oficiales generales* (general official communications), and *órdenes* (orders). Use catalogs or collection inventories to determine the various categories into which such documents may be organized, if the orders of promotion and/or transfer have been published, and what records exist. Where none are available, write directly to the military archives or to that portion of the military responsible for military histories, such as the *Servicio Histórico Militar* in Madrid, Spain. These records may also be found in state or provincial historical archives for militia units.

5. *Listas de Quintas o Conscripciones* (conscription lists): These were lists of new recruits or of all individuals available for military service, indicating those who were actually selected. In some countries these are housed in the national military archives, but they are most frequently found in the municipal archives. In the latter case, where parish records or other available records have been destroyed, a listing of all adult males eligible for military service can be a valuable ongoing census of the male residents of the town.

6. *Filiaciones* (enlistments): These are individual listings (in most cases on separate sheets called *hojas de filiación*) of the soldiers in the army, as distinguished from the officers. Generally, *filiaciones* have the names of the soldier and his parents, his birthplace, place of residence, religion, whether he is married, and a physical description. In most cases it will also contain information such as the *hoja de servicio*, showing various places where he has served. Unfortunately, unless arranged alphabetically as part of the initial filing, these *filiaciones* are much less likely to be indexed and therefore aren't as accessible. For this reason, in dealing with a non-officer it is important to note any information relative to military service encountered in local or family records. The location of enlistment, or the regiment in which a particular soldier served, may be the key to finding his record.

In Spain the records covering at least the period since 1836, and often much more recent records, are now housed in the Archivo General Militar de Guadalajara, a new archives created in the late 1970s. Most records of soldiers were transferred there from the Archivo General Militar de Segovia and the regional military archives. These records are arranged alphabetically by major enlistment districts, so that it is necessary to indicate a specific geographical area of origin for the soldier/ancestor if possible, as well as a specific time period and both surnames. Written requests for information on a specific soldier can be addressed directly to the Archives at Guadalajara or to the Servicio Histórico Militar, Calle Martires de Alcala, Madrid, Spain, which oversees activities at both the Guadalajara and the

Segovia archives. Both of these archives should be searched for any individual soldier in the event that he became an officer. In many cases personnel files of soldiers remain at Segovia, mixed with those of officers with similar names.

7. *Padrones* (censuses) and *Listas de Revistas* (review lists): Frequently, especially in outlying areas, censuses were taken of military personnel (both officers and enlisted men) who served at a particular post, as well as of their families. In addition, it was common to review all the members of a unit in frontier areas, such as the southwestern United States, where censuses of the *presidios* (frontier posts) frequently included all of the citizens under the responsibility and protection of that unit, as well as all the soldiers. A 1748 census for the presidio of Sinaloa, Mexico appears as figure 12-4.[6]

WHERE TO FIND MILITARY RECORDS

Locating the records of your ancestors who served in the military may require some diligence but is well worth the effort. The major difficulty in looking for a military record is that the records tend to have been preserved in archives corresponding to the type of military service. This means that, for those serving in the Spanish regular army in colonial areas, or serving as officers in provincial or militia units, the records are likely to be found in the archives of Spain. For enlisted personnel in colonial regiments and for national armies after independence, the records may be found in national archives other than those of Spain. In addition, those for militia units may be found in state provincial or large municipal archives.

Military census records, reports, promotion lists, and other administrative records were frequently prepared in duplicate or triplicate, especially during the colonial period. One copy was kept locally, a second was sent to the regional *capitanía general*, and the last one was sent to colonial administrators in Spain. While this pattern makes it somewhat difficult to determine in what archives the records you are searching may be filed, it has proved fortunate in areas where local archives have been destroyed. It is possible to find Latin American military records that were primarily local in nature in Spanish national archives. An excellent example of this are the military records of the American South and Southwest during the Spanish colonial periods, which are preserved in the Archivo General de las Indias in Seville[7] as well as in the archives at Simancas.[8]

In looking for a particular military record, the pattern of research should be as follows:

1. Identify those archives containing military records for the country you are searching. To help you make this initial identification, the following list has been compiled of the principal archives where records of a military nature can be found for the countries of Latin America.[9] For the

Spanish-American Genealogist Annual 1979 (31-34) Page 559

Archivo General de la Nación, *Inquisición*, Volume 1292, p. 423.

En La Villa de Sinaloa en beinte y nueba Dias de El mes de Junio de mill setecientos Quarenta y ocho an^{s}; Yo D^{n} Juan de Goycoechea Thë^{te} Gnral Politico Y militar de Este Muebo Reyno y Prouincias de Sinaloa Para Efecto de Elejir Y nombrar Cap^{n} y oficiales Suhalternos a la Compania Miliciana de Españoles de esta dha Villa; tengo Probeydo autto y promulgado Por Bando, el dia Veinte y quatro deel Corriente mes mandando La Coucurrencia en este Real Presidio Para El dia de oi, en obserbancia de la Prouidencia; dada Por El ss^{or} LL^{do} D^{n} Joseph Raphael Rodrigues Gallardo Abogado dela Real Audien^{a} de Mexico, Y Visitador delos Presidios de Esta Governa^{on} En Virtud de despacho que Por el Exmo ss^{or} Virrei de esta nueba españa Se le cometio con fha de veinte y dos de Enero deste Presente año para El destino que en el se Refiere, y echa La eleccion de dhos oficiales, Prosedi a Pasar la Muestra en la forma y Manera siguente, Primera Mente

Cap^{n} D^{n} Miguel Carlos de Mollinedo Por Muerte de D^{n} Sebastian Lopes de Ayala y Gusman

(Marginal note: Este se puso con titulo de cap^{n} sin haverlo admitido)
Thef^{e} D^{n} Ygn^{o} de Lugo Por Renuncia de D^{n} fran^{co} Peñuelas
Alfrs D^{n} Manuel de Billa ViSencio
Sarg^{to} D^{n} fran^{co} Bohorques todos estos oficiales manifestaron armas y caballos necesarios

5. Cabo de Esquadra Ygn^{o} de Castro Con Armas y Caballos
6. Cabo de Esquadra Ylario de Espinosa Con lo mesmo
7. Cabo Antt^{o} Sotelo Con Armas y Caballos
8. Cabo de Esquadra Ju^{o} Diego de Castro Con todas armas Y Caballos
9. El Cap^{n} Reformado D^{n} Pedro Antt^{o} Albares de Asebedo Thodas armas y Caballos
10. El Cap^{n} D^{n} Sebastian Antt^{o} de Ascarraga Thodas armas y Caballos
11. El Cap^{n} D^{n} Joseph de angulo Thodas Armas y Caballos—
12. El Cap^{n} D^{n} Thomas de Hujdobro, todas armas y Caballos
13. El Cap^{n} D^{n} Feliesino Antt^{o} de Ascarraga Thodas armas y Caballos
14. D^{n} Joseph Man^{l} Lopes todas armas y Caballos
15. D^{n} Ju^{o} del Balle Thodas armas y Caballos
16. D^{n} Ju^{o} Alberes de Asebedo todas armas y Caballos
95. ...ando Goycoechea todas armas y Caballos
96. Ygn... todas armas y Caballos
97. Esteban Boho... armas y ...ballos
98. Pedro Barcelon sin ... ...llos
99. Joseph Baldes sin armas do...
100. Ju^{o} Antt^{o} Romo Lanza y adarga do...
101. Antt^{o} de Uria, sin armas seis Ca...
102. Ju^{o} Man^{l} de Castro todos armas y ...llos
103. Nicolas Antt^{o} Redondo sin armas t... Caballos
104. Nicolas de Alaxo sin armas todos C...allos

Ausentas D^{n} Jua^{o} Maria de Alcala todas Armas tres Caballos

1.
2. D^{n} Ju^{o} Joseph Bon todas Armas y Caballos
3. D^{n} Manuel Gutierres todas Armas y Caballos
4. francsico de Espinosa Con Armas y Caballos
5. Juan de Acosta
6. Joseph de Uria
7. Ygn^{o} de Uria
8. Antt^{o} Felis con Todas Armas y Caballos
9. D^{n} Claudio Brism Con todas Armas y Caballos
10. D^{n} Joseph Garcia todas armas y Caballos
11. D^{n} Santiago Bernardo Garcia
12. D^{n} Juachín Ganas Maldonado con todas Armas dos Caba^{os}

Todos los Quales en la conformidad que se Refiere en El Extracto que anttesede Pasa con la Muestra Con assistencia de Su Thef^{e} D^{n} Ygnacio de Lugo y sub alternos, Por aucencia de el Cap^{n} y Por que se adbierte en muchos de ellos Caresar de Armas les mande se apersiban los tales dentro de El termino de Tres meses desde la fha de este ala menos de lanza, Y Adarga Bajo dela Pena de seis pesos, que se les sacaran Yrremisiblemente no lo hasiendo y de que a Su Costa se manderan haser Para que en dho termino se Presenten con ellos y que en Las Urjencias o Ymbasiones que se ofrescan puedan hallarse Preuenidos Para La Defensa, y Para que Conste Lo Puse Por Dilixencia que la firme con los testigos de mi asisten^{a} Ynfraescriptos de q^{e} doy fee—

Juan de Goycoechea (rubríca)
Franz^{co} Lopes Peñuelas (rubríca) Joacqin Lopes Peñuelas (rubríca)

Figure 12–4 ***Padrón del Presidio de Sinaloa,*** **published in** ***Spanish American Genealogies,*** **1979, pp. 559, 561**

colonial period, records might also be available for any of the following countries in the archives of Spain, which are discussed in detail below.

Argentina: Archivo General de la Nación in Buenos Aires, *archivos provinciales*, *archivos diocesanos*.

Bolivia: Biblioteca de la Universidad Mayor de San Andreas, in *archivos militares*. (Note that in the Archivo de las Indias in Seville, Spain, the *audiencias* of Charcas, Buenos Aires, and Lima should be consulted for military records of this country.)

Chile: Archivo Nacional in Santiago; *archivos militares*, *históricos*, and *provinciales* throughout Chile, Argentina, and Peru.

Colombia: *Archivo Nacional de Historia* in Bogotá.

Costa Rica: Archivo Nacional in San José. For certain periods also check the Archivo General de la Nación in Mexico, and the Archivo General de Centroamerica in Guatemala.

Cuba: Archivo Nacional de Cuba in Havana; Archivo Historico Nacional in Madrid, Spain; El Archivo General Militar de Segovia in Segovia, Spain; Archivo del Vicariato Castrense in Madrid, Spain.

Ecuador: Archivo Nacional de História in Quito; Archivo Histórico de Guayas and Archivo Histórico de la Biblioteca Municipal in Guayaquil.

El Salvador: Archivo General de Centroamerica in Guatemala City; Archivo Militar, which forms part of the defense military in San Salvador.

Guatemala: Archivo General de Centroamerica in Guatemala City.

Honduras: Archivo General de Centroamerica in Guatemala City, Archivo General Militar in Tegucigalapa.

Mexico: Archivo Histórico Militar Mexicano, Archivo Histórico de Hacienda, Archivo General de la Nación, and Archivo Histórico del Instituto Nacional de Antropología e História, all in Mexico City.

Nicaragua: Archivo General de Centroamerica, Guatemala City, Guatemala; Archivo General Militar, Managua, Nicaragua; National Archives in Washington, D.C.

Panama: Archivo Nacional de Historia, Bogotá, Colombia.

Paraguay: Archivo Nacional and Archivo Militar in Asunción; Archivo General de la Nación, Buenos Aires.

Perú: Archivo Histórico Militar, Archivo General de Guerra y Marina, Archivo General de la Nación, Biblioteca Nacional, in Lima; in *archivos notariales* and *históricos y departamentales* throughout Peru.

Puerto Rico: Archivo General de Puerto Rico; Archivo General Militar de Segovia in Segovia, Spain; National Archives in Washington, D.C.

Republica Dominicana: Archivo General de la Nación, Santo Domingo.

Uruguay: Archivo General de la Nación, Montevideo.

Venezuela: Archivo del Ministerio de Defensa Nacional, *archivos departamentales*, and Archivo General de la Nación in Caracas.

The military archives of Spain are reviewed in great detail in the book *Archivos militares y civiles en donde se conservan fondos de caracter castrense relacionados con expedientes personales de militares*, a reprint of the appendix to volume nine of the officers' index of the *Archivo General Militar de Segovia.*[10] The detail provided therein is limited to descriptions of the sections of Spanish archives containing military records. It is currently somewhat out of date since there have been significant changes in military archival organization.

2. If possible, determine whether the individual you are seeking was an officer or an enlisted soldier. This will indicate the availability of records, the possibility of an available index to those records, and even in which archives you should search.

3. If the information known about a particular ancestor indicates he served in a specific military unit, search for records in the archives that would correspond to that military unit first. Recognize, however, that many soldiers and officers served in several units, and records may appear in more than one archives.

4. In cases where you know nothing about the military unit in which your ancestor served, or even if he served, the following priority is suggested:

a. For Spain and for colonial periods in Cuba, Puerto Rico, and the Philippines, search the index of officers in the Archivo General Militar de Segovia (see above), which provides a rapid and excellent means of identifying officers who served in the Spanish military in the late eighteenth century, throughout the nineteenth century, and into the early twentieth century.[11] For Spain and all of the colonies during the eighteenth and into the early nineteenth century, the Archivo de Simancas should also be reviewed. Several of the military sections of that archives are indexed, but only one of those indexes is published: *Secretaría de Guerra, hojas de servicios de América,*[12] which covers the service records of personnel, primarily officers, who served in the colonies during the late eighteenth century and the pre-independence years of the nineteenth century.

b. For periods after independence, and for colonial periods when you know, or are fairly certain, that your ancestor did not serve in the regular Spanish army or as an officer in the local units, the national archives of the country of service should be reviewed. In many cases service records found in these archives will be arranged in alphabetical files for personnel. It may also be possible to identify lists of personnel serving in particular areas, or originating from particular areas, in the *listas de reclutamiento* (recruitment lists) and the *revistas* (reviews). Because many such lists are organized alphabetically, and also because in many cases indexes exist for such collections, these records may be more accessible than others and may provide a means of identifying the military unit in which your ancestor served, thereby facilitating research in that unit's records. Some countries still have a non-access policy for military archives,[13] but a letter requesting information should always be sent to both.

c. If initial searches in the indexes of the above entities have not yielded results, check the provincial, state, or (in the case of large cities) municipal archives. Military records in these archives are most likely to be limited to recruitment lists, lists of personnel who served in particular units originating from or stationed in the local region, and personnel records for the provincial state or urban militias.

The emphasis of this chapter has been on finding *ejercito* (army) records. Those for the *marina* (navy) are frequently found in separate collections, and may even be found in separate archives. Before doing extensive research in records marked "Military Records," be certain that they do in fact contain those of naval personnel. For Spanish naval records, the Archivo Central de la Marina in Madrid and the Archivos de los Departamentos Marítimos in El Ferrol, Cadiz, and Cartagena have collections of documents similar to those contained in the Archivo General de Segovia for the late nineteenth and twentieth centuries. The Museo Don Alvaro de Basa in Ciudad Real contains personal documentation, service records, pension records, enlistment records, and other documents relating to naval personnel for the period before 1775. In Mexico the navy also has a separate archives.[14]

---

1. Instituto Salazar y Castro, *Archivo General Militar de Segovia, Indice de expedientes personales*. 9 vols. (Madrid: Hidalguía, 1959).

2. Lyman D. Platt, "The Mexican Military," *Latin American and Iberian Family and Local History, Volume 9 of The World Conference on Records* (Salt Lake City: The Church of Jesus Christ of Latter-day Saints, 1980), #713.

3. *Guía del Investigador del Archivo de Simancas* (Madrid: Ministerio de Cultura, 1980), 198–200.

4. James R. Scobie, *Argentina, A City and A Nation*, 2nd ed. (New York: Oxford University Press, 1971), 75.

5. A good description of each of these can be found in the corresponding entry in the *Gran Encyclopedia: Ilustrado Universal Espasa-Calpe* (Madrid: Espasa-Calpe, 1923).

6. *Spanish American Genealogist*, 31–34 (1979): 559–561.

7. Vicente de Cadenas y Vicent, *Archivo militares y civiles donde se conservan fondos de caracter castrense relacionados con expedientes personales de militares* (Madrid: Hidalguía, 1975), 97–98.

8. Archivo de Simancas, *Secretaría de Guerra (siglo XVIII), hojas de servicios de América* (Valladolid: Patronato Nacional del Archivo de Simancas, 1958).

9. The resource papers published by The Church of Jesus Christ of Latter-day Saints as Series H (as described in full in chapter 4) and *Una guía genealógico-histórica de Latino America* by Lyman D. Platt were the main sources used in compiling this information. These books should be consulted for greater detail as to specific types of records, time periods covered, and even titles of specific sections of the archives containing military records.

[10] Vicente de Cadenas y Vicent, *Archivo militares y civiles donde se conservan fondos de caracter castrense relacionados con expedientes personales de militares* (Madrid: Hidalguía, 1975).

[11] Ibid.

[12] See endnote 10, supra.

[13] For example, see Eulalio Fonseca Orozco, "Creación y desarollo del Archivo Histórico de la Secretaría de la Defensa Nacional," and Gloria Martin, "Situación y perspectivas del Archivo Histórico de la Secretaría de Marina," *Balance y prospectiva de los Archivos Históricos de México* (Mexico, D.F.: Archivo General de la Nación, 1994), where two military archives in Mexico City are discussed, describing the collections and inadequate facilities, mentioning no investigation or consultation rooms and, in one case, stating there is no copy machine.

[14] Ibid.

CHAPTER 13

Notarial Records

> *To look in a notarial register is like observing from a high hill all the panorama of Spanish life and to depart with its people, famous and humble, who, confiding in professional secrecy, laid before us their weaknesses and also at the same time their beautiful virtues.* — A.G. de Amezua y Mayo[1]

Hispanic parish records are so exceptional, and the government records so complete, that many family historians tend to overlook another even richer source of documentation — the notarial records. Unlike most other record sources, which are limited in scope, notarial records cover the full breadth and depth of life. The following types of documents are examples of what is included in the archives of a notary: wills, sales of rural and urban land, proof of purity of blood, dowries, sale of slaves, marriage contracts, sale of cloth, sale of horses, apprenticeship papers, and contracts with teachers. You will find significant family history in the records of the notary "because it would be difficult to find any human act in private or public life in which the pen of the notary did not intervene to give faith and testimony [to that act]."[2] Many people did not have property or personal reasons to use the notary to provide legal validation of transactions; however, for those whose ancestors had sufficient social or financial status to use notarial services, these records will provide the greatest amount of human interest and daily life information about their ancestors.

The history of the notaries in Spain goes back to the Roman origins of Spanish civilization. By Visigothic times the writers and validators of legal documents were already known as *comes notarium*, *lector scriba*, or *notarius*. By the time of the publication of such fundamental documents in the Spanish legal system as the *Fuero Real* and the *Siete Partidas*, the role of the notaries, or *escribanos públicos* as they were by that time known, was clearly formulated.

By the end of the Middle Ages, four separate classes of notaries had developed:[3]

1. *Escribanos reales* (royal notaries) were notaries whose function was specialized and limited to preparation and formalization of the documents that originated from the king and his councils and advisors.

2. *Escribanos públicos o de número* (public notaries) served the same function as the *notarios públicos* in modern times; they wrote and veri-

fied documentation for private legal transactions and, in so doing, created permanent register books called *protocolos*.

3. *Escribanos de provincia o del criminal* (provincial or criminal notaries) served as appendages to the various courts, performing a wide variety of administrative and judicial functions in both criminal and civil matters.

4. *Escribanos eclesiásticos y apostólicos* (ecclesiastical and apostolic notaries) were limited in their activities to canonical affairs. However, the wide breadth of involvement of the Catholic Church in every level of Spanish life gave these notaries a diversified practice. Their work encompassed all the types of documents that the other three notaries handled, with the only restriction being that the document involved the Church in some aspect, giving the Church an interest in drawing up and formalizing the document. These documents can be distinguished from those drawn up by the *escribanos de número* primarily by the seal at the head of the page, which in the case of the ecclesiastical notary was a pair of keys with a motto in Latin, and in the case of the public notary was a small cross. In addition, these ecclesiastical documents were generally written in a more formal and elegant style of writing.

SPANISH NOTARIAL LAWS

As they did with many other areas of Spanish life, the Catholic monarchs Ferdinand and Isabel and their successors attempted to impose some type of order on the notarial system. All notaries had to receive royal appointment, which was not granted until an examination was taken before the *Cámara del Consejo de Castilla* (Exchequer of the Council of Castile). *Escribanos reales* (royal notaries) were required to have sixteen years of apprenticeship service, part of which was with the *corregidores* (the local judicial representatives of the king). After the year 1609, the *escribanos de número* were required to have two years of experience in drafting notarial documents before being allowed to take the examination.[4]

In spite of such restrictions, there remained a certain amount of disorder within the notarial system. Prior to 1609 the *protocolos* (bound register volumes) were considered to be the property of the *escribano* and he could will them to anyone, generally to his oldest son. This meant that former records were frequently not available to the new notary who succeeded the *escribano* if the heir was unable to pass the examination or meet all of the other qualifications. Frequent attempts were made by the kings of Spain to enforce the preservation of the *protocolos*, and by the time of Charles III when a system of inspections was established (in 1788), the practice of maintaining some type of notarial archives had become nearly universal.

During the nineteenth century in most Hispanic countries, a *Ley de*

Notaría (Notarial System Law) was passed, imposing restrictions and new order on the private portion of the notarial system.[5] The name of *notario* was given to the *escribanos de número*, who functioned in the private sector outside of the judicial court system, and a system was set up whereby they became public fiduciaries and professionals in the legal system on a par with *abogados* (attorneys). The function of document drafting performed by American attorneys is handled in Hispanic countries by the *notario*, as is the function of recording such documents and making them available for public record.

The notarial system was implanted in the colonies by Spain. After independence most Latin American countries followed the Spanish and French example and set up notarial laws like those adopted for Spain. To this day, the notarial practice of Latin America continues to closely parallel that of Spain. Those interested in the details of the notarial history of a particular country should check the Internet libraries for books on notaries in individual Latin American countries. In many frontier areas where notaries did not exist, the local *alcalde* (mayor) or military *comandante* prepared legal documents and maintained them in book format just as the notaries did.

LOCATING THE RECORDS OF A SPECIFIC NOTARY

Because the conservation laws adopted by most countries in the early years of the twentieth century have not been uniformly followed, the most difficult problem confronting the researcher using notarial records can be locating them. Such records can be found in four different types of archives. Although the archives of Spain are used most often as examples in the following discussion, *protocolos* may be found in similar types of archives throughout Latin America, and a search for specific notarial records like that described below will be necessary in any Hispanic country.

1. Provincial or state historical archives. The records found in these archives are those in which the Spanish 100-year rule has been faithfully observed, and the district notary has submitted all *protocolos* in his control to the provincial archives when they became 100 years old. In some provinces where the local provincial archivists have been energetic, such as in Caceres or Barcelona, nearly all such records will be limited to those found in the provincial archives. In others, for example in Valencia, the primary notarial collections will be from the area surrounding the capital city. In still others, practically no effort has been made to gather notarial records into a provincial historical archives. In some cases other large historical archives may contain sections of notarial records that one would expect to find in the provincial historical or notarial archives. A good example of this is the collection of *protocolos* from parts of the province of Barcelona, which is found in the Archivo de la Corona de Aragon and not in the Archivo Notarial Histórico del Colegio Notarial de Barcelona.

2. District historical archives or the district notarial office. Records may frequently be at the district level, where they have been submitted to the district notarial office in accordance with the twenty-five year rule. In cases where the records are found at this level, the district's notarial archivist has generally not sent these records into the provincial archives, either because such an archives has not been set up or because an adequate archives has been provided for the records at the district level. Frequently, local pride and/or the interest of a local historian has prompted the creation of such archives, or discouraged the practice of submitting the records to the provincial historical archives.

3. Local archives or notarial offices. The same factors (listed above) that resulted in the creation of district archives also caused the creation of local notarial archives. In addition to those factors, mere failure to follow the outlined procedure, or general inertia, sometimes resulted in the retention of the records in their original locality. The preservation of records at this level varies dramatically — from the ordered or well-protected preservation of such records in a proper library setting, to a random or careless storing of the records in any available space, either in the notarial office or in nearby government or private facilities (most frequently in the local city hall). Many notarial records for Mexico will be found in the municipal archives. Notaries of large cities often grouped together to create historical archives for the *protocolos*. If you are looking for a notarial record from a particular city, it may be necessary to consult that archives, not the provincial historical archives.

4. Private, ecclesiastical, or government archives. Notarial records, especially those from before 1609, can be found in any of these categories of archives, because such records were the private property of the *escribano* who drafted the records, and not the property of the *notaría* itself. These other archives may also contain collections of wills, contracts, or other documents normally found in the notarial archives, because in addition to their official functions *escribanos de provincia* or *escribanos eclesiásticos* performed the functions of an *escribano público*.

This wide variety of locations where notarial records can be found presents a challenge to the researcher desiring to locate information about his family in the *protocolos*. Whether in Spain or Latin America, the researcher will usually be attempting to locate records from a particular locality; in some cases, for example where a death record has already indicated the specific notary, he may even be looking for a particular notary. First check the Family History Library Catalog to determine if the records have been microfilmed. Search under the locality, the state, and the state capital. Also, if the name of a notary is known, check in the Author/Title search of the microfiche edition of the Family History Library Catalog under the name of the notary. If the records have not been filmed, you should check first with the regional, provincial, or district archives to ascertain what records may be available. This can be done either by letter or in person.

Provincial historical archives have now been created in forty-one of the fifty provinces of Spain. Of the nine without provincial archives (Barcelona, Baleares, La Coruña, Granada, Guipúzcoa, Madrid, Navarra, Sevilla, and Valencia), four have regional archives with notarial collections (Baleares, La Coruña, Granada, and Valencia), two have *archivos históricos de protocolos* (Guipúzcoa and Madrid), and extensive collections of local notarial records are found in the Archivo de la Corona de Aragon in Barcelona. The volume of records collected varies dramatically from archives to archives, with only thirty-seven meters of shelf space occupied by notarial records in Castellón, and over 4,706 meters in Madrid. In some provinces, such as Huelva, no notarial records have been gathered into the provincial archives, but in others, such as Caceres, nearly all such records have been collected.[6]

In Mexico, Argentina, and Venezuela, the preservation and availability of notarial records follow patterns similar to those in Spain, with records originating in the middle of the nineteenth century or before located in provincial, state, or municipal governmental archives. In other countries, such as Bolivia, Chile, Colombia, Costa Rica, El Salvador, Guatemala, Nicaragua, and Uruguay, all or the vast majority of such older records have been gathered into national archives. Newer *protocolos* are retained by the notarial offices in nearly all countries. In some countries, such as Costa Rica, El Salvador, Guatemala, Mexico, Paraguay, and Peru, either all or portions of the oldest *protocolos* have been indexed. For greater details on a country-by-country basis, the Latin American researcher should consult the Series H Major Genealogical Resource Papers published by The Church of Jesus Christ of Latter-day Saints.

For those areas of Spain or Latin America where notarial records have not been collected into formal archives, or where the established archives do not have records for a particular locality or notary, a letter to the *notario* of the nearest town with a *notaría*, as well as to the provincial historical archives, may help the researcher locate the particular notary who generally served the people of that town. The local notary may be aware of records that he himself has, or that may be in some other archives, governmental or private, which relate to the locality or to a particular notary who served in that locality. Since many smaller localities did not have a notarial office, the researcher should identify the larger towns that may have had notaries. For Spain this can be accomplished by consulting the list of *notarías* found in chapter 18 of George R. Ryskamp's *Tracing Your Hispanic Heritage*.[7] For other countries a good atlas can help identify the principal town, often the *cabecera* of the municipality, near the locality from which an ancestor came.

In some cases, where a locality was equidistant from two major towns, people may have gone to either or both of the towns for legal transactions, in which case it would be necessary to check the notarial records in each town. Of course, if the researcher is in the country itself, this information can be obtained by going to the local notary. Be sure to remember, however, that these individuals are busy professionals, just as lawyers are in this country, and it may be necessary to make an appointment to visit with them. Generally, if you approach the notary with respect, but with confidence that you will be allowed to consult the records over 100 years old, you will find the notary to be very receptive and helpful. Unfortunately, the notaries are generally not interested in, or trained for, searching the records. If a researcher is unable to personally consult the records, and the records have not been microfilmed and made available in the United States, the services of an experienced historian, genealogist, or record searcher will have to be obtained.

Spanish notarial legislation states that a notary must provide the means for a legitimate historical investigator to make use of those *protocolos* over 100 years old. Those that are less than 100 years old require special permission and the possible payment of a fee, or you may have to request a form from the Registro de Ultimas Voluntades in Madrid prior to being able to consult the record. If you want to consult documents under 100 years old, it is frequently advisable to have the notary read the document or indicate the facts of genealogical interest. These regulations concerning documents less than 100 years old are provided as a means of protecting the privacy of individuals whose names appear in such documents.

ARRANGEMENT AND INDEXING OF *PROTOCOLOS*

Protocolos are always arranged under the name of the notary who produced them. Frequently, until the late eighteenth and nineteenth centuries, the documents for a specific year were merely bound or tied together in *legajos* (files or bundles of paper). There was a movement in Spain to have all of the *protocolos* bound, following the Notarial Law of 1869, which ordered the creation of district notarial archives. At this point many of the older *legajos* were organized and commercially bound, so that today *protocolos* are generally found in bound volumes containing all of the documents drafted by a single *notario* (notary) during a specific year, or series of years. In a notarial office where the notary had extensive work, there may be separate volumes for certain classes of documents, such as testaments or contracts.

Since all notarial documents are arranged under the name of the notary, it can be very helpful to know the names of the notaries serving a particular locality during a specific time period. There are two ways that these names can be learned. One is to make note of any mention of the town notaries that appears in the parish or other records. Most frequently, these will appear where the family of the notary is involved in the parish ordinance work, where the notary himself serves as a godfather or witness, or where the notary who writes the will of the deceased is named in the death certificate of that person. In the latter case the date when the will was written may also be given. When this occurs it is imperative that the researcher write down any information about the notary, especially his name.

All of the major historical archives have a list of the notaries whose records appear in their collections. In many archives, although not all, these lists are arranged in two separate sections. The first is an alphabetical listing of the notaries by surname, containing all of the notaries whose *protocolos* appear in the archives, with an indication as to the years such *protocolos* cover and frequently the name of the locality in which the *notario* or *escribano* served (see figure 13-1). The second is a geographical listing of all of the towns from which *protocolos* have been assembled in a particular archives. Under the name of each town will appear the name

PROVINCIA DE MADRID
RELACION POR LOCALIDADES, DE ESCRIBANOS, FECHAS Y SIGNATURAS

Escribanos		Fechas	Signaturas
ALAMO, EL (Dist. Navalcarnero):			
RECIENTE	Marcos	1624	30.911
PÉREZ BELTRÁN	Felipe	1741/1751	30.912/30.913
CASTELLANOS Y GONZÁLEZ	Manuel	1787/1799	30.914
IZQUIERDO	Lorenzo	1853/1866	30.915/30.917
ALCORCON (Dist. Getafe):			
VERGARA	Martín de	1575/1581	32.045
VERGARA	Diego de	1582 y 1583	32.046
BARRANCO	Pedro	1589-90-95	32.047
CONDE	Juan	1613 y 1618	32.048/32.049
CAMACHO	Juan	1647/1649	32.050
ROBLEDO	Bernabé	1663	32.051
CAMACHO	Mateo	1663 y 1664	32.052
QUIÑONES	Tiburcio de	1680 y 1681	32.053
TORRES	Manuel	1688/1690	32.054
GALLARDO	Bartolomé	1699/1701	32.055
MALNERO	Manuel Francisco	1732/1768	32.056/32.058
ALDEA DEL FRESNO (Dist. Navalcarnero)			
HERNÁNDEZ	Antonio	1599/1617	30.918
CARRIÓN	Juan	1701/1720	30.919
ARANJUEZ (Dist. Chinchón)			
SUÁREZ	Juan	1584/1587	29.372
AUÑÓN	Matías de	1589/1610	29.373/29.374

Figure 13-1 First page of list of notaries from the province of Madrid, Spain, Antonio Matilla Tascón, *Inventario General de Protocolos Notariales* (Madrid: Ministerio de Cultura, 1980), p. 171

of the notary or notaries from that town whose records appear in the archives, generally with an indication as to the years their particular *protocolos* cover.

A third type of indexing or listing of *protocolos* is an inventory, usually found at the beginning or end of each volume or year within a volume, listing all of the notarial records by types of records. In some cases these lists have been compiled into separate volumes arranged under the name of each specific notary. Such a list is shown in figure 13-2. On rare occasions there may be a fourth type of index, which is an alphabetical listing of the persons and/or subject matter dealt with in each of the documents in the *protocolos*. A number of archives in Mexico have taken this one step further and published extracts of entire notarial collections. Figure 13-3 is a page from a volume of published extracts of documents found in the *protocolos* in the Archivo Municipal in Monterrey, Mexico.[8]

The above indexes and inventories may be found in printed catalogs and in handwritten inventories or lists also found in the archives itself. In order to select the particular notary for the time period and the town in which his ancestor lived, the researcher will need to consult whatever listing exists of specific notaries. A system of reference numbers will exist for each archives with a number identifying each specific bundle or bound volume, which may cover one of the several years of documents produced by a particular notary. The researcher can copy from the appropriate catalog card inventory, or published page, the reference number to request the specific volume or volumes he wishes to consult.

As a further aid each volume of legal documents frequently contained, either at the beginning or the end, an inventory of all the specific documents contained in that particular volume. Such inventories, as appear in figure 13-2, indicate the nature of the document (testament, contract, etc.), the name of the parties involved, and in some cases, the date of the document. When actually consulting a particular volume of *protocolos*, the researcher can rapidly review the principal parties to all of the documents the volume contains by merely reading the inventory page. In those volumes in which more than one year of records are bound, it is likely that a separate inventory will appear for each year in the volume. These may be found at the beginning or the end of the volume, or at the beginning or end of each individual year.

NOTARIAL DOCUMENTS — GENERAL FORMAT

Legal transactions recorded in *protocolos* are of many different types, as indicated in the introduction to this chapter. In spite of this fact, a system of standard forms and usages was developed, since one of the purposes of the notarial system was to assure that the transactions recorded would be legally recognized and binding. First, all documents drafted from 1673 on had to be drafted on specially stamped paper, the cost of which

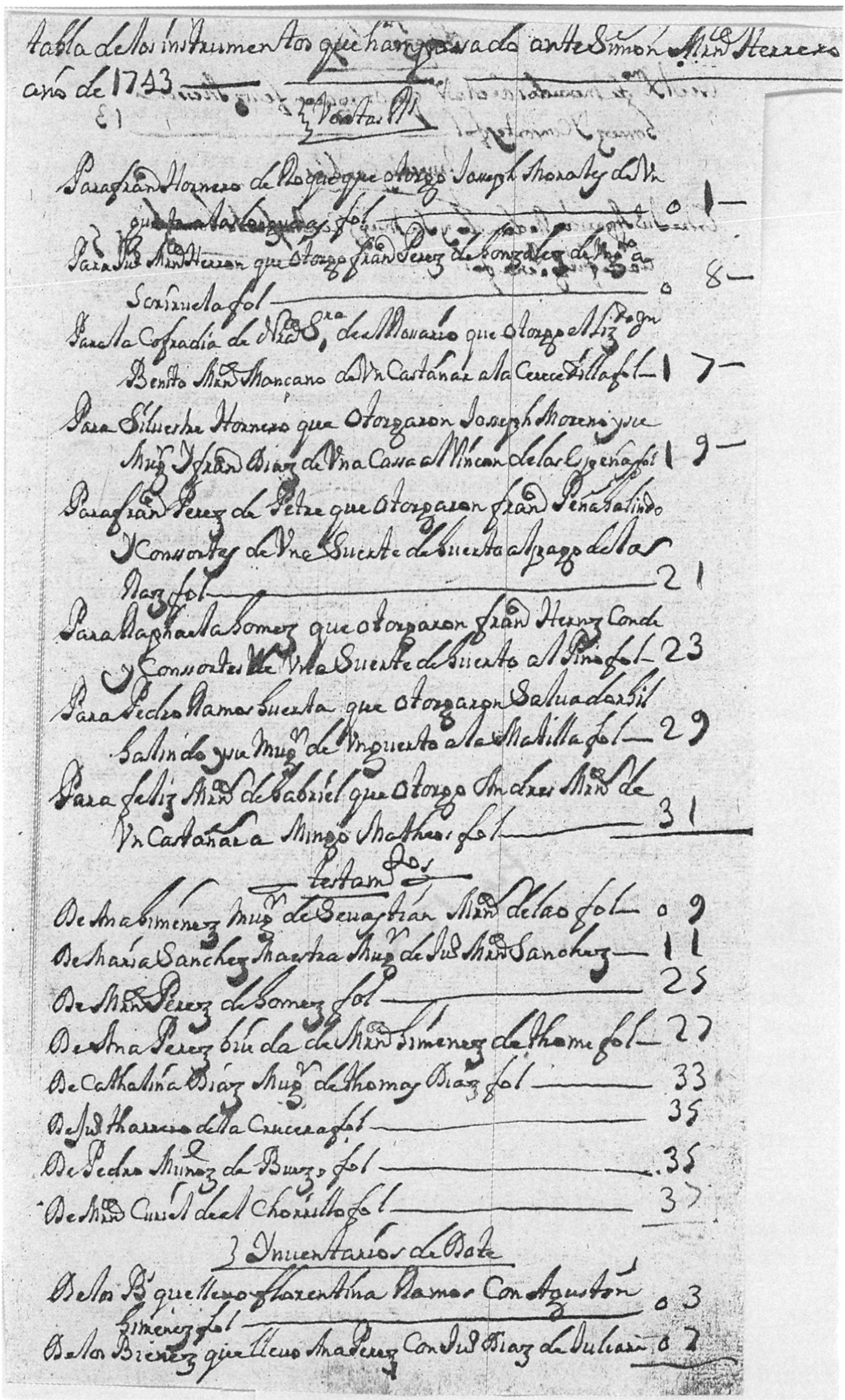

tabla de los instrumentos que han pasado ante Simon Mrn Herrero
año de 1743

Ventas

Para Fran Herrero de [illegible] que otorgo Joseph Moralez de Vn [illegible] fol — 1

Para Jul Mrn Herrero que otorgo Fran Perez de Gonzalez de [illegible] Serrezuela fol — 8

Para la Cofradia de Nra Sra del Rosario que otorgo Mig Benito Mrn Mancano de Vn Castañar a la Cerca Villa fol — 17

Para Silvestre Herrero que otorgaron Joseph Moreno y su Mug y Fran Diaz de vna Casa al Rincon de la [illegible] fol — 19

Para Fran Perez de Petre que otorgaron Fran Peña Galindo y Consortes de vna Suerte de huerta al [illegible] de las Naz fol — 21

Para Raphaela Gomez que otorgaron Fran Herrez Conde y Consortes de vna Suerte de huerto al Pino fol — 23

Para Pedro Llamas huerta que otorgaron Salvador Gil Galindo y su Mug de vn huerto a la Matilla fol — 29

Para Feliz Mrn de Gabriel que otorgo Andres Mrn de Vn Castañar a Mingo Matheos fol — 31

testamentos

De Ana Gimenez Mug de Sebastian Mrn de la O fol — 9

De Maria Sanchez Martha Mug de Jul Mrn Sanchez — 11

De Mrn Perez de Gomez fol — 25

De Ana Perez biuda de Mrn Gimenez de Thome fol — 27

De Cathalina Diaz Mug de Thomas Diaz fol — 33

De Jul Herrero de la Cuerca fol — 35

De Pedro Muñoz de Burgos fol — 35

De Mrn Cuial de al Chorrillo fol — 37

3 Inventarios de Bote

De los Bienes que llevo Florentina Llamas con Agustin Gimenez fol — 3

De los Bienes que llevo Ana Perez con Jul Diaz de Juliana — 7

Figure 13-2 Index page from a *protocolo* (author's copy)

ARCHIVO MUNICIPAL DE MONTERREY

1755] XII, fol. 284, no. 114: Don Mateo de Lafita y Berri, vecino del real y minas de Santiago de las Sabinas, se constituye en fiador de don Alonso Ignacio de Aragón y Abollado, del cargo de alcalde mayor y capitán a guerra de aquel real que le ha conferido el gobernador don José Antonio Fernández de Jáuregui y Urrutia; comprometiéndose a responder por él si no cumpliere cuando le sea tomada residencia de su empleo. Ante José Fernández Fajardo, escribano público y de cabildo. Testigos, Antonio Ladrón de Guevara, Manuel de Larralde y Juan Roel. **Monterrey, 9 de mayo de 1735.**

1756] XII, fol. 286, no. 115: Juan José Sánchez Roel, vecino de esta ciudad, otorga fianza de su residencia a favor de Juan José Rodríguez de Montemayor, del cargo de alcalde, mayor y capitán a guerra del valle de Guajuco, que le ha conferido el gobernador don José Antonio Fernández de Jáuregui y Urrutia. Ante José Fernández Fajardo, escribano público y de cabildo. Testigos, Alejandro de Uro y Campa y Antonio Ladrón de Guevara. **Monterrey, 12 de mayo de 1735.**

1757] XII, fol. 287, no. 116: José Antonio Guerra, vecino de esta ciudad otorga fianza de su residencia a favor de José Cayetano de Ayala, del cargo de alcalde mayor y capitán a guerra del valle de Santa Catarina que le ha conferido el gobernador don José Antonio Fernández de Jáuregui y Urrutia. Ante José Fernández Fajardo, escribano público y de cabildo. Testigos, Alejandro de Uro y Campa, Antonio Ladrón de Guevara y Manuel de Larralde. **Monterrey, 18 de mayo de 1735.**

1758] XII, fol. 288 vto., no. 117: Don Valentín de la Garza, vecino de la juris dicción de esta ciudad, otorga fianza de residencia a favor de Francisco Cantú, a quien el gobernador don José Antonio Fernández de Jáuregui ha conferido el empleo de alcalde mayor y capitán a guerra del valle de las Salinas; comprometiéndose a responder por él cuando le sea tomada residencia de dicho cargo. Ante José Fernández Fajardo, escribano público y de cabildo. Testigos, Alejandro de Uro y Campa, Antonio Ladrón de Guevara y Pedro de Alcántara Guerra. **Monterrey, 27 de mayo de 1735.**

1759] XII, fol. 289 vto., no. 118: Diego de Guzmán, vecino de esta ciudad, otorga fianza a favor de Abito José Fajardo de Quintanilla, a quien el gobernador don José Antonio Fernández de Jáuregui ha designado alcalde mayor y capitán a guerra de la villa de San Felipe de Linares; comprometiéndose a responder por él en caso de incumplimiento cuando le sea tomada residen-

-42

Figure 13-3 Published extracts from notarial records, Israél Cavazos Garza, *Catalogo y Sintesis Archivo Municipal de Monterrey, 1726–1756* (Monterrey, Mexico 1986), p. 42

varied depending on the type of document to be drafted. Only paper stamped with the particular year of issue could be used. Only in times of isolation from Madrid, i.e., during war or internal revolution, was paper from a preceding year used. This, in and of itself, is indicative of an interesting but difficult period in the history of a locality.

A basic format for writing notarial documents developed by the end of the Middle Ages.[9] Every notarial document was to contain the following six elements:

1. Date and locality of the transaction.
2. Reception of the parties by the notary.
3. Identification of the parties; usually names, surnames and residences, and often marital status and/or occupation or title.
4. Standard legal language specific to the type of transaction. This was so standardized that by the sixteenth century books were published setting forth specific formats for the notary to copy.
5. Witnesses to the transaction, giving identification for them similar to that of the parties.
6. Authentication of the transaction by the notary.

Figure 13-4 illustrates a typical physical arrangement of a notarial document. At the very top, and generally in the center, appears the day and month in which the document was drafted (the year could be obtained from the seal). Note also the small cross that appears at the top of the document, indicating it is a public notary and not an ecclesiastical notary, as discussed earlier. Unlike most documents, the one in figure 13-4 did not give the specific date, but merely states "during the reign of his Majesty Don Carlos IV." The number appearing in the upper left-hand corner of the page is the page number of the bound volume; this was added when all of the loose documents for the year were bound together. In the left-hand margin appears a brief description of the document; for example, the one in figure 13-4 reads, *Testamento que otorga Don Jeronimo Sanchez Saso presbítero de esta villa* (Testament executed by Don Jeronimo Sanchez Saso, priest of this town). In cases where the document is a contract or other transaction between two parties, the names of both parties will generally appear in this description of the contents of the document.

Following the description, the body of the document begins. The body of the document also followed certain formats established for that particular class of document. Familiarity with some of the more significant types of documents and their basic formats can be gained by reading the examples provided below. Once he becomes familiar with these basic formats, the researcher can rapidly analyze the information contained in a document to evaluate if it should be read carefully and in its entirety. The basic body of the will in figure 13-4, which was several pages long, has been omitted.

As with the beginning portion, the final page had a set format. In the last paragraph the *escribano* personally recognized and gave validity to

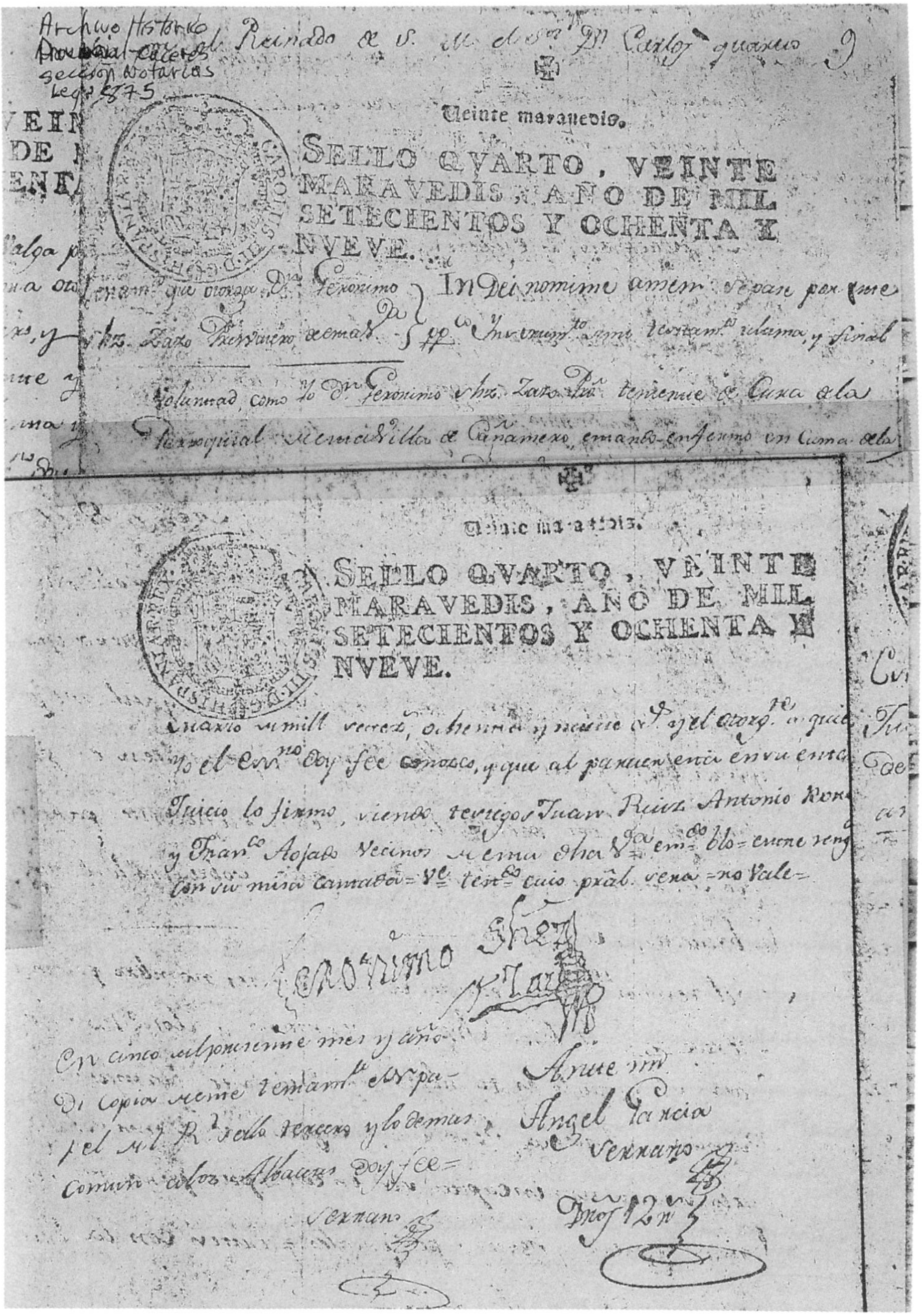

Veinte maravedis.

SELLO QVARTO, VEINTE MARAVEDIS, AÑO DE MIL SETECIENTOS Y OCHENTA Y NVEVE.

Veinte maravedis.

SELLO QVARTO, VEINTE MARAVEDIS, AÑO DE MIL SETECIENTOS Y OCHENTA Y NVEVE.

Figure 13-4 Format of notarial documents (author's copy)

the document, and signed it before certain witnesses whom he names. The document then was signed by the party or parties involved, after whose signatures appeared the words *paso ante mi*, (given before me, or before me), followed by the signature of the notary and his rubric (the peculiar flourish identifying an individual's signature).

At the end of the document, there very frequently appeared a comment such as the one in figure 13-4, *derechos doce reales* (fees: twelve reales [money units]), indicating the amount paid to have the legal document drafted. In addition, if any copies were made of the document, a notation should appear on the original document at the bottom or in the margin indicating the date the copy was made and the amount paid for it, with the signature of the notary and again his rubric. Because of the uniformity in the beginning and ending of documents, a researcher can quickly survey a large number of documents in looking for those that relate to his particular family. This is fortunate, since practically no general indexes exist as to the names of the parties involved, and for many volumes even the yearly inventories do not appear.

NOTARIAL DOCUMENTS — SPECIFIC TYPES

A. *Testamentos* (Wills)

Wills accounted for a significant portion of the work done by notaries. In some notarial offices where a large amount of work was done in a single year, these testaments were bound in a separate volume.

As evidenced in figure 13-4, the introductory and closing formats of a will follow those of all notarial documents. The body of the will also follows a general pattern. It begins with "*In Dei Nomine, Amen*," which is Latin for "In the name of God, Amen," or the Spanish equivalent, "*En el nombre de Dios, Amen*." The initial paragraph then states the name of the testator (the individual writing the will and testament), with an indication as to his or her place of residence and, occasionally (especially for women), the name of his or her spouse and/or parents and their residence. Frequently, the individual makes a statement as to his health, usually that he is sick or in some other way fearing death, but that he is of sound mind. The will then contains a long sentence in which the testator indicates his belief in Catholicism and its basic tenets, and in which he wills his soul to God. This is followed by a series of orders that the testator wants carried out following his death. There will be an order as to where he wants to be buried, generally in the parish church. He frequently indicates any *cofradías* or other social organizations of which he was a member. In addition, he specifies the types of masses he wants celebrated in the Catholic Church. These instructions as to specific masses may cover from several paragraphs to several pages. All of these portions should be read carefully, since many times the name of a departed relative, such as a child, parent, sibling, or an in-law, may be mentioned among the masses given for those who are already deceased.

Following the instructions as to masses, the will then grants specific bequests to family members and friends. Such bequests of property can provide extensive information about the testator's family, especially when there was a large amount of property to be given, and it was distributed not only to his children and spouse but also to cousins, nephews, nieces, etc. After the specific bequests, the *albaceas* or *testamentarios* (executors) are named. At least one of these will generally be the testator's spouse, son, son-in-law, and/or brother. The power to act as executor is generally given to all, and to each of them individually (*a todos juntos y a cada uno de por si*). The testator then names his legitimate, sole, and universal heirs (*mis legítimos únicos y universales herederos*), who will generally be his living descendants. These descendants will be named with an indication as to the parents of each person, especially where the testator was married more than once, or where one of his children has died, leaving one or more descendants.

The concluding clause is usually a statement that no other testament or testaments or codicils written by the testator prior to that time shall have any effect. The attestation clause of the notary then follows in which the names of the witnesses are set forth, as discussed earlier for all notarial documents.

Because wills always involve at least two generations of a family, they are extremely important genealogical sources. In the detailed descriptions of property given, which may frequently include everything from the bed in which the person is dying to major pieces of real estate, wills also provide the human interest that, as a family historian, you are seeking. Wills of elderly unmarried siblings, aunts, or uncles of direct-line ancestors are especially valuable, as they often provide extensive detail about family members and relationship, both by blood and by marriage, covering several generations.

B. *Capitulaciones Matrimoniales* (Marriage Contracts of Pre-nuptial Agreements) and *Inventarios de Dotes* (Dowry Inventories)

Under Spanish law inheritance rights were retained by married women. As a result, marriage contracts or dowry inventories were common even among the lower class, but especially in families with good social position, having enough property to be concerned about its disposition through marriage. These contracts were entered into by the bride and groom and their parents, generally prior to the marriage or soon thereafter.

There are two forms these documents can take. One is a bilateral contract between the bride and groom, the former frequently represented by one of her parents or an older brother. This document indicates the disposition of any property she brings into the marriage, in the event she should die childless before her husband or in the event that following her death their children should die before having children of their own. Similar provisions are also included as far as the inheritance rights to the property of the husband. The more common type of marriage contract is a two-way contract between the respective families. These contracts will generally be entitled *inventario de dote*, rather than *capitulación matrimonial*. There will frequently be two documents, one signed by the parent or brother of the bride and the other signed by the father of the groom or the groom himself. These marital contracts often list specific items such as pillows, quilts, sheets, pots, dishes, and clothing, giving us a glimpse of daily life and the couple's economic status at the beginning of their marriage.

C. *Compra-ventas* (Purchases and Sales)

Sales and purchase contracts make up a large portion of most *protocolos*. In the opening paragraph the parties to the transaction are set forth and the legal language to transfer property is stated, followed by a description in detail of the property being sold. In cases where real estate is involved, there will be a careful delineation of the property boundaries, usually specifying the owners of adjacent property. There will also be a description as to the consideration paid for the property and, frequently, as part of the description of the property itself, an indication of how the current owner received such property. The latter can be of particular interest to the family historian, since many pieces of property are inherited. In such cases the sales contract may indicate the person who willed the property to the seller and give the relationship of that person to him. You can also use these sales contracts to identify particular pieces of property owned by your direct-line ancestor. With that description you could perhaps locate and photograph the property, making your family history more interesting.

D. *Inventarios de bienes de difuntos o de menores* (Inventories of the estate of decedents or minor children) *Partición de bienes* (Division of Assets) and *Curadurías* (Guardianship)

The processes of accounting for and dividing up a decedent's estate and of handling the guardianship of a minor and his estate — both handled under the jurisdiction of the probate court in the American legal system — were handled in Spain and Latin America by notaries. The executors of a decedent's estate filed an inventory of the estate's assets with the notary, and the local *tasador* (appraiser) determined its value. A *partición de bienes* was prepared, dividing and distributing the person's assets among his heirs. This last process is especially significant if the person died intestate (without a will), as it may be the only document setting forth names of the heirs.

When a property owner was a minor (under age twenty-five), or in some way legally incapacitated, a *curador* (guardian) was appointed. In such cases the notary notified the relatives of the minor that a guardianship was being sought, and they were given an opportunity to object. The notary, taking into account the objections, decided whether to issue the documents necessary for the *curador* to take power over the minor and his assets. In cases of guardianship, inventories and accountings appear often, even annually, from the time they are issued until the person's minority is ended. All of these documents were filed by the notary in his *protocolos*.

Both executors and guardians could sell assets of, and buy for, the estate. In addition they could exercise other contracting powers on behalf of the estates they represented. These documents also appear in *protocolos*.

The following translation of the document appearing as figure 13-5 illustrates the detailed content of death inventories.[10] Notice how much we can learn about this person's daily life from the complete list of her physical possessions at the time of her death.

> In the town of Garganta La Olla on the eighteenth day of the month of December of the year one thousand seven hundred thirty nine Francisco Garcia de Pinto, local magistrate of the [town] having received notice that Pauline Sanchez, widow of Juan Herrero Matheos [and] neighbor of that town, is dead and has passed from this present life to the other, having gone through her time of necessity in the company of the present notary and of Pedro Martin de La O her lay minister, at the residence of said deceased, which is in this town in the section of the mills. It is bordered by the houses of Matias Diaz and of the widow of Francisco Martin Regidor; and in order to inventory the assets that said deceased left because she has left a minor child of less than fourteen years; and in order that it might be set forth for all time; and entering in said house there were found and inventoried the following goods:
>
> First, a pig [weighing] about four *arrobas*[11] and three small pigs about one half *arroba* One new large earthen jar about fifteen *arrobas*.[12] A large cracked earthen jar about four *arrobas*. A large earthenware jar about ten *arrobas* which contained about five *arrobas* of wine. One large cover. [Unknown word]. One weeder. One pruning hook. One small tin funnel. One rope basket about three measures[13] and with a broken lock. A skein of tow[14] 3/4 cured. One large pitcher. One small old rope basket. One medium-sized small box with lock. One skein of linen about one half pound, cured. One rope box with cover and lock about eight measures [twelve bushels]. About one pound of prepared tow in balls. About one pound of prepared thread in balls. About one-fourth measure of dried figs; one broken small jar about one and a half *arrobas* somewhat old and in it two small measures of linseed. A medium-sized axe. About a half *arrobas* of [word illegible]. About a pound and a half of combed flax. One half pound of remnants of tow. One clamp. One small crucifix [words unknown]. A small relicary. One small old pillow without stuffing. Two bed benches with pedestal. One day bed. One used mattress of tow. One new sheet of tow. One white, lightweight bedspread. One old and broken cow lock. One strainer with legs. One old stainer. One used yellow ladle, about one kilo. One roller. One used medium-sized broth pot. One broken clay pot of about two *arrobas*. One broken old hand trough. One sieve frame. One broken, small cork box, one half measure. One glazed earthenware bowl one half *arrobas* year old of fine porcelain and rough earthen ware. Approximately six measures of green chestnut. About

Figure 13-5 ***Inventario de bienes de difunto* from *Archivo Histórico Provincial de Caceres, Protocolos, Legajo* 1615, year 1739, p. 77 (author's copy)**

one kilo of olives. Two flax combs. One small round table. One small pitcher. One small hatchet. And there were found no other assets in said house even though an oath was received from all parties and interested persons and the said assets which her husband ordered placed with and were placed with said Juan Herrero Matheos who, being present, really and with full effect, he accepted the receipt of them and agreed to serve himself as the trustee of all of them, and guaranteed himself [i.e. bonded] by his person and moveable goods and real property, and of [those] his heirs successors; to have them ready and available to turn them over to him who in law ought to have them at the time of his majority, or because a competent judge so orders, for the execution and fulfillment [of which] he extends his power in its fullness to the justices and judges of his majesty who are competent, in order that they might compel and oblige him and fine him for any violation under the law without exemption from the laws in his favor and that which by right exists; and which testimony he set forth before me the present public notary, witnesses being Matheo Muñoz de Rogos, Pedro Martin de la O and Fernando Norberto Martin Herrero, neighbors of this town, I the notary give faith I know the grantor. He said he does not know how to sign for himself and upon his request a witness signed. Francisco Garcia de Pinto, Fernando Norberto Martin Herrero before me Simon Martin Herrero.

E. Other Documents

It is impossible to even briefly review all of the many types of documents found in the *protocolos* of a notary. Only those most frequently found, or those of particular genealogical significance, have been discussed. When unfamiliar documents not discussed above are found, first check the Glossary in the back of this book to see if the type of document you have found is defined there. If not, check a good unabridged Spanish language dictionary, such as that published by the Academia Real de la Lengua Española in Madrid, Spain, to define the type of document it is.

JUDICIAL, GOVERNMENTAL, AND ECCLESIASTICAL NOTARIES

Most family history researchers will find all of the information they seek in the *protocolos* of the *notarios publicos* or *escribanos de número* who had offices in the town or near the town in which their ancestors lived. However, as mentioned earlier, these public notaries were not the only notaries functioning in Spain throughout its history. Records prepared by judicial and governmental notaries are to be found in the respective archives of the judicial or governmental units that they served. These records are almost entirely documents prepared for the presentation of a particular court case, or for the filing of a petition with an administrative body. Since they are not well indexed as to particular individuals involved in the cases, you will most likely only find it practical to consult these documents when you are aware that a particular ancestor was involved with a suit in a specific court, or with a petition to a specific governmental council. Because they will be rarely used, no further description is given here of these records. If you find it necessary to consult them, talk with the personnel of the particular archives where the records are kept, since they will be familiar with the various kinds of information to be found in these records.

Apostolic or ecclesiastical notaries worked in the various dioceses and prepared documents for presentation at canon law courts. They also prepared the various petitions which were sent both to Rome and to the local bishop. In addition, they prepared any contracts and testaments involving the church and its property. Many of the documents, such as testaments and contracts, very closely parallel those prepared by public notaries. Most of these documents are kept in either diocesan or cathedral archives.

---

1. Agustin G. de Amezua y Mayo, *La vida prívada española en el protocolo notarial* (Madrid, 1950), 9.
2. Miguel Muñoz de San Pedro, *Reflejos de siete siglos de vida estremeña en cien documentos notariales* (Caceres, 1962), 485.
3. Ibid., 484.
4. Ibid., 282–295.
5. Ibid., 295–302 and 424–429.
6. Olga Gallego Domínguez and Pedro Lopez Gomez, *Clasificación de los fondos de los archivos Históricos Provinciales* (Madrid: Ministerio de Cultura, 1980).
7. George R. Ryskamp, *Tracing Your Hispanic Heritage* (Riverside, Calif.: Hispanic Family History Research, 1984), 698–712.
8. Israel Cavazos Garza, *Catálogo y síntesis de los portocolos de Archivo Municipal de Monterrey, 1726–1756* (Monterrey, Mexico: Ayuntamiento de Monterrey, 1986), 44.
9. "Bibliografía del Notariado en España," *Estudios históricos y documentos de los archivos de Protocolos* (Barcelona: Colegio Notarial de Barcelona, 1974), 195–198.
10. Archivo Histórico Provincial de Cáceres, Sección Protocolos, Legajo 1616, año 1739 folio 77.
11. An *arroba* equaled about 25 pounds of weight.
12. An *arroba* equaled about 3 gallons of liquid.
13. This measure of dry grain equaled about 1.5 bushels.
14. Tow is hemp or flax used for making cloth.

Glossary

abad - 1) An abbot; 2) in some provinces the rector of a parish
abadengo - abbey
abuelastro/a - step-grandparent, parent of the stepfather or of the stepmother
abuelo/a - 1) grandparent; 2) ancestor, forefather; 3) old person
aceptación - 1) acceptance; 2) approval, approbation
acta - 1) official act; 2) recording of an official act
adelantado - 1) colonial title used for the following: governor of a frontier province, supreme justice of the kingdom, captain general in times of war; 2) a discoverer, founder; 3) pacifier of Indian lands
administración - administration
adulterio - adultery, violation of the marriage vows
adviento - Advent, the four weeks preceding Christmas
adyacente - adjoining
afinidad - relation by marriage
agregacion - 1) addition; 2) attachment; 3) appointment, assignment
ajuste - 1) settlement, arrangment; 2) hiring
alabardero - Spanish Royal Guard
albacea - executor of a will
albino - 1) blood mixture, Spanish and **Morisco**; 2) albino
alcalde - 1) mayor; 2) magistrate; 3) official to whom mayor delegates his powers in a certain section of a city
alcalde constitucional - local magistrate during nineteenth century
alcalde ordinario - mayor, the highest municipal office of a town council or municipal district
alcalde mayor - 1) justice of the peace; 2) the administrative and judicial magistrate of a province or district (in some cases the **corregidor** exercised this function); 3) local magistrate
alcalde pedanco - junior judge
aldea - village, hamlet
alferez - 1) ensign; 2) army officer lower than lieutenant, sub-lieutenant; 3) in Bolivia and Peru a municipal office in the Indian villages
alguacil - 1) constable, baliff, officer who carries out the orders of the **alcalde**; 2) minister of justice who executes the orders of the justices and tribunals
alma - 1) soul; 2) person
almoneda - 1) public auction; 2) clearance sale
alqueria - hamlet

alteza - an honorary title given to the kings, princes, and officials of the high court (**audiencia**) and to some of the royal councils, your highness

altitud - altitude

amonestación matrimonial - proclamation published during three successive Sundays before marriages, banns

amparo - 1) the act of protection of the Indian by the Spaniard, specifically teaching him a trade, bringing him up; 2) duty of the **encomendero** or **patron**

anejo - 1) annex; 2) a church dependent upon another one; 3) rural district joined to a borough

anima - 1) soul; 2) those spirits consigned to purgatory; 3) in the plural **animas** sometimes refers to the death mass or the tolling of the bells to summon people to pray for a recently deceased person

año bisiesto - leap year, the years in which the last two numerals of the year are divisible by four

año secular - the centenary years: 1500, 1600, 1700, 1800, 1900, and 2000 (the years 1600 and 2000 are also leap years)

ante - 1) before, in front of, in the presence of; 2) in view of, with regard to

ante todo - above all, first of all

anteiglesia - 1) atrium or portico (of a church); 2) parish church; 3) parish or district

antiguo/gua - old

apartamiento - judicial act or declaration by which one removes himself from a legal action or right

apeamiento - 1) surveying; 2) shoring up of a building

apodo - nickname, sobriquet

apostólico - apostolic

appellido - surname, family name, last name

aprendizage - apprenticeship

aprendizo/za - apprentice, beginner

aprobación - document establishing the proof or certainty of a fact, such as a proof of the nobility of a person's family

arancel - official tariff or custom

archivo - 1) archives, place where records are kept; 2) (office) files, file

arciprestazgo - land under jurisdiction of an archpriest composed of several parishes

arcipreste - archpriest, a parish priest who also presides over several other parish priests

arrendamiento - rent, letting, lease

arroba - 1) weight measure equivalent to 25 lbs. of 16 oz. each; 2) liquid measurement equivalent to about 3 gallons; 3) the fourth part of a quintal

artículo - article

arzobispado - archbishopric, ecclesiastical territory under the jurisdiction of an archbishop

arzobispo - archbishop, the bishop of a metropolitan church to which other bishops are subordinate

ascendencia - ascendancy, a series of ancestors

asiento - 1) seat on a tribunal or council; 2) contract or obligation made to provide money or goods for the army

audiencia - 1) regional high court; 2) civil tribunal that dealt with the civil and criminal actions of last resort (In the absence of a colonial viceroy this high court became the executive branch that represented the king.)

ausente - 1) absent; 2) absentee, missing person

ausente sin licencia - military, absent without leave

auto - 1) judicial sentence; 2) warrant; 3) edict; 4) various legal documents both judicial and administrative, not including wills or inventories

autos de bienes de difuntos - processing of assets of the deceased

auto de fe - a public procedure in which those accused by the Inquisition were sentenced

ayuntamiento - 1) municipal government; 2) town council; 3) city hall

bachiller - 1) graduate of the equivalent of junior college in the U.S.; 2) holder of a bachelor's degree, baccalaureate; 3) applied to priests who have graduated from the seminary

banda - proclamation, publication of marriage banns

bautizar - to baptize, to christen

behetría - free town under its own chosen prince or seigneur

beneficencias - 1) beneficence, charity; 2) welfare organization or institution, charity organization, public welfare office

beneficio - 1) benefit, profit; 2) development, cultivation (of land); 3) ecclesiastical benefice; 4) a position that is purchased; 5) (law) right by law or privilege

beneficio de deliberar - (law) opportunity of deliberation in which the heir can postpone acceptance of inheritance until inventory has been made

beneficio de inventario - (law) benefit of inventory, right granted to heir to accept inheritance without being obligated to pay debts amounting to more than the inheritance

beneficio simple - ecclesiastical sinecure

bisabuelo/la - great-grandparent

bisnieto/ta - great-grandchild

bozal - caste name given to Negros in Panama

braza - length measure, length formed by having both arms of a person open and extended—which commonly is taken to be 6 feet of width

bula - papal bull or proclamation

caballería - 1) military cavalry; 2) knightly order, knights, e.g., **la caballeria de Santiago** (the Knights of Santiago), knighthood, rank and privileges of a knight; 3) knight's fee, a grant of land made on the condition of maintaining one mounted man-at-arms; 4) land measure (in Spain about 95 acres, in Cuba 33, in P. Rico 194, in Mex. 106)

caballero - 1) nobleman; 2) knight; 3) member of military order

cabeza - head

cabildo - 1) municipal or town council; 2) chapter of a cathedral or collegiate church

cabildo abierto - meetings of the town council and the citizens of the town

cacicazo - the territory governed by and/or the authority of a **cacique**

cacique - 1) the chief or ruler of some Indian tribes; 2) local ruler

cambio - 1) change, alteration; 2) interchange, exchange; 3) (law) exchange of posts by two holders of government jobs or ecclesiastical benefices

cambujo/ja - blood mixture: Indian (1 part), Negro (1 part), and Chinese (2 parts)

cambur/ra - blood mixture: Spanish (1 part), Indian (2 parts) and Negro (1 part); taken from the parish registers of Mexico

canonicatos - canonry (canons collectively), canonship

capellán - a priest who has a chaplaincy, or says mass in a private chapel and who is paid by a trust fund or private individual to administer the affairs of said fund or individual

capellanía - 1) benefice or foundation subject to certain obligations; 2) lay foundation without ecclesiastical intervention

capital - 1) assets; 2) principal of a trust fund

Capitán General - supreme commander of a military region

capitanía general - 1) captaincy general; 2) territorial demarcation governed by a Capitán General during the colonial era; 3) major military administrative unit in Spain

capitulación matrimonial - marriage contract

capítulo matrimonial - marriage articles, marriage contract, civil marriage

carga - weight measurement, a certain portion of grain, which in Castile is 4 fanegas = 138, 074 kg.

carga de tabaco o algodón - weight measure equivalent to 92 kg

carta de pago - receipt (for payment)

carta examen - diploma; license (to practice a trade or profession)

casa solar - ancestral home, manor house

casado/da - married to

casamiento - marriage, wedding

casería - rural house with dependencies and lands, comonly used in the Basque countries

caserío - hamlet

casta - 1) caste; 2) lineage; 3) each one of the closed classes in which a society is divided (see the various "blood mixture" definitions in this Glossary)—in many cases the caste distinctions are social rather than literal

castillo - castle

castizo - 1) of a good caste; 2) in Puerto Rico, a blood mixture of **mestizo** and Spanish; 3) in Guatemala, a blood mixture of Spanish (15 parts) and **Criollo**

catastro - 1) census; 2) census of the lands and resources

Catastro de Ensenada - census ordered in 1749 by the **Marqués de Ensenada** for Charles III for the entire area ruled by Castile

catedral/catedra - Episcopal church of a diocese or archdiocese; cathedral

caudillo - military leader, captain, **cacique**

cedula - 1) royal decree; 2) document, manuscript

cedula personal - **documento nacional**, identity card, identification papers

celemín - dry measure equivalent to four cuartillos—4.625 liters

cementerio - 1) cemetery; 2) a place in the countryside where Christian Indians, slaves, and other poor persons are buried; 2) a churchyard burial ground, behind, beside, or sometimes in front of the church; 3) places within the churches—in the floor, the walls, and special crypts, etc.; 4) civil burial grounds which date from the beginning of civil registration within each country

censo - 1) census of population, etc.; 2) official register of citizens having the right to vote; 3) head-tax, tribute, tax; 4) annual stipend paid formerly by some churches to their prelates; 5) (law) living pledge, contract, whereby an estate is pledged to payment of an annuity as interest on a loan without transfer of title.

certificado (de nacimiento, de casamiento, de defunción) - 1) certificate (of birth, of marriage, of death); 2) registered mail

certificación - certification, attestation

chancillerías - supreme tribunals of justice prior to the nineteenth century; courts of original jurisdiction for proof of nobility

chino/na - in Peru, blood mixture: offspring of a mulato and an Indian

cholo/la - in Peru, blood mixture: offspring of a **mestizo** and an Indian

ciudad - city

cimarron/na - in Mexico and Guatemala, blood mixture: Spanish (1 part), Indian (1 part), and Negro (2 parts); in Panama, a rebellious slave

clase - 1) class, type, kind; 2) (military) non-commissioned officers

clérigo - 1) clergyman; 2) those who have been received into a sacred order (in military orders this is distinguished from **caballero**)

cobdicilio - codicil

cofradía - 1) congregation or brotherhood of religious individuals; 2) guild; 3) trade union

colector - collector of taxes, or of collection for the church

colecturía - death records listing collections of payments for funeral and masses

colegiata - collegiate church

colegio notarial - notarial college

colonial - 1) time period beginning at the conquest and ending with the wars of independence, or approximately 1492–1825 (1899 for Puerto Rico, Cuba, and the Philippines); 2) of or relating to that time period; 3) relating to a colony

comadre - 1) midwife; 2) godmother

comandancia general - military administrative unit, commandery

compañía - 1) a legal association or society of several persons united for a single purpose, commercial, social, or ecclesiastical; 2) military unit

compraventa - contract of purchase and sale

compromiso - 1) pledge, commitment, promise; 2) engagement (to be married); 3) (law) compromise, arbitration, agreement

comunidad - 1) community, particularly a religious group; 2) village, commune, community

concejo/concejil - council

concierto - 1) agreement, contract; 2) arrangement, settlement

concuñado/da - spouse of one's own spouse's brother or sister

condado - 1) earldom, courtship (dignity, jurisdiction or possessions of an earl or count); 2) county

conde - 1) count, earl; 2) overseer

confirmación - 1) confirmation, affirmation, corroboration; 2) the religious sacrament of confirmation administered by the bishop

congregación - 1) congregation; 2) assembly; 2) Religious Brotherhood; 4) committee of cardinals, or of a religious order

conocido - known

conquistadores - Spanish conquerors of the New World in the 16th century

consanguinidad - consanguinity, kinship, blood relationship, measured in degrees in canon law by counting from each person to the common ancestor

consejero - counselor, advisor

consejo - council

Consejo de Castilla or **Real** - Council of Castile, Royal Council, supreme administrative body in Spain

Consejo de Indias - royal council that governed the colonies

consentimiento - consent, compliance, acquiescence

consignación - 1) consignment; 2) deposit (of money)

consorte de - 1) spouse; 2) partner, associate

constar - to be recorded or registered

contratación - 1) making a contract; 2) trade; 3) **Casa de Contractación,** Spanish government entity located in Seville and overseeing all commercial activity and the colonies, 1503–1790

contrato - contract, agreement enforceable by law

contrato de apprendizaje - contract of apprenticeship

contrayente - contracting party, such as in a marriage

contribución - tax

convenio - agreement, covenant, pact

convento - convent

conyuge - spouse, consort; (pl.) married couple

copia literal - literal or word-for-word copy

cordillera - mountain range

corregidor - 1) Spanish magistrate, mayor appointed by the king; 2) governor of the district

corregimiento - 1) occupation of the **corregidor**, the territory in which he exercises his jurisdiction

corriente - current, present (week, month, year)

cortesana - court hand; paleographic term referring to the writing used in the courts during a period between 1500 and 1650 A.D.

cortesano - courtier, royal attendant

cosa - 1) thing, something; 2) affair, business

coto - group of estates with one owner

coto redondo - group of estates with one owner

coyote - blood mixture, Spanish (4 parts), Indian (3 parts), and Negro (1 part), taken from the parish registers of Mexico

criollo/a - 1) Creole; 2) Latin-American colonial born of European parents

crisma - chrism, consecrated oil

cronista - chronicler, historian

cuadra - 1) stable; 2) city block

cuaresma - 1) Lent, the 40 days before Easter beginning on Ash Wednesday; 2) collection of lent sermons

cuarteado - blood mixture: Spanish (2 parts), Indian (1 part) and Negro (1 part); the offspring of a **mestizo** and a mulatto.

cuarteron - blood mixture: Spanish (3 parts) and mulatto (1 part), at times called **morisco**

cuarteron de chino - in Peru, blood mixture: Spanish and **chino**

cuarteron de mestizo - in Peru, blood mixture: Spanish and **mestizo**

cuartillo - dry measure equivalent to 1/4 celemín, or 1.156 liters

cuate/ta - in Mexico, the word used for twins; usually the Spanish word is **mellizos**

cuatrero - blood mixture: Spanish (1 part) and Indian (3 parts); the offspring of a **mestizo** and an Indian

cuatrillizos - quadruplets

cuenta - account, bill, report

cuerpo - 1) body, volume, book, body of laws, of writings, of people; 2) corps (diplomatic and military)

cuñado/a - brother-in-law, sister-in-law

cura - parish priest, vicar

curato - parish

curia - administrative and judicial organization under the bishop

cursivo - paleographic term: cursive, flowing handwriting, italic

dado - as long as, provided that, given that

de los mismos - of the same, usually refers to previous wording, such as month and year

de primera instancia - (court) of original jurisdiction

de repente - suddenly

decanato - deanship, deanery (post and residence of university dean)
declaración - declaration, statement, affidavit
defensor - defense, counsel
defunción - death
dehesa - pasture land
delación - 1) relinquishment, abandonment; 2) (law) assignment
delegación - 1) delegation (delegating of power); 2) group of delegates
demanda - demand, claim
departamento - department; one of the districts into which a country is divided
depósito - deposit, depository
derecha - right
desconocido - unknown
descripción - description
despachar 1) to finish or shorten at a section; 2) to resolve or determine the causes; 3) to send a person or thing
despobado - unpopulated
dia de los reyes - Day of the Kings of Magi, Twelfth Night, January 6
diccionario corográfico - geographic dictionary
dicho/cha - 1) said, the above mentioned; 2) (law) declaration, statement made by witness
difunto/ta - deceased, dead
dignidades reales - 1) Your Royal Highnesses; 2) royal concessions or grants
digo - I say, frequently used by scribes in records to correct errors as they wrote
diligencia matrimonial - premarital investigation conducted by parish priest
diócesis - diocese, unit of Catholic Church presided over by a bishop
diputado - deputy
discernimiento - 1) judgment; 2) appointment of a guardian
dispensa apostólica - apostolic dispensation or grant given by a pope or bishop, depending upon its nature
dispensa de su santidad - apostolic dispensation from a pope or bishop
dispensa matrimonial - exception to canon law regulation given by bishop to bride and groom to permit marriage, e.g. , for being related within the 4th degree
disposición - arrangement, disposal
dista/distante/distancia - distance (from)
distrito - district
divorcio - divorce
doctrina - 1) doctrine; 2) ritual; 3) a village of Indians that as yet has not been designated as a parish (**curato** or **parroquia**), a district under the direction of a priest expressly called to indoctrinate the Indians; 4) Latin American parish

documento nacional de identidad - personal identity document issued by the civil government (used throughout much of the Hispanic world)

don - title of respect prefixed to Christian names, which prior to 1832 usually referred to nobility or to political or ecclessiastical office holders

doña - 1) lady (see don); 2) woman; 3) (Chile) gift, bequest; 4) (pl) bridegroom's presents to the bride

donación - donation, gift, grant

dotación - endowment, dowry

dote - dowry, that property which a woman takes into marriage

ducado - 1) the coin of gold or silver that the Catholic monarchs created, established in the value of 375 **maravedis** de **vellón,** which varied; 2) dukedom, duchy

ducado de plata - its value was of 375 maravedis of silver and corresponded in vellón with the variety — according to the increase or decrease which silver had at different times

duque - duke, title of honor which follows that of prince

eclesiástico - ecclesiastical

edad - age

ejecutor/ra - executor

ejecutoría - court or administrative body that issues **ejecutorios**

ejecutorios - 1) legal patent of nobility; 2) (law) writ of execution (of a judgment)

emancipación - emancipation, the act of freeing from servitude

embarcar - 1) to pack, crate, bale; 2) to go abroad in a vessel

emigración - emigration, population movement, leaving one's native country to go and establish oneself in another country

en tierra - on land

encapetamiento - 1) registering, inscribing; census-taking; 2) tax-roll; 3) heading (of a will)

encomendero - one who had Indians assigned to him in an **encomienda** during the first centuries of the colonial era (see **amparo**)

encomienda - 1) patronage, commandery; 2) dignity of military order to which a geographical territory and certain income therefrom was attached; 3) a village or territory of Indians that was under the jurisdiction of an **encomendero** who was charged with the supervision of the moral and civil education of a group of Indians in exchange for a tribute collected from the Indian labor

entierro - burial, funeral, interment

episcopal - of the bishop

escribanía - 1) notary office; 2) court clerkship, office of court clerk; 3) writing desk

escribano - 1) notary; 2) court clerk, judge's secretary

escritura - 1) writing, handwriting; 2) document, e.g., deed; 3) instrument, contract, indenture

escritura encadena - chain writing, a form of handwriting used extensively before the sixteenth century

español/a - 1) in colonial records, that individual born of Spanish parents in peninsular Spain; 2) the Spanish language; 3) of or relating to Spain; 4) in colonial records, white or of pure Spanish blood

español criollo - Spanish creole; that individual born of Spanish parents within the Spanish colonies

espera - (law) adjournment

esposo/sa - spouse

estado - 1) status, e.g., marital status; 2) state, nation, country, government

este - east

examen - *see* **carta examen**

exhumación - exhumation, removal of a corpse from its grave, niche, or mausoleum

expediente - 1) the written proceedings of an particular action; 2) petition; 3) file

expediente de quinta - 1) conscript's file; 2) the written conscription proceedings

expediente matrimonial - marriage proceeding or application

expósito - abandoned, foundling child (frequently used as the surname for such children)

extracto del certificado - summary or abstract of the certificate (not a literal copy)

extrema unción - extreme unction, last rite (fifth of the Seven Sacraments) administered to a gravely ill person, usually just before death

fábrica - 1) factory; 2) construction; 3) church property funds

familia - 1) family; 2) all persons of the same blood, such as uncles, cousins, nephews, etc.

familiar - 1) pertaining to a family; 2) domestic; 3) servant of the clergy; 4) local representative or servant of the Inquisition

fanega - 1) unit of measure equaling 1.5 bushels; 2) dry measurements—12 **celemines**, which is equivalent to 55.5 liters; 3) weight measurement—measurements of grain and other seeds, it is the fourth part of what in Castile is called a "carga" of wheat, because this has about 4 **arrobas**

fecha - date

feligres/a - parishioner, person belonging to a given parish

feligresia - 1) parish; 2) district of a parish

ferrería - iron works

fianza - deposit, guarantee, bond, bail

fichas - index cards

fichero - 1) filing cabinet; 2) index-card system, filing-card system, card-catalog

filiación - 1) military register of a soldier; 2) parental ties between parents and children

filial - 1) relating to a son; 2) dependent institution

finiquito - closing of an account

folio - page of a book, notebook or bundle (**legajo**)

fornicación - fornication, sexual union outside of the marriage contract, where the persons involved are not married

foro - 1) tribunal court; 2) bar, legal profession; 3) lease, rent

fortalez - fortress

fuero - 1) jurisdiction; 2) right, the privilege of the clergy and military to be tried in their own courts; 3) traditional regional law

fundación - foundation endowment

gemelo/la - twin; word used to distinguish one of two or more children born at the same time

gobernación - government, governing

gobernador - governor, the supreme ruler of a province, department, city or territory

grado - degree, grade, rank

gran - grand, great, large

gremio - guild, society, association, brotherhood

guardia - 1) guard, body of soldiers; 2) keeper, custodian

guia - 1) guide; 2) advisor, instructor, trainer

habitante/s - inhabitant/s

hace ya dos años - two years ago

hacienda - 1) farmstead, estate, a rural establishment; 2) the Treasury Department

herederos - heirs

hermandad - brotherhood, confraternity, fraternity, sisterhood

hermano/na - brother (sister), born of the same parents, or of the same father, or of the same mother

hermano/a carnal - brother (sister), born of the same parents

hermano/a político/ca - brother-in-law (sister-in-law).

hidalgo/ga - noble, of noble blood, gentry; from **hijo de algo** literally "son of something"

hijo/ja - child, son/daughter (usually appears in documents modified by some adjective such as **legitimo**, **ilegitimo**, **natural**, etc.)

hijo/ja adoptivo/va - adopted child, a person that legally uses the name of another

hijo/ja legitimo/a - legitimate child, a child born of a legal union

hijo/ja natural - common-born child, a child born of unwed parents who could have been legally married if they had desired, an illegitimate child

hijo/ja político/ca - son-in-law (daughter-in-law)

hijodalgo - see **hidalgo**

hijuela - 1) document listing the assets that a person is to receive from a decedent's estate; 2) the assets to be received from a decedent's estate; 3) little daughter, little girl

hipoteca - mortgage, pledge

Hispaniola - colonial name for Haiti and the Dominican Republic

hoja - leaf, sheet of paper, page of book

hoja de servicios - service record, document containing the personal and professional antecedents of government employees, used extensively in the military

hoja familiar - family group sheet

iglesia - church

igual - equal

impedimiento - 1) obstacle, hindrance, obstruction; 2) impediment, in particular one of those imposed by canon law to prevent marriage by related persons, married persons, etc.

imponible - taxable

incógnito/ta - unknown, unrecognized

indemnidad - indemnity (security or protection against injury, damage, or loss)

Indias - Indies; the Americas, including the Caribbean, Mexico, Central and South America

índice - written index, list, catalogue

indio/dia - Indian, a person living with the Indians who adopts their customs, a social designation

industria/industrial - industry/industrial

infacie ecclesiae - Latin phrase meaning before the church; used in marriage documents to describe full church marriage

información matrimonial - a bundle of papers or an entry in a parish book which originates from pre-marriage proceedings that include the publication of banns (**amonestaciones matrimoniales**), declarations by the contracting parties and witness, and at times a copy of the marriage ceremony, copies of baptismal records of bride and groom, and consents of parents to the marriage or copies of their death records

infrascrito/ta - 1) written hereafter; 2) undersigned person

inhumación - burial

inmigración - immigration, population movement between two countries, entry to a foreign country with the intention of establishing permanent residence there

instancia - petition, request

instancia, corte de primera - lower court, court of original jurisdiction

intendencia - intendancy, territorial division under the direction of the **Intendente**, which originated in the Americas during the last quarter of the eighteenth century under the reign of Carlos III and continued until the Independence Era

intestado - intestate, without testament

inventario - inventory, list

inventario de bienes de difunto - inventory of the deceased person's assets

investigador - 1) investigating, researching; 2) investigator

Islas Fortunatas - colonial name for the Canary Islands

itálica - paleographic term, italic, cursive script introduced during the sixteenth century in Spain and the Americas

izquierda - left

jornalero - day laborer

juez - 1) judge, juryman; 2) governor of Castile

juramento - oath

jurisdicción - jurisdiction

jurisdicciones - 1) jurisdiction; 2) boundary; 3) district

juros - 1) right of perpetual ownership, perpetual annuity; 2) pension

justicia - 1) justice, rightness, fairness; 2) court (of justice); tribunal

juzgado - local court

juzgado de comarca - region or district court

juzgado de primera instancia - court of original jurisdiction (the first petition)

ladino/a - 1) blood mixture: Spanish (3 parts) and Indian (1 part); 2) a name given to those Indians who speak Spanish; 3) in Panama, a Christian Negro who spoke Spanish; 4) in Costa Rica, a name indicating a social position, or a Spaniard with a small amount of Indian blood

lasto - receipt given to a person who pays for someone else

latifundia - large landed estate typical of Andalucia and large parts of Latin America

latitud - latitude

legajo - bundle of loose papers that are usually tied together because they deal with a common subject; most common unit of filed papers in Spanish archives

legítimo/ma - legitimate, lawful

legua - 1) league (3½ miles); 2) length—land measurement which varies depending on the nation, equivalent to approximately 5.572 m.

lengua - language, tongue

liberación - exoneration, exemption from taxes or obligations

libertad - 1) freedom, liberty; 2) privilege, right

libra - 1) weight measure, weight which commonly is 16 oz., even though it can change depending on the place; 2) the measurement by which some liquids, such as olive oil, are sold—it is divided in 4 cuarterones, which is the same as 16 ounces (in the drug stores this measure has 12 ounces)

libramiento - 1) deliverance; 2) warrant or order of payment

libranza - draft, bill of exchange, money order

libro de actos - minute book

libro de familia - book of the family, often issued by the government for recording births, marriages, and deaths

libros sacramentales - parish registers

licencia - 1) permission, authority; 2) leave, furlough

licenciado - 1) release; 2) licensed, authorized 3) licentiate, holding a master's degree

limite/limita - limit, boundary

limpieza de sangre - 1) purity of blood; a phrase used in the records of the Inquisition, civil fraternal orders, and some other governmental employment records indicating that a person and his ancestry were not contaminated with heretic religion nor the blood of Moors, Moriscos, Jews, or Negros; 2) records showing the purity of ancestry of the person applying for a position

liquidación - 1) liquidation, winding up; 2) liquidation of debts

lobo/ba - blood mixture, Indian (1 part) and Negro (3 parts)

longitud - longitude

lonja - public exchange, market

lugar - 1) village, hamlet; 2) place, spot, site

madrastra - stepmother, the woman with respect to the children of her husband born of another marriage

madre política - mother-in-law, stepmother

madrina - godmother, a woman who assists in one of the sacraments of baptism, marriage, etc. (many times the godmother is a near relative), sponsor, protectoress

magistratura - judgeship

mancipación - transfer of property

mandas - bequests

Mar del norte - 1) the North Sea; 2) the Atlantic and Caribbean in early colonial records

Mar del sur - the South Sea, the Pacific

maravedi - ancient Spanish coin, sometimes it has been understood by a certain coin and others by number or quantity of them. Their value varied at different times, because of their different quality and metal; because they were of gold, silver, and copper. In eighteenth-century Spain there were 34 **maravedis** in one **real**.

margen - margin

marido - husband

marina - Navy

marino - sailor

marítima/mo - maritime

marques - marquis; in ancient times, a lord over the lands situated on the frontiers of a kingdom; in later times, a noble title between that of count and duke

más - more

materno/na - maternal, pertaining to the mother's family.

matrícula - register, list, roster, roll census

matrimonial - matrimonial, relating to marriage

mayorazgo - 1) family estate, entailed on the eldest son; 2) a legal term indicating priority right to authority, inheritance, or succession; 3) first-born son with the right of primogeniture

media anata - payment made to obtain a title position or benefice originally equal to one-half year's income from the title, position, or benefice

medio hermano/na - half-brother (sister), being brother (sister) only by father or mother

mejora 1) special bequest, additional bequest; 2) development, improvement

mellizo/za - twin, (pl.) two children born of one pregnancy

memoria - 1) memory, recollection; 2) report; 3) study account

menor - 1) younger, youngest; 2) smaller, smallest

menos - less

merced - grant or privilege given by the monarch or lord to his vassals; these came to be associated with control over income-producing property and required an initial payment as well as payment when a transfer was made by death, gift, or sale to another person (see **media anata**)

merindad - 1) jurisdiction and post of a district judge; 2) district whose interests were looked after by the chief town within that territory; 3) township district

meritos - 1) merit; 2) accomplishments

mestizo/za - 1) a person born of parents of different races, usually Spanish and Indian; 2) crossbreed

militar - 1) pertaining to the military or to war; 2) a person serving in the army

mismo - 1) the same; 2) as expressed; 3) equal

mita - 1) tribute paid by the Indians of Peru and Bolivia; 2) forced labor in the mines, factories, and on public works for which the Indians were selected by lot during Inca and Spanish dominion—minor compensation was sometimes given (see **repartimiento**)

monasterio - monastery

moreno/na - blood mixture: Spanish (2 parts), Indian (1 part), and Negro (1 part); offspring of Spaniard and **zambaigo**

morisco/ca - 1) Moorish, those baptized Moors that lived in Spain and the colonies; 2) Mexico, blood mixture: Spanish and mulatto

mozo/za - 1) single, unmarried, bachelor; 2) lad, young man; 3) the younger, or junior

muerte - death

mujer - 1) woman; 2) wife

municipal - of or relating to the **municipio**

municipio - municipality, the territorial jurisdiction which includes the inhabitants governed by a town council

murió - died, third person past tense of **morirse**

nacer - to be born

nacimiento - birth

nació - past tense of **nascer**, he was born

nacionalidad - nacionality, citizenship

natural - 1) native of, born in a given locality; 2) born outside of the marriage contract

naturaleza - 1) nature; 2) nationality; 3) place of origin

nave - 1) ship; 2) nave, aisle

necesidad - necessity, need

negro/ra - Negro, black or dark-skinned, native of various tribes of Africa

negro fino - blood mixture: Spaniard (1 part) and Negro (3 parts); offspring of mulatto and Negro.

nobiliario - 1) nobiliary, peerage list; 2) pertaining to the nobility

nombramiento - appointment, election, nomination, commission

nombre de pila - name, Christian name, e.g., name given at baptismal font

nordeste - northeast

noroeste - northwest

norte - north

notable - notable, noteworthy, outstanding

notario - notary, authorized official for preparing and certifying public actions, contracts, deeds, bonds, wills, etc. Before 1869 those using this title were usually ecclesiastically appointed, and the civil notaries of that era were generally called **escribanos**.

nuera - daughter-in-law, wife of the son

nuestro/ra - our, of ours, ours

Nueva Andalucía - 1) region of Tierra Firme between the Cabo de la Vela in the gulf of Uraba or Darien in modern Colombia; 2) the region and city of Cumana, Venezuela

Nueva Castilla - The northern part of colonial Peru, its southern boundary 25 but not more than 60 leagues south of the San Juan de Chincha River

Nueva Córdoba - Venezuela during the early colonial era

Nueva España - colonial Mexico

Nueva Extremadura - 1) early colonial Chile, the northern part of Chile; 2) the territory of Coahuila, Mexico

Nueva Galicia - colonial Aguascalientes, Jalisco, and parts of Durango, Zacatecas, Nayarit, San Luis Potosi, and Coahuila, Mexico (its capital was Guadalajara)

Nueva Navarra - the Californias in the early colonial period

Nueva Vizcaya - separated from Nueva Galicia 1573–1576, included Sinaloa, Sonora, Durango, Chihuahua, and parts of Coahuila, Mexico (its capital was Durango)

Nuevo Leon - Nuevo Leon, Mexico and its surrounding areas, including part of Tamaulipas

Nuevo Santander - the northern part of colonial Colombia, northeastern Mexico State of Tamaulipas and Texas south of Nueces River during period before 1848

Nuevo Toledo - 1) the southern part of colonial Peru, that jurisdiction which from 1559 was known as the **Audiencia de Charcas**, its southern boundary being the straits of Magellan; 2) Chile

nupcias - nuptials, marriage, wedding

obispado - bishopric, episcopate

obispo - bishop, spiritual and ecclesiastical leader of a diocese

óbito - death

obituario - obituary, book wherein are registered deaths and burials, section of death notices in the newspapers

obligación - 1) obligation, responsibility, duty; 2) liability, bond

obras pias - foundation or donation created or given for church work or for charitable works, literally, pious works

oeste - west

oficio - 1) occupation, job, work, craft, trade; 2) office, post, position; 3) function; 4) written communication

oidor - magistrate who, in the royal courts (**audiencia**), heard and sentenced disputes and lawsuits

óleo - blessed oil used in the ceremonies of the Church

onza - 1) weight that is worth 16 adarmes and is equivalent to 287 decigrams; 2) the twelfth part of a Roman libra

onza de oro - a Spanish ancient gold coin minted from the time of Felipe III until that of Fernando VII and worth 320 reales, meaning 80 pesetas

originario - native of a given place

oro - gold

otorgar - to set forth, establish, offer, grant, stipulate or promise something, usually used when the notary is preparing the actual document

otrosi - 1) furthermore, besides, moreover; 2) (law) each additional petition after the principal one

padrastro - stepfather; the man with respect to the children of his wife born in another marriage

padre - 1) father; 2) (pl.) parents; 3) (pl.) ancestors

padre político - father-in-law; stepfather

padrino - godfather, a man who assists in one of the sacraments of baptism, marriage, etc., usually a friend or relative; pl., godparents

padrón - list or census of the residents or inhabitants of a village or parish

paleografía - paleography, study of ancient handwriting

panteón - cemetery, funeral monument where the dead are buried

pardo/da - blood mixture: Spaniard (1 part), Indian (2 parts), and Negro (1 part)

parecer - 1) to appear, seem, look; 2) manner of viewing, e.g., **anuestro parecer**

párrafo - paragraph

párroco - parish priest

parroquia - 1) parish, territory covered by the spiritual jurisdiction of a parish priest; 2) the church of the parish

parte - 1) part, fragment; 2) part, share, portion

partición - 1) division, partition, separation, especially a division of assets following death

partido judicial - district, usually made up of several villages in a province, in which a judge exercises original jurisdiction over civil and criminal judicial matters (judicial district)

párvulo/la - a small child

paterno/na - paternal, from the male line

pechero/ra - 1) taxable, taxpayer; 2) plebeian, commoner

pedimiento - 1) petition; 2) petition or claim presented to judge and each separate case therein

peninsular - peninsular, born in Spain or Portugal

perdón - pardon, forgiveness, grace, reprieve

permuta - 1) exchange, usually of two public or ecclesiastical offices or benefices; 2) interchange, barter

peseta - Spanish monetary unit

peso - 1) weight; 2) Spanish coin used in colonies

pie - length measurement which in Castile was equivalent to 28 cm., and today in England to 30.5 cm., in France to 33 cm.

pieza de indias - 1) one slave in good condition; 2) various young slaves or women in poor condition

plata - silver

plaza - 1) main square of a town; 2) space or place for a person with others of similar type; 3) office, position, employment

plazo - 1) term, period of time; 2) installment

pleitos - lawsuit, suit, court or judicial action or proceedings

población - population

poder - 1) power, strength; 2) power of attorney; 3) (pl.) authority

político/ca - when applied to a term of blood relationship, indicates the same relationships by marriage, e.g., **padre político** (father-in-law)

por - 1) by, for; 2) through, along, over, by way of, via, around, about, in, at; 3) by means of, with, in exchange for, in return for; 4) times, multiplied by

portero - doorman

posesión - 1) possession (in all senses); 2) (pl.) possessions, property, estate

postura - 1) posture, position, attitude; 2) bid, offer; 3) agreement; 4) stake, wager, bet

prelado - prelate, ecclesiastical dignitary, superior of a convent

presente - present, current

presidente - head or leader of the courts (**audiencias**) and chancery (**chancilleria**), one of the titles of the viceroy, president

pretendiente - 1) claimant, seeker, petitioner; 2) candidate (for office); 3) suitor (for a woman's hand)

previsto - anticipated

primo/ma - cousin, child of an uncle or aunt

primo/ma carnal - first cousin, child of an uncle or aunt

primo/ma hermano/na - first cousin, child of an uncle or aunt

primogénito - firstborn

priorato - priorate, priory

privilegios - 1) privilege, grant, concession; 2) exemption; 3) franchise, patent

probanza - 1) (law) prove, proving; 2) (law) proof, evidence

procesal - 1) (law) legal, of a trial; 2) paleographic term, handwriting style used in Spain from 1300 to 1550, replaced by **itálica**

proceso - 1) process; 2) (law) trial, lawsuit, action

productos - products

prohijación - adoption of a child as one's own

promesa - 1) promise, offer; 2) vow, pledge

prorrogación - extension or postponement for a specified period of time

protesta - protesta, protestation, declaration, affirmation

protesto - declaration made before a notary or judge to protect one's rights, declaration made before a notary when a letter of exchange is not paid to protect one's rights

protocolo - book generated and preserved by the notary publics

provincia - province, territorial division representing different extensions of jurisdiction depending on the country

Provincias Internas - Interior Provinces; that region of northern Mexico which included the states of Durango, Coahuila, Chihuahua, Nuevo Leon, Nuevo Mexico, Sonora, Tamaulipas, and Texas

pueblo - 1) town, village, population; 2) in the colonies, a geographical area under the administration of royal officials as compared to the **encomienda** or **mission** which were administered by private and ecclesiastical personnel, respectively.

pulgada - length measurements, measurement that is the twelfth part of a **pie**

quarterón de mulato - in Peru, blood mixture: Spanish and mulatto

quinta - 1) country house, manor, villa; 2) (Peru) group of town houses with a common entrance; 3) (Sp.) annual draft, induction of recruits for the army

quintal/quintales - 1) weight measurement, equivalent to 100 pounds or 4 arrobas, even though it varies in some places; 2) the fifth part of a hundred

quinterón - in Peru, blood mixture: Spaniard and **cuarteron**

ratificación - ratification, confirmation

real - 1) royal, of or pertaining to the Crown; 2) a kind of Spanish coin

real audiencia - the supreme court or tribunal of the colonial Americas, the court of last resort. It served as a representative of the king; its decisions were final and only the king could reverse them.

reales - coin of value of 34 maravedis, which were called real de vellon or, in some places, the silver real

rebisabuelo/a - great-great-grandparent

rebisnieto/a - great-great-grandchild

recepción - 1) reception, receiving, receipt; 2) admission; 3) (law) examination of witnesses

recibo - 1) receipt (document acknowledging payment)

reclamación - 1) claim, demand; 2) objection, protest, complaint; 3) (law) remonstration

reconocimiento - 1) recognition, admission, acknowledgment; 2) inspection, examination

redención - 1) redemption, salvation; 2) (com.) redemption (of a pledge, mortgage, etc.)

redondilla - paleographic term; the round hand, distinguished by its straight and circular strokes

reducción - 1) reduction; 2) a village of Indians converted to Christianity, usually directed by a religious order such as the Jesuits

regimento - military unit headed by a **colonel**

registro - 1) register, record, record book; 2) registration, registry; 3) examination, inspection, search; 4) entry, record, register

reglamento - 1) regulation; 2) regulations, bylaws

reina - queen

reinado - reign

reino - kingdom, realm

religioso/sa - 1) religious; 2) one who has taken the vows of an order, i.e., monk, priest, or nun

renta/s - 1) revenue, income; 2) rent; 3) annuity; 4) government bonds, public debt

renunciación o renuncia - 1) renunciation; 2) resignation; 3) (law) waiver, disclaimer

repartimiento - 1) distribution of lands after reconquest; 2) the assessment of work assignments and the subsequent distribution of those so assessed to their work stations in the mines, haciendas, public works, etc. In many cases this was an involuntary servitude, especially by Indians in the colonies

repudiación - repudiation

requerimiento - 1) request, requisition, demand, summons; 2) (law) injunction

requinterón - in Peru, blood mixture: Spanish and **quinteron**

requinterón de mestizo - in Peru, blood mixture: Spaniard and **quinteron de mestizo**

residencia - review of a colonial official at the end of his term

residente - residing in

resguardo - 1) protection, shelter; 2) security, voucher; 3) frontier customs guard

retatarabuelo - a great-great-great-grandfather

revista - review, inspection of troops

revocación - 1) revocation, abrogation; 2) annulment; 3) (law) reversal

rey - king

riachuelo - stream

rio - river

sacramento - 1) sacrament (e.g., baptism, marriage, etc.); 2) the Eucharist

sacristan - sacristan, sexton, the individual who took care of the ecclesiastical cemeteries

sala - 1) parlor, hall, lounge, salon; 2) court, tribunal

santo/ta - 1) holy, saintly, hollowed, sacred, blessed, 2) saint

secretaría - office of the secretary, secretariate

secretario/ria - secretary

segundo/da - second, secondary

seguridad - 1) safety, security; 2) certainty, assurance; 3) surety bond

seguro/ra - 1) safe, secure, steady; 2) insurance, insurance policy; 3) permit, warrant, license

señalamiento - designation, appointment, indication (of place, time)

señorío - domain

septentrion/al - northern, septentrional

sepultura - 1) interment, burial; 2) tomb, grave; 3) burial place, sepulchre

servicio - 1) service, serving; 2) voluntary donations given to king or state; 3) (pl.) emergency direct tax

sigla - paleographic term, abbreviation by use of initial letter to represent entire word

signatura - 1) filing mark (to facilitate filing of documents), library number; 2) (ecc.) Roman-Catholic court of justice and pardons

sínodo - ancient name given to the ecclesiastical councils of a diocese

sitio de ganado - place or part of the land which the cattle occupies

situación/ situado/a - location

sobrino/na - nephew (niece), child of a brother or sister (known as first nephews/nieces or **sobrinos carnales**) or of a cousin (known as second nephews/nieces or **sobrinos segundos**)

sobrino-bisnieto/ta - great-grand nephew (niece); that relationship of an individual to his great-grand uncle (the brother of the great-grandfather)

sobrino-nieto/ta - grand nephew (niece), the relationship of an individual to his grand uncle (the brother of the grandfather)

solar para casa - 1) portion of land that has been constructed on, or where one is going to build; 2) stockyard or orchard adjacent, or around, the home

soldada - 1) salary, wages; 2) soldier's pay

soldadera - female soldier

soldado - 1) soldier; 2) (mil.) private

soltero/ra - 1) single, unmarried; 2) bachelor, unmarried woman

subrogación - subrogation, substitution

subsecuente - subsequent

sudeste - southeast

sudoeste - southwest

suegro/a - parent-in-law

sufragáneo - suffragan, one who is under the jurisdiction or authority of another

sur - south

sustitución - substitution, usually an agreement for one man to fulfill the military service of another

tarjeta - 1) card (visiting, personal, or invitation card); 2) index card, etc.; 3) heading, title (on a map)

tasación - appraisal, appraisement, valuation

tasador - public appraiser

tatarabuelo/la - great-great-grandparent

tataranieto/ta - great-great-grandchild

teniente - 1) assistant, deputy, substitute; 2) (mil.) lieutenant

tercero/ra - 1) third; 2) (ecc.) tertiary; 3) third party

término - 1) term, word, expression; 2) end, finish, conclusion; 3) limit, boundary, landmark; 4) time limit, term, period, space of time; 5) district

terrritoro/territorial - territory

testador - testator, person who writes a will

testamentario - executor, person who oversees distribution of decedent's assets in accordance with last will and testament

testamento - will, a document in which one declares his last will and in which he disposes of his property and makes other arrangements for after his death

testamento abierto o nuncupativo - will that is dictated by a dying person before witnesses and in some cases the notary and is later recorded by the notary in his **protocolo**

testamento adverado - a will—in accordance with local law (**dereho foral**), especially in Galicia—dictated before the **párroco** and two or more witnesses, and later recorded by the **párroco** in his parish records or by the notary in the **protocolo** to make it a public record

testamento cerrado - a will that is written in secret and then sealed before a notary and witnesses to be opened after the death of the testator

testamento ológrafo - holographic will, written and signed in the hand of the testator

tio - uncle, the brother of the father or mother

tio-abuelo/la - grand uncle, the brother (sister) of the grandparent

tio-bisabuelo/la - great-grand uncle (aunt), the brother (sister) of the great-grandparent

tio carnal - cousin of the father or mother, in English the equivalent of first cousin, once removed

titulo - 1) title, name, sobriquet; 2) caption, heading; 3) section (into which laws and regulations are divided); 4) (law) title, such as a title of nobility; 5) diploma

traducción - translation

transacción - 1) transaction, negotiation; 2) settlement, agreement, compromise

traspasos - transfers of property not involving a sale

tres dias festivos sucesivos - three successive Sundays or holidays; a phrase used in marriage documents referring to the three successive Sundays or holidays in which the publications or banns are made

tributo - 1) tribute, tax; 2) tribute, respect

trillizos - triplets, each one of the three children born of one pregnancy

trinidad - trinity

trueco - trade

tutela - 1) guardianship,the authority conferred by law to an individual to care for the fortune and at times the person of a minor; 2) the documents generated from the guardianship

tutela dativa - (law) guardianship by court appointment

tutela ejemplar - (law) guardianship of the mentally incapacitate

universidad - university

ut supra - (Lat.) as above

vara - length measurement equivalent to 835 millimeters and nine tenths

véase - look at

vecindad - neighborhood, local area

vecindario - 1) persons taken together, who reside in the same vicinity or neighborhood; 2) list or census of the residents of a town

vecino/na - 1) legal resident, citizens of a local town, village, or city, usually owning a home and contributing to the local tax collections; by law this status was available only after residing for a fixed number of years in the town; 2) neighbor

velación - 1) vigil, watch; 2) (Ecc.) veiling ceremony of bride and groom in nuptial mass

velado/da - 1) veiled; 2) having received the **velación**

vellón - 1) copper coin, real de vellón; 2) mix of silver and copper of which the coin was made in ancient times

venta - 1) sale, selling

vicaría - 1) vicarage; 2) the territory over which a vicar presides, an area similar to a parish in size but not yet advanced in its development sufficiently to be elevated to the position of a parish; a vice-parish

vicario - vicar, the religious functionary who, as an assistant, takes full charge when his superior is gone, the functionary in charge of a parish at times

vicario general - vicar general, the alternate bishop or assistant to the chief judge of the diocesan courts and head of the **curia** of the diocese

villa - town or small populated area that has been granted privileges which distinguish it from **aldeas** and **lugares**

vínculo - 1) bond, tie, link; 2) (law) entail, entailment in which assets are linked to a family or position (civil or ecclesiastical) according to the instructions of the creator or donor

virreinato - viceroyalty, the territory governed by a viceroy

virrey - viceroy, the personal representative of the king in colonial America

viruela - 1) smallpox; 2) pockmark

visita - visit, call, inspection

viudo/da - 1) widowed; 2) widower, widow

vizconde - viscount, a title of nobility which follows that of count in its rank

vuelto/ta - verso, reverse side

yerno/na - son-in-law (daughter-in-law), the spouse of one's child

zambaigo - blood mixture: Negro (1 part), Indian (1 part); sometimes in Mexico 1 part Chinese, 1 part Indian

zambo - in Peru, blood mixture: offspring of a Negro and mulatto; in Venezuela, blood mixture: Indian (1 part) and Negro (1 part); in Chile and Colombia this admixture is called mulatto

zambo de indio - in Peru, blood mixture: offspring of Negro and Indian

APPENDIX

Hispanic Genealogical Societies in the United States

Los Bexareños Genealogical Society
P.O. Box 1935
San Antonio, TX 78297
Periodical: *Los Bexareños Genealogical Register*
Other Publications: No

Los Californianos
4002 St. James Place
San Diego, CA 92103-1630
Periodical: None
Other Publications: No

Cuban Genealogical Society
P.O. Box 2650
Salt Lake City, UT 84110-2650
Periodical: *Revista*
Other Publications: Yes

Los Descendientes del Presidio de Tucson
P.O. Box 50871
Tucson, AZ 85703
Periodical: newsletter
Other Publications: No

El Paso Genealogical Society
El Paso Main Public Library
501 North Oregon Street
El Paso, TX 79901
Periodical: *Rio Grande Researcher*
Other Publications: No

Genealogical Society of Hispanic America
PO Box 9606
Denver, CO 80209-0606
Periodical: *Nuestras Raices*
Other Publications: Yes

Genealogical Society of Hispanic America — Southern California Branch
P.O. Box 2472
Santa Fe Springs, CA 90670
Periodical: *Huellas del Pasado*
Other Publications: Yes

The Hispanic Genealogical Society
P.O. Box 1792
Houston, TX 77251-1792
Periodical: None
Other Publications: No

Society for Hispanic Historical and Ancestral Research (SHHAR)
P.O. Box 5294
Fullerton, CA 92635
Periodicals: *Somos Primos*
Other Publications: Yes

Spanish American Genealogical Association
P.O. Box 5407
Corpus Christi, TX 78405
Periodical: None
Other Publications: Yes

American Portuguese Genealogical and Historical Society
Box 644
Taunton, MA 02780
Periodical: *Bulletinboard;* Cecilia Rose, Newsletter Ed.
Other Publications: No

Portuguese Ancestry
Ed. Rosemarie Capodicci
1155 Santa Ana
Seaside, CA 93955
Periodical: Quarterly newsletter
Other Publications: No

Portuguese Genealogical Society of Hawaii
Doris Nomeau, President
2117 Awiktwik Street
Pearl City, HI 96782
Periodicals: No
Other Publications: No

Portuguese Historical and Cultural Society
P.O. Box 161990
Sacramento, CA 95816
Periodical: *O Progreso*
Other Publications: No

Index

abandoned children 174, 175
abbreviations 31, 34, 43, 48, 49, 50, 82, 93, 95, 96, 170
abogado 237
abuelos 154, 171, 185
Academia Real de la Lengua Española (see *Real academia de la lengua española*)
accent marks 97
accuracy 6, 7
admoniciones 196–97, 199
Advent (see *Adviento*)
Adviento 199
affinity 196
Africa 3, 42, 139
Aguascalientes 58
Aguilar 99, 100
Alabarderos 222
albaceas 179, 248
Albacete 49
alcalde 105, 237
aldea 86, 124, 140
alemana 82, 83
alien registration 15, 77, 78
alquiler 15
alternate spellings 94
American Geographical Society 113, 124, 142
Americas, The 114
Amezua, y Mayo, A.G. 235, 253
amonestaciones (see admoniciones)
analysis 31, 82, 111, 112, 116, 117, 118, 119, 121, 124, 126, 154, 164, 167, 169, 184, 207
  locality 112, 113, 114, 115, 116, 169
  people 111, 121
  records 117, 118, 119, 120, 121, 122, 123, 167
Ancestral File 22, 40, 41, 61
Ancestry's Redbook 64
Andalucia 88, 104
Andorra 142
apellido de la mujer 4, 101–2
apellido materno (see *apellidos*)
apellido paterno (see *apellidos*)
apellidos 4, 48, 52, 98, 99, 101, 104, 105, 159, 178, 179
apodo 99
Aragon 237, 239
archdiocese 191, 206, 207
Archives (see *archivo*)
Archives of the Indies (see *Archivo General de las Indias*)
archivo 25, 54, 121, 122, 123, 132, 139, 143, 168, 191, 206, 212, 213, 220, 221, 226, 228, 229, 231, 232, 233, 234, 237, 239, 242, 244, 251, 253
Archivo de Centroamerica (Guatemala City) 231
Archivo de la Corona de Aragon 237, 239
Archivo General de las Indias (Seville) 123, 229
Archivo General de la Nación (Mexico) 121, 123
Archivo General Militar de Guadalajara 228
Archivo General Militar de Segovia 220, 221, 228, 231, 232, 233
Archivo General de Simancas 229, 232
Archivo Histórico de Hacienda (Mexico) 231
Archivo Histórico Nacional (Madrid) 123,168
Archivo Histórico Provencial (Caceres) 251, 253
Archivo Histórico Provincial (Santander) 251,253
Archivo Notarial Histórico de Colegio Notarial de Barcelona 237
Archivos de Protocolos (Madrid) 253
Archivos militares y civiles en donde se conservan fondos de caracter castrense (see Cadenas y Vicente)
archivos parroquiales (see parish records)
Arciprestazgo 116
Argentina 3, 42, 53, 99, 103, 114, 117, 129, 130, 131, 138, 142, 146, 172, 200, 205, 209, 216, 217, 231, 233, 239
Arizona 64, 65, 66, 67, 68, 123, 142, 154, 217
arroba 253
Asia 42
Asturias 99, 175
Atlas grafico de España (see Aguilar)
atlases 113, 114, 129, 130, 131, 132, 133, 134, 135, 136, 137, 138, 139, 140, 141

Audiencia (colonial) 222, 231
Audiencia (judicial) 222, 231
Augustan Society (see Spanish American Genealogist)
autobiographies 18
Automated Archives, Inc. 23
Avila 26
Ayuntamiento 117, 121, 122, 253

bachiller 105, 106
Bahamas 42
Bancroft Library (UCB) 123
Banner Blue 77
Banns (see *admoniciones*)
Baptisms (see *bautismos*)
Barcelona 10, 140, 173, 189, 191, 206, 237, 239, 253
Basque countries (see *Vascongados*)
Basque language 23, 49, 88, 173
Basque surnames 23, 25
batch number 47
bautismos (see also parish records—extract forms) 4, 11, 13, 122, 160–175
Bebout, Jeri 28, 29, 32, 34, 35
beneficios 189
beginning 9
Belize 42
Bermuda 42
bibliographie 52, 123
Biblioteca Nacional 25, 123, 231
biographical dictionaries (see dictionaries, biographical)
biographies 11, 18, 22, 23, 52
biography cards 34, 36
birthplace 169
births (see *nacimientos*)
bishop (see *obispo* and diocese)
Bolivia 42, 53, 117, 130, 146, 231, 239
border crossing records 69, 72, 73
Bowman, Peter 24, 26
Branch Genealogical Libraries (LDS) 119
Brazil 3, 42, 53, 117, 119, 130, 142, 206
breadth 6, 7, 235, 236
Brigham Young University 80, 129
Brøderbund 77
burial (see *entierros*)

Cabezas Moro, Octavio 8
cabildo capitular 188
caballeria 170, 222
Cáceres 253
Cadenas y Vicent, Vicente de 1, 7, 27, 38, 233, 234
Cadiz 233
calendar 104, 126
California 23, 28, 38, 54, 68, 69, 70, 72, 73, 75, 79, 80, 123, 124, 142, 185, 211, 217, 255
cambio 15
Canary Islands (Canaries) 42
Canton 117
Cape Verde 42
capellanias 189
capitalization 94, 95
Capítania general 222
capitulaciones matrimoniales 15, 206, 248
Caribbean 1, 42
casamientos (see *matrimonios*)
casa solar 106
Castile (see Castilla)
Castilian language 87
Castilla 88, 236
Catalan 89, 103, 182
Catálogo de los archivos españoles en que se conservan fondos genealogicos y nobiliarios (see Larios Martin, Jesus)
catastro 209, 211
Catastro de Ensenada 211
cathedral 183, 188, 189, 253
cathedral archives 253
Catholic Church 4, 63, 64, 118, 119, 120, 157, 185, 194, 195
Catholic Church records 157
Catholic monarchs (see Ferdinand and Isabel)
Causas Pias 189
cavalry 170, 220, 222
Cavazos Gavza, Israel 253
cedula personal (see *documento nacional de identidad*)
cemeteries 120, 150, 153
censo 121, 122, 133, 136, 143, 209, 218
Censo guia de archivos españoles 121, 122
census records 58, 64, 67, 68, 118, 120, 121, 123, 186, 209, 210, 211, 216, 217, 218, 219, 229
Central America 53
certificates 2, 4, 6, 11, 75, 106, 150, 154, 178
cesion 15
Chancillerías 95
Chancillería Real de Valladolid 209
Charitable donations 189
Chihuahua 55, 60
Chile 42, 53, 68, 117, 131, 142, 146, 216, 222, 231, 239
Chinchilla 132
Church of Jesus Christ of Latter-day Saints 11, 22, 24, 33, 37, 39, 40, 41, 61, 62, 63, 86, 109, 119, 190, 191, 218, 233, 239
  CIDOC collection 114
  publications 26, 61, 62, 63
Church records 64
citizenship records 13, 15

City council minutes 120
city hall (see *ayuntamiento*)
Ciudad Real 171, 233
civil records 28, 61, 150, 155
civil register 4, 10, 18, 58, 109, 118, 120, 121, 124, 126, 145, 146, 147, 148, 149, 150, 151, 152, 153, 154, 155, 160, 161, 162, 163
  births (*nacimientos*) 147
  deaths (*defunciones*) 153
  marginal notes 175
  marriages (*matrimoniales*) 150
  (see also parish records—extract forms)
clergy 195
Coahuila 55, 117
cofradías 36, 118, 186, 187, 247
colecturias 176
colegio 16, 237, 253
Colombia 42, 53, 117, 132, 146, 216, 231, 239
Colorado 255
composite surnames 100, 101
compra-ventas (see *ventas*)
computer 22, 23, 27, 33, 36, 37, 39, 49, 51, 52, 61, 113, 116, 121
computerized catalogs 25, 51
conde 105, 106
confirmaciones 183–84
confirmations (see *confirmaciones*)
confusing letters 91, 92, 93
consanguinity 118, 189, 196, 202
conscripciones 228
Consejo de Castilla 236
continuity 3, 4, 5
contracts (see *contratos* and *ventas*)
contractions 96
contratos 15, 206
conventionalisms 96
Cordoba 197, 198
corregidores 236
correspondence 81, 105–9, 153, 154, 228
  general 105
  guidelines 105
  with archives or library 81
  with civil register 153
  with distant family members 19
  with military archives 225, 228
  with parish priest 185
correspondence log 108
cortesana 82, 83
Coruña 187, 239
Costa Rica 13, 42, 53, 117, 132, 133, 142, 146, 154, 216, 231, 239
Council of Trent 4, 173, 194, 195, 196, 197
Count (see *conde*)
court records 56, 73, 75, 120, 121, 193, 205
Cuaresma 199
Cuba 3, 11, 42, 53, 63, 69, 117, 119, 133, 136, 142, 146, 219, 220, 222, 225, 231, 232, 255
cuentas (see *libros de cuentas*)
curador (see *curaduría*)
curaduría 249, 250
curia 189
Curso de genealogica (see Larios Martin, Jesus)

death announcement 13, 69
deaths (see *defunciones*)
Defense Mapping Agency 113
defunciones (see also parish records—extract forms) 122, 145, 153, 176–183
defuntos (see *defunciones*)
departamento 117, 124, 138, 233
descent chart 27
diaries 18, 19
Diccionario biográfico de Saltillo 23, 25
Diccionario de abreviaturas hispanas 109
Diccionario geográfico de Guatemala 124
Diccionario geográfico del Salvador 114, 115
Diccionario onomástico y heraldico basco (see Querexeta, Jaime de)
dictionaries 22, 23, 56, 86, 91, 113, 114129, 130, 131, 132, 133, 134, 135, 136, 137, 138, 139, 140, 141
  biographical 22
  geographical 86, 113, 114, 129, 130, 131, 132, 133, 134, 135, 136, 137, 138, 139, 140, 141
  language 81
  surname 91
diligencias matrimoniales (see marriage information)
diocesan archives 118, 120, 123, 183, 188, 190, 191, 202, 205, 206, 216, 217
diocesan records 51, 58, 60, 116, 119, 157, 188, 189, 190, 191, 205, 206, 207
  locating 190
  matrimonial petitions 189, 201 205
diocese 51, 55, 60, 64, 109, 114, 116, 142, 169, 173, 183, 184, 185, 186, 188, 189, 190, 191, 201, 202, 203, 205, 206, 207, 210, 253
discharge (see military records)
divorces 190

documento nacional de identidad 18
Dominica 47
Dominican Republic 42, 53, 117, 133, 142, 146
Don 27, 104–6, 149, 170, 197, 233, 245
Doña 104–6, 170
donación 15
double letters 93
double surname system 49, 99, 100, 103
duke (see *duque*)
duque 105, 106
Durango 60, 117
Duron Jimenez, Martha 75

ecclesiastical directories 114, 116, 129, 130, 131, 132, 133, 134, 135, 136, 137, 138, 139, 140, 141, 142
ecclesiastical divisions 116, 121
ecclesiastical records 90, 188
Ecuador 42, 53, 82, 117, 134, 142, 145, 146, 216, 231
Editorial Aquilar (see Aguilar)
El Salvador 42, 53, 114, 115, 117, 134, 142, 146, 174, 231, 239
emigration 16, 24, 54
empleos 224, 228
encyclopedias 114, 178
engineers 222
England 41, 61
Enciclopedia heraldica y genealogica Hispano-Americana (see Garcia Carraffa)
entierros (see also parish records—deaths) 120, 176, 178
escribano 96, 105, 106, 177, 179, 189, 235, 236, 237, 238, 241, 245, 252
escribano eclesiástico y apostólico 236, 238, 253
escribano provincial (criminal) 236, 238, 252
escribano publico 238
escribano real 235, 236
ethnic histories 116
evaluating information 27
Excelsior 23
executors 179, 182, 248, 249, 250
expedientes matrimoniales (see parish records—marriage petitions; or marriage dispensations)
extractos bancarios 15
extrema unción 182
Extremadura 101, 103, 117

fabricos (see *libros de fábricas*)
Family Group Records Archives (LDS) 22
family groups 7
family group sheets 10, 27, 30, 31, 34, 35, 36, 60, 164, 172, 177
family historian 1, 5, 6, 9, 11, 15, 27, 36, 37, 55, 81, 98, 99, 100, 103, 104, 111, 142, 177, 182, 184, 185, 187, 188, 193, 201, 202, 209, 219, 235, 248, 249
family histories 1, 2, 3, 4, 5, 6, 7, 9, 10, 11, 15, 16, 18, 19, 20, 21, 22, 23, 24, 25, 28, 31, 33, 37, 39, 40, 41, 47, 48, 51, 52, 54, 60, 61, 62, 64, 72, 77, 80, 81, 98, 107, 109, 111, 112, 114, 119, 121, 123, 124, 126, 129, 143, 157, 164, 166, 176, 184, 188, 189, 191, 207, 217, 235, 238, 249, 252, 253
family history centers 24, 39, 51, 77, 119, 124
family history, definition 1
Family History Library (Salt Lake City) 24, 39, 51, 164, 191
Family History Library Catalog 24, 39, 40, 51–62, 64, 77, 80, 119, 123, 124, 164, 184, 189, 217, 226, 238
family members 4, 11, 12, 16, 18, 19, 20, 21, 22, 24, 25, 36, 72, 166, 176, 211, 248
family sources 11, 18, 40, 124
Federal Census, U.S. (1900) 64, 67
Ferdinand and Isabel 220, 236
filiaciones 228
filing systems 27, 28, 30, 31
Filipinas (see Philippine Islands)
Florida 63, 123, 124, 133, 205, 217, 218, 222
flourishes 94
forms 27, 28, 33, 34, 64, 77, 81, 82, 87, 90, 91, 93, 95, 97, 160, 178, 211, 231, 242, 248
French 89
Fuentes principales de registros genealogicos (see Major Genealogical Resource Papers)
Fuero Real 235
funerals (see *misas*)

Galapagos 42
Galicia 89, 96, 101, 103, 104, 175, 187
Gallego 253
Garces, Jorge A. 82, 97, 109
Garcia Carraffa 23, 25, 52
gazetteers 13, 129–143
Genealogical Library, Salt Lake City 39
genealogical societies, Hispanic 25, 119, 279

genealogist, professional 1, 2, 7, 9, 11, 23, 33, 37, 64, 80, 108, 113, 119, 123, 126, 150, 224, 230, 233, 240
 hiring 5, 123
genealogy computer program 37
genealogy—definition 1, 2, 3, 5, 7, 8, 27, 33, 35, 37, 56, 57, 63, 80, 143
GEO net Names Server 113
Geografia politica y eclesiastica (see Larios Martin, Jesus)
geographical dictionaries (see dictionaries, geographical)
geography (Spain) 56, 58, 64, 113, 114, 136
geography
 physical (Spain) 113
 political (Spain) 116
Gerona 49, 206
Gibraltar 42
gifts (see *donación*)
given names (see *nombres de pila*)
Godparent (see *padrinos*)
Gonzalez Salas, Carlos 25
gothic numerals 98
Granada 191, 206, 239
grandparents (see *abuelos*)
Greenwood, Val D. 5, 8, 63, 80, 128, 140, 143
Grenada 42
Guadalajara 10, 55, 60, 116, 191, 203, 206, 207, 228
Guam 42
guardian (see *curaduría*)
Guatemala 2, 42, 51, 53, 114, 115, 117, 124, 125, 135, 142, 146, 222, 231, 239
Guerra, Raul 297
Guía de archivos municipales de Tamaulipas 121
Guía de la Iglesia en España 121, 191
Guía Familiar de Baja California (see Martinez, Pablo)
Guiana 42
guides to archives 121
Guipuzcoa 23
Guyana 42

Hacienda 214, 231
Haiti 42, 133
Hamilton-Edwards, Gerald 8
handwriting, guidelines 5, 56, 81, 82, 83, 84, 85, 86, 91, 94, 96, 107, 159, 160, 173
 special problems; confusing letters 91
 alternate spelling 94
 flourishes 94
 double letters 93
 linking letters 94
 suppression of ‘e’ 94
Handy Book for Genealogists 64
Herederos 15
Herrero Mediavila, Victor 26
hidalgo 60, 209, 224
Hidalguía (publisher) 7, 8, 24, 233, 234
hijo natural 170, 174
Hispanic American Historical Review 116
Hispanic American Index (HAPI) 116
Hispanic Americans 21
Hispanic, definition 257, 1, 2, 3, 4, 5, 8, 9, 11, 12, 15, 16, 18, 21, 22, 23, 24, 25, 27, 30, 39, 40, 41, 42, 43, 47, 49, 51, 53, 55, 58, 60, 61, 63, 64, 72, 80, 98, 100, 106, 107, 109, 111, 112, 113, 114, 116, 118, 119, 121, 123, 124, 126, 129, 142, 145, 153, 154, 157, 167, 172, 185, 189, 191, 193, 207, 209, 210, 214, 216, 217, 219, 224, 225, 235, 236, 237, 239, 253, 255
histories (see local histories)
hoja de servicio 221, 224, 226, 228
home sources 18, 19, 219
Honduras 42, 53, 117, 135, 136, 142, 216, 231
Huelva 239

Iberian peninsula 191, 233
identification number 33, 35
IGI (see International Genealogical Index)
ilegítimo (see *legítimo*)
illegitimate children 174, 175
immigrant 3, 12, 15, 18, 19, 21, 24, 63, 64, 69, 72, 73, 80, 99, 100, 103, 219
immigration 3, 24, 54, 63, 68, 72, 120
Immigration and Naturalization Service 72, 73, 74, 77, 78
impediments 195, 196
in facie eclesia 200
In Search of Ancestry (see Hamilton-Edwards)
Index to Map of Hispanic America (see American Geographical Society)
Index to Marriage Investigations of the Diocese of Guadalajara (see Guerra, Raul)
indexes 11, 22, 25, 51, 54, 56, 57, 64, 72, 77, 87, 118, 121, 123, 158, 159, 205, 210, 216, 232, 233, 242, 247
Indians 99, 100, 169, 201, 211
Indice Biográfico de Espana, Portugal e Iberoamérica 23, 26
Indice geobiografico de . . . pobladores de la América hispana (see Bowman, Peter)

Indios 100, 200
infantería 222
infantry 222
informaciones matrimoniales (see parish records—marriage petitions; and marriage information)
ingenieros 222
Inglis, G. Douglas 55, 191, 218
Inquisition 54, 60, 100, 118, 120, 123
Instituto Genealógica e Historico Latinamericano 119
interchangeable letters 87–89
International Genealogical Index (IGI) 22, 39, 40–49, 51, 61, 62
International Vital Records Handbook 64
Internet 25, 38, 113, 121
interviews 11, 19, 20, 21, 195
interwoven 96
inventario de bienes de difuntos 248, 249, 250, 251
inventario de dote 249
inventarios 15, 186, 206, 248, 249
Isabel (Queen of Spain) (see Ferdinand and Isabel)
Italian 89
Italica 82, 83
Italy 3, 194

Jaen 137
Jalisco 55
juez 155
juzgado 122

Knights of Columbus 80

LDS Church (see Church of Jesus Christ of Latter-day Saints)
La Coruña 187, 239
land records 120
language 2, 21, 55, 57, 64, 81, 84, 86, 87, 88, 89, 90, 91, 107, 143, 182, 195, 245, 249, 252
  interchangeable letters 87
  latin influences 90
  letter "h" 89
Larios Martin, Jesus 2, 5, 7, 8, 38
Latin 89, 90, 91
Latin America 2, 3, 11, 23, 24, 30, 41, 63, 81, 82, 99, 103, 105, 113, 114, 116, 117, 119, 142, 145, 146, 150, 157, 169, 170, 171, 172, 173, 186, 188, 191, 194, 200, 205, 211, 217, 218, 222, 225, 229, 233, 237, 238, 239, 249
Latin American Census Records 217, 218
Latin American Studies Handbook 116
legajo 226, 240, 251, 253
legal papers 15
legitimación de hijos natrales 149
legítimo 197, 201
Lent (see *Cuaresma*)
Leon 48, 54, 173, 207
letters 15, 16, 19, 23, 28, 34, 48, 49, 81, 82, 84, 87, 88, 91–97, 106–9, 142, 144, 154, 159, 185
libraries—general 24, 25, 53, 54, 56, 112, 113, 114, 121, 123, 129, 142, 217, 237
  letter to 25
Libro de Behetrías 209
libros de cofradías 186
libros de cuentas 186
libros de fábricas 186
libros de familia 12, 153
licenciado 96, 105, 106, 173, 197
limpieza de sangre 6, 120
linking letters 94
Listas de Revistas 229
local census records 123
local histories 7, 114, 116, 142, 186, 187
locality analysis (see analysis, locality)
locality report 116
locating census records 216
Louisiana 205, 222
Lowrey, Joan 38
Lugo 49, 164, 165, 166
Luking, Sandra 26

Madoz, Pascual 140
Madrid 7, 8, 25, 38, 82, 123, 133, 136, 140, 141, 168, 169, 171, 172, 191, 210, 214, 216, 222, 225, 227, 228, 231, 233, 234, 239, 240, 241, 245, 252, 253
maiden surnames (see *apellidos de la mujer*)
Major Genealogical Resource Papers (Series H) 239
Málaga 121, 123, 185
maps 55, 57, 58, 80, 86, 113, 114, 129, 130, 131, 132, 133, 134, 135, 136, 137, 138, 139, 140, 141
marital status 13, 68, 69, 147, 150, 153, 167, 178, 179, 182, 196, 202, 210, 216, 245
marques 105, 211, 214
marquis (see *marques*)
marriage conflicts and disputes 120, 205
marriage contracts (see *capitulaciones matrimoniales*)
marriage dispensations 120, 189, 201–205
marriage impediments (see impediments)
marriage information 120, 150, 152, 153, 193, 194, 195, 206

marriage records 145, 150–153, 193–207
Martinez, Pablo 138, 141
Martinique 42
masses (Catholic Church) (see *misas*)
maternal surname (see *apellidos*)
Matilla Tascon, Antonio 241
matrícula 186, 209
matrimonios 60, 120, 122, 176
medical records 18
memberships 18
memorandum 27, 38
Memorandum de la genealogica familiar (see Cadenas y Vicent, Vicente de)
Mendiguchia 23
México 1, 3, 7, 10, 14, 15, 19, 22, 23, 26, 39, 40, 42–64, 68, 72, 83, 88, 100, 113, 114, 116, 117, 121, 123, 136, 137, 142, 143, 145, 146, 150–52, 154, 164, 189, 191, 202, 203, 205–7, 209, 210, 211, 212, 216, 217, 218, 225, 229, 231, 233, 234, 238, 239, 242, 244, 253
microfilmed records 51
milicias provinciales 222
military divisions 222, 223
Military Index 22, 40
military orders (see *ordenes militares*)
military ranks 223, 224
military records 4, 6, 16, 28, 30, 54, 57, 77, 106, 118, 120, 121, 123, 210, 211, 219–34
Millares Carlo, Agustin 82
misas 176
Mormons (see Church of Jesus Christ of Latter-day Saints)
Morocco 42
Mozambique 42
municipality (see *municipio*)
municipio 58, 116, 117, 124, 136, 154
Muñoz de San Pedro, Miguel 253

nacimientos 122, 145, 147–50, 169
names 1, 4, 6, 12, 13, 21, 22, 23, 28, 34, 35, 36, 40, 41, 42, 43, 45, 48, 49, 50, 52, 55, 57, 60, 61, 77, 84, 86, 87, 91, 94, 98, 99, 100, 104, 113, 114, 119, 121, 139, 142, 147, 150, 153, 159, 165, 166, 167, 169, 170, 171, 172, 173, 174, 175, 177, 178, 179, 182, 183, 184, 187, 193, 196, 197, 199, 202, 204, 209, 211, 217, 219, 225, 228, 229, 240, 245, 247, 248, 250
names (see *nombres de pila*)
Narro Etcheguray, Ignacio 25
national archives 123
National Archives, Washington, D.C. 72, 120, 146, 217, 219, 231
national census records 68, 123, 211
naturaleza 150, 171
naturalization 13, 64, 67, 68, 70, 72, 73, 74, 75, 77, 120
Navarra 239
navy 233
Nayari 43, 45
Neofitas 211
Netherland Antilles 42
New England Historical and Genealogical Register 41, 61
New Mexico 206, 218
New York 1, 26, 80, 109, 135, 233
newspapers 16, 57, 68, 219
Nicaragua 42, 53, 55, 117, 137, 142, 146, 231, 239
Nichols, Elizabeth L. 61
nobility 18, 57, 105, 106, 118, 120, 169, 170, 209, 210, 211, 218
nombramientos 122
nombres de pila 103, 104, 159
notario 4, 30, 51, 52, 54, 55, 57, 58, 60, 118, 119, 120, 121, 122, 177, 178, 190, 206, 210, 219, 220, 231, 235, 236, 237, 238, 239, 240, 341, 242, 244, 245, 246, 247, 248, 253
notarial archives 206, 236, 237, 238, 240
notarial law 236, 237, 240
notarial office 238, 239, 240, 247
notarial records 4, 51, 52, 55, 57, 58, 60, 118, 119, 120, 121, 177, 190, 210, 219, 220, 235, 237, 238, 239, 242, 244
  format 242, 245, 246
  indexing 240–44
  locating 55, 237
notario 179, 201, 237, 239, 240, 241
  history of
  use of
notario eclesiástico 252
notary (see *notario* and *escribano*)
Nueva atlas de España (see Aguilar)
Nuevo Atlas Porrvade la Republican Mexicano 113, 147
Nueva España 136, 222
Nueva Granada 222
Nueva Vizcaya 117
numbers 3, 24, 33, 34, 35, 36, 47, 48, 58, 72, 84, 97, 98, 126, 142, 149, 150, 159, 160, 167, 169, 216, 219, 220, 224, 242

obispo 183, 188, 189, 194
obituaries 68
occupation 147, 149, 170
occupation records 16
oficinas del Registro Civil 145
oficinas municipales 145
oral sources 5
ordenación 189, 196
ordenes militares 168
  administrative records 219
organizing information 27
orphans (see abandoned children)

padres 93, 96, 171, 173, 179
padrinos 172, 174, 196
padrón (see census records)
Palacio Real 171
Paleografía diplomática española y sus peculiaridades en América 82, 97, 109
paleography 52, 82, 86
Pamplona 140
Panama 42, 117, 133, 137, 142, 146, 216, 231
Paraguay 42, 53, 117, 130, 138, 142, 146, 231, 239
parental consent 150, 206
parish 3, 4, 5, 6, 28, 30, 31, 45, 46, 47, 48, 49, 51, 52, 53, 54, 58, 60, 61, 64, 66, 82, 84, 86, 90, 91, 95, 96, 99, 100, 101, 104, 106, 108, 109, 113, 114, 116, 118, 119, 120, 121, 123, 124, 126, 128, 142, 145, 147, 149, 153, 157, 158, 159, 160, 161, 162, 163, 164, 165, 166, 167, 169, 170, 171, 172, 173, 175, 176, 177, 179, 182, 183, 184, 185, 186, 187, 188, 190, 193, 194, 195, 196, 197, 198, 199, 200, 201, 202, 209, 210, 211, 216, 217, 219, 220, 225, 228, 235, 240, 247
Parish and Vital Records List 48
parish priest (see *parroco*)
parish records (see also *bautismos, defunciones, matrimonios, padres, abuelos, legítimo, padrinos*) 96, 119, 120, 124, 157–189
  extract forms 30, 160–163
  indexes 158, 159
  inventory 159
  locating 184, 185
  marriages 196–202
  marriage petitions 60, 186, 193–195
  military 225
  organization 30, 157, 158
  research in 164–167
  visita pastoral partición 15, 249
parroco 185
parroquias 116, 131, 132, 139
passenger lists 54, 69, 71, 72, 120
passports 12, 13, 14, 15, 54, 118, 120
paternal surname (see *apellidos*)
patronymic system 98, 99
Paz, Julian 129, 130
pedigree charts 27, 31, 33, 36, 172
pensions 120
people analysis (see analysis, people)
periodicals 24, 56, 57, 114, 119, 123, 142, 217
Personal Ancestral File 37, 38, 40
personal visit 19, 154, 155
Perú 4, 42, 53, 117, 138, 209, 216, 222, 231, 239
Philippine Islands 2, 42, 53, 63, 222, 225, 232
Phillip II 95
photographs 12, 21
physical geography (see geography, physical)
places 1, 4, 5, 6, 7, 11, 12, 13, 15, 16, 21, 22, 30, 31, 34, 35, 36, 37, 39, 40, 41, 52, 60, 61, 63, 64, 68, 69, 72, 73, 77, 80, 84, 86, 87, 85, 98, 103, 1-4, 106, 109, 111, 112, 113, 116, 124, 126, 136, 147, 149, 150, 153, 164, 169, 171, 172, 173, 174, 176, 177, 178, 179, 182, 183, 188, 193, 194, 199, 200, 201, 202, 205, 209, 219, 220, 225, 228, 247, 255
Platt, Lyman D. 23, 24, 26, 119, 137, 143, 191, 217, 218, 233
political divisions 113, 117
political geography (see geography, political)
Portugal 2, 3, 11, 23, 26, 42, 53, 63, 101, 117, 119, 139, 175
Portuguese 3, 25, 42, 68, 255
preliminary survey 9–25
pre-marriage investigations *prendas* 194
prenuptial agreements (see *capitulaciones matrimoniales*)
Preserving Your American Heritage (see Wright, Norman)
presidios 211, 229
priesthood ordination 120
printed materials 13, 24
probate 120
procesal 82, 83

professional genealogist (see genealogist, professional)
proof 6
property records 15
protocolos 236, 237, 238, 239, 240, 241, 242, 249, 250, 251, 252, 253
public employment records 120
Puerto Rico 42, 53, 114, 117, 139, 140, 142, 146, 216, 222, 225, 231, 232
punctuation 94, 95, 96
purity of blood (see *limpieza de sangre*)

Querexeta, Jaime de 23, 25
questionnaire 19
quintas 122, 210, 228

race 69, 172, 200
Real academia de la lengua española 87–88
records 3, 4, 5, 6, 7, 10, 11, 12, 15, 16, 18, 21, 27, 28, 30, 31, 36, 39, 40, 42, 43, 45, 47, 48, 49, 51, 52, 53, 54, 55, 56, 57, 58, 59, 60, 61, 63, 64, 66, 68, 69, 72, 73, 77, 80, 81, 82, 84, 86, 87, 89, 90, 95, 97, 99, 100, 101, 103, 104, 105, 106, 111, 114, 116, 117, 118, 119, 120, 121, 123, 124, 126, 128, 142, 145, 146, 149, 150, 153, 154, 155, 157, 159, 160, 164, 165, 166, 167, 169, 170, 171, 172, 173, 174, 175, 176, 177, 178, 179, 182, 183, 184, 185, 186, 187, 188, 189, 190, 191, 193, 194, 196, 199, 200, 201, 202, 205, 206, 207, 209, 210, 211, 216, 217, 218, 219, 220, 224, 225, 228, 229, 231, 232, 233, 235, 236, 237, 238, 239, 240, 241, 242, 244, 252, 253
records analysis (see analysis, records)
redonda 82, 83
Reflejos de siete siglos de vida extemeña en cien documentos notariales (see Muñoz de San Pedro, Miguel)
regimental histories 222
Registro Civil (see civil register)
registro de últimas voluntades 240
religiosas 141
religious maturation 2
Republica Dominicana (see Dominican Republic)
research:
  calendar/log 126, 127
  notes 28
  process 9–11
  reports 126, 127
Research outlines 63
Researcher's Guide to American Genealogy, The (see Greenwood, Val D.)
Revista del Instituto Genealógica e Historico Latinamericano (see *Instituto* of the same name)
Riesco, Terrero, Angel 109
RLIN 25, 116, 121
roman numerals 98
Romance languages 89
Royal Chancellery Court Archives, Valladolid (see *Chancilléria Real de Valladolid*)

Saint Lucia 42
Saint Vincent 42
sale (see *ventas*)
Sanare, Jose 191
Santander 12, 49, 69, 207
Santiago 131, 146, 169, 172, 231
school records 16, 80
secretario 105, 154, 155
Secretario del registro civil 154, 155
  letter to
Seed, Patricia 207
seguros 15
señor 96, 107, 154, 173, 201
Series H (see Major Genealogical Resource Papers)
Servicio Histórico Militar 222, 225, 227, 228
Sevilla 149, 191, 239
Siete Partidas 235
siglas 96
Sinaloa 230
Social Security Death Index 22, 40, 77
Social Security records 73, 76
Society for Hispanic Historical and Ancestral Research 22
Sonora 41
Sosa system 33, 34
Source, The (see Szucs)
sources 5, 6, 9, 10, 11, 18, 19, 22, 23, 24, 31, 35, 40, 48, 49, 51, 54, 55, 56, 57, 63, 68, 69, 84, 100, 103, 105, 111, 116, 119, 123, 124, 126, 128, 178, 217, 219, 233, 235, 248
  original 6
  primary 6
  secondary 6
South America (see Latin America)
Spain 1–5, 10, 11, 12, 15, 16, 21, 23, 28, 30, 31, 39, 40, 42, 49, 51–55, 63, 64, 83, 88, 89, 98, 99, 101, 103, 104, 114, 117, 118, 119, 121, 123, 136, 140, 142, 143, 145, 147, 148, 150, 157, 168–173, 175, 181, 186, 187, 188, 191, 194, 197, 198, 205, 206,

209, 210, 211, 213, 214, 217, 219, 220, 222, 225, 227, 228, 229, 231, 232, 235, 236, 237, 238, 239, 240, 241, 249, 252

Spanish American Genealogist 119, 230, 233

Spanish language—general 81, 87, 88, 89, 90, 252
  history of 81

Spanish Records Extraction 84, 169

Spanish Sahara 142

status 3, 5, 13, 16, 24, 68, 69, 105, 106, 121, 147, 149, 150, 153, 167, 170, 175, 176, 178, 179, 182, 193, 196, 202, 205, 210, 214, 216, 224, 235, 245, 249

success 3, 5

sucesión 15

superpositions 96

Surinam 42

surname dictionaries (see dictionaries, surname)

surnames (see also *apellidos*) 3, 4, 10, 22, 23, 24, 34, 45, 48, 84, 86, 89, 91, 98, 99, 100, 101, 103, 104, 105, 147, 150, 153, 159, 164, 166, 167, 169, 170, 172, 175, 178, 196, 211, 220, 228, 245

surnames of women (see *apellidos de la mujer*)

suspensions 96

Szucs, Loretto 24, 26, 63

Tamaulipas 58, 121

Tarragona 206

tax records 120, 121

TempleReady 40

tercios 220

Teruel 30

testamentarios 179, 248

testamentos 15, 186, 247

Texas 3, 72, 113, 123, 207, 217, 218

thoroughness 6, 7, 68

Timor 42

titles 104

Tobago 42

Toledo 87

tradition 5

transfers 225, 227

Tratado de Paleografía Espanola 82

travel (trip) to ancestral homeland (see personal visit)

Tribunal 289

Trinidad 42

tutoria 15

United States 1, 2, 3, 15, 18, 24, 25, 28, 39, 40, 42, 54, 55, 63, 64, 68, 69, 72, 73, 77, 78, 99, 106, 107, 113, 114, 116, 118, 123, 124, 129, 139, 217, 229, 240, 255

United States Army Map Service Select Series 113

university archives 16, 120

University of Texas 113, 123

U.S. Board on Geographic Names 142

Uruguay 3, 11, 16, 42, 53, 117, 141, 142, 146, 231, 239

utility programs 37, 38

Valencia 123, 132, 140, 237, 239

Valladolid 209, 211

Vascongados 23, 49

Vazquez, Nadine 207

Vela, Baldamero 207

Vela, Saul 3, 8

velaciones 199

Venezuela 42, 55, 117, 141, 142, 146, 216, 222, 231, 239

ventas 249

virreinatos 223

vital records 11, 64

Vizcaya 23

Voting records 68, 120

Wagner, Sir Antony 3

Waloons 222

Weber, David J. 80

West Africa 42

Wills (see *testamentos*)

work permits 13, 15

WORLDCAT 25, 116, 121

World Wars 77, 79

written sources 5

Wright, Norman 63

Zorilla, Fidel 25